Colonial Rule and Social Change in Korea, 1910–1945

HONG YUNG LEE, YONG CHOOL HA,

and CLARK W. SORENSEN, Editors

Center for Korea Studies Publications

The Northern Region of Korea: History, Identity, and Culture
Edited by Sun Joo Kim

Reassessing the Park Chung Hee Era, 1961–1979:
Development, Political Thought, Democracy, and Cultural Influence
Edited by Hyung-A Kim and Clark W. Sorensen

The Center for Korea Studies Publication Series published by the University of Washington Press is supported by the Academy of Korean Studies Grant funded by the Korean Government (MEST) (AKS–2011–BAA–2101).

이 논문 또는 저서는 2012년도 정부(교육과학기술부)의 재원으로 한국학중앙연구원의 지원을 받아 수행된 연구임(AKS-2012-BAA-2101).

The Center for Korea Studies Publication Series is dedicated to providing excellent academic resources and conference volumes related to the history, culture, and politics of the Korean peninsula.

Clark W. Sorensen | Director & General Editor
| Center for Korea Studies

Colonial Rule and Social Change in Korea, 1910–1945

Edited by

**HONG YUNG LEE,
YONG CHOOL HA, and
CLARK W. SORENSEN**

A CENTER FOR KOREA STUDIES PUBLICATION

UNIVERSITY OF WASHINGTON PRESS | SEATTLE & LONDON

Colonial Rule and Social Change in Korea, 1910–1945
Edited by Hong Yung Lee, Yong Chool Ha, and Clark W. Sorensen
© 2013 by the Center for Korea Studies, University of Washington
Printed in the United States of America
18 17 16 15 14 13   1 2 3 4 5

CENTER FOR KOREA STUDIES
Henry M. Jackson School of International Studies
University of Washington
Box 353650, Seattle, WA 98195-3650
http://jsis.washington.edu/Korea

UNIVERSITY OF WASHINGTON PRESS
P.O. Box 50096, Seattle, WA 98195 U.S.A.
www.washington.edu/uwpress

LIBRARY OF CONGRESS CATALOGING-IN-PUBLICATION DATA
Colonial rule and social change in Korea, 1910–1945 / edited by Hong Yung Lee, Yung Chool Ha, and Clark W. Sorensen.
    p. cm. — (A Center for Korea Studies publication)
  "A Center for Korea Studies publication."
  Includes bibliographical references and index.
  ISBN 978-0-295-99216-7 (pbk. : alk. paper)
  1. Korea—History—Japanese occupation, 1910–1945. 2. Korea—Social conditions—1910–1945.
  3. Social change—Korea—History—20th century. 4. National characteristics, Korea. I. Lee, Hong Yung, 1939– II. Ha, Yong-ch'ul, 1948– III. Sorensen, Clark W., 1948–
  DS916.55.C65 2012
  951.9'03—dc23   2012031647

Colonial Rule and Social Change 1910–1945 is dedicated to Mr. Kim Chong Un (1920–2000). Mr. Kim served as president of the Korea Research Foundation from March 1995–1998. He was a renowned specialist on English literature and taught at Seoul National University. He served as president of Seoul National University from 1991–1995.

Contents

Acknowledgments

This book has had an unusually long history from its inception to its publication. Scholarly attention has long been directed at Japan's experiences with rapid economic development; in the 1990s, increasing evidence of South Korea's remarkable economic success, combined with widespread scholarly interest in Japan's colonization of Korea, resulted in a trend towards attributing South Korea's economic development to Japan's colonial legacy. This scholarly trend led Hong Yung Lee to write a paper on and organize a panel around the subject of appraising the Japanese colonial legacy in Korea at the Association of Asian Studies annual meeting.

Meanwhile, Yong chool Ha was working a paper that examined the origins of high school ties in Korea. Finding no materials on the topic, Ha felt the need to do further research into the colonial era, the period when high schools first opened in Korea. Realizing that our research interests dovetailed into one another, we agreed about the need to study the social legacy of the colonial era, not only in terms of the Korean economy, but also in terms of Korean institutions and modernization as a whole. One glaring absence in U.S. and European scholarly debates about the Japanese colonial legacy has been the perspective of Korean scholars from Korea; as such, we decided to launch a project that would introduce non-Korean audiences to research being done by Korean scholars on these issues. Unfortunately, the difficulty of accessing the work of Korean scholars on Korea persists to this day—so while late in coming, this publication is still very much worthwhile.

For making this project possible, we would like to acknowledge the late Jong Woon Kim, former President of the Korea Research Foundation. Mr.

Kim understood the importance of this project from the outset and was extremely generous in providing support for it. Without his understanding and encouragement, this book would never have taken shape. We would thus like to dedicate this volume to him.

Funding provided by the Korea Research Foundation enabled Ha to organize a research group consisting of ten scholars, most of whom have authored chapters in this volume. A series of regular discussion sessions were held at Seoul National University between 1996 through 1999, and the first international workshop was held on July 15, 1997, with Korean scholars presenting their first drafts at the University of California, Berkeley. The second international workshop was held in Seoul in 2001 for which Clark W. Sorensen served as discussant, and who agreed to add his contribution and to bring the papers to publication.

On the Korea side, Myung Gyu Park has for many years been instrumental in not only organizing the group, but also in coordinating its discussions. The contributions that he has made to this project are greatly appreciated. At UC Berkeley, the Center for Korean Studies has provided generous support in accommodating various workshops associated with this project over the years. Many of the scholars who participated in those workshops have made numerous valuable contributions over the years. Among them are: Ken Jowitt, Peter Duus, and Lowell Dittmer. Their kind but critical comments and questions have been extremely helpful in honing and polishing these papers.

Over the years, the editors of this volume have accumulated quite a debt of gratitude to the numerous students, administrators, and editors who have worked on it. Yumi Moon, now an assistant professor at Stanford, worked as the initial coordinator for this project, and Sunil Kim, JeongWhan Lee, and Kyung Jun Choi have all helped us at different stages. Without their tireless support, this project would never have come to fruition.

The Center for Korea Studies at the University of Washington took over the task of polishing and editing the papers for publication under the direction of Clark W. Sorensen. The complicated origin of this manuscript has made this final editing task unusually laborious. We have spent much time smoothing out differences between Korean and American world processing systems, and citation practices. Thanks go to the Korea Librarian of the University of Washington, Hyokyoung Lee, for helping us track down illusive Korean and Japanese language citations. To make the articles from Korean contributors more accessible to English-speaking audiences, we have endeavored to reorganize articles to conform to American academic writing expectations and smooth the English into as natural-sounding a form as possible. Josh Van Lieu, Cindi Textor, and Hyokyoung Lee at the University of Washington provided *yeoman* service tracking down and standardizing Korean, Japanese, and Chinese Romanization.

Special thanks go to Tracy Stober, the managing editor of this volume, who was tireless in communicating with and keeping track of contributors in Korea, Japan, and various parts of the United States. The Associate Director of the Korea Center, Youngsook Lim, was helpful in tracking some of the more elusive contributors down.

Wayne de Femery has been a talented typesetter for the publications of the Center for Korea Studies. And finally, we must thank the staff, students, and collaborators at the Center for Korean Studies—Joseph Buchman, Laura Burt, Amy Courson, Stephen Delissio, Jeremiah Dost, Teresa Giralamo, Alexander Martin, Janet Fisher, Karen Lavery, Jan Mayrhofer, Jeanna McLellan, Julie Molinari, Susan Pavlansky, Nelli Tkach, and Barbara Wagamon—who provided three rounds of proofreading for the entire manuscript before it went to press.

List of Illustrations

Introduction: A Critique of "Colonial Modernity"

HONG YUNG LEE

It is not surprising that people who have been colonized often view their colonial past in ways that are diametrically opposite to those of the colonizers. Despite Japan's official apology for their annexation of Korea, Japanese rightists have continued to insist that colonialism played a positive role in Korean history. Colonialism transformed Korea "from a potentially degenerate kingdom to a well-ordered society; from a backward and poverty-stricken country to a productive and flourishing land; and from a helpless pawn of power politics to a secure and protected member of a virile imperialist system."[1] In contrast, Koreans view Japanese colonialism as a humiliating experience that had little benefit for Korea.

These different perspectives on the recent past have remained a bone of contention between Japan and South and North Korea, delaying diplomatic normalization between the two countries until the mid-1960s and continue to impede not only closer collaboration between these three geographically close neighbors, but also any positive movement toward regional cooperation and integration in the region despite the increasing economic interdependence and globalization of international politics. The ongoing dispute over Japanese textbooks, tension over contested territories such as the Tokto/Takeshima Islands, and recent controversies over Koizumi's yearly visits to the Yasukuni shrine all demonstrate how the legacy of the region's colonized past continues to shape international relations among the East Asian countries.[2]

Such seemingly basic questions of responsibility and consequences pose almost insurmountable methodological, historical, and theoretical challenges. However, an objective and impartial assessment of the controversial issue of Japan's colonial legacy agreed upon by the international academic community, has the potential to help reduce differences in perception and historical memory, thereby facilitating a more congenial East Asian community. Thus the question of how to evaluate the Japanese colonial legacy, is not only intellectually challenging, but also has profound political implications for the future of regional politics in East Asia.

COLONIZING ONE'S CLOSEST NEIGHBOR

The unique characteristics of Japan's colonization of Korea have made reaching a consensus about the Japanese colonial legacy, particularly as it pertains to Korea's modernization, nearly impossible. First of all, Japanese colonial rule lasted only thirty-six years, less than all modern instances of colonization.[3] When this short period of colonization is seen in the context of Korea's two-thousand-year history as, for the most part, a continuously distinctive political community, the brevity of Japanese rule becomes even starker. Still, brief though it was, Japan's colonization of Korea took place from 1910–45, a critical period as far as modernization is concerned. If the first half of the twentieth century was transformative for Western nations, it was even more so for Asian nations, which had come into contact with the West in the middle of the nineteenth century, and had spent the next fifty years adapting their traditional, social, political, and economic structures to the challenges posed by the West. The first part of the twentieth century thus became perhaps the most critical juncture for nation building, modernization, and industrialization throughout East Asia.

Probably there is no precedent for one country colonizing its closest neighbor, particularly when that neighbor boasts two thousand years of distinctive cultural, historical, political, and ethnic identity. One could argue that the development of Japan and Korea had been roughly parallel up until the West came to Asia around the middle of the nineteenth century. Both maintained their own political identities that shared broadly defined Confucian values and reached a comparable level of technological and economic development, although their specific political and social institutions differed. For this reason, one scholar commented that "Japan colonized their neighboring states with whom they shared racial and cultural traits; it was as if England had colonized a few, across-the-channel continental states."[4] The continental states, which were not far behind England in terms of industrialization, did in fact manage to catch up without being colonized by the British. On the other hand, any chance Korea might have had to "catch up" was arguably forestalled because of Japanese colonization.

That Japan did end up colonizing Korea could be largely attributed to the fact that Japan was the first of the two to successfully transform itself from a centralized, feudal, political system into a modern nation-state after opening up to the West. Using its newly acquired military and economic muscle, which it had "built up through economic and intellectual exchange with European powers," Japan was capable of colonizing its closest neighbor, which it came to view as a hopelessly backward country that needed to be "civilized."[5] For their part, Koreans believed that Japan had been able to colonize Korea merely because of its marginal advantage as the first Westernized Asian country and so did not concede either Japan's cultural superiority or its political legitimacy. Although Koreans might have been impressed with Japan's successful transformation into a strong modern state, this did not translate into an acceptance of the necessity for Japanese colonialism.

Because of these unique characteristics, applying theories derived from other colonial studies has become more difficult. Two issues are particularly relevant to the broadly defined counterfactual question of what Korea's potential for modernization might have been if Japanese colonialism had not been imposed. First, there is the issue of the minimal cultural gap between the two; and second, there is the fact that Japanese modernization occurred several decades earlier, enabling it to colonize Korea. These two points can, in turn, lead to two opposite conclusions: one could argue that Korean acknowledgement of Japanese modernization lead to Korean cooperation with Japan in working towards modernization. However it is also possible to argue that Korea did not need Japanese colonialism to make a break with the past and embark on the path to modernization. Separating out Japanese influence from the normal processes of modernization and industrialization that Korea might have experienced without colonization is quite a difficult task.

To further complicate matters, Japanese colonial rule in Korea went through three distinctive phases characterized by different strategies.[6] During the initial phase, Japan relied on force to ruthlessly subjugate any Korean resistance, did not allow any freedom or autonomy to Koreans, and totally disregarded Korean traditions and interests. This phase is known as the period of "military rule." During the second phase, Japanese colonial policy changed to "cultural rule," which employed tactics of appeasement and divide and rule, while tolerating limited cultural and social freedom for Koreans. In the last phase, Japan relied on a tactic of total mobilization for its war effort while attempting to make Koreans into Japanese through the forced assimilation policy known as *naisenitai* (Japan and Korea as one). Unlike other colonial nations that were content with economic exploitation and political domination, Japan's colonization did include attempts to completely assimilate Koreans into Japan and to eradicate Korea's ethnic and cultural identity. Any analysis of Japan's colonial legacy in Korea will thus depend on which period is being emphasized, and whether the particular evidence being examined is an isolated piece of information or takes into account the totality of the colonial situation.

The Korean Nation as an Imagined Community

Inextricably related to the question of Korea's potential for modernization is the controversy of whether Koreans developed any notion of a national identity before Japanese colonization. There are two conflicting views on this question. One school of thought—generally associated with the school of colonial modernity and largely driven by theoretical considerations rather than empirical facts of Korean history—tends to stress the decisive role that Japanese colonialism played in shaping the modern notion of nationalism.

According to this line of reasoning, it was during the Japanese colonial period that Korea became a nation-state. The colonial administration introduced a national system of schooling, transportation, and communication. This was done primarily through the introduction of print capitalism, by which each Korean came to realize themselves as members of a Korean nation.[7] In other words, according to this view, Korean nationalism was based on an "imagined" or "constructed community" intentionally devised by Korean nationalists as a way of challenging Japanese colonialism.[8]

In contrast, many Korean historians tend to believe that Koreans had already developed some sense of national identity by the time the Japanese took over, even though it might not have been identical with modern nationalism. For instance, observing that "the Korean Peninsula has had an extraordinarily long experience of unified political rule" since the seventh century up until the end of Chosŏn Dynasty in 1910, John B. Duncan insists that not only the traditional elites, but the non-elite social strata had developed a national identity despite their wholehearted subscription to "cardinal Confucian social values in the second half of the dynasty."[9] After carefully analyzing folk stories about the Imjin War, Duncan asserts that the stories reflect "some degree of awareness among the non-elites of Chosŏn that they constituted a social and political collectivity distinct from those of their neighbors and some degree of awareness, albeit strongly negative, of the role the state played in their lives." Despite the absence of communication channels among Korean commoners, "a sense among non-elites of a larger Chosŏn identity emerged, at least in part, in contradiction to Japan and China." Duncan continues: "While this is hardly the same as sitting in one's home in Cherbourg and reading about events in Marseilles in the morning newspaper, nonetheless it indicates a certain popular awareness of the other parts of Chosŏn and how they were affected by the war."[10]

Andre Schmid concurs with Duncan's view that Korea's unique history helped in the formation of a pre-modern national identity, while specifically rejecting the argument that Korean nationalism was based on an "imagined community."[11] He writes: "Yet by describing the origin of the nation as a move from and to the essential categories of modern and the tradition respectively, these approaches [i.e. the approaches of those who insist on the thesis of an imagined community] have tended to neglect the interactions between the nationalist and pre-nationalist discourse, thereby oversimplifying the genealogy of modern nation." Although he does not deny the modern element of Korean nationalism, he also equally stresses pre-modern nationalism in Korean history. "By the time the Western powers arrived, the centralized state bureaucracy of the Chosŏn Dynasty had administered a relatively stable realm for well over four centuries. Out of administrative practice and geographical studies . . . a sense of territory had already developed well before the concept of sovereignty arrived. Works on territory and history written since at least the seventh century, if not earlier, had created a sense of space that transcended any single dynasty." This subjective awareness "was crucial in the late-nineteenth century, since it meant that early nationalist writers did not need to imagine from scratch the nation as a spatial entity."[12] That Japanese colonialism further aroused Korean nationalism does not necessarily mean that Japanese colonialism led Korean nationalists to artificially construct the idea of a Korean "nation."

Education as Contested "Material Domination" of Modernization

Colonial authority education is always a double-edged sword for both the colonized and colonizer. The former knows that education is the only means by which an individual or nation can gain its independence and survive in modern society. At the same time, education does not deal only with knowledge, science, and technology, but also shapes the minds of people by helping them to define their social relations, as well as their relation to their traditions, culture, and self-identity. Similarly, colonizers have always recognized the need to educate the colonized in order to make them economically productive, while eradicating their cultural and national identity, thereby making them loyal to the colonizing authority. But a modern education not only makes it possible for the colonized to survive and get ahead in the social hierarchy, it also has the potential to awaken the colonized to the ironies of colonialism, and can even make them feel proud of their own cultural and national traditions. The double-edged nature of this problem becomes even more acute when the cultural gap between the colonized and colonizers is not that wide, as was the case with Japan and Korea.

There is no dispute that the Japanese colonial authority introduced a modern educational system to Korea. This fact is frequently cited as a good example of Japanese modernization efforts in Korea, largely because the number of schools founded, the number of students trained, and the fact that the literacy rate can be easily measured, and that human capital is a known factor for any development.[13] However, one has to remember two crucial points. First, Japan introduced a modern educational system into Korea with one of the most proactive educational traditions in the world. Korea's unusual zeal for education did not originate from Japanese colonialism, but rather from Korea's Confucian tradition, which has continued to this day among Korean Americans in the United States, for example.

Second, the Japanese educational policy discriminated against Koreans, even while intending to make Koreans loyal subjects of the Japanese emperor. For instance, in 1939, all Japanese in Korea attended high school, whereas only one out of 220 Koreans attained a junior high school level education.[14] More Japanese were educated than Koreans in Korea and the number of Koreans trained in the sciences were inadequate and could not accommodate Korea's needs. After carefully studying Korean scientific and technical manpower growth during Japanese colonialism, Kim Kŭnbae found that pre-colonial Korea, which was urgently in need of scientific and technological knowledge, established mining, postal, and electric schools and produced nearly 3,600 survey engineers by 1910.[15] However, Japanese colonialism converted these schools to practical knowledge centers that carried out low-level training. Even when the Japanese colonial state set up specialized colleges for science and engineering in Korea, only one-third of the schools' enrollment was allocated to Koreans.[16] Keijō University established a school of science in 1941. As a result, by the time of Korean liberation, the number of B.S. degree holders in Korea totaled only 125; most of these students studied engineering, while only thirty-two majored in the sciences.[17] Another study estimates that only 5 percent of Korean college graduates majored in science and engineering—about 200 people. If you include those Koreans who had obtained B.S. degrees in other countries, the total number grows to 300 by the time of liberation. The total Korea Ph.D. degree holders in the natural sciences numbered only twelve—eight in the sciences and four in engineering during the thirty-six years of Japanese rule. In contrast, as early as 1920, the total number of Japanese Ph.D. holders in the field was 543—177 in the sciences and 466 in engineering. By way of comparison, the total number of Chinese who received Ph.D.'s outside China reached 845 in the same period.[18]

According to 1938 records, there were only 360 Korean experts in the field of science and technology, less than 10 percent of the total number of scientists and technicians in Korea; among those 360, only ninety-five had graduated from college—mostly from colleges in Japan—and the rest were graduates of specialized high schools. By the time of national liberation, the total number of technicians working in big factories in the Hamhŭng area was 1,012, but only fourteen of these people were Korean. In contrast, Japanese scientists and technicians working in Korea numbered about three thousand—one for every 100–200 Japanese adults in Korea. It is on the basis of this data that Kim rejects the thesis that Japanese colonialism laid down a foundation for Korea's future industrialization.

After the Japanese defeat, the Engineering School of Seoul National University opened up with a few Korean scholars who had only bachelor degrees. If the training of technical and scientific personnel is one of the most critical factors for economic development, then the University of California, which has trained hundreds of Korean Ph.D.'s since 1950, could be given more credit for the Republic of Korea's economic development than the entire Japanese colonial authority.

Colonial Modernity

It is almost inevitable that current economic and political concerns tend to influence the selection of research agendas and the interpretation of past history. Even a self-conscious historian finds it difficult to avoid reinterpreting the past according to current criteria and needs. The more complex the topic of debate the more room there is for present circumstances to color evaluative judgment. Therefore it is not surprising to see that evaluations of the Japanese colonial legacy in Korea have fluctuated with the changing times.

The original concept, shared by pre-war conservative Japanese and some Americans, viewed Japanese colonialism as an essentially positive experience.[19] During the Pacific War, however, American perceptions changed to view Korea as a ruthlessly exploited victim of Japanese imperialism.

After Korea's liberation, Korean scholars questioned the view that South Korea's modernization was made possible by Japanese colonization and labeled such historiography as a "colonial historical perspective" (singminji sagwan) intentionally fostered by the Japanese colonial authority. These scholars advocated instead for a nationalist interpretation of modern Korean history. For instance, Shin Yong Ha argued that both the British style of indirect colonial rule and the French style of direct colonial rule resulted from the preoccupation with economic exploitation. The ethnic and cultural traditions of the respective colonial territories were thus left largely intact. Japanese colonial rule of Korea, on the other hand, took the form of direct rule and aimed to eliminate Korea as an ethnic and cultural entity through forced assimilation.[20]

However, the economic miracles in Korea and Taiwan in the 1980s, based in large part on Japan's strategy for economic success, encouraged some scholars to revive the pre-war thesis that Japanese colonialism had laid down the basic infrastructure for modernization in Korea. According to this view, the economic, social, and industrial developments in Korea undertaken by Japan in the 1920s and 1930s played a positive role in South Korea's more recent economic development.

Among South Korean scholars, An Pyŏngjik, an economist once known as a Marxist, challenges earlier nationalist interpretations with his detailed analysis of economic data collected by the colonial administration. These analyses lead him to conclude that if Japan had not colonized Korea, Korea would have never gotten rid of their traditional constraints and embarked on a plan of economic development. Moreover, since it is difficult to separate out Japanese from Korean ownership in pre-liberation Korea, whatever the Japanese did in Korea should be considered as part of Korea's industrialization and modernization.[21]

Other scholars reached similar conclusions by focusing on different aspects of the colonial legacy. Some economists paid attention to the Japanese colonial administration's construction of basic infrastructure, claiming that this was the vital factor for South Korea's successful economic development.[22] Comparing the economic performance of the last days of the Chosŏn Dynasty with that of Korea under Japanese colonialism, this line of reasoning argues that during the thirty-six years Japan was in Korea, it invested a total of $8 billion for roads, railways, and other institutions that laid the groundwork for Korea's industrialization in 1970s.

Other scholars attribute the Republic of Korea's economic development to the chaebŏls, trace the origin of these Korean-style entrepreneurs to a few successful Korean businessmen from the Japanese colonial period, and stress the parallels between the contemporary and colonial era businessmen in terms of their close ties with and the financial favors received from the state.[23] Still other scholars subscribe to the thesis of a "developmental state." According to this idea, South Korean economic success can be attributed to the implementation of a strong state that was relatively autonomous from the dominant ruling class, and capable of carrying out an economic development strategy. This strong state is then traced back to the colonial administration that had replaced the ineffective, incompetent, and corrupt Chosŏn Dynasty.[24]

Some left-leaning scholars subscribing to the broadly defined world system and dependence theory that was quite fashionable in 1970s and 1980s joined the school of colonial modernity through different reasoning processes. According to the dependency theory, South Korea could not have developed its national economy independently because its dependency on the United States should have resulted in a similar fate to that of Latin American countries. However, contrary to the predictions of dependence theory, South Korea and Taiwan succeeded in their economic development. In another contradiction to dependency theory, the South Korean state turned out to be nationalistic and capable of controlling not only its capitalist class, but also of holding its own with foreign governments and capital, thereby promoting the South Korean national economy.

Some scholars have tried to explain this theoretical anomaly by stressing Korean experiences with Japanese colonialism and the "flying geese" model of Japanese development strategy. More specifically, this view emphasizes the incorporation of the Korean economy into the world system through Japan during the colonial period and in the postwar period through the transfer of Japanese sunset industries to Korea according to the logics of production cycle. Such scholars modify the implications of the world system theory to match South Korea's economic development, while at the same time applying the basic logic of world system theories to the Korean independence movement and the division of Korea. For instance, Bruce Cumings stresses class cleavages over nationalism as the driving political forces in colonial Korea, while attributing nationalism to the working class, thereby condemning Korean elite as Japanese collaborators. This line of reasoning leads him to view North Korea as a revolutionary regime and the Korean War as "the national liberation war."[25]

The latest work espousing colonial modernity is a collection of essays called *Colonial Modernity in Korea*, edited by Gi-Wook Shin and Michael Robinson.[26] Noting that colonialism, anti-colonial nationalism, and modernization took place almost simultaneously in Korea, they propose to conceptualize the Japanese colonial period as a complex historical process that underwent drastic transformation through modernization. Yet, these scholars viewed these complex and profound changes during the colonial period as the process of modernization introduced by the Japanese colonial authority as being totally disconnected from Korea's prior history.

Consequently, the interaction of nationalism and modernity, particularly the question of how nationalism had cooperated or competed with colonialism for modernization, or how the Japanese used modernization to justify their colonial rule over Korea, is not clearly laid out in such a framework. In other words, to paraphrase Dong-No Kim, the work fails to distinguish between modernization that took place during the Japanese colonial period, and colonial modernity, or the colonial nature of modernity introduced during the same period.[27] As a result, Shin and Robinson seem to argue that any modernization that occurred in Korea during Japanese colonial rule should be credited to the Japanese colonial authority.

Figure o.1 Gi-Wook Shin and Michael Robinson's view on the Relationship Among the National, the Colonial, and the Modern.

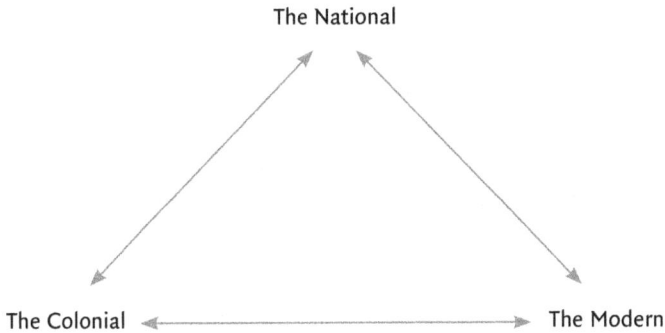

The National

The Colonial ⟵————————————⟶ The Modern

Source: "The Historical Field," Gi-Wook Shin and Michael Robinson, eds., *Colonial Modernity in Korea.* (Cambridge, MA: Harvard University Asia Center, 1999).

One of the frequently overlooked complexities in the master narratives of Korean nationalists, according to Shin and Robinson, is the notion of hegemony that the Japanese colonial authority developed while governing the Korean people. This idea of hegemony contrasts with the characterization of Japanese colonialism by Korean nationalists as "uniquely coercive Japanese political repression, economic exploitation, and its debilitating cultural policies."[28] But what is overlooked in such an analysis is that this hegemony, at least in the eyes of the Korean people, was based largely on Japan's coercive power and on the actual performance of the Japanese colonial administration in introducing modern systems, institutions, and technology that the Koreans themselves wanted. In this respect, Shin and Robinson neglect to distinguish between the Japanese colonial administration's efficacy in introducing modernity for which Koreans willingly gave credit to Japan for, and its legitimacy, which most Koreans refused to recognize.

In the eyes of most Koreans, Japan neither possessed cultural superiority nor succeeded in developing a persuasive ideological justification for its colonial rule. If the colonial administration hoped to develop hegemony by introducing modern institutions and technology, it was futile because the kind of modernity Koreans wanted was irrespective of Japanese colonial legitimacy, and Koreans felt that they could do much better without Japanese colonial rule. For this reason, this introduction will argue that in spite of the serious intellectual mistakes of oversimplification that nationalist narratives might have made, scholars espousing colonial modernity have also failed to squarely address the essential question of how the political considerations of the colonial rulers, in the absence of their legitimacy, would have affected the actual modernization processes that took place during the colonial period.

A similar observation can be made with regard to the multiple identities that Korea might have developed in addition to a national identity. No one, including nationalist historians, would deny that Korean society underwent profound transformation—e.g. social stratification and professionalization—during the colonial period, resulting in the emergence of multiple identities based on such diverse criteria as class, gender, race, culture, and nation. The relevant question, therefore, is how the colonial context distorted, colored, and otherwise affected the emergence and relative weight of such identities.

All the works cited above share several commonalities. First, they are almost exclusively based on data collected by colonial authorities. Given the nature of colonial rule, it is inevitable that the data collected by the colonial regime would tend to focus on its achievements while overlooking its negative aspects. As such, this data has a good chance of being biased, if not outright distorted. As a result, some Korean scholars have stated their refusal to "draw their verdict from official statistics and self-serving government reports, because they suspect that the records carefully compiled by colonial administrative officials reveal that Japanese policy was above all devoted to uplifting Korea, but unfortunately not its people."[30]

This is symptomatic of a more fundamental error: the colonial modernity school tends to underscore the economic aspects of colonialism, while completely neglecting its political dimension. As a result, these scholars tend to assume that whatever modernization happened during the colonial period came about largely due to the policies of the colonial authority—Koreans are only portrayed as passive recipients. Such an argument becomes possible when a total discontinuity between the colonial period and preceding Korean traditions is implied.

The weakest point in this line of reasoning is the linkage between two separate events—Japanese colonialism through 1945 and South Korea's economic explosion in the second half of the 1960s—a period separated by almost twenty years. Some scholars point to institutional similarities between business organizations or the role of the state during these two distinct periods. However, they also have to rule out the possibility that Korea might have merely learned from the Japanese model—something that would have been possible even without the experiences of Japanese colonialism. It is absolutely necessary to make distinctions between Japanese colonialism per se, and the inspiration exerted by Japanese political, economic, and intellectual successes vis-à-vis the modernized West. It is, therefore, one thing to argue that Korea followed Japan on its path of industrialization and used the Japanese model as means of catching up to the West, but it is another to argue that Japanese colonialism supplied the foundation for future economic development in Korea.

If Korea copied the Japanese model of economic development, the next logical question is, where did the Japanese model come from, and why did the Japanese model work for Korea? These questions might in turn have caused scholars to consider the shared characteristics of late industrializing countries or the many shared cultural traits of Japan and Korea, rather than attributing all of Korea's modernization to the specific legacy of colonialism.

In addition, these analyses fail to discuss the profound disruption and discontinuity caused by such drastic and systemic changes as the division of the peninsula, the civil war that destroyed more than 80 percent of South Korea's industrial capacity, and the massive aid received from and consequent close relations with the United States—all of which could be said to have had their roots in the legacy of Japanese colonialism. Such studies tend to be oblivious to the possibility that despite structural similarities between the institutions of the two countries, the actual operation and practice of those institutions—for example, developmental states—were quite different. While stressing the parallels between the colonial experience and South Korea's strategy for economic development, these scholars are silent on the puzzling question of how to explain the economic failure of North Korea, where the Japanese industrial legacy was more conspicuous. If South Korea had failed to develop its economy, as North Korea did, would this also have been due to Japan's colonial legacy?

Any empirical study of the modern institutions and physical infrastructure introduced during the Japanese colonial period is itself a legitimate intellectual enterprise, but any evaluative extrapolation from such study requires cautious judgment, especially in the context of colonialism. In other words, merely describing what took place during the period of colonial rule does not help solve the question of how colonialism's legacy should be appraised. To justify such studies by saying that they are needed to correct the nationalist master narratives, for which Korean scholars from both South and North Korea are equally guilty, is to argue the strawman fallacy rather than to provide productive proof of an argument.

METHODOLOGICAL PROBLEMS

Modernization, Nationalism, and Colonialism

The question of how to view relationships among colonialism, anti-colonial nationalism, and modernity is key to any objective evaluation of Japanese colonialism. Chatterjee and Schmid's conceptualization differ from Shin's and Robinson's scheme.[29]

The problem with Shin's and Robinson's conceptualization is that it tends to overlook that modernization is an almost inevitable process in the long run, although the choice of a political leader or nation may impede or facilitate this process. Chatterjee makes an eloquent plea for the need to distinguish between colonialism and modernization. "The idea of colonialism was only incidental to the history of the development of modern institutions," whereas the modern state and "technologies of power in the countries of Asia and Africa are now very much with us."[31] This, according to him, is the reason why "we now tend to think of the period of colonialism as something we have managed to put behind us, whereas the progress of modernity is a project in which we are all, albeit with varying degrees of enthusiasm, still deeply implicated."[32] In other words, modernization is a universal phenomenon that even colonized people eagerly subscribe to, particularly when they know that their colonization resulted from their country's failure to modernize. As such, it's no real surprise that nationalist reformers of the late Chosŏn Dynasty, the Korean independence movement activists during the colonial era, and Koreans in the postwar era have all supported modernization as the only way to assure the survival of the nation. In other words, the modernization that took place during Japanese occupation has as much to do with the timing of Japanese colonialism as it does with Japanese colonial authority's decision to modernize Korea. If modernization was a historical inevitability, colonialism

Figure 0.2 Chatterjee and Schmid Representation

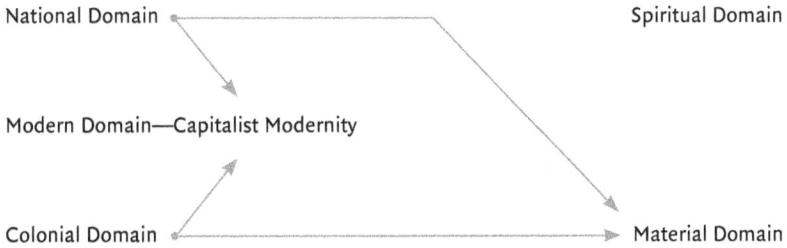

National Domain ← ⟶ Spiritual Domain

Modern Domain—Capitalist Modernity

Colonial Domain ← ⟶ Material Domain

Source: Partha Chatterjee, *The Nation and Its Fragments: Colonial and Postcolonial Histories* (Princeton, NJ: Princeton University Press, 1992).

would be a contingent phenomenon imposed on a select number of countries. It is, therefore, absolutely necessary to separate the experience of colonialism from the process of modernization. In other words, even if colonialism and modernization happened to take place simultaneously in Korea, it would be a mistake to look at the relationship as being causal.

Once we understand modernization as a universal phenomenon anticipated and accepted by even those being colonized, the question then shifts to whether or not pre-colonial Korea had the intention as well as the capacity to pursue modernization, and how the colonial process that did historically take place affected the development of modernization in Korea. Since modernization implies "the Enlightenment, rationalism, citizenship, individualism, legal rational legitimacy, industrialism, nationalism and the nation state, the capitalist world system, and so on," any study of colonial modernization has to address how the colonial authority's political imperatives influenced these politically sensitive dimensions of modernization.[33] Since colonialism, by definition, refers to foreign rule largely backed by coercive power, the basic nature of colonialism can only tolerate selective modernization: in other words, the notion of colonial modernity is predicated on the fact that the modern ideas and institutions introduced by the colonizing force should not undermine the political supremacy of its colonial rule. Thus, the most critical question underlying colonial modernization is to what extent the colonial situation distorted modernization. In the Korean case, this means that any comprehensive evaluation of the Japanese colonial legacy must address the political issues of citizenship, legal rights and authority, and discrimination on the basis of ethnicity.

Both of these two ideas—that modernity is generally desired, even by nationalists (though apparently not by reactionary nationalists), and that colonialism, by definition, can introduce only selective, limited modernization—lead us to the logical conclusion that colonial modernization tends to destroy "any equilibrium among the various components of modernity." Chatterjee recalibrates the relationship between nationalism, colonialism, and modernity by distinguishing between modernization in the "material domain"—which refers to "the domain of the 'outside,' of the economy and of state craft, of science and technology," as well as the structure of the economy—and the domains of the "spiritual" represented by "'inner' bearing the 'essential' marks of cultural identity."[34] Korean nationalists might have accepted colonial modernization in the material domain, but they vigorously defended their prerogative in the spiritual domain. For instance, as Chatterjee points out, the nationalist "thinks of its own language as belonging to that inner domain of cultural identity from which the colonial introducer had to be kept out: language therefore become a zone over which the nationalist first had to declare its sovereignty and then had to transform in order to make it adequate for the modern world."[35] In lieu of developing the spiritual domain of modernization, nationalists wanted to develop a modern, rational, and effective state in which, according to Chatterjee, "power is meant not to prohibit but to facilitate the process " of modernization.[36] The colonial state is, however, constrained from performing this normal mission, for it is "an agency that was never destined to fulfill its normalizing mission of the modern state because the premise of its power was a rule of colonial differences, namely, the preservation of the alienness of the ruling group."[37] Here one can clearly see the double-edged sword of the colonial state, whose first imperative was the perpetuation of its rule rather than leading society down the path of modernization.

Andre Schmid follows Chatterjee's line of analysis in his book, *Korea Between Empires, 1895–1919*.[38] Focusing squarely on the issue of how a Korean national consciousness developed amid the disintegration of the Chinese empire and the rise of modern Japan in 1910, Schmid's book draws information from newspapers in which the modernizing Korean elite advocated *munmyŏng gaehua* (civilization and enlightenment) as a means of strengthening the nation state, which faced internal and external threats. His conclusions, reached on the basis of careful study of the modernization of the elite at the last days of the Chosŏn Dynasty, depart from the school of colonial modernity in significant ways.[39] According to Schmid, both nationalists and colonialists endorsed and pursued capitalist modernity, but for different reasons: the nationalists thought modernization would strengthen their own national survival, whereas the colonialists used it as justification for colonial rule. Because he looks closely at the arguments advocated by pre-colonial Korean nationalists, Schmid is able to assimilate the pre-colonial Korean nationalist plan for modernization into the overall process of Korean modernization, thus avoiding the logical traps of colonial modernity. According to Schmid, Korean nationalist reformers

> had appealed to as a higher authority to strengthen the nation was now cited by Japanese colonial authorities as a higher authority to extinguish Korea as a nation. Satirize as they did Japanese colonial discourse and decry the contradictions between rhetoric and action, these writers were caught in the double bind of "civilization and enlightenment."[40]

To put it more bluntly, Korea's failure to modernize allowed the Japanese to "hijack" modernization as a means to justify the takeover of Korea. According to Schmid, "Japanese justification for colonizing Korea was framed in the very same vocabulary of civilization employed by Korean intellectuals in their own rethinking of the nation."[41]

After Japan managed to successfully appropriate an agenda for the buildup of a modern administrative structure, some Korean nationalist writers began "moving away from a state-centered definition of nation to contemplate an alternative location, one variously called the national soul (*kukhon*) or the national essence (*kuksu*)."[42] Faced with the overwhelming coercive power of the colonizers, Korean nationalists tried to preserve the autonomy of the spiritual domain while accepting modernity in the material domain as a universalizing trend that every nation, with or without colonialism, must move toward.[43] "This spiritually defined nation offered a form of resistance rooted not in civilizing reform but in the cultivation of language, religion, and especially history."[44]

Long Korean History versus Thirty-Six Years of Colonialism

Another methodological question holding significant implications for the interpretation of Japan's colonial legacy is how to compare the relative influence of Korea's long history and cultural tradition with the influence of Japan's thirty-six years of colonialism. Undoubtedly, to ask what would have happened to Korea if Japan had not colonized Korea would be a counterfactual question. However, scholars of colonial modernity build their argument on an opposite counterfactual assumption—that if Japan had not colonized Korea—the Chosŏn political system would have remained incompetent, factionalized, and isolated from the outside the world.

What would have happened to Korea if it had not been annexed by Japan? How one answers this hypothetical question depends on one's view of Korea's situation at the time of annexation, as well as the kind of international environment we can assume to have surrounded Korea. Even without Japanese colonization, the international environment at that time would not have allowed Korea to stay with its traditions intact and immune to external changes. Korea's elite had to respond to external pressures, and the only way to respond was to have its entire system reformed, either drastically or gradually. In the worst-case scenario, such drastic changes might have sparked a civil war or revolution. Nonetheless, it is unlikely that Korea could have remained immune from the international environment with its faction-ridden elite and conservative Neo-Confucian ideology intact.

During the waning days of the Chosŏn Dynasty, particularly negative criticisms were reserved for the Chosŏn Dynasty elite, known as yangban, who frequently served as a convenient metaphorical device used by both nationalists and colonialists to critique traditional Korean culture. Korean nationalist reformers shared similar views with Japanese colonizers about the yangban, but they differed about the goal of such images: "in one case it was to urge the population to reform away from particular types of behavior, and in the other it was used to show that such practices made international reform unthinkable."[45]

James Palais appears to take a position between these opposite views about the traditional elites' potential for modernization. Stressing that the yangban class was more loyal to Confucian culture under a dynasty that had always been subject to China, than to the Korean nation, he argues that far from conforming to a modern notion of a nation state, the Chosŏn Dynasty was actually quite weak. At the same time, Palais repudiates the Japanese colonialist view that Korea "was condemned to stagnation and backwardness."[46] According to him, efforts by nationalist Korean intellectuals to prove Korea's capacity for development and progress were not "unwarranted, just exaggerated." However, "the charge of Japanese and Western scholars in the first half of the twentieth century that Korean society was incapable of any change was more a product of prejudice than fact."[47]

In dealing with this hypothetical question, it may be worthwhile to remember that over the previous two thousand years, the Korean people had successfully responded to a changing international environment, and also that they have proven themselves able to adjust to the new international environment since Korea's liberation. Although Korea fell victim to Japanese aggression, it possessed the potential to ride the inevitable wave of modernization. Social stratification was less rigid in Korea, and its political structure was more centralized than in Japan. It also boasted many modern features such as the merit-based recruitment of officials through civil service examinations. Despite stark differences between the yangban and commoner classes, pre-colonial Korea was relatively homogeneous and without the ethnic and religious cleavages that could be seen in, for example, India. Even though the state's administrative capacity was quite limited, it had maintained a centralized bureaucratic state for at least five hundred years during the Chosŏn Dynasty.

Totality versus Case Study; Continuity versus Beginning;
Beginning versus Causation

Another difficult methodological issue is whether an appraisal of the Japanese colonial legacy should be attempted in a totalistic fashion—relating all the costs or benefits—or whether a more fragmented appraisal is acceptable. Is it possible to interpret a piece of empirical information in light of the total colonial experience? By discussing only Japanese contributions to the development of Korea's economic infrastructure during the colonial period, we may lose perspective about the costs paid by Korea in the process of that development.

Those advocating colonial modernity have stressed empirical evidence to justify their views. However, a war waged on empirical cases does not help clarify the bigger question of evaluation. For instance, Carter Eckert's detailed empirical study of Kyŏngsŏng Textile Company demonstrates that Kim Sŏngsu had developed close ties with the Japanese governor-general and had benefited from the Japanese War against China, which in turn created huge demands for the textile industry. He writes: "It was war, however, that ultimately led to improvement in the quality and status of the Korean workers," then goes on to assert that this, in turn, contributed to the success of Korea's postwar industrialization.[48] The crucial critique of this position is not whether the Japanese War effort led to an improvement in employment opportunities for the Koreans, but rather how to establish a linkage between war-induced industrialization and postwar Korean economic development and how to simultaneously address the massive costs paid for by the Koreans during Japan's aggressive war.

Can the Japanese colonial authority's tolerance of the expansion of Kim Sŏngsu's business be considered proof of Japan's colonial contribution to South Korea's economic development almost three decades later? It is one thing to contradict the nationalist portrait that some Korean historians have painted of Kim Sung Soo. However, it is a totally different matter to attribute recent Korean industrialization to the Japanese colonial administration and its policy of total mobilization for the war effort. That Kim Sŏngsu was the first Korean bourgeoisie does not means that he is responsible for the emergence of the Korean chaebŏl in the 1960s. Here one has to make a clear distinction between beginnings and causes. In fact, Eckert fails to provide any linkage between the origin of the Korean bourgeois and its contribution to Korea's economic development in the 1960s. What is the linkage between the increased number of the workers and technicians due to the Japanese war effort and Korean industrialization in the 1960s and 1970s? In Ho Kim argues that the pre-liberation industry was not connected to post-liberation industrialization in Korea. For instance, in Japan, airplane manufacturing skills and knowledge were used to produce a rapid train system, but the incipient industrialization of the aviation industry was not connected to any consequences after Korea's liberation.[49]

Carter Eckert also asserts that the textile industry introduced to Korea by the Japanese colonial administration played an important role in Korea's economic development. "The essential industrial infrastructure maintained and became the basis for postwar economic reconstruction in the 1950s, and a great new spurt of industrialization," he writes. "Nowhere is this more evident than in the textile industry. On the contrary, it represents the culmination of a process of development that had begun during World War I and blossomed in the 1930s after the Manchurian Incident. The postcolonial contribution of American aid to this process was essentially to provide the capital and technology with which to reconstruct and expand the colonial base."[50] Another crucial question thus becomes how much postwar American aid should be credited for the development of the South Korean economy. Although Eckert acknowledges the positive role that American aid played in the Republic of Korea's economic development, his overall thesis tends to underscore Japan's colonial legacy as being more significant.

This line of reasoning totally disregards the historical fact that all late industrializing countries—including China—start with light industries, in particular the textile industry. His argument also seems to presuppose that the origin of any industrialization is the key for its eventual success. In other words, he implies that industrialization, once started, is an automatic process. By mistaking beginnings for causality, he fails to recognize that modernization is a process that requires continuous leadership. Even granting that Japanese colonial industrialization provided some basic infrastructure, much of this the Korean War destroyed, the origins of which can be also traced back to the Japanese colonialism. On the other hand, the infrastructure of heavy industry left behind in the northern half of the peninsula by Japanese colonialism did not lead North Korea to sustain successful economic development. This, in turn, indicates that South Korea's economic success has more to do with developing the processes of industrialization rather than the origin of industrialization.

Overall Cost and Benefit of Colonialism

Debate over whether colonial modernization was beneficial or a constraint is a misdirected question. The right question is not what was started in Korea during the Japanese colonial period, but to what degree industrialization was realized; whether the structures Japan laid down were such that these foundations would have had the capacity to develop into a national economy. Another critical question that every scholar attempting to appraise Japan's colonial legacy has to confront is whether or not Japanese colonialism was the best means for Korea to enter the modern world system in 1910.

This means that it is absolutely necessary to consider the cost of Japanese colonialism together with any and all possible positive benefits to Korea. No one questions that the Japanese colonial policy was highly exploitative and that living conditions for Koreans, particularly during the war period, were very harsh. For instance, by 1933, Korea was exporting 66.3 percent of its rice to Japan, while its importation of Manchurian millet reached about 1.72 million sok. The total volume of Korea's imports and exports rose rapidly, but 98.5 percent of all exports and 94.2 percent of all imports were with Japan and its colonies, including Manchuria.[51] This trade pattern indicates that the Korean economy became more dependent on Japan as time went on. If these figures are used to support the argument that Japan's colonial legacy helped Korea's economic development, more direct credit should go the United States, which kept its domestic market open to Korean and Japanese products during the postwar era.

In addition, one has to remember that Koreans were discriminated against under Japanese colonialism. By the time of national liberation, about 80 percent of Korean wealth belonged to the Japanese. Korean wages were 50 percent less than those of the Japanese. Colonialism further deepened class cleavages as land ownership became further concentrated in the hands of influential landlords. In addition, there is ample evidence that the colonial policy aimed at tying Koreans to an agricultural economy, while helping the Japanese to occupy all the key positions of power and wealth on the Korean peninsula.[52] Although some Koreans might have benefited from colonialism, they were still discriminated against in comparison to the Japanese. Koreans were kept in the bureaucratic lower echelons and were always placed under Japanese supervision. For example, Koreans supplemented the Japanese military police force. Initially, most Japanese migrants to Korea were from the poorest sectors of Japan, but by 1940, 45 percent of Japanese citizens residing in Korea were employed in the government apparatus or in professional fields, whereas Koreans in those same fields amounted to only 4 percent.[53]

Given such a context, any study of the few successful Korean businessmen from that period who collaborated with the Japanese colonial authorities can hardly prove that Japan's colonial legacy is positively related to South Korea's postwar economic success.

The political cost of Korea's colonial experience was too high compared with its largely speculative advantages. Many Koreans believe that Japanese colonialism, aimed at direct rule and total assimilation, was much worse than the British style of indirect rule or the French style of direct rule. Both of these European colonial regimes were interested in economic exploitation, leaving the ethnic and cultural traditions of their respective colonies largely intact. Japanese colonialism split the Korean elite into two camps: those who were anti-Japanese versus collaborators. This split was superimposed on the class cleavages that any industrialization process produces, while simultaneously depriving Koreans of any opportunity to learn about self-rule. In other words, such colonial experiences further strengthened rather than weakened neo-familism, according to Yong chool Ha, who contributes the leading chapter to this volume.[54]

To sum up, I believe that the scholars who stress the positive role played by Japanese colonialism up to 1945 need to be more self-critical about their methodological assumptions. Such a simplistic view that whatever existed historically is therefore justifiable cannot be used to effectively explain South Korea's historic economic development two decades after Japanese colonialism.

Problem of Extrapolation: "The Nationalistic Narrative" as a Strawman

The most serious problem with colonial modernity scholarship lies not in empirical findings, but rather in the tendency to extrapolate the implications out of the context of the colonial situation. Instead of demonstrating awareness of the methodological dilemmas and complexity required in evaluating specific empirical findings for the overall evaluation of Japanese colonial legacy, colonial modernity scholarship tends to use the "nationalist narrative" as a strawman in order to elevate the theoretical implications of their findings to a more general level, and in turn this makes it possible for the evaluation of Japanese colonialism to become the focus. Such intellectual maneuvers are then justified as correctives to the nationalistic influence of Korean academics—what Carter Eckert calls "exorcising Hegel's ghost."[55]

In this instance, the only concrete examples of a "master nationalist narrative" that Eckert offers is the "spontaneous sprout of capitalism," a theory that assumes that the Chosŏn Dynasty possessed the potential to develop capitalism even without external influence, and that, in fact, capitalism managed to sprout in the last days of dynasty. This theory is, in many ways, the most extreme of the differing nationalist discourses. By setting it up as representative of South Korean scholarship as a whole, Eckert is able to condemn South Korean scholarship for its "nationalist paradigms" that "have obfuscated, subsumed, or obliterated virtually all other possible modes of historical interpretation" by using "a myopic nationalist lens" proven to be "a narrow and unforgiving gate through which the facts of history, as well as the historian must pass."[56] In this categorical condemnation of South Korean scholarship, even the fundamental differences between South and North Korean scholars are totally lost, as if both were equally guilty of pursuing nationalist trends at the cost of empirical data. It is one thing to say that South Korean society may have a tendency to be nationalistic, given its historical experiences, and the contemporary situation of division. But condemning the entire body of South Korean scholarship on colonialism without specifying particular authors is quite a different matter.

While criticizing Korean scholars for their politicized master narratives, Eckert promises "scholarship with a focus on the complex relations between colonialism, modernity, and nationalism," declaring that "evidence does matter," as if those he criticizes had been totally "impervious [. . .] to contrary empirical evidence," while pleading for a "pluralistic" and "inductive method." Eckert lectures that "a historian has to have two kinds of passion: passion for the truth, a zeal for finding out what happened, and the second passion is for the historical interpretation being put forward."[57] However, he does not follow the principles he advocates. According to his writing, it is essential to interpret facts in the context of the historical stage of a given moment. Any study of colonialism requires a comprehensive context in order to fully elaborate the implications any historical facts may have for a broader intellectual issue. The "colonial modernity" argument appears to make the same intellectual mistake attributed to the Korean nationalist discourse, namely extrapolating the implications of findings beyond what the findings warrant. It is absolutely necessary for any scholar working on the Japanese colonial legacy to be sensitive to the complexity involved in the seemingly simple intellectual task of evaluating what took place during the age of modernization, as Partha Chatterjee eloquently argues. Being able to detect the subtleties, gray areas, and contradictions of the period, while not losing overall perspective of the basic nature of colonialism is what is required from good scholarship. Good scholarship further requires that one not exaggerate any implication of one's own empirical findings, regardless of how valid they are empirically. Instead, a proper interpretation of the theoretical implications of one's findings must be made without losing sight of the peculiar context of colonialism.

In other words, finding what took place is only the first step in any historical research. The more important step is to interpret those findings in a historical context. For instance, Eckert underscores his empirical findings that Korean laborers saw a quantitative increase in numbers during the last phase of colonialism, after Japan embarked upon total mobilization for their desperate war efforts. The above statement is not itself wrong, but it is inadequate. If this increase in laborers included Koreans conscripted as comfort women or as workers in Japanese mining facilities and factories when able-bodied Japanese workers were sent to the front line, what claims can be made about how Korea benefited from this increase, particularly in regards to the Republic of Korea's industrialization twenty years later?

No one would challenge that Kim Sŏngsu was very close with the colonial government and even collaborated with the Japanese authority in order to expand his business enterprises. It is well known that without collaborating with the Japanese authority, no business could grow during that period; the successful operation of any Korean business, not to mention any expansion, was out of the question without this kind of collaboration. But the implicit implication of the Eckert argument—that without Japanese colonialism, the Korean bourgeoisie would not have started enterprises during this period—is controversial. Again, what is being contested is the question of how to interpret empirical findings, and whether or not such interpretation changes when viewed in the total context of colonialism. It seems that Eckert makes a quantum jump from the case study of Kim Sŏngsu to the origins of the South Korean bourgeois, and then again to the South Korean chaebŏl of the 1960s and 1970s, and finally to the Republic of Korea's eventual economic success. All Korean businessmen of a certain age group in the 1960s must necessarily have started their career before 1949. In order to establish a link between the

Kyŏngsŏng Textile Company of the Japanese colonial period and the chaebŏl of the 1960s, which played the role of engine for economic development, he needs to relate his case study of Kim's business in 1930s to the South Korean economic development in 1960s and 1970s more directly.

Some of the ultra-nationalistic historian's mistakes do not offer justification for extrapolating one's findings to make them theoretical significant beyond what the evidence warrants. It does not make sense to challenge a simplistic view with another simplistic view taken out of the totality of colonial context. Eckert's passionate plea to exorcize Hegel's ghost sounds hollow, because Hegel's ghost proves to be a real ghost without any substance, one only used to exaggerate the implications of specific empirical findings, totally taken out of the context of Japanese colonialism and Korean history. Some of the obviously politically motivated forms of nationalist discourse, such as the "spontaneous sprout of capitalism," are used as a strawman to condemn the entirety of Korean scholarship, while justifying the exaggerated implications of some empirical findings that are themselves not controversial. If one is not careful to extrapolate the implications of one's own empirical findings, the school of colonial modernity is in danger of becoming the school of neo-colonial historiography.

Implication of China's Rise and
Need to Re-conceptualize East Asian Modernization

The recent rise of China casts doubt on the validity of the underlying assumptions of the debate around Japan's colonial legacy and underscores the need to reexamine East Asian modernization and economic development using a new framework.[58] If the previous debate assumes that Korea, and for that matter China, did not have the will or capacity to embark on modernization and economic development and instead had to wait for Japan to initiate these processes, a new conceptual framework should be built upon a macro view of modernization—an ongoing historical process that each of the Asian countries struggled to deal with since they came into contact with Western civilization and its industrial and military powers.

Such a macro historical perspective would be grounded on empirical findings from the comparative study of the three nations. On the basis of this, it would become possible to accumulate generalizations, eventually relating them into a coherent theoretical argument. This approach offers several intellectual advantages.

First, the conceptual framework enables us to accommodate the differences in each country's histories, traditions, and cultures, as well as take note of other factors in the initial conditions of each country's social and political structure that might have resulted in different responses to and degrees of success with modernization. At the same time, such a framework will allow us to be sensitive to the fact that these three East Asian countries shared similar cultural and institutional heritages, including a history of autonomous, paternalistic states whose origins can be traced to the beginnings of each society; the tradition of recruiting bureaucrats from the best-educated segments of society; shared experiences of national humiliation that engendered strong nationalism, thus enabling the state to mobilize its population for economic development; and the destruction of dominant classes that may have hampered the relative autonomy of the state. They also shared the similar problems of all late industrializing countries that have to figure out how to survive and develop among advanced industrialized countries. On the basis of these shared attributes, these three nations adopted policies by drawing upon their traditions for economic development, effectively utilizing and mobilizing their own resources for their own modern needs and exploiting trade opportunities offered by the existing international system.

Such a framework can also help to explain why it has taken different lengths of time for each country to find, adopt, and implement the right formula and strategy for its own development. Doubtless, Japan was the first East Asian country to achieve successful modernization, even though it took advantage of this early modernization to embark on imperialist campaigns against its neighboring countries. The Republic of Korea has achieved economic development and modernization in spite of the division and destruction caused by the Korean War, and the heavy defense burden that has resulted from its confrontation with North Korea. In contrast, North Korea has failed so far to transform itself into a modern state with a record of successful economic development, despite the fact that most Japanese industrial investments had been located in the northern half of the Korean peninsula. The North Korea situation demonstrates again the importance of political leadership and correct but flexible strategies rather than the path taken by the Japanese colonial authority a half century ago vis-à-vis the Korean peninsula.

Third, we can easily recognize the active roles played out in Japan, South Korea, and China by their people, who utilize their own unique historical legacies and traditions, while exploiting the opportunities provided by the international environment. Only by giving agency to each nation does it become possible to relate to the struggles of South Korean and Chinese nationalist reformers who passionately advocated for modernization as the only way of preserving a national political community. This line of argument also readily accommodates Chatterjee's and Schmid's arguments that colonialism is a historical accident, whereas the process of modernization is a universal phenomenon that even nationalist reformers actively advocate, and that postcolonial societies continue to pursue of their own will.[59]

Fourth, this perspective can effectively address the question of where the Japanese model of economic development came from. Is it based on a unique Japaneseness, or is it based on Japanese attempts to catch up to the industrialized West within the constraints imposed on Japanese history and traditions? If the Japanese model was appropriate for the Korean case, was this due to Korea's colonial experiences, or was it because Korea shares similar cultural traditions and faced similar challenges? If one conceptualizes the Japanese model as a successful combination of its own cultural and institutional traditions and the conditions of later industrializing countries, one needs to explain why the Japanese model worked in Korea, instead of arguing that Japanese colonialism lay down the foundations for Korea to adopt the Japanese model. Korea's colonial experience might have been the worst possible way of learning the Japanese model. Saying that Koreans learned and imitated the Japanese model because it was suitable to the Korean condition is totally different from asserting that the colonial legacy was the mechanism for spreading the Japanese model.

Lastly, by conceptualizing the modernization processes of these three East Asian countries this way, we can prepare a more systemic comparison of the similarities and differences of these three countries, particularly regarding the question of how similar questions are approached differently in each country, as well as other questions of continuity versus discontinuity of traditions in modern times, or the relative ability of each country to adapt to the changing international environment—in other words, the types of questions that will determine the fate of each nation in the coming years.

ORGANIZATION OF THE BOOK

The chapters collected in this volume were initially presented in a brainstorm session sponsored by the University of California at Berkeley, Center for Korean Studies. The contributors then met twice more to discuss and revise the papers. We believe that this collected work is quite different from what we have described as works of colonial modernity scholars.

First of all, all the authors in this volume—except for Hong Yung Lee, Yong chool Ha, Clark W. Sorensen, and Mark E. Caprio—are Korean scholars residing and teaching in South Korea. These works represent their first attempts to present their view on Japanese colonialism in English. Although they do not represent the entire spectrum of South Korean scholarship, it is fair to say that they reflect a majority of Korean scholars' views on the sensitive issue of Japan's colonial legacy.

Second, these scholars rely heavily on Korean data as much as possible, while considering data from the Japanese colonial administration within the total context of the colonialism. Instead of narrowly focusing on economic issues during the colonial period and their implications on South Korean economic development almost twenty years later, the chapters collected here focus squarely on social and institutional changes brought about by modernization under colonial rule. Rejecting the linear view of colonialism leading directly to modernization, the authors detail how the idea of modernization was contested over by both the colonial authorities and the nationalists in certain areas, although for different goals, and how these contests affected—and distorted—the actual practice of certain modern institutions. In other words, instead of simply accepting modern institutions as something fixed, the authors in this volume criticize them, detailing the modern institutions' multiple dimensions as well as the subtle transformations they underwent during the actual process of their operation.

Such an approach inevitably privileges the question of how institutions introduced by the Japanese colonial authority actually operated in the context of colonialism rather than what type of modern institutions were introduced. In the view of these essayists, modernization was not a simple process initiated and introduced by Japanese colonialism, but rather a universal goal of progress that many Koreans actively pursued, often for their own hidden nationalistic agendas. By conceptualizing modernization this way, these scholars are able to incorporate into their analysis the historical fact that the modern institutions introduced from Japan became Korean institutions operating in a Korean way, rather than being a "carbon copy" of the Japanese. This, in turn, leaves room for Korean tradition, culture, and temperament to exert influence on the modernization process, even during the colonial period.

Third, these chapters tend to assume the continuity of Korean history prior to and through the Japanese colonial period, instead of viewing the pre-colonial and the colonial periods as two disjointed and distinctive stages in Korean history. As a result, authors are able to pay more attention to the concrete and specific aspects of Japanese colonialism in the context of Korean history instead of drawing upon general implications from any theoretical perspective. By stressing the continuity of Korean history, these chapters tend to focus on the unique characteristics of Japanese colonialism in Korea.

In the leading chapter of this volume, "Colonial Rule and Social Change: The Paradox of Colonial Control," Yong chool Ha proposes to divide the realm of human activities under colonial rule into three distinctive spaces: superstructural, functional, and social. Since the primary concern of the colonial authority was to preserve its alien rule, the degree of coercion employed by the colonial power and the level of compliance such coercion produced varied from sphere to sphere. In the colonial superstructure, the colonial authority endeavored to develop ideological justification and legitimacy for its own rule, while refusing to tolerate any dissent and challenge from the colonized. However, in the "functional spaces"— similar to Charteerjee's "material domain of modernization"—both colonizers and colonized found their interests to be parallel, albeit for different goals. For instance, the colonizer introduced modern institutions to make their domination more effective and efficient, whereas the colonized realized the need for such modern institutions as a means of strengthening their potential for independence and self-rule. In the social sphere, Japan's predominant concern with its own rule resulted in unintended consequences for some of the modern institutions introduced by the Japanese authority. For instance, the Japanese colonial authority established a modern school system, while prohibiting students from organizing any cross-campus and cross-generational associations. This, in turn, facilitated the development of secret associations based on personal ties to which contemporary South Korean society's preoccupation with school ties can be traced.

Yong-Jick Kim, in his chapter "Politics of Communication and its Colonial Public Sphere in 1920s Korea," uses Habermas's concept of the public sphere to analyze colonial space in Korea. Kim speculates that Korea's public sphere "failed to perform its critical function" (p. 79) of being the social arena through which colonial demands and requests were met. He shows that although colonial Korea was allowed to have a public sphere in the 1920s under so-called cultural rule, even then this sphere could not be categorized as liberal or Confucian. Rather it was, according to Kim, uniquely colonial and uniquely Korean.

Seong-cheol Oh and Ki-seok Kim examine the question of whether the expansion of formal educational opportunities during the Japanese colonial period should be credited to the modern education system introduced by the Japanese colonial authority or to Korea's well-known zeal for education. What would have happened to Korean education if Japan had not colonized Korea? Even before Japan took Korea over, several different types of schools—including Western missionary schools, state schools, private schools established by Korean elites, and traditional *sŏdang*—existed. By showing that the increase in the public schools was accompanied by a proportional decrease in enrollment in other types of schools, this chapter implies that if educational opportunities had not been expanded by the Japanese public school system, missionary and private schools would have filled the educational gap for the Korean people. Furthermore, since the goal of colonial education was to train Koreans to be low-grade laborers who were politically submissive to the Japanese colonial authorities and the Emperor, this chapter implicates the colonial education system in discrimination against the Koreans that, indeed, was even more serious in institutions of higher education.

Dong-No Kim's chapter discusses the most controversial question in the entire history of Marxist movements: How did national and class identities intersect in the colonial setting? Lenin's thesis of imperialism is based on the notion that class struggle can be postponed in a country where capitalism has not advanced very far, but is facing foreign aggression. Chinese communist success is thus attributed to the successful combination of class and anti-imperialistic struggle. This depended on what the major conditions were at a given moment. For this reason, Dong-No Kim pleads that since modernization does not necessarily imply progress, the question of what type of modern institutions were introduced during the colonial period is more important than the debate between exploitation versus modernization. His data shows how Korea's peasant identity changed from the peasants revolting against excessive taxation to class-based challenges with landlords. Due to modern notions of property rights, particularly the concept of ownership that the Japanese helped introduce with the land survey, the taxation system changed from a collective to an individual liability, thereby disintegrating collectivity and creating more individualized peasants. As a result, the focus of protests changed from being anti-state to anti-landlord, wherein the modern impersonal relationship between the landlords and tenants resulted in worsening economic conditions for most Korean peasants. In this sense, the living conditions of peasants deteriorated in contrast to the colonial modernization theory that underscored that the increase in agricultural productivity would lead to an improvement of peasants' living standards.

Mark E. Caprio discusses the importance of colonial government reforms enacted in response to the March 1919 movement in his chapter titled "The 1920 Colonial Reforms and the June 10 (1926) Movement: A Korean Search for Ethnic Space." Even though King Sunjong's funeral gave Koreans an avenue similar to the 1919 funeral of King Kojong through which to express their dislike and distrust of the Japanese, this June 10 movement was not comparable to 1919. Caprio maintains that the period between Sunjong's death and funeral provided both sides (Japan and colonial Korea) the ability to test the reforms put in place after the March First movement.

Keongil Kim's chapter compares the "thought conversion" in Korea with Japan and highlights Japanese difficulties in establishing hegemony, largely due to the refusal of Koreans to recognize Japanese cultural superiority outside of those areas where it had successfully modernized. Another reason for Japan's failure to establish hegemonic dominance over Korea was an ironic inconsistency in its propaganda. One the one hand, Japan condemned Koreans as backward, lazy, and undisciplined, and on the other hand, it believed that the cultural and other gaps between the two peoples were narrow enough to make the Korean people Japanese through its *naisen ittai* policy.

Keunsik Jung's comparison of the Japanese "directory regime" and the Western "tutelary regime" in the management of modern leprosaria reveals that even in the process of modernization in the "functional sphere," the Japanese management system stressed "absolute isolation, vasectomy based on eugenics, arbitrary punishment, and compulsory labor"—a sharp contrast with the Western style where "relatively mild isolations, patient autonomy, and Christianity were the predominant methods of social control." His chapter eloquently demonstrates how the overall goals of Japanese imperialism shaped their policies, even in colonial functional spaces, thereby underscoring the need to view colonial modernity in the overall context of Japanese colonialism rather than focusing on fragmented information about specific institutions taken out of the colonial context.

In "Colonial Body and Indigenous Soul: Religion as Contested Terrain of Culture," Kwang-Ok Kim examines how the colonizers and the colonized contested the areas where the colonial superstructure and social space overlapped. The colonizers tried to reshape the Korean mind, filling it with Japanese religion in the name of science and modernity, whereas Koreans exploited their native religious practice, known as shamanism, to resist, ridicule, and subvert forced cultural assimilation by the colonial authority in their daily lives. Pretending to be the voice of a spirit, Korean shamans frequently expressed a derogatory view of the Japanese, views that were not allowed in ordinary discourse. Kim's work once again eloquently describes the difficulties the Japanese colonial authority encountered in its attempts to establish hegemony in these fields.

Finally, Clark W. Sorensen discusses the Korean family, modernity, and colonial assimilation in his chapter titled "The Korean Family in Colonial Space—Caught between Modernization and Assimilation." He notes that the colonial period significantly altered the modern Korean family toward the Japanese model of a "corporate house system" as opposed to one based on patrilineages that leaves the exact boundaries of the household unit vague. "[C]hanges motivated by administrative convenience and modernization—especially those changes that were the result of administrative interpretation of customary practice—quickly became part of the system" (p. 330) while those changes perceived to have been motivated by Japanese assimilationist impulses were reversed after liberation.

In conclusion, this text provides refreshingly various accounts on the history of the colonial period of Korea. Such research is essential. It not only provides historical information to the academic community, but also offers a portal through which current relationships in East Asia can be viewed. This text, then, has given scholars and politicians alike some of the resources necessary to facilitate communication and dialog in order to continue the formation of amiable relationships throughout the region.

NOTES

1. Hyman Kublin, "The Evolution of Japanese Colonialism," 67–84. For Japanese leaders' view on colonialism in Korea, see http://www.nanet.go.kr/japan/h_fact/facto2.html.

2. For the latest dispute over Japanese colonial legacy in Taiwan, see Norimitsu Onishi, "Japanese Remarks about Taiwan Anger Beijing," *The New York Times*, February 6, 2006.

3. Yu Sŏkch'un, "Singmin chibae ŭi tayangsŏng kwa t'alsingmin chibae ŭi chŏn'gae" 44–45.

4. Atul Kolhi, "Where Do High Growth Political Economies Come From?" 1269–93.

5. Terauchi Masatake, the first governor-general said in 1910 that "the purpose of Korean annexation was to direct and develop Koreans to be civilized people," A. Hamilton, Herbert Henry Austin, and Masatake Terauchi, *Korea: Its History, Its People, and Its Commerce.*

6. Carter Eckert, and Ki-baek Yi ed., *Korea, Old and New.*

7. Henry Em, "Nationalist Discourse in Modern Korea."

8. Benedict Anderson, *Imagined Communities.*

9. John B. Duncan, "Non-Elite Perceptions of the State in the Late Chosŏn."

10. Ibid.

11. Andre Schmid, *Korea Between Empires, 1895–1919.*

12. Ibid., 18–19.

13. For the latest dispute on Japanese educational contribution to Taiwan, see see Norimitsu Onishi, "Japanese Remarks about Taiwan Anger Beijing," *The New York Times* February 6, 2006.

14. Wonmo Dong, "Assimilation and Social Mobilization in Korea," 161.

15. Kim Kŭnbae, *Ilche sigi Chosŏn kwahak kisul illyŏk ŭi sŏngjang.*

16. Kim Keun Bae, "20-segi singminji Chosŏn ŭi kwahak kwa kisul," 297–313.

17. Kim Kŭnbae, *Ilche sigi Chosŏn kwahak kisul illyŏk.*

18. Kim Keun Bae, "20-segi singminji Chosŏn ŭi kwahak kwa kisul," 297–313.

19. Andre Schmid, "Japanese Propaganda in the United States from 1905." Conference paper. Workshop on the International Impact of Colonial Korea, University of Washington–Seattle, November 19, 2010.

20. Shin Yong Ha, *Ilche singminji kŭndaehwaron pip'an.*

21. An Pyŏngjik and Chungch'on Ch'ŏl [Nakamura Satoru], *Kŭndae Chosŏn kongŏphwa ŭi yŏn'gu, 1930-1945*; An Pyŏngjik, "Han'guk kŭnhyŏndaesa yŏn'gu ŭi saeroun p'aerŏdaim: Kyŏngjesa rŭl chungsim ŭro."

22. Young-Iob Chung, *Korea under Siege.*

23. Dennis L. McNamara, *The Colonial Origin of Korean Enterprise*; Carter Eckert, *Offspring of Empire.*

24. Atul Kolhi, "Where Do High Growth Political Economies Come From?" 1269–93.

25. Bruce Cumings, "The Origins and Development of the Northeast Asian Political Economy"; Bruce Cumings, "The Legacy of Japanese Colonialism in Korea."

26. Gi-Wook Shin and Michael Robinson, eds., *Colonial Modernity in Korea.*

27. Kim Tongno, Singminji ŭi minjokchuŭi rŭl nŏmŏ kŭndae ro." For work discussing how colonialism has affected the inner space of Korean writers, see Ji Won Shin, "Recasting Colonial Space," 51–74.

28. Gi Wook Shin and Michael Robinson, eds., *Colonial Modernity in Korea,* 7.

29. Hyman Kublin, "The Evolution of Japanese Colonialism," 67–84.

30. Partha Chatterjee, *The Nation and Its Fragments: Colonial and Postcolonial Histories;* Andre Schmid, *Korea Between Empires, 1895–1919.*

31. Partha Chatterjee, *The Nation and Its Fragments,* 14.

32. Ibid.

33. Ibid., 9.

34. Ibid., 6.

35. Ibid., 7.

36. Ibid., 5.

37. Ibid., 10.

38. Andre Schmid follows Chatterjee's line of analysis in his book, *Korea Between Empires.*

39. Ibid.

40. Ibid., 14.

41. Andre Schmid, *Korea Between Empires.*

42. Ibid., 15.

43. Ibid.

44. Ibid.

45. "The danger for nationalists was that their own critique of past cultural practice, due to its representational overlap with colonial critiques, could be harness to the very colonial enterprise they were now resisting." Andre Schmid, *Korea Between Empires,* 14–15.

46. James Palais, "Nationalism: Good or Bad?" 214–27.

47. Ibid.

48. Carter Eckert, "Total War, Industrialization, and Social Change."

49. Kim Inho, T'aep'yŏngyang chŏnjaeng sigi Chosŏn kongŏp yŏn'gu, 424.

50. Carter Eckert, "Total War, Industrialization, and Social Change."

51. An Pyŏngjik and Chungch'on Ch'ŏl [Nakamura Satoru], Kŭndae Chosŏn kongŏphwa ŭi yŏn'gu, 1930–1945, 12.

52. Stephen Haggard, David Kang, and Chung-In Moon, "Japanese Colonialism and Korean Development," 867–81.

53. Ibid.

54. See chapter 1 by Yong chool Ha.

55. Carter Eckert, "Exorcizing Hegel's Ghosts," 363–78.

56. Ibid.

57. Ibid.

58. For the rise of China, see Zheng Bijian, "'Peaceful Rising' to Great-Power Status," 18–24.

59. Partha Chatterjee, *The Nation and Its Fragments*; Andre Schmid, *Korea Between Empires*.

1

Colonial Rule and Social Change in Korea: The Paradox of Colonial Control

YONG CHOOL HA

Studies of Japanese colonial rule (1910–45) in Korea have long been preoccupied with the economic impact of both development and exploitation. Important as the economic issues may be, the debates have preempted equally important efforts to understand the nature of social changes that occurred during colonial rule. This chapter is an attempt to create a bridge between economic and social impacts in our understanding of Japanese colonial rule in Korea. It will be argued that in understanding colonial society it is essential to see the inherent contradictions created by the conflicting needs of colonial rule and the intersectoral imbalance or disequilibrium arbitrarily imposed by colonial control. It will be also argued that generalizations based on any single or monosectoral analysis, such as an economic study, are not adequate for understanding the colonial social whole. This chapter contends that a different conceptual and theoretical framework is needed that will reveal the complex social dynamics among different sectors under colonial control.

In what follows I present a critical review of major arguments related to the impact of Japanese colonialism on Korea and propose an alternative framework for understanding this colonial society. Two cases of colonial social changes—school ties and family issues—are presented to illustrate the importance of the unintended social consequences and contradictions inherent in colonial rule, the reasons for which can be clarified only through an intersectoral approach.

Studies of Japanese colonial rule in Korea have long been dominated by two diametrically opposed paradigms that may be described as orthodox and revisionist. Orthodox interpretation, well known for its nationalist coloration, focuses on political dependency and arbitrariness, social control and repression, and economic exploitation and the loss of cultural identity. The revisionist approach is largely concerned with positive economic change, modern sociocultural influences under Japanese rule, and cultural hegemony. Criticizing the orthodox interpretation as too nationalistic, the revisionists trace the colonial origins of Korean economic development and argue that colonial rule left legacies such as capital and infrastructure accumulation, as well as a strong state and its modern bureaucracy, all of which became instrumental in designing and implementing Korean economic development plans during the 1960s.[1]

Despite fundamental differences, the two approaches share common methodological and substantive assumptions. Both are monosectoral in their scope of analysis, with their focus primarily on economic issues. Each has also conducted a "war of case studies," typical of monosectoral analysis, in which one case of exploitation is countered by another case of development. As such, both approaches lack a theoretical framework within which to understand the broader institutional and social consequences of colonial rule.

The exploitation-centered orthodox approach rightly emphasizes the suffering imposed by discrimination and physical and psychological controls, but it is not clear what the enduring psychological, institutional, and social consequences of this suffering were. In fact, most such studies are limited only to the colonial period itself.[2]

Problems with the revisionist approach are equally serious. Revisionist research proceeds as if dealing with the economic sector is tantamount to dealing with the whole. It further applies Western sociological concepts and categories to characterize Korean colonial society and thereby fails to acknowledge the unique aspects of Korean colonial society. By linking the institutions of the colonial era to those in present-day Korea—a strong state, economic development, and the emergence of management styles—revisionists commit the error of "reverse teleology," or reading history backwards.[3] The studies cannot do justice to the complex nature of colonial institutions and societies as they actually existed because their interest in the colonial society of Korea is limited to explaining postcolonial economic development. It is not surprising, therefore, that revisionist studies have not paid attention to social institutions developed during the colonial era and how they have affected both society and subsequent patterns of economic development in Korea.

A more recent approach focuses on interactions among national, colonial, and modern arenas in colonial Korea. It criticizes the orthodox approach's exclusive focus on nationalistic interpretations of colonial social changes. According to this view, colonial society was involved in a constant tug of war among the national, colonial, and modern arenas. It attempts to show how the Korean people, though limited by individual leverage, were not simply coerced but interacted on their own volition with the other spheres. On the opposite side, Japanese hegemony was not completely based on force.[4]

It accurately points out the limitations of nationalistic historiography by focusing on colonial modernity but is less successful in suggesting conceptual frameworks for understanding the complexity of colonial society. By treating the colonial arena as one of only three interacting arenas, this approach underestimates the centrality of the effects of the colonial arena on colonial society. Put differently, the colonial arena is subsumed under the interactive aspects of colonial social change. If anything, this view has further parceled the field by referring to cases and situations that do not illuminate the core characteristics of colonial rule. Further, it, regardless of its original intentions, is bound to be linked to the nationalist-revisionist debate and most likely will be strongly identified with the latter, because its emphasis on the active history-making aspect of a colonized people tends to be critical of the nationalist interpretation of repression and exploitation. In the midst of the ongoing emotional polemic, the interjection of this seemingly value-neutral view confuses rather than enhances our understanding of the colonial situation. In this regard, one scholar`s admonition is apt:

> For those of us in exile, when negotiating the intellectual production in our places of origins (whether Latin America, Africa, or Asia) and the intellectual conversation in our place of residence (the United States or Western Europe), the question arises of whether our function should be that of go-between, promoting the importation of "new theories" into our "backward" countries, or whether we should "think from" the post-colonial experiences in which we grew up. My concern is to understand the point that "colonial and post-colonial discourse" is not just a new field of study or a gold mine for extracting new riches but the condition of possibility for constructing new loci of enunciations as well as for reflecting that academic "knowledge and understanding" should be complemented with "learning from" those who are

living in and thinking from colonial and post-colonial legacies. Otherwise, we run the risk of promoting mimicry, exportation of theories, and internal colonialism rather than promoting new forms of cultural critique and intellectual and political emancipation.[5]

It is clear from the previous discussion that studies of Korean society during the colonial period presented and made generalizations based on a fragmented reality, and institutional legacies have not been systematically analyzed. A new conceptual framework is needed within which to capture colonial complexities and subtleties, positioning all these monosectoral analyses in such a way that we may understand Korean society during this period from the perspective of the whole.

A CONCEPTUAL FRAMEWORK: COLONIAL SPACE

The complexities of the colonial experience require a clear understanding of what exactly constitutes the colonial situation. Balandier's remarks on Africa are still useful.

> Any present day study of colonial societies striving for an understanding of current realities and not a reconstitution of a purely historical nature, a study aiming at a comprehension of the condition as they are, not sacrificing facts for the convenience of some dogmatic schematization, can only be accomplished by taking into account this complex we have called the colonial situation.[6]

Balandier further itemizes the components of the colonial situation as follows:

1. Domination imposed by a racially (ethnically) and culturally distinct foreign minority in the name of racial and cultural superiority;

2. The linking of radically different civilizations into some form of relationship;

3. A mechanized, industrialized society with a powerful economy, a fast tempo of life, and a Christian background imposing itself on a non-industrialized, "backward" society;

4. The fundamentally antagonistic character of the relationship between two societies resulting from the subservient role to which the colonial people are subjected as "instruments" of the colonial power; and

5. The need to retain essential dominance both by outright coercion and the creation of a system of pseudo-justification and stereotyped behavior.[7]

This summary contains accidental and essential elements, with only the latter being applicable to the Korean case. Thus, while Christianity is accidental, the essential elements of Japanese colonialism in Korea include foreign dominance, in which the domestic and numerical majority is controlled by a foreign and numerical minority with the intent of economic and strategic exploitation based on an overwhelming disparity in coercive force.

Balandier's main concern—to remind us that ethnic components are crucial in understanding the colonial social whole in the African context—can be easily extrapolated in more general terms: to maintain discrimination through control, colonial authorities reserve the right to launch arbitrary interventions in any area of human action as the need for control arises. As a consequence, system boundaries among political, economic, and sociocultural activities become unclear and blurred under colonial control. Put differently, in the colonial situation any activity can be made political through the colonial authorities' pervasive politicizing of even mundane issues. Such formulations underscore the unique aspect of colonial social changes, particularly social distortions caused by a foreign minority's rule over a local majority, discrimination, and an overwhelming reliance on the force to control.[8]

The blurring of system boundaries is closely related to colonial disequilibrium. Colonial disequilibrium refers to the artificial blockage of intersystem spillover. Colonial disequilibrium arises where conscious efforts are made to avert or forestall the flow of institutional change from one area into another. Without such efforts, control over the colony itself becomes difficult, if not impossible. For instance, colonial authorities permitted economic activities only through prior considerations of political control and blocked the spontaneous emergence of social groups based on economic interactions. Thus noncolonial differentiation among political, social, and economic sectors is artificially disrupted by an overarching imperial imperative and arbitrary political intrusion. According to Mercier, the most important factor in understanding postcolonial African society is the dilution of class relationships by the superimposition of the colonized/colonizer axis upon the subordinate society.[9] In the African context, tribal and kinship ties are found to be the most salient factors affecting social relations. MacCarthy also deals with how colonial bureaucrats' interest in control hindered market development in Tanganyika.[10]

Blurred system boundaries and the consequent artificial blockage of intersystem spillover mean that system boundaries can shift, and thus we have the difficulty of understanding colonial society in single, macro-structural terms. Put differently, colonial society is potentially so fluid that it cannot be conceptualized by any one single "total concept."[11] To approach the colonial situation as a whole means understanding that colonial society is based on this fluidity. Thus, efforts to understand any one element—particularly such essential elements as foreignness, imposition, control, and unnaturalness—and to generalize the whole therefrom will not produce an accurate picture. A distinct aspect of the colonial situation is the difficulty we have in ensuring congruence among sectors, such as between economics and social consequences.

The abnormally fragmented nature of colonial society emerges here as a conceptual constraint on the discussion of colonialism by postcolonial scholars, diverting understanding of the essential dysfunctionality of colonial/postcolonial society into an endless and sterile intellectual debate on accidentals. Thus it is necessary to examine the intended and unintended social and institutional consequences of blocking change from one sector to another.

Such considerations shape the crucial contours of the argument that follows. While all colonial societies share colonial disequilibrium, the contents of social consequences are unique to each colonial society because of their different historical contexts and colonial experiences. The artificial blockage of flow between sectors forces the analyst of colonialism to forsake many standard social science concepts and formulate new and context-specific social categories to understand a given colonial society. Colonial control may prove to be the link, for example, between the introduction of an apparently modern institution and a totally different consequence in another area. Thus, if class formation were seriously skewed because of anticolonial nationalism, the situation might require a different conceptualization applicable to a skewed class society. The concept of "class" is either subsumed by a higher-level, colonialism-specific category or acquires new and variable meanings depending on the individual characteristics of the precolonial, indigenous society. What is treated as an independent variable elsewhere becomes a dependent variable here. In addition, the fragmented nature of colonial society ensures that concepts of social cause and effect can no longer be taken for granted. Instead, causal determinants become a highly empirical enterprise. This circumstance accounts for the strong emphasis on empirical case studies that characterize the present analysis.

Taking into account the factors of the colonial situation—disequilibrium and totality—the general framework of the present theory may be adequately expressed as constituting a colonial space, where:

- *Colonial* denotes the fact that the colonial power sets the priorities, makes decisions, and implements them according to its goals, which may or may not be relevant to a colonial society.

- *Space* indicates the general field of human interactions where systemic boundaries are fluid and blurred.

The term *colonial space* is used to help us to understand the colonizer's perception and imperative that colonial control involves and requires the uninhibited crossing of boundaries, in the same sense that a computer operator can freely erase and redraw his creations in cyberspace. Thus in the noncolonial situation we may justly speak, for example, of political, social, or economic systems with relatively firm and definable boundaries. That is, *space* is used to denote a totality of living patterns where fixed and predictable system differentiation is inconceivable.

Thus colonial space implies the usurpation of coherent structuration and system building through purposeful fragmentation and disequilibrium. Although there may be surface resemblances to economic or political space, these subordinated spaces are neither fixed nor stable. Where the noncolonial system is recognized and defined by its spontaneity, logic, and coherence, colonial space is recognized and defined by its artificiality, discontinuity, and arbitrariness. External coercion and control are substituted for integral necessity and organic development; force replaces logic. In colonial space, one cannot automatically rationalize or model any outcome according to necessary cause or effect. Colonial space may be characterized as a kind of Frankenstein's monster concocted for purposes divorced from anything that may be imputed to the surrounding human environment. It is independent of human need and satisfies the latter only intermittently and accidentally. For this reason, it is meaningless to point to isolated instances in which indigenous populations may benefit accidentally from the arbitrary mechanisms and functions obtained within colonial space.

In colonial space, foreign authorities manipulate system boundaries at will whenever their focus of interest and attention shifts, leaving the indigenous population helpless to affect the most fundamental conditions of their lives.[12] At the same time, colonial authorities maintain artificial boundaries between one system and another depending on the outcomes of interactions with the colonized population. Colonial space in this sense is highly dynamic and volatile. Especially in the Korean context, where the old social structure was rapidly disintegrating, it was easier to block the emergence of such large-scale social units as class. Thus what emerge from colonial space are groupings of people who share similar experiences but no organizational connections. Under colonial rule, people are arbitrarily grouped or regrouped according to their shifting functions within spaces defined by, and furthering the interests of, the colonial power.

The cumulative effect of such overwhelming arbitrariness on individuals, society, culture, and national and ethnic identity cannot be overestimated. More generally, the arbitrariness of colonial space preempts the possibility of acquiring a rational sense of cause and effect, divorces people's actions from results, and preempts almost every possibility of developing a meaningful sense of self-as-actor. All of these are the legacies of every once-colonized people, including Koreans.

The Functional Structure of Colonial Space

Given the colonialism-specific logic just described, colonial space can be divided into three areas: Colonial Superstructural Space, Colonial Functional Space, and Colonial Social Space. These spaces differ primarily in (1) the changing threat perception of the colonial authorities with respect to such elements, i.e., does a given element comprise a greater or lesser degree of accommodation or resistance? and (2) the scope and intensity of direct colonial control over the relevant elements, in which control is equivalent to arbitrary interference and thus increased disequilibrium within the affected element. The structures may be distinguished as follows:

Colonial Superstructural Space (CSuS) is the space in which the colonial authority attempts, within the inevitable constraints of material possibility, to establish its hegemony over the colonized and to inaugurate institutional, societal, and ideological arrangements to implement and maintain such hegemony. Examples of efforts to further Japanese hegemony include the Japanese equivalent of the "white man's burden," the concept of the Greater East Asia Co-Prosperity Sphere, tendentious distortions of Korean history, the attempt to assimilate the Korean people into Japan through Japan-Korea unity and identity, anthropological studies treating Korean people as "natives," forcing Koreans to use Japanese names, the imposition of emperor worship, and the use of the Japanese language. The bureaucracy and other organizations that support such ideological impositions are also elements of CSuS.

Acts associated with CSuS are undertaken where an element is crucial to the mechanisms of colonial control or where relatively less essential elements are perceived to contain a relatively high degree of potential threat. In this sense, CSuS is the most colonial and least indigenous aspect of colonial space. Moreover, because high levels of surveillance and control over "normal" elements of an indigenous society are required to establish colonial hegemony, CSuS is innately hostile to indigenous institutions. CSuS is highly pragmatic and opportunistic, and thus its boundaries are exceptionally fluid and arbitrary admitting blatant contradictions. For instance, the contradiction between treating Koreans as cultural brothers deserving assimilation and treating Koreans as inferior "natives" never occurred to the Japanese colonizers, as indeed it need not have, as long as the conclusion (the colonization of Korea) remained the same, irrespective of the premises.[13]

Colonial Functional Space (CFS) is the space in which the functional arrangements necessary to accomplish the primary goal of economic exploitation by the colonial power are made. It exists where the mechanisms of colonial society are either routine or the perceived threat level is low, or both. Here belong familiar phenomena, such as coerced economic policies and institutions along with a coerced educational system and curriculum that in various permutations and combinations always characterize colonial systems.

CFS resembles Ekeh's category of migrated institutions in that it often combines such foreign structures as centralized educational systems or modern production practices with indigenous traditional systems or divisions of labor.¹⁴ Thus, this is a space that differs little on the surface from similar structures in noncolonial situations.

What makes CFS colonial, however, is the fact that the functional goals and means of implementing policies are those of the colonizers, who are again those empowered to make such decisions. The overriding goal is to maximize economic exploitation within a highly controlled and thus stable and friendly environment. The means involve incentives to engage colonial people in economic efforts but within an overarching logic of discrimination and material control. The colonial power needs to educate the colonized population to pursue its economic goals cheaply, and it limits the goals of colonial education to suit this need. As one former French principal of an Algerian school expressed it, the goal of French colonial education was neither to transform Algerians into true French nor to permit them to remain true Algerians, but to land them in a nowhere zone somewhere in between.¹⁵

Since arbitrary intrusions of coercive power are relatively rare in this space and the perceived threat potential of its elements is tolerable, CFS becomes the area of maximum interaction and dialectic between the colonizers and colonized. It is the arena in which objective functional needs, common to all societies, contend and conflict with the imperative of colonial control. Regardless of the given colonial situation, both the colonized and the colonizer must engage each other in this area, either for survival or for exploitation. The need for colonial control frequently contradicts the logical consequences of functional activities, such as industrialization and education. The unintended emergence of colonial modernity raises thorny issues of control. The colonial power has to deal with workers in materially modern factories and graduates of modern educational systems. Colonial education, however tightly or expertly controlled, inevitably creates challenges arising from the cognitive disjunction between colonial discrimination and universalism acquired through education.

Colonial Social Space (CSS) can be regarded as a residual space that the colonial power leaves least controlled after carving out its position in the other two spaces. CSS is not uncontrolled, but it is the least controlled because that is necessary for the purpose of control. Empirically, CSS contains the traditional sector, but as Ekeh pointed out, even if the degree of control is relatively minimal, the remaining traditional orders also suffer qualitative changes. Thus, what constitutes CSS must be empirically defined in terms of time and place. In the Korean case, the family system is a good example of this space. As will become clear later, Japanese colonial authorities left the Korean family system virtually intact, not because they wanted to protect it but because it was much more beneficial to do so in the interest of their ability to facilitate colonial control.

Boundary Blurring and Categorical Variability

These three categories, CSuS, SFS, and CSS, constitute the logical abstractions most suitable for expressing the peculiar nature of colonial space as discussed in the relevant literature and as refined on the basis of this author's own empirical observations and reflections. In employing them, it is, above all, necessary to avoid the trap of conceptual rigidity. Attempts to instantly categorize confront the blurring of boundaries discussed earlier, which is an intentional and invariant feature of colonial systems. It should be stressed that the colonial power alone is the ultimate definer of the specific content of colonial space. Depending upon the colonial power's perception of colonial reality, spatial boundaries can move arbitrarily. This fluidity of boundaries is what makes it difficult to apply fixed sociological categories to the elements, and this variability makes each of them (e.g., religion) potentially a Colonial Superstructural Space (CSuS) category. It is either the new goals set by the colonial power or the reactions of the colonized that determine new boundaries between the spaces without changing the fundamental imperative of economic exploitation. The fluidity defined by the colonial power is what prevents coherence between socioeconomic actions and socio-institutional consequences.

The Primary Dynamic Artifact: Accommodation and/or Resistance

As noted, CSuS, CFS, and CSS are distinguished primarily by their innate importance to the colonizers and/or the perception of potential threat within subordinate colonial spaces. This raises the question of what constitutes the perception of threat in a colonial context. We may define all human interactions loosely in terms of power: either intentional actions are capable of producing systemic effects, however small, or they are not. Within such a general definition, it is clear that colonial systems offer their members both the lower and upper limits on the axis of power: at the low end is the near powerlessness of the colonized; at the high end, the vastly overextended power of the colonizer. In fact, within such systems there is only one primary category in which the colonized are guaranteed power to effect changes within the colonial system. This category lies along the axis of accommodation/resistance. If the colonized accommodate, they ensure the stability of the colonial status quo (given that this stability is defined as the continuance of the colonizer's ability to effect arbitrary, systemic change unimpeded by consideration of the colonized). If they resist, they force the colonizer to address their resistance, thus adding another quantum of control to the characterization of the status quo and possibly increasing the cost of maintaining the colonial system. Since this is the only invariant axis along which the colonized may be assured—anything resembling "power" in a colonial system—it is necessary to discuss its application to the present model.

Applied to the colonized, *accommodation* is defined as accepting the premises of colonial rule and thus does not create the need for negative sanctions from colonial authorities. This definition assumes that it is hard to imagine complete identification with the colonial power, either because it is impossible for the colonized or because it is not desirable for the colonizers. *Resistance* is defined as refusing to acknowledge colonial rule and thus either launching a struggle against it or remaining aloof from it. The former strategy of *accommodating resistance*, involves a willingness to participate in colonial spaces, but with the ultimate goal of resisting or rejecting colonial rule. The latter, *resisting accommodation*, means to accommodate reluctantly because one has no other choice, or to exert passive resistance. Thus each space has two types of social consequences: institutions that function to support the space and human groups surrounding these institutions. Following Ekeh, the nature of institutions can take traditional, migrated, and emergent forms.[16]

In each kind of colonial space, options are more or less clearly limited. Colonial Superstructural Space (CSS), for example, largely relates to elite groups in the sense that it is defined by the colonial power. In this space, options for reaction are limited; either resistance or accommodation (collaboration) is a choice, largely because of the sensitivity of the colonial authorities to this space and the constant pressure to choose effectively. From this space emerge nationalist groups who resist colonial control and collaborators who accommodate the colonial power. In this space, many different kinds of colonial institutions serve to promote justification of colonial rule, but all can be reduced to the category of colonial bureaucracy because almost all were implemented under colonial rule and its auspices.[17]

In Colonial Functional Space (CFS) one can theoretically imagine four different kinds of reactions by the colonized. The predominant reaction pattern, however, is *accommodating resistance*. Since this space is about survival and gaining status, the colonized are obliged to accept reality. Once they are engaged in CFS, however, their reaction patterns may vary depending on their original positions and their relationship with the colonial power. Even among capitalists under colonial rule there can exist different groups and orientations toward the colonial power. The unique ethos of the capitalists may also emerge, something not imaginable in a noncolonial situation—the feeling that they are betraying the nation, for example—is overshadowed by the justification that what they do ultimately serves to strengthen the nation. Workers whose jobs were created as a result of colonial economic changes are prevented from uniting to follow certain ideologies that may threaten colonial rule, and thus these workers' organizations become fragmented. Workers themselves also develop a colonial ethos that requires them to consider national liberation and their own interests simultaneously.[18] Because there are different kinds of capital and worker groups, making generalizations about workers is extremely difficult. Thus capitalist and market system institutions are strongly colored by colonial control.

Colonial education produces an ironic predicament. Those who accept colonial schooling show accommodation in doing so, but a modern education gives them the tools to resist the colonial power, either overtly or covertly. Likewise, the colonial government needs educated people but cannot support the institutional principles that a modern education inevitably teaches, such as equality, justice, and autonomy. The result is a seemingly modern educational system that is strongly influenced by colonial control; separate from the progressive curriculum, it features punishment and a strong authoritarian relationship between teachers and students.

After the most sensitive areas of traditional elements are defined as parts of the Colonial Superstructural Space (CSuS), Colonial Social Space (CSS) encompasses those traditional social elements that the colonial authorities are indifferent to. This might be called resistant traditionalism, in which the masses use elements of tradition as symbols of resistance although the colonial authorities themselves use it for purposes of control. If the first two colonial spaces challenge many traditional values and institutions, CSS reinforces tradition unintentionally, a fact that is normally not well understood in most nationalist historiography. In everyday life, it may take what Goffman called "secondary adjustment" in the context of total institutions, such as prisons and mental hospitals, in which, without directly challenging the authorities, "forbidden satisfactions [are obtained or permitted] by forbidden means."[19]

Enough has been said about the complexity in the interactions between colonial rule and traditional institutions and values. Due to the inconsistency inherent in colonial rule, it is hazardous to generalize the impact of colonial rule on tradition. At a micro-level, understanding the impact of colonial rule on tradition requires close examinations of the intentions of the colonial rule and its consistency in relation to each case of traditional values and institutions. The macro picture regarding the relationship between colonial rule and indigenous traditions will take on a mosaic form in terms of degree of control and consequences. Traditional values and institutions may go through different trajectories under colonial rule. Following Blumer, they can take different paths to reinvention: rejective, disjunctive, assimilative, supportive and disruptive.[20] To do a comprehensive work on the impact of the colonial rule on Korean tradition requires the collection of the cases in relation to changes in tradition. Given the uneven and limited number of the cases, the following examples are here drawn as an effort to demonstrate the complex interplays between colonial rule and traditions.

EDUCATION AND FAMILY IN COLONIZED KOREA

This section analyzes two institutions under colonial rule: colonial education and the Korean family. The former is a case of colonial change and the latter a case of colonial nonchange. In analyzing these institutions the focus is not on detailing historical facts but on how the colonial situation changed or did not change these institutions. Examining colonial education and its social consequences in Korea will reveal how colonial control constantly created contradictions between CSuS and CFS, that is, between colonial modernity and colonial control; it will further show how colonial contradictions brought about long-lasting social consequences. In contrast, analysis of the Korean family under colonial rule will demonstrate why Korean traditional family ties were paradoxically strengthened in spite of apparent socioeconomic changes. These examples also help to explain the institutional legacies of the colonial era, especially in relation to Korean economic development. In spite of rapid industrialization, strong and enduring high school and family ties have prevented the emergence of a true modern society and cannot be understood without examining their historical link to the colonial past.

Colonial Education, Colonial Control, and the Emergence of High School Ties

Within the threefold model outlined here, Colonial Superstructural Space (CSuS) expresses most intensely the essential contradiction of the colonial situation. Colonial contradiction occurs wherever the strategies necessary for achieving the primary goal of economic exploitation automatically produce an increase in resistance from the colonized. Such contradictions are inevitable artifacts of the logic of colonialism. Contradiction is therefore the locus of conflict. It transforms the colonial context and is the most obvious mechanism for generating unintended social consequences.

An outstanding example of the contradictions inherent in CSuS is the institution of colonial education. In the Korean context, both the colonizer and the colonized needed formal education, but the educational enterprise took on contradictory significance to the two participating parties. Education inevitably became one of the most intense fields of perceived threat to the Japanese authorities, as demonstrated by the broad scope of repressive measures taken against students and schools. It is this repression that justifies locating education firmly within CSuS. More crucially, it was within the institution of education that uniquely Korean, postcolonial, social artifacts were forged and refined. I refer to the emergence of the singular Korean phenomenon of a network of social ties of mutual cooperation, trust, and assistance generated not between university students, as in Japan, but within high schools.

The colonizers needed an educated workforce to increase the usefulness of selected colonized persons and schools that would teach unquestioning respect for authority.[21] The colonized needed a modern education because it was one of the few paths to an economically successful life open to Korean people. The fact that the colonial power limited the number of educated Koreans to a minimum speaks eloquently to Japanese sensitivity to the potential threat inherent in the educational process. Even though it was a strategy designed to counter the contradictions of the colonial educational enterprise, the strategy itself merely localized and intensified the paradox: "In fact, one of the functions of school selection was to make education scarce, thus increasing its value and the demand for it."[22] And selection was biased in favor of colonial loyalty over academic excellence. For the colonial authority to maintain "proper social distance" from the colonized and to preserve colonial control along with explicit discriminatory measures, neither too much acculturation nor too much local orientation was allowed in selecting students. Thus there existed inherent limits to any assimilation policy.[23]

Nevertheless, the increased perceived value of education generated by this policy of creating an artificial scarcity could not help but also increase the perceived value of its unintended artifacts: knowledge of the wider world and increased political sophistication, both of which were intellectual tools suitable to affirming or debunking Japanese colonial ideology. By artificially limiting the number of educated persons, the Japanese unintentionally enhanced the perceived charisma and authority of persons who elected to use their newly educated minds in the service of Korean nationalism and anti-Japanese resistance.

Like the Japanese colonizers, the Korean colonized were also ambivalent toward colonial education. They were fascinated by new knowledge in general and by knowledge of housing, agriculture, hygiene, and health in particular. Further, they understood the need for knowledge in resisting the colonial power. On the other hand, the decision to receive a colonial education meant acknowledging colonial rule, a typical example of the contradiction between accommodation and resistance.

The goals of technical education and raising loyal "servants for the emperor" in colonial Korea were persistently pursued in spite of several changes in the Educational Edict and Laws.[24] But the educational opportunities given to the Korean people were severely limited both in number and in content. In 1939, only two out of one thousand Korean children were enrolled in primary school, while the enrollment figure in Japan was three times as high: in high schools, fourteen times, in universities, 111 times.[25] According to Henderson,

In thirty-one years the number of students at all levels increased over sixteen times, from 110,800 in 1910 to 1,776,078 in 1941. Over 50 percent of Korean children were not receiving compulsory education. Only 5 percent of Korean children went beyond the primary education. At liberation little over 20 percent of Koreans had received any formal schooling, as opposed to three quarters of the Japanese population of Chosen; some ten times the proportion of resident Japanese as of Koreans had secondary education.[26]

In addition, vocational schools, such as those that taught technical, business, and agricultural trades were given priority over general education. Japanese students were kept remarkably segregated from Korean students, and moral education was emphasized along with the Japanese language.[27]

The geographic distribution of high schools is significant. As Table 1.1 shows, only one or two high schools were established in each province.

Over time, the attitudes of Koreans toward colonial education shifted from an initial general denial and resistance to gradual acceptance. In the early 1910s, when public primary schools opened, the authorities had a hard time recruiting students because Korean parents refused to send their children to the new schools, partly from lack of understanding but mainly because of their resistance to Japanese rule.[28] This phenomenon was especially widespread among upper-class Koreans, who still insisted on the curriculum taught in traditional Korean schools; most students participating in Japanese-run schools thus came from the middle or lower classes.[29] As a result, public primary schools were called the "schools of the poor."

The situation shifted rapidly in the 1920s, however, when people began to show more interest in sending children to the new schools.[30] As the number of applicants increased, schools were able to begin selecting the students they wanted. This was a dramatic contrast to the previous decade, when they had to make an effort to recruit students. There are three reasons for this change. First, at the end of the March First Independence movement in 1919, most people began tilting toward the new ideology, which emphasized the need for self-strengthening to save the country (a compromise to full resistance). Second, because Korean society, regardless of Japanese colonial rule, was facing social turmoil with the decline of the yangban, the old ruling class, people tried to reestablish their social identity through education. As Henderson aptly put it: "The hectic years of late Yi over, education came to be

Table 1.1 Korean High Schools (Non-Vocational) in 1937

	Male	Female	Male	Female
Chunbuk	1	3	1	0
Chungbuk	1	1	0	0
Chungnam	1	2	0	0
Chunnam	1	2	0	0
Hamnam	1	3	1	2
Kangwon	1	1	0	0
Kyungbuk	1	2	0	0
Kyunggi	2	3	6	6
Kyungnam	2	3	1	1
Pyoungnam	2	2	1	1

Source: Chōsen Sōtokufu, Gakumukyoku, Chōsen shogakkō ichiran, Shōwa jūyonnen [Prospectus of Schools in Korea] (Keijō: Chōsen Sōtokufu, 1939).

the only path for ambition, and all the schools were oversubscribed several times. For the young, forming one's ambitions in terms of the Japanese world and one's career within Chosen became almost inevitable, even where resentment and hurt lasted."[31] Third, Korean society had maintained a long tradition in which education equaled a shortcut to governmental positions; a tradition that strongly motivated many to acquire it.[32]

A Locus of Colonial Contradiction:
High Schools and the Development of Resistance

Educational opportunities, as mentioned, were limited in colonial Korea, but they were especially limited beyond the primary school level. Remarkably, throughout the colonial period no more than 3 percent of primary school graduates went on to high school. Even as late as 1942, the number of Korean middle school and high school students hovered around twenty-five thousand, which was less than 2 percent of primary school graduates. Of the 1,218,367 Korean primary school graduates (girls and boys), only 28,878 were allowed to attend high school.[33]

The number of public and private high schools increased from five in 1910 to forty-five in 1935 (girls' schools included) and 142 in 1942 (including middle schools and Japanese schools).[34] High school graduates, especially public high school graduates, were nationally or regionally selected and well positioned to play important roles regardless of whether they received a college education. The importance of high school thus increased in Korea far beyond its corresponding value in Japan or China.

In this way schools, especially high schools, naturally evolved to become organization centers of Korean colonial society. This trend was strengthened by default, since on-campus associational organizations were difficult to establish under the strict Japanese regime and were often quickly suppressed once established. Continuity became, therefore, a value in itself. In addition, Korean high school students shared with their non-colonial peers all the customary traits of youth: a new awareness of the importance of social groups and the desire to participate in activities according to their own interests. In addition, they were undistracted by outside interests and thus freer in their choice of activities. The relative scarcity of university students and particularly university graduates, meant that high school students were by default the most well-educated group in Korean society; they were among the privileged elite who learned "new knowledge," such as math, science, history, and geography.

Thus it was the high school graduates, who thought most keenly about and most often articulated, the colonial contradiction, and they came to internalize the colonial contradiction in an acute and personal manner.[35] Having accommodated the colonizers in deciding to participate in this education, they found that the same education was equipping them with the knowledge and organization necessary to resist both the Japanese educational system and the colonial system as a whole. High schools were theaters of conflicting values, strains, and double standards. It must also be said that the crude Japanese propaganda dispensed in the schools, and the oppressive and heavy-handed manner in which ideologically doctrinaire teachers inculcated it, was often an education in itself, and the lesson taken by its recipients was one entirely unintended by the Japanese.

Korean Student Movements during the Colonial Period

A detailed history of anti-Japanese Korean student movements is not necessary because it is available elsewhere.[36] It is sufficient here to provide a brief survey of these movements as they relate to the institutional and social consequences of high school education in Korean colonial and postcolonial society. Both the patterns and the content of student resistance changed over time in response to the transformation of the colonial environment. This environment is empirically quantifiable as educational policy changes and changing patterns of police surveillance, organizational suppression, and arrests, but on a more immediate level the transformation came down to the level of individual students and teachers and the increasing tensions between them. A crucial artifact of external organizational and policy changes was the corresponding transformation of high school students' sense of identity—what it actually meant to be a high school student. Increasingly, their identity began to formulate itself along the axis of resistance.

The March First Independence movement was the first opportunity for students to demonstrate the significance of their political and social role. After that uprising, students played a leading role in nationwide political movements against Japanese rule in the June Tenth Appeal for Independence incident in 1926 and the Kwangju student uprising in 1929. But as time went by, student movements became less centralized and began to be organized around local school groups. Before the March First movement, student organizations took the form of mutual friendship societies among students who stayed in Seoul but were from various parts of the country. For example there were groups named the North-West Student Friendship Society, the Honam (Southwest) Student Organization, and so on.[37] During the 1920s, communism and nationalism became two ideological pillars, though the two were not easily distinguishable. During the 1920s and early 1930s, however, organized groups and slogans made the communist influence more visible. As colonial control intensified from the late 1920s until the end of colonial rule in 1945, the student movement, regardless of ideological orientation, became narrowly focused on schools and secret organizations. Open protests organized by nationwide organizations gradually gave way to local high schools and secret organizations.

The most popular form of student protest over this period was the strike, in which high school students refused to attend school until their demands were heeded. About half of the strikes between 1921 and 1928 were staged by high school students. More important, high schools throughout the provinces of the country participated in them (See Table 1.2).

Table 1.2 Student Strikes by Province, 1921–28

Province/School	Number of Strikes
Kyunggi	77
South Hamgyong	51
Hwanghae	42
South Kyungsang	38
Kangwon	29
North Cholla	29
South Cholla	28
North Pyongan	24
South Pyongan	20
South Chungchong	20
North Chungchong	17
North Hamkyung	15
North Kyungsang	13

Source: Chōsen Sōtokufu, Keimukyoku, *Chōsen ni okeru dōmei kyūkō no kōsatsu* [A survey of student strikes in Korea] (Keijō: Chōsen Sōtokufu, 1929), 6–7, 43–46.

Student demands embraced various issues: educational facilities, the rejection of teachers, school administration, and ideological issues. Among them, the rejection of teachers and ideological and nationalistic issues loomed largest. From 1921 to 1928, there were 434 instances of teacher rejection and seventy-four ideology-related strikes.[38] Because most of the teachers were rejected for discriminating against Koreans and making derogatory remarks about Korean culture and Koreans personally, practically all strikes carried a strong anti-Japanese message.

In the July 1927 strike, students of Hamhŭng Public High School issued the following statement to the school authorities demanding the removal of three Japanese teachers.

Not only these teachers, but the rest of the faculty are merely preaching the superiority of Japan and the inevitable disappearance of Korean people. We

do not regard this as a true education which would satiate our zeal for
knowledge. For those of us who are dependent upon our parents for school,
our hope has turned to despair. Schools have become forts, teachers behave
as if they were military police and secret agents and plant fear into our
minds. We come to school every day with a feeling that we are falling into a
hole. As Pestalocci showed, educators should educate students transcending
national boundaries, based on a humanitarian spirit.[39]

In addition, students were challenging parochial discrimination by way of
universal principles, such as equality and human rights, a clear contradiction
of colonialism, which students gained through colonial education.

Student strikes continued throughout the 1930s. There were 107 strikes in
1930 and 102 in 1932, but as Japanese pressure and surveillance on students
became more severe after the Manchurian invasion, the number began to
decline, decreasing to thirty-six in 1935.[40] In the first half of the 1930s, students adopted a new strategy of establishing secret organizations, most of
which, regardless of ideological orientation, were composed of high school
students and graduates. It is likely that communist organizational skills, such
as strict discipline, impersonalism, and secret contacts were used among
socialist and communist-oriented students in organizing secret organizations. From the latter half of the 1920s, even nationalist-oriented students had
to go underground because of heightened colonial control and surveillance
of all organizations, communist or not. Among fifty known secret organizations, forty-three were organized around high schools. The same trend continued in the second half of the 1930s. Thirty-three out of thirty-four known
secret organizations were organized by high schools all over the country.[41]
One regional situation and one specific organization will illustrate how secret
organizations were formed and operated.

The regional example took place in Northern Kyŏngsang Province between
1928 and 1945. There were eleven cases of secret student organizations that
were suppressed by the police; their members were later prosecuted and sentenced (see Table 1.3).

Five different local high schools were involved in the Taegu student secret
organization. The case became known to the outside world in 1928, when the
police arrested 105 students. The organization began in 1927 as a secret lec-
ture series that nine Taegu high school students attended. After three lectures,

fifteen members organized the Sinu Tongmaeng (新友同盟 New Friend Alliance); thereafter, the group kept changing its name to secure secrecy, first to Hyŏgu Tongmaeng (革友同盟 Revolutionary Friend Alliance) and again to Chŏgu Tongmaeng (赤友同盟 Red Friend Alliance). Ideologically communist in orientation, this organization was dedicated to the anti-imperialistic struggle against Japan.[42]

The local example was the arrest of twelve members of the so-called Evergreen Association (Sangnokhoe 常綠會) of Ch'unch'ŏn High School in 1939. All were graduates of Ch'unch'ŏn High School, all were classmates except one, and all were from either the same city or province. The main charges against them were organizing a secret organization and a reading group to promote nationalistic spirit through reading books and discussions. After four classmates agreed to start the organization, they recruited their junior students at the same high school. All were sentenced to jail terms from one and a half to two and half years for violation of the Public Order Maintenance Law (Chian yujibŏp).[43]

A regional analysis tells us that in most cases secret organizations were formed by a single high school but rarely by several schools jointly. In the case of the Sangnokhoe, it can be surmised that personal connections based on trust were the link rather than schools themselves. The data show that none of the secret organizations could last long under the watchful eye of the colonial police. It is also interesting that even communist organizations had to rely on high school ties, a fact that indirectly demonstrates how important high school ties were as bases for establishing trust. Most organizations were small in scale, ranging between two and forty members, so as to evade surveillance of the police, and most were started by classmates of the same year, again to secure trust. Thus, even though they were dealing with national and international issues, their regional backgrounds were narrow and uniform. When these groups were forced to limit membership to close schoolmates, they surreptitiously introduced the local or regional factor, yet another aspect of the colonial paradox.

Placed in a wider perspective, the institutional significance becomes clearer. The colonial situation in Korea was an environment in which association, publication, and speech activities were severely limited by various regulations, such as police, domestic security, newspaper, and the publication laws, the temporary order for carrying subversive documents, the

Table 1.3 Secret Student Organizations in North Kyŏngsang Province

Schools	Type of Group	Date of Arrest	No. of Arrests
Taegu (T.) High School	TSSC[1]	April 6, 1928	105
T. Commerce Vocational School	TSSC	April 6, 1928	
T. Agricultural High School	TSSC	April 6, 1928	
T. Middle School	TSSC	April 6, 1928	
Private Kyŏngnam School	TSSC	April 6, 1928	
Kyŏngbuk (K.) Provincial Normal School	bimil kyolsa (secret organization)	March 30, 1933	6
K. Taegu Normal School	Teacher and Student org.	January 26, 1932	37
K. Ŭisŏng Primary School	Secret organization	August 28, 1933	2
K. Public Agricultural School	Red Students Vanguard	December 2, 1933	27
K. Taegu Normal School	Taehyŏktang & Yeongu Hoe study groups	August 1, 1941	300
K. T. Normal School	Muwoo won (Care free Garden)	June 29, 1943	?
K. Taegu Public Commerce School	Taeguktan	May 23, 1945	36
K. Andong Public Agricultural H.S.	Taehanminguk Hoebok yeongu dan[2]	March 1, 1945	41

Source: Kyŏngsang-pukto Sa P'yŏnch'an Wiwŏnhoe. Kyŏngsang-pukto sa [The history of North Kyŏngsang Province], 3 vols. (Taegu: Kyŏngsang-pukto Sa P'yŏnch'an Wiwŏnhoe, 1983, 457.

[1]Taegu Haksaeng Pimil Kyŏlsahoe (Taegu Secret Student Coalition,TSSC).

[2]Korean Independence Restoration Study Group.

assembly order, and so on. Violations of the notoriously restrictive Domestic Security Law, which covered political activities, increased substantially.[44] Under such circumstances, modern associational groupings were rare, and it was difficult to find large-scale social units as sources of identity. As Henderson remarked,

> Underneath the top level, the long history of Japanese surveillance with its war finale worked its own will on the form of those organizations outside governmental mobilization. The Japanese were superbly informed and had excellent distribution of information within their hierarchies. Korean group-ings were in constant fear of infiltration and discovery. In self-defense, the small group, the friendship circle, the gang, sworn in brotherhood, became the social unit.[45]

High school ties cemented under colonial rule added special meaning to the fact that students shared these formative years in their lives. They also shared a sense of mission, aspirations, frustrations, and guilt about what they could or could not do about their colonial situation, regardless of whether they participated in the secret student movements. Further, given the limited sources of identity foundation outside school, solidarity based on common school experiences and locality became a much stronger basis for trust and mutual help. In this regard, it is important to note that even local landlords tried to establish school networks to protect their own interests.[46]

The suppression of nationwide student organizations led to the gradual narrowing of organizational scope we have been examining. The fact that general and universal issues had to be discussed in secret local organizations illustrates the important theoretical point of colonial disequilibrium: colo-nial control produced students with modern knowledge who had to rely socially on very restricted school and regional ties to express their views. This case also points out the dangers of monosectoral analysis because it illustrates dramatically how colonial modernity combined with the need for control can bring about one consequence in one sector and the opposite consequence in another sector. In relation to the concept of colonial space, Korean colonial education started as a part of Colonial Functional Space (CFS), then challenged Colonial Superstructural Space (CSuS), and finally ended up in Colonial Social Space (CSS) with the institutional legacy of social relations based on high school ties. The long-term implications of this discussion can only be understood in conjunction with the consequences of colonial control.

Japanese Colonial Rule and Korean Familism

Both nationalistic and revisionist interpretations share the perception that Korean society underwent many changes as a consequence of the introduction of new institutions and policies under colonial rule. Important institutions and policies introduced new administrative mechanisms such as the *myŏn* (the lowest unit of administration), the land survey, new agricultural cultivation techniques, the new school system, industrialization, and urbanization. Among them, the impacts of the land survey were the most far reaching: land with ambiguous or disputed ownership transferred to state ownership, which further impoverished the peasants and created more migrant workers. The nationalistic approach highlights the exploitation and destruction of traditional cultures, whereas the revisionists emphasize development. Conspicuously absent in both interpretations, however, is any characterization of what survived these changes after colonial rule. After all, Korean society remained predominantly rural in terms of economic and population structures at the end of colonial rule: in 1938, 85.5 percent of the Korean population lived in rural areas, and agriculture accounted for 46.4 percent of the whole economy.[47] Those tenant farmers who could not be absorbed into industrial sectors had to stay in the villages.[48] How are we to understand this vast portion of the population in social and institutional terms?

Many studies have focused on the economics of the landlord-tenant relationship as it affected this majority of the Korean population.[49] There is no denying that this relationship was important to the survival of tenant peasants. But although their suffering was from time to time expressed in the form of landlord-tenant disputes, for the most part peasants had to endure and abide by the larger institutional mechanisms that the landlords and the colonial power jointly created and maintained. The traditional family system that the yangban landlords perpetuated reinforced these mechanisms. For this reason, both the changes in and continuity of the Korean family system cannot be understood adequately without considering the adjustments that the old ruling class, the yangban, made in the context of the village. At the same time, the colonial power's strategy with regard to the traditional family system should be taken into account.

The yangban class had been disintegrating as a cohesive group since the late nineteenth century. Its decline manifested itself in a further "yangbaniza-tion" of society. For example, in the Taegu region at the end of the seventeenth century, yangban, commoners, and untouchables constituted 8.3 percent, 51.5 percent, and 40.6 percent of the population, respectively; in the middle of the nineteenth century, 65.5, 32.8, and 1.7 percent. Officially, the 1895 Kabo Reform abolished the yangban system based on official positions and land ownership, and colonial rule arrived in the midst of status confusion. With the weakening connection of the yangban to the land, the middle and commercial class began to emerge as new landlords. Thus the extent to which the old yangban survived as landlords is very important in understanding the continuity of yangban domination during colonial rule. One survey shows that during the colonial period 73.8 percent of the most powerful landlords came from the yangban class, demonstrating a high rate of successful adaptation to a new situation, whereas commoners and merchants constituted 17.1 percent and 7.3 percent, respectively.[50] But because many official titles were bought up at the end of the Yi Dynasty, the non-yangban proportion could have been much higher than 25 percent.

Thus Korean colonial society can be characterized as undergoing a confusing shift. The yangban, though politically meaningless (at the central level) and suffering from socio-political shock, survived economically and were still socially influential, as one Japanese source described: "With annexation, the old status differentiation was abolished, and the trend is gradual disappearance of class distinctions, but the yangban, who used to enjoy privileges and respect, are still respected, maintain influence, and are scattered around various places in the local areas."[51] Because social and economic categories frequently did not match, the colonial authorities used these categories in approaching Korean colonial villages: landlords versus tenants on one hand and yangban villages versus commoners and other types of villages on the other.[52]

The degree to which the concept of yangban ceased to function differed widely depending on the area. At new schools, for example, the concept was rapidly fading.[53] Many public high schools kept detailed records of their students' status and backgrounds until 1930s; thereafter, economic criteria became more important. Following our concept of colonial space, it can be surmised that in CFS the disappearance was faster, while in CSuS and CSS it was quite slow. From a young student's perspective, for example, the world surrounding him must have been confusing enough: at school he learned modern knowledge, and in the village he was a traditional young man whose identity was defined by which family he belonged to. The core sources of the maintenance of this notion of the Korean family were the yangban landlords in the villages throughout Korea.

The phenomenon of yangban resilience is well-documented by many Japanese sources. Most frequently cited is the extent and persistence of clan villages and extended families during the colonial period. One study pointed out that Korea, unlike China and Japan, was unique in the predominance of clan villages, which numbered fifteen thousand in 1940.[54] The extended family was an important component of these clan villages. Usually large, ranging from six to more than twenty members, the extended family was based on strict patriarchal power and blood ties; in 1930, the number of extended families was 4,747.[55] These clan villages and extended families underwent many changes as a consequence of economic changes and war mobilization during the 1930s and 1940s, but they did not disappear completely—not a surprising fact considering the size of the rural population—at the end of colonial rule.

These clan villages were under the strong influence of yangban landlords because prominent yangban established the villages several centuries earlier. Clan villages under colonial rule received positive marks from the Japanese authorities. Although the negative aspects of clan villages were pointed out, such as their exclusiveness, conservatism, and concealment of crimes, these demerits were outnumbered by their merits: unity based on clear leadership, progressive education, facilitation of agricultural policies, and kye (rotating mutual help).[56] In short, "clan villages are excellent self-governing entities."[57]

This reputation did not come without some effort from yangban landlords, who were actively involved in local political, administrative, and economic affairs. The yangban served on various advisory committees and associations related to schools, forestry, the Red Cross, fire stations, and farmers' associations and were leading members of financial institutions and myŏn chiefs. They utilized their positions to strengthen their status in clan villages by promoting clan activities, such as clan assembly and the publication of books on clan genealogy.[58] Their contribution to clan organizations served several purposes. First, it protected yangban interests in that the trust they gained helped them to play an intermediary role between the colonial power and the villages, thereby enhancing their status in dealing with the colonial power for their own gain. Second, their activities took on a facade of preserving Korean tradition and a quasi-anti-Japanese outlook while consolidating clan cohesiveness. And sometimes they performed social welfare functions that were not available outside clan villages.

It is no wonder that one Japanese visitor in 1922 observed that:

> looking at the myŏn system, one cannot but feel that there is a clear confusion between Korean tradition and the new colonial system. Although I have not visited many places, it is impossible to deny that myŏn officials are members of the big extended families of the local areas. It is especially so in the southern part of the country. Changing local decentralization into clan-based decentralization is against the true spirit of the myŏn system.[59]

The yangban landlords' adaptation strategies may not have been possible without the colonial authorities' judicious calculations as to how to treat Korean traditional institutions. The colonial authorities chose landlords as their social base,[60] and the overlapping of landlords and the yangban class meant that the colonial authorities already permitted the continuity of tradition in the service of economic interests. In fact, the colonial authorities were extremely cautious about changing Korean customs. The Japanese authorities were wary of possible reactions and resistance from conservative forces in Korea. Therefore they decided to take a gradual approach that was particularly visible in the introduction of new civil codes. The guiding principle was that Korean customary laws were permitted to continue to operate with very few exceptions.[61] The core elements of the Korean family system prohibited the changing of family names, marriage between a couple with same family name, and the adoption of a child with a family name different from the adopter. Attempts were made to change these statutes in 1940, but no fundamental changes were made to the old system at that time.[62]

There is much evidence to support the notion that Japanese colonial authorities had decided to take advantage of the old system in order to maintain control. According to one contemporary Japanese account, the Village Alliance for National Mobilization, ku (subunits of myŏn) and various kye organizations were based on village organizations that were frequently part of, or related to, clan organizations; in many cases, one person occupied multiple leadership positions in these organizations. In ku meetings, village elders and Confucian scholars were invited and seated ahead of officials.[63] Also, in the selection of village leaders for the New Guidance for Villages Project, family background was the second most important criterion. Those with yangban family background were preferred.[64]

Average peasants, other than the yangban landlords and those who went abroad or migrated to Manchuria, survived mostly in the context of the extended family, and there are several reasons why they remained family centered under colonial rule. First, dwindling land agriculture became much more labor intensive and thus demanded more family cooperation. The whole family, including children, had to work to survive: "In early spring poor peasant children had to plough, care for the cows, fertilize the crops, and feed the animals, all tasks forcing them to work so hard their bones did not grow straight. They could not go to school and had to spend their life illiterate."[65] Second, social welfare was poorly developed under colonial rule. Unlike in Japan, until 1944 emergency aid in-kind and supplementary support were made only to those in need; those who lacked a family. Therefore family members had to support each other.[66] The customary range of support was extensive, reflecting the extended family system: parents, grandparents, spouse, sons, daughters, grandsons and granddaughters, siblings, first uncles, and aunts on the father's side, nephews and nieces, cousins, second cousins, grandparents on the mother's side, and the wife's parents in that order.[67]

Another reason for the reinforcement of the family system among peasants was education. It is well known that Korean families sacrificed whatever they had to educate sons (especially the eldest son). During the colonial period, families below middle peasant status had a difficult time supporting primary school attendance; unable to pay even 1 yen a month for education.[68] Thus they were frequently in debt. The other side of the coin was the perception of success. If one family member succeeded after finishing his education, the success was regarded as that of the whole family, and the successful person was obligated to support the family. One Korean author of the 1920s commented that if one received an education, he could make money, achieve power, and let his family's name be known to the world: his family could enrich itself through his influence.[69]

To sum up, for the average poor Korean peasant, village life during colonial rule probably looked like this: politically he had to be silent, economically he had to suffer under tenancy, and socially he could not liberate himself from the village-wide clan order and close family obligations. While he might have heard or read about the outside world (if he received an education), in reality he was confined to his narrow village boundaries, feeling a great gap between the cognitive world and the world that he actually experienced because his travel radius was limited. As Grajdanzev noted,

> The per capital annual average number of trips in Korea in 1937 was 2.1; that in Japan was 25.1, twelve times as many. If only 69,000 workers commuted to work everyday, 341 days a year, this would account for the 47 million trips made in a year. This clearly shows how little the life of Koreans is affected by the railways. It is interesting to note that the average fare paid by passengers in Korea was 78 *sen* as compared with 22 *sen* in Japan.[70]

It is clear that the Japanese colonial authorities decided to promote their economic interests in the context of not disrupting the traditional authority structure and family relationships they encountered in Korea. In fact, they exploited the preexisting social structure. This strategy was in marked contrast to the serious discussions under way in Japan, in line with pursuing modernization tasks since the early Meiji, about how to redefine the status of the Japanese family. The main issue was to what extent modern Western elements could be incorporated and, conversely, how Japanese traditional *bushi* (samurai) family norms and systems should be retained. At the end of this long deliberation, the final decision was to retain the basic tenets of the Japanese the household unit, the first fundamental element of Japanese society. Further discussions involved how to reflect these values in schools. The social and economic status of the family was constantly revised and redefined to cope with new tasks, such as the labor movement and ideological currents. In short, family issues in Japan were viewed as part of broader sociopolitical issues in redefining Japanese tradition.[71] This discussion started in 1870, and after two decades of preparation, a new civil code was finally put in effect in 1890.

In contrast, no such discussions took place in colonial Korea, largely because maintaining the old system was beneficial in securing Japanese eco-

nomic interests and control. For the Korean people, maintaining family traditions was regarded as an act of passive resistance to the colonial authorities.
So there was neither a conscious effort to change the family system, as there
had been in Japan; nor, thanks to the colonial situation, was there any spontaneous flow of economic change into the family structure and function, as
there had been in England. In short, the Korean family system is a case of
colonial non-change par excellence.

CONCLUSION

This chapter has attempted to demonstrate how colonial social changes are
closely related to colonial control, which in turn causes colonial disequilibrium, where the social implications of change in one area are not fully played
out in others. The concept of colonial space has been proposed to emphasize
how problematic it is to apply fixed, conventional, sociological concepts and
categories to the colonial situation. The example of the new Korean educational system introduced to facilitate colonial rule shows how its inherent
contradictions caused students to challenge the colonial authorities, and how
the coercive responses of the colonial authorities in turn brought about unexpected social solidarity among the narrow, school-based elite. The Korean
traditional clan structure and family system, on the other hand, were used to
promote the interests of the colonial authorities. These two cases clearly show
the unsatisfactory nature of monosectoral analysis; instead, we need to think
about how changes in one sector affect the interspatial priorities set by the
colonial power. The two cases also show how difficult it is to make predictions about social change under colonial rule.

As for colonial studies in and about Korea, this study urges investigators
to shed the predetermined methodological and value orientations so prevalent
in the field. They are urged especially to take a second look at the practice of
academic pilfering, whereby colonial materials are used out of context to
explain issues of current economic development. Colonial history is not
something that can be used to justify elements of a current society without
careful analysis. Multifaceted colonial society evades easy formulations, and
the imposition of fashionable methodologies and theories will not help us
understand it. Colonial history is a field of human suffering on which present-day scholars should not perform theoretical experiments. Careful efforts

are needed to reconstruct the complete picture of colonial society by excavating meaningful sociological fragments.

Lastly, the theoretical implications for postcolonial Korean society must be identified. We need to know, for example, how the institutional legacies of the colonial era have interacted with South Korean patterns of economic development. South Korean politics is played out in the regional arena: ownership of the Korean chaebŏl is notoriously monopolized by families, and most elite behaviors are based, as in the colonial era, on high school ties. In this study there was not enough space to discuss the colonial origins of regionalism, but the point has been made that high school ties are intrinsically regional and that the importance of the locality-bound family has serious implications for regional identity, especially given the scarce sources of multiple identity. Finally, the living patterns of Koreans in Manchuria and Japan require serious examination, not merely in terms of the issue of uprootedness but also from the perspective of the reinforcement of regional ties. It is well known that Koreans in Manchuria lived in different regions depending on their provincial origins in Korea.

This analysis suggests other avenues of investigation as well. Strong high school ties, familism, and regionalism were the main sources of social trust at the time of liberation. And this complex of familial ties provided the social conditions for the state-led economic development of the 1960s. South Korean society anticipated the emergence of a phenomenon I call "neofamilialism," which developed during the economic development of the 1960s and 1970s from the interaction between the state and the social legacies of colonial rule. Thus we need to carefully trace the colonial sources of the present phenomenon of neofamilism and how they interact with South Korean economic development.[72] Only by doing this, rather than simply imposing Western sociological categories on South Korean society, will we better understand both the Korean people and their society.

NOTES

1. For detailed discussion of the two positions, see Carter J. Eckert, *Offspring of Empire*, Chapter 1. For recent debate, see Cho Sŏkkon, "Sut'allon kwa kŭndaehwaron ŭl nŏmŏsŏ," 355–70; Chŏng T'aehŏn, "Sut'allon ŭi songnyuhwa sok e sarajin singminji," 344–57; Sin Yongha, "'Singminji kŭndaehwaron' chaejŏngnip sido e taehan pip'an," 8–38; and An Pyŏngjik, "Han'guk kŭnhyŏndaesa yŏn'gu ŭi saeroun p'aerŏdaim," 39–58. The fact that

the development-exploitation argument intensified in proportion to Korean achievement of extraordinarily high and rapid economic growth (in effect, raising the political stakes) again suggests that a political agenda has been interposed between data and theory.

2. A critical remark on colonial studies made in another context is also relevant to the Korean case. "Modernity was never itself the object of a non-teleological criticism. This is what the post-colonial present demands. Rather than the anticolonial problems of overthrowing colonialism (or the West) what is important for this present is a critical interrogation of the practices, modalities, and projects through which modernity inserted itself into and altered the lives of the colonized." David Scott, "Colonialism: Anthropological Approaches to Colonialism," 453–62.

3. Bruce Cumings, "The Origins and Development of the Northeast Asian Political Economy."

4. See, for example, Gi-Wook Shin and Michael Robinson, eds., *Colonial Modernity in Korea*, Introduction and Chapter 3.

5. Walter D. Mignolo, "Colonial and Postcolonial Discourse: Cultural Critique or Academic Colonialism?" 128.

6. Georges Balandier, "The Colonial Situation: A Theoretical Approach," 51.

7. Ibid., 54.

8. Of course, Balandier's main concern was the way ethnic groups or tribes were treated in the African context, as if they were a part of a social whole without considering the colonial situation. His inter-ethnic premise of the colonial situation can be extrapolated into a more general level of issues between different sectors, such as political, social, and economic sectors. I thank Clark W. Sorensen for reminding me of this point.

9. P. Mercier, "Problems of Social Stratification in West Africa," 341.

10. D.M.P. MacCarthy, *Colonial Bureaucracy and Creating Underdevelopment: Tanganyika, 1910–1940*.

11. Georges Balandier, *The Sociology of Black Africa: Social Dynamics of Central Africa*, 28.

12. Colonial and totalitarian realities differ in intention, ideology, and planning. Totalitarian control is based on clearly defined systematic ideological principles and consistent modes of changes in all aspects of human life, with the intention to improve the situation at a given time; colonial control is inconsistently and unevenly extractive, coercive, instrumental, and invidious with shifting areas of benign neglect.

13. For the case of American Indians, see Thomas R. Burger, *A Long and Terrible Shadow*.

14. Peter P. Ekeh, *Colonialism and Social Structure*, 17.

15. Fanny Colonna, "Educating Conformity in French Colonial Algeria," 362.

16. Ekeh suggested three forms of institutions in a colonial society as an example of the fragmentation of colonial society (indigenous institutions; migrated institutions; emergent social institutions). Peter P. Ekeh, *Colonialism and Social Structure*, 15.

17. For details see Crawford Young, *The African Colonial State in Comparative Perspective*, Chapter 1.

18. Landlords were not easily able to transform themselves into capitalists because of the colonial power's interest in control over the rural areas. Bruce Cumings, "The Legacy of Japanese Colonialism in Korea," 492.

19. " . . . secondary adjustments, namely, practices that do not directly challenge staff but allow inmates to obtain forbidden satisfactions or to obtain permitted ones by forbidden means. These practices are variously referred to as the angles, knowing the ropes, conniving, gimmicks, deals or ins. Such adaptations apparently reach their finest flower in prisons, but of course other total institutions are overrun with them, too. Secondary adjustments provide the inmate with important evidence that he is still his own man, with some control of his environment; sometimes a secondary adjustment becomes a kind of lodgment for the self." Erving Goffman, *Asylums: Essays on the Social Situation*, 55.

20. Herbert Blumer, *Industrialization as an Agent of Social Change: A Critical Analysis*, 89ff.

21. Fanny Colonna, "Educating Conformity in French Colonial Algeria," 354.

22. Ibid., 358.

23. Ibid., 362.

24. Chŏng Chaech'ŏl, *Ilche ŭi tae-Han'guk singminji kyoyuk chŏngch'aeksa*, Chapter 6.

25. Andrew J. Grajdanzev, *Modern Korea*, 265.

26. Gregory Henderson, *Korea: The Politics of the Vortex*, 89. Korea was referred to as Chōsen in Japanese during the colonial rule.

27. An analysis of the school records of Kyŏnggi High School reveals that as colonial rule progressed, a more sophisticated list of items to check student behaviors developed. For instance, in 1918 there were nine items, such as personality, behavior, strength, weakness, hobbies, facial appearance, uniform, language, and punishment; by 1930 there were eleven. These included character, will power, behavior, language, skills, strength, weakness, special features, hobbies, punishment/reward, and student activity. Yong chool Ha, *An Analysis of School Registrars Preliminary Summary*.

28. Han Uhŭi, "Pot'ong hakgyo e taehan chŏhang kwa kyoyukyŏl," 63. Parents' primary objections were to (1) the policy of taking children to Japan after education to work as soldiers and slaves, and (2) learning the Japanese language.

29. Ibid., 65.

30. In 1915, only 17.7 percent of school-aged children in the urban areas and 2.6 percent of the rural areas entered primary schools; in 1926, it changed to 33.8 percent and 16.2 percent respectively. Han Uhŭi, "Pot'ong hakkyo e taehan chŏhang kwa kyoyungnyŏl," 67.

31. Gregory Henderson, *Korea: The Politics of the Vortex*, 90.

32. Many Japanese officials referred to this phenomenon. Chōsen Sōtokufu, Seikatsu jōtai chōsa: Suigen gun ich, 110; Chōsen Sōtokufu, Chōsenjin no shisō to seikaku, 153.

33. Andrew J. Grajdanzev, *Modern Korea*, 266.

34. Annual Government-General's Office Statistical Reports, respective years. Quoted from Hashitani Hiroshi, "1930–40 nyŏndae Chosŏn sahoe ŭi t'ŭkchil e taehayŏ," 398.

35. Tongnip Undongsa P'yŏnch'an Wiwŏnhoe, *Tongnip undongsa 9: Haksaeng tongnip undongsa*, 300.

36. See, for example, Chŏng Sehyŏn, *Hang-Il haksaengsa*; Kim Sŏngsik, *Ilcheha Han'guk haksaeng tongnip undongsa*; and Cho Tonggŏl, "Han'guk kŭndae haksaeng undong chojik ŭi sŏnggyŏk pyŏnhwa," 317–97.

37. Cho Tonggŏl, "Han'guk kŭndae haksaeng undong chojik ŭi sŏnggyŏk pyŏnhwa," 326–27.

38. Chōsen Sōtokufu. Keimukyoku, *Chōsen ni okeru dōmei kyūkō no kenkyū*, 6–7 and 43–46.

39. Ibid., 52–53.

40. Tongnip Undongsa P'yŏnch'an Wiwŏnhoe, *Tongnip undongsa*, vol. 9, 696.

41. The numbers were recounted based on data in Cho Tonggŏl, "*Ilcheha Han'guk haksaeng tongnip undongsa*," 326–91.

42. Ibid., 458–60.

43. Pak Kyŏngsik, ed. *Chōsen mondai shiryō sōsho*, 544–52, For similar patterns in other cases, see Cho Tonggŏl, "Han'guk kŭndae haksaeng undong chojik ŭi sŏnggyŏk pyŏnhwa," 450; and Kyŏngsang-pukto Sa P'yŏnch'an Wiwŏnhoe, *Kyŏngsang-pukto sa*, 460.

44. Pak Kyŏngsik, *Ilbon chegukchuŭi ŭi Chosŏn chibae*, 314.

45. Gregory Henderson, *Korea: The Politics of the Vortex*, 111.

46. Social networks were formed through school ties to protect their interests; Sollin High School graduates, many of whom became employees of the Chōsen Shokusan Ginkō [Korean Shokusan Bank], looked after each other in terms of promotion and transfer, reflecting a limited social trust basis for all leading elite groups in a dynamic environment. For the landlord case, see Hong Sŏngch'an, "Ilcheha chijuch'ŭng ŭi chonjae hyŏngt'ae," 350–61.

47. Andrew J. Grajdanzev, *Modern Korea*, 84.

48. In this regard, an article by *Tonga ilbo* is revealing: "Industrial development draws rural people to cities. Rural youth's dream is to leave the villages to enjoy cultural activities in cities. What of the Korean situation? There is no pull of rural youth from industrial sectors, but land is being taken away from peasants and exploitation of landlords is becoming more severe and threatening the lives of peasants." April 12, 1927, quoted in Kim Yŏnggŭn, "1920-nyŏndae nodongja ŭi chonjae hyŏngt'ae e kwanhan yŏn'gu," 147.

49. Sin Yongha, *Han'guk hyŏndae sahoesa yŏn'gu*; and Chu Ponggyu, *Ilcheha nongŏp kyŏngjesa*; and Cha Kibyŏk, ed., *Ilche ŭi Han'guk singmin t'ongch'i*.

50. Kim Yŏngmo, "Ilchesi taejiju ŭi sahoejŏk paegyŏng kwa idong," 110–11.

51. Chōsen Sōtokufu, *Seikatsu jōtai chōsa: Kōryō-gun*, 196.

52. Practically all the official publications on rural conditions used these categories. For examples, see notes 59 and 60.

53. Yong chool Ha, *An Analysis of School Registrars*.

54. Zenshō Eisuke, "Chōsen ni okeru dōzoku buraku no kōzō (1)," 20.

55. Zenshō Eisuke, "Chōsen ni okeru dōzoku buraku no kōzō (3)."

56. Keikidō Naimufu, *Keijidō nōson shakai jijyō*, 26, 27, 29.

57. Ibid., 28.

58. Hong Sŏngch'an, "Ilcheha chijuch'ŭng ŭi chonjae hyŏngt'ae," 359; and Hong Songch'an, *Han'guk kŭndae nongŏp sahoe ŭi pyŏndong kwa chijuch'ŭng*, Chapter 1.

59. Inaba Iwakichi, "Chōsen no bunka mondai," 6, 76, 80–81. He further observed that there are no extended families without yangban.

60. Hong Sŏngch'an, "Ilcheha chijuch'ŭng ŭi chonjae hyŏngt'ae," 359.

61. Yasuda Mikita, "Chōsen ni okeru kazoku seido no hensen," 9–10.

62. Nomura Chōtarō, "Chōsen kazoku seido no suii," 21.

63. Suzuki Eitarō, "Chōsen no nōson shakai shūdan nit tsuite," [On rural social organizations in Korea], *Chōsa geppō* [Research monthly] September (1943), 7. Cited in Hashitani Hiroshi, "1930–40 nyŏndae Chosŏn sahoe ŭi t'ŭkchil e taehayŏ" [On the nature of Korean society in 1930s and 1940s,] 409.

64. Masuda Shūsaku, "Chōsen ni okeru buraku chūshin jinbutu ni tukiteno ichi kōsatu," 92; and Chōsen Sōtokufu, *Seikatsu jōtai chōsa go: Chōsen no juraku zenhen*, 593.

65. Mun Sojŏng, "Ilcheha nongch'on kajok e kwanhan yŏn'gu," 18.

66. Ha Sangnak, "Ilche sidae ŭi sahoe pojang."

67. O Ch'ŏng, "Chōsen no Shinzoku Kankei," 103.

68. Chōsen Sōtokufu, *Seikatsu jōtai chōsa go: Chōsen no juraku zenhen (5)*, 110.

69. Ki Ch'ŏn, "Chugŭl saram ŭi saenghwal kwa sal saram ŭi saenghwal," 2–3, quoted in O Ch'ŏng, "Chōsen no Shinzoku Kankei," *Chōsen* 151 (December 1927), 63.

70. Andrew J. Grajdanzev, *Modern Korea*, 187.

71. Kawashima Takeyoshi, *Kawashima Takeyoshi chosaku shū 10: kazoku oyobi kazokuhō 1 kazoku seido*, 205–25; and Patrick Beillevaire, "The Family: Instrument and Model of the Japanese Nation," 242–43.

72. Yong Chool Ha, "Late Industrialization, the State and Social Changes," 363–82.

2

Politics of Communication and the Colonial Public Sphere in 1920s Korea

YONG-JICK KIM

The first decade 1910–19, of Japanese rule in Korea was a period of military rule (*budan seiji*) during which Koreans did not have any political freedom or liberties. Japan's colony of *Chōsen* was outwardly tranquil, and it seemed that the status quo could be perpetuated without much difficulty. However, in the spring of 1919, the March First movement broke out. This national independence movement, which began as peaceful mass demonstrations in Seoul and other large, northern cities, spread rapidly throughout the Korean peninsula and mustered explosive energy from the active participation of more than two million people. Despite brutal suppression by the colonial gendarmerie, the uprising lasted for several weeks and covered the entire peninsula. Independence struggles on a local scale continued to arise sporadically long after, and the gendarmerie, even after receiving reinforcements from home, did not regain control until May.

The third governor-general, Saitō Makoto (1919–27), instituted a new policy of cultural rule (*bunka seiji*) in 1920 that lasted for a decade. Cultural rule introduced a new era that permitted the rebirth of Korean newspapers and political magazines. Governor-General Saitō recognized the fact that the total absence of indigenous, political, social, and media rights in Korea was not so much a sign of success, but rather a major cause of the failure of former Governors General Terauchi and Hasegawa's administrations. Japanese rule was, according to Governor-General Saitō, moving toward a stage of civilized rule owing to his own a new benevolent decision. As a result of this decision Saitō revived the vernacular press in the early 1920s to address key issues of colonial society. This tentative liberal policy of the colonial authorities, however, gradually turned more and more into a sophisticated system of manipulation and control by the end of the decade.

How to interpret the give-and-take between vernacular discursive space and colonial repression has always been a difficult issue. Robinson (1984) argued that in the end the cultural nationalists were co-opted by the colonial authorities. More recently in looking at the 1930s Robinson and Shin have argued that Korea developed a kind of "colonial modernity" that "produced cosmopolitanism without political emancipation."[1] In the cracks between the official ideology of cultural rule and the growing vociferous demands of the colonial residents, the vernacular media in the 1920s could plant nationalist views on various colonial issues. In fact, through the contentious battle against the colonial authorities, nationalist cultural elites constituted at that time what could be termed a *public sphere*. Though vernacular newspapers existed throughout the period of Japanese colonial rule, the incipient public sphere of the 1920s should not be interpreted as a part of the linear and unbroken development of modernity through colonialism. The severity of official censorship was heavier and more extensive not only before but also after the period of cultural rule. The media, thus, lost their initial critical function and became truly "colonized" by 1926, which in turn lead to the demise of the colonial public sphere.

THE PUBLIC SPHERE UNDER COLONIALISM

In modern times the constitution of the public sphere has depended critically on the media (newspapers and political journals) which can provoke a forum for debate and communication among citizens.[2] In addition to the media, the socio-political space of the public sphere includes public activities such as assemblies, forums, debates, and interactions between individuals, as well as communication in the public media. When a public sphere develops, as was persuasively explicated by Habermas, information and arguments come into focus to constitute public opinion in a society.[3] Public opinion in turn became one of the most important political tools which helped build a new age modern, democratic society.

The assumption of modernization theorists that the rapid increase of communication and spread of print media in developing societies will guarantee progressive changes toward a modern and industrial society requires close scrutiny and verification, however. The colonial public sphere in Korea was a modern, politico-social phenomenon which was achieved in the early 1920s by the critical journalism of vernacular newspapers and political magazines. Yet, at the same time it was a politico-social, colonial phenomenon in that it had to be constantly renewed through struggle with the colonial authorities. With a solid foundation based on widespread readership and subscription, Korean newspapers for the first four years of cultural rule constituted a public sphere that could attack the colonial government in genuine critical tones and arguments. But two years of serious confrontations with the authorities in the mid-1920s nipped these developments in the bud. After 1926 there was a return to an autocratic era. On the one hand, the continual manipulation of colonial newspapers and magazines through systematic censorship distorted the role of the vernacular press. On the other, the radical critique of the socialists hampered the development of a public sphere after the *Tonga ilbo*'s fatal, scandalous editorial incident in the spring of 1924.

As the example of colonial Korea confirms, the mere quantitative increase of the communication and flow of information in a colonial society does not demonstrate that a society is becoming either democratic or developing. Recognizing this, modernization theory scholars sometimes call colonial society transitional rather than modern.[4] For many nationalist historians, on the other hand, the absence of any genuine representative political mechanism in colonial societies obviously proves that a public sphere did not exist.[5] The assessment that a public sphere did not exist, however, unduly overstates the capacity of the colonial government in Korea as well as grossly underestimates the power of Korean nationalist critical journalism in the early 1920s. Korea may be somewhat exceptional in this regard because it had already developed a strong tradition of publicity and public communication before the advent of colonialism.[6] This made it difficult for colonial authorities to completely ignore demands for a free press and thereby the creation of a public sphere.[7]

An increased quantity of communication in colonial society is a necessary condition, but this alone is not sufficient to prove the existence of the public sphere. Habermas' model of a public sphere, which relies on the development of the capitalist economy and growth of bourgeois political activity, in fact, treats the public sphere as a contingent rather than a permanent or stable phenomenon. What makes one consider that colonial Korea had a public sphere? Here we assume that so long as the media treated controversies that enabled the formation of a critical and rational public opinion for some extended duration of time, a public sphere existed.

The concept of the *colonial public sphere*, in fact, is of immense utility for the analysis of the period of cultural rule. This sphere's barometric role in public political communication is critical for understanding Korean nationalism in the 1920s, because it was a social arena in which colonial demands and requests, as well as the views of the colonial government, were presented. The public sphere, thus, was a site of ideological struggle between nationalist and imperialist discourses. Here we will examine how critical public discussions evolved into a counter hegemonic discourse, and how this trend later was reversed. We will also examine why the public sphere failed to perform its critical function so that society descended into an abyss of distortion and frustration during the last fifteen years of colonial rule.

COMMUNICATION TRADITION AND THE CHALLENGE OF COLONIAL RULE

The Tradition of Public Spheres and Public Communication in Premodern Korea

The Chosŏn Dynasty (1392–1910) had a tradition of political communication institutionalized in the three ministries of the central government or Censorate. The Office of Special Advisors (Hongmun'gwan) provided research on administrative and legal precedents; the Office of the Censor-General (Saganwŏn) advised the king; and the Office of the Inspector-General (Sahŏnbu) conducted social surveillance. The officials of these ministries were empowered to speak in royal councils and could even remonstrate with the king. There was a recognized communication process known as ŏllo (言路 way of speech). It was a built-in part of the central bureaucratic mechanism, but it was also an instrument to regulate the free flow of communication in society. Thus at times when a certain faction or a strong clan restricted the flow of communication at the institutional level, the political process itself was affected. If the government was not addressing pressing concerns, literati, whether in or out of office, could take direct action by sending memorials (sangso 上疏) to the court. The increasing volume of petitions in the latter days of the Chosŏn Dynasty indicates that literati communications, as well as those of the lower classes, were not well incorporated in the political process at that time.[8]

Thus, at the turn of the twentieth century, Korean society had three distinct mechanisms of public communication. (1) Because the traditional Confucian public in the early and mid-Chosŏn Dynasty participated in the *yuhyangso* (a local public administrative arena that was the government's liaison office) the literati were an entrenched part of the local community. In the last centuries of the dynasty, the literati also used the Confucian academies (*sŏwŏn*) to which they summoned other scholars in order to initiate public political actions in the form of memorials to the king. (2) During the 1894 Tonghak Rebellion, for a time, rebels created directorates (*chipkangso*) made up of ordinary people who were tasked with reforming the administration. (3) And at the very end of the nineteenth century, reformers demanding a constitutional monarchy rallied around the activities of the Independence Club (Tongnip Hyŏphoe) and the newspaper *Tongnip sinmun* (The independent). The Independence Club introduced to Korea a modern bourgeois political public sphere in which even nonofficials could discuss and make recommendations on state policies. The Independence Club also established the first modern vernacular daily newspaper, a landmark in the development of print capitalism in Korea.

In the first decade of the twentieth century, patriotic enlightenment movements led the national awakening through a variety of modern newspapers and private academies. Among the more than a dozen major vernacular newspapers, the influence of the *Cheguk sinmun* (Imperial post) and the *Taehan maeil sinbo* (Korea daily news) was prominent. Other daily newspapers such as the *Hwangsŏng sinbo* (Capital gazette), the *Maeil sinbo* (The daily news), and the *Kŭrisŭdo sinmun* (Christian news) were also popular and gained broad readership. Relying on the efforts of the reformist and anti-Japanese patriotic movements, the modern, nationalist communicating with the public rapidly gained popularity, and nationalist newspapers such as the *Taehan maeil sinbo* (The Taehan daily news) emerged as a symbol of anti-Japanese struggles in the last days of the Chosŏn Dynasty.

The Japanese administration, since the early years of the Protectorate (Chōsen tōkanfu, 1905–10), imposed systematic control on communication through the promulgation of the Newspaper Law (1907) and the Publication Law (1909) and launched an extensive surveillance policy. When the Japanese government proclaimed formal annexation of Korea in 1910, all political organizations and mass media, except those owned by the Japanese, were dissolved.

After a decade of quiescence, the March First movement in 1919 provided a sudden outburst of the nationalist demand for independence. The nationalist struggles by radical Korean independence groups never ceased thereafter, although the Japanese gendarmes put down most of the popular national uprisings after the first two turbulent months. The repercussions of the Japanese Army's brutal oppression of the March First movement and particularly the reactions to the massacre of Cheam-ni in which twenty-nine people were herded into a church which was then set on fire, were extremely unfavorable and criticized by the United States and England.[9] The new Governor-General Saitō, hence, had to promise "a liberal and righteous administration" in his inauguration speech to wipe out the negative image of his predecessor.

GOVERNOR-GENERAL SAITŌ'S CULTURAL POLITICS AND COMMUNICATION POLICY[10]

The repression of freedom following the annexation by Japan in 1910 had caused a sharp break in the upward trend of the modern social communication process which had been led by patriotic reform movement leaders in the first decade of the twentieth century. It was only after the March First movement in 1919 that high-level officials in the colonial government understood and accepted the importance of indigenous communication. It was when the new governor-general was inaugurated that deference to public opinion was included in a reform agenda.[11] The new Governor-General Saitō moderated the military rule of the preceding administrations and promised reforms, such as measures that would render respect to native culture and customs, nondiscrimination between the Japanese and Koreans, freedom of speech, and freedom of the press.[12]

Saitō's cultural rule policy was a compromise measure to handle the colonial crisis and earn the favor of the Korean population while continuing to maintain a firm grip on Korea.[13] In December 1919, Saitō's colonial administration decided to give permits to Koreans to publish vernacular newspapers, thinking that the increasing discontent of the colonial population would have been detected earlier if the colonial society had had the "safety valve" of vernacular media. Cultural rule was not designed as a unified set of policies when Governor-General Saitō initially proposed it. The obvious aim was to settle the rebellious Korean situation and not to aggravate the elevated feelings of popular animosity toward colonial rule. Throughout his tenure Saitō worked his way towards solidifying Japanese colonialism by recasting the rationale and legitimacy of colonial rule in Korea in a systematic and complex way. Rather than being predetermined, concrete policies were undertaken in response to subsequent incidents that took place.

The Colonial Crisis and the Hegemonic Project: Saitō's Communication Policy

The political atmosphere of Korea in the fall of the 1919 was very tense as demonstrated by the bombing incident on the inauguration of the new governor-general. Overseas Korean independence organizations had sent secret agents into Korea. Local administrative offices and police stations were often attacked by armed bands of "independence agitators."[14] Governor-General Saitō recognized that he needed a grand plan to propagate his new governing doctrine and to further implement a reform agenda.

Some prominent Japanese, such as Yoshino Sakuzō of Tokyo Imperial University, blamed the military rule of former Governor-General Hasegawa for the March First demonstrations; even Japanese Prime Minister Hara recognized the need for a change in Japanese ruling methods in Korea.[15] The failures of the old colonial administration were closely studied, and it became increasingly clear that colonial rule could not be based on force alone. The cultural rule proclaimed by the governor-general laid claim to civilized government, putting great emphasis on the equal treatment of Koreans and Japanese, the extension of Japanese rule to Korea, and permanent peace of the Far East. This policy, however, simply masked the ruling ideology that had always been premised on assimilation. The colonialists' strategy was basically designed as a two level strategy. The surface level being a doctrine of cultural politics or "civilized rule," such as suggested by the reform measures of the new governor-general. The hidden level, which was never officially acknowledged, was a project of building hegemony and co-opting Korean elites through incentives and manipulation.[16] Japan's covert project for building cultural hegemony has been understood and criticized by nationalist historians as a policy of "divide and rule," or as a policy of "appeasement and manipulation." What these analysts often do not notice is that this two-level policy was not a contradiction, but rather something that was consciously designed to make up for the weakness of the cultural rule doctrine.

Saitō's communication policy stemmed from his grand strategy to establish long-term colonial rule on the basis of persuasion and consent.[17] First and foremost this hegemonic strategy was designed to establish a governing coalition that incorporated some pro-Japanese Korean elites. Propagation of communication either favorable to or positive of the colonial ruling ideology was considered to be a vitally important part of Governor-General Saitō's ruling strategy. Saitō worked on propaganda activities by personally attending and summoning local magnates to offer propaganda seminars. Nationally well-known figures such as Pak Yŏnghyo, Yun Ch'iho, and Song Pyŏngjun were often selected as guest speakers and used as unofficial Korean spokesmen for the colonial government. Initial efforts to create pro-Japanese public opinion by holding political propaganda seminars did not show much success owing to the lack of the speakers' influence on the native population.[18] However, the colonial authorities continued to resort to similar methods in the 1920s by covertly influencing conservative local magnates.[19]

The colonial government understood the importance of rural areas where the majority of the population remained in a traditional life style, and it tried every means available to separate local publics from the influence of the national anti-colonial movements. Governor-General Saitō himself made regular "propaganda trips" to the provinces. In his eight years in office, Saitō paid visits to the provinces thirty-five times, spending 171 days. During these visits Saitō met and explained culture rule to various opinion leaders of the provinces, such as landlords, literati, evangelists, and local magnates.[20]

The Japanese felt they needed a semi-public command post to build the hegemony and created, in November 1920, the Information Committee (jōhō iinkai) under the Governor-General Saitō's second-in-command, Administrative Superintendent Mizuno Rentarō. Saitō's colonial communication policy was unofficially, yet systematically, designed not only by key officials of the colonial government, but also by civilians who had been well known as experts in colonial internal affairs for many years.[21] The committee was in charge of collecting and analyzing vast quantities of information on nationalist activities as well as spreading political propaganda both inside and outside the Korean peninsula.[22]

Lastly, manipulating cleavages of class and ideology was an unwritten policy of Saitō's colonial rule in Korea. The favored allies sought by the colonial government were reactionary, conservative forces: the landlord class, the literati, peddlers,[23] former government officials, and the yangban from the last years of the Chosŏn Dynasty. Creation of pro-Japanese groups from among these social allies was an essential measure on which the colonial government in Korea relied. As a result, these pro-Japanese elements acquired important influence in colonial society particularly at times of political crisis. Among the pro-Japanese groups sponsored by the colonial government, early key examples are the School Spirit Society (Kyop'unghoe), the National Society (Kungmin Hyŏphoe), and the Comrades of Greater East Asia (Taedong Tongjihoe). One example of a pro-Japanese Korean is Min Wŏnsik, who had organized the National Society in 1920, with the help of one Maruyama, a Japanese official in the police department.[24] Min ran the *Sisa sinmun* (Current affairs daily), a pro-Japanese newspaper reporting on current events in 1920, and he later initiated a controversial petition movement asking for Korean representation in the Japanese Diet. In times of crisis the colonial government mobilized these pro-Japanese organizations systematically. The primary goal of the propaganda activities of the government media was to divert people from the information and news of the nationalist newspapers, which might stimulate national sentiment or trigger anti-Japanese reactions.

Dissemination of propaganda on official policies and reform achievements of the Government-General of Korea (Chōsen Sōtokufu) was the major activity of these propaganda networks. The more than thirty propagandist media sources were effective means through which the colonial authorities could contradict and attack the claims of the nationalist newspapers and promote the ideology of assimilation and cultural rule. The Information Committee tried to create a semblance of modernization and benevolent cultural rule in the colony, but this was not easy in a colonial society where the critical journalism of nationalists as well as other more militant independence movement groups posed diversified challenges to colonial rule.

THE COLONIAL PUBLIC SPHERE: GENESIS, STRUCTURE, AND PHASES

The Renaissance of National Movements and Genesis of the Public Sphere

Although a new era for Korean nationalism had begun when the Saitō administration allowed the publication of three vernacular newspapers in 1920: the *Tonga ilbo* (East Asia daily), the *Chosŏn ilbo* (Daily), and the *Sisa sinmun*, there was no "liberal" change of regulations and laws in regulating media and publication. The colonial government did, however, loosen its policy of banning all vernacular newspapers and political magazines. "Print capitalism," which Anderson (1991) identified as the chief impetus to the spread of nationalism in countries around the world, had developed rapidly in late nineteenth-century Korea, before being cut off by Japanese repression in 1910. Japan's new policy on publication freed cultural nationalists to once again embark on a reformist project. Newspapers were most important for the formulation of public opinion because they cut across all walks of life and served to overcome or confirm misgivings and skepticism about the leadership of national figures.

The corresponding increase of social communication in the 1920s was phenomenal. Among the various new magazines published in the 1920's were *Kaebyŏk* (Creation) published by the Ch'ŏndogyo church, *Asŏng* (Our voice) of the Korean Youth League, and *Ch'ŏngch'un* (Youth) edited by Ch'oe Namsŏn. In the first three years of the cultural rule (1920–23) some seven thousand organizations were created. Among the daily newspapers in colonial Korea, the most widely read was the *Tonga ilbo* with thirty-seven thousand subscribers. The official government gazette, the *Maeil sinbo*, had a circulation of only about twenty-three thousand. The circulation of the *Chosŏn ilbo* and *Chosŏn chungang* was about twenty-three thousand and fourteen thousand respectively. The total number of subscriptions to the four major newspapers steadily increased until 1929 when it reached one hundred thousand within the national population of twenty million.[25] As in the period before 1910, newspapers were the heart of the nationalist revival in the period after 1920.

The Main Features of the Colonial Public Sphere

The early 1920s were unique in having the least repression during colonial rule in Korea, and this moderate level of repression allowed for the appearance of a public sphere in the colonial space.[26] The boundary of the public sphere, however, was determined by the colonial police authorities who classified communism and anarchism as radical ideologies beyond the limits of the law. Extreme right nationalists in exile in Manchuria, Shanghai, and Beijing relied on direct action by occasionally dispatching armed bands of guerillas from outside the northern Korean-Chinese border. Within Korea radical groups of left-wing journalists appeared in 1922 and rapidly spread in subsequent years, but they could not disseminate their messages beyond a limited range due to the harsh repressive control of the colonial police. Prominent nationalist journalists, whose social status and orientations were typically those of the bourgeois upper class, led the colonial public sphere. These were progressively oriented intellectuals whom Robinson[27] termed "cultural nationalists" because they typically thought that the Korean nation could strengthen itself under colonialism and gradually become independent. Their activities were focused on the *Tonga ilbo* and *Kaebyŏk*.

An important characteristic of the colonial public sphere was that it was not built on a stable legal foundation but on an unstable balance of forces between national movements and the colonial government. Since the governor-general ruled by decree, the capricious will of high-level colonial bureaucrats could be decisive. From the mid-1920s, reform of publication and newspaper laws became a regular demand among the resolutions passed at meetings of journalists and attorneys. However, even after 1940 when Korean newspapers were completely abolished, arbitrary repression outlasted criticism and survived. This shows that weakness and vulnerability to oppression and manipulation was a second and important feature of the colonial public sphere.

The colonial public sphere became a buffer zone, a zone where discursive battles took place between the indigenous population and the colonial power. It was a zone of negotiation that absorbed the impact of radical demands and harsh measures for both the ruling authorities and the colonial cultural elite. After the *Sin saenghwal* (New life) incident of 1922, when six writers from *New Life* magazine were imprisoned, repressive measures on socialist ideas became common phenomenon in Korea. The colonial authorities regarded left-wing intellectuals as a danger to colonial security, and socialist and communist discourses were denied access to the colonial public sphere.[28] Anarchists, in fact, never even attempted to put their demands in the public sphere at all. Instead, they relied on direct action, staging terrorist bombing and assaults, for example the bombing of the Chongno police station in Seoul by Kim Sangok, a member of the Ŭiyŏltan (Righteous brotherhood) on January 12, 1923.

Phases and Limits of the Colonial Public Sphere

The fact that a public sphere emerged during the first four years of Saitō's cultural rule was a remarkable phenomenon in the history of modern Korean nationalism. The activities of the "defiant Korean press" began to stimulate national consciousness when their rekindled public discourse filled the opinion sections of the nationalist newspapers.[29] In July 1920, the colonial government confiscated the *Tonga* editorial that protested against the order to dissolve the itinerant lectures of the Tokyo Foreign Student Friendship Society (Tonggyŏng Yuhaksaeng Haguhoe). This was the first *Tonga ilbo* editorial dealing with the freedom of the press. The colonial police not only banned the Tokyo Foreign Student Friendship Society's final event in Seoul, they also prevented the publication of protesting opinion.[30] The *Chosŏn ilbo* editorial on the occasion of a U.S. Congressmen's visit to Korea led to the suspension of its publication. In both cases it was apparent that the colonial authorities were determined to minimize outside influence on colonial society. Among the confiscated Korean newspaper articles in 1920 and 1921, approximately 48 percent were on international relations.[31]

The influence of prominent cultural nationalists, such as Kim Sŏngsu, Song Chinu, Ch'oe Namsŏn, and particularly Yi Kwangsu and Ch'oe Rin, was most decisive in shaping the character of the colonial public sphere. This group, which was associated with the *Tonga ilbo* and its nationalist followers, proposed two agendas for the nationalist movement: the Korean Products Promotion movement (Chosŏn Mulsan Hangnyŏ Undong)—designed to promote the purchase of Korean-made products—and the Movement to Establish a People's University (Millip Taehak Sŏllip Undong). The failure of these two movements in the summer of 1923 attests to the stark reality that the moderate nationalist movements faced internal critics, as well as the expected arbitrary interference of colonial authorities. The degree of success of these educational and cultural programs was immensely important given the weakness of Korea's infrastructural foundation at that time.

For the colonial authorities, consolidation of colonial control generally overrode Korean cultural nationalist demands. Strengthening the economic value of Korean national assets was not on the Government-General agenda. The governor-general of Korea officially welcomed these nationalist plans, but secretly tried many means to undermine them. Throughout September

1922, the colonial government allowed publication of *Chosŏn chi kwang* (Light of Korea) and four other journals that were licensed with the right to deal with issues of current political and economic affairs. This liberal era, the first phase in the development of the colonial public sphere, lasted no more than a few months. Yet, by having allowed the brief publication of these political magazines, the colonial authorities unwittingly enabled additional media for the next several years to aid the creation of a public sphere.

The second phase in the development of the colonial public sphere was a two year period of turbulence (1924–25) over control of the public sphere. The period began with the novelist and columnist Yi Kwangsu serializing in January 1924, an essay titled "National Statecraft" ("Minjokchŏk kyŏngnyun") in the *Tonga ilbo*. In this essay Yi criticized Korea's leaders and outlined a "hundred year national plan" to build modern industry, education, and politics for the nation. In the resulting scandal he was forced to resign from the *Tonga ilbo*, and massive seizures of reports and editorials subsequently began to hamper public discussions through the media.[32] The colonial authorities applied the Newspaper Law and the Publication Law as effective instruments of censorship and manipulation and in 1925 introduced another notorious law, the Peace Preservation Law (Chian ijihō). The law, designed to punish radical and dangerous activists such as communists and anarchists, had an immediate impact on colonial Korea. Although in April 1925 the Annual Conference of the Korean Reporters and Journalists protested this new law, the third indefinite suspension of *Kaebyŏk* (August 1925) and the publication ban on the *Chosŏn ilbo* (September 1925) put effective straitjackets on the press. Afterward, the number of editorials that directly dealt with current political affairs decreased conspicuously.

This illustrates the functional limit of the public sphere in a colonial society that lacks a powerful private sphere comparable to the bourgeoisie's expanding role in the civil society of Europe, a powerful role that provided a stable basis for the public sphere in the eighteenth century.[33] After a liberalized era of only three months, which began with the issuance of political magazines, the colonial government in Korea tightened its media policy by punishing socialist journalists in judicial proceedings.[34] The newly applied policy for newspapers and magazines was a "policy of permit and control," a policy that was outwardly permissive, but its essence remained highly authoritarian.[35] A third period of general decline and decay of the colonial public sphere appeared well before the end Saitō's administration in 1927. Once again the *Tonga ilbo* was subjected to an indefinite publication ban, and this time the indictment of the publisher, Song Chinu and a chief editor, Kim Ch'ŏlchung, followed.

Discursive Struggles in the Public Sphere: The Nationalist Challenge to Colonialism

While a public sphere did open up for a time in colonial Korea, limitations on the freedom of the press made the existence of this colonial public sphere precarious. Gramsci's notion of hegemony is useful here to grasp the nature of communication under colonialism.[36] While the Korean nationalist media were able to produce critical discourses, which in turn constituted the public sphere of the colony, this autonomous public opinion could emerge only by overcoming Japanese colonial discourses. Public opinion emerged fitfully through discursive struggles between the colonizers and indigenous nationalists in the vernacular Korean newspapers and other media.

The Struggle for Hegemony between Colonial Ideology and Cultural Nationalism

Nationalist cultural elites and agents of colonial ruling ideology were in constant confrontation in the realm of public communication. The official ideology of the Saitō administration was "a policy of extension of the imperial territoriality." Governor-General Saitō, having faced mounting political pressures both from home and the colony, emphasized the efforts to abolish discrimination between Japanese and Koreans at all policy levels and to execute institutional reforms. This followed from Japanese Prime Minister Hara Kei's recommendation for the strict application of the assimilation policy (*dōka seiji*). Assimilation was an ideology of Japanese colonialism, a social Darwinist idea that manifested, for the Japanese, as a mission to civilize and guide the "lesser" races of East Asia. The doctrine was included in the concept of Japanization, yet colonial authorities discriminated against Koreans and limited the scope of assimilation by excluding measures that provided political rights or political autonomy to the Korean colony.

The colonial government initially countered the critical Korean press by presenting the ruling ideology of assimilation and Saitō's cultural rule policy with propagandistic logic imbued with modernization theory. Later Japan countered with a strategy of propagating a hegemonic discourse by relying on government media, such as the Japanese language newspaper *Keisei shimbun* (Current affairs), the Japanese monthly, *Chōsen*, the Korean language daily, the *Maeil sinbo*, and the English language *Seoul Press*.

The *Tonga ilbo* and other vernacular newspapers for their part repeatedly criticized various ruling policies of the Government-General of Korea. The Korean nationalist press assailed the colonial immigration policy numerous times by demanding the abolition of the Oriental Development Company (Tōyō Kaitaku Kabushiki Kaisha) that sponsored Japanese agricultural immigration to Korea. They also criticized the industrial and educational policies of the colonial authorities in general. Although the governor-general of Korea promoted the assimilation policy with repeated assertions of nondiscrimination, ethnic discrimination against Koreans was, in fact, never abandoned in the administrative practices of the Government-General of Korea.[37] The majority of the messages delivered in the official and ruling political communication process were authoritarian, paternalistic, and coercive rather than conciliatory.[38]

CULTURE AS NATIONALIST DISCOURSE IN COLONIAL SPACE

The *Maeil sinbo*, a government-owned vernacular daily, presented the ruling perspective by publishing the official standpoint. Early editorials were steeped in discourses of modernity and modernization. Articles frequently dealt with material progress or modern facilities to be installed in Korea. Frequent editorial subjects were reform measures of the new administration, establishment of facilities and committees for public libraries, railways, roads, an imperial university, and so forth.[39]

The *Tonga ilbo* in its inaugural issue, on the other hand, declared culturalism (*munhwajuŭi*) as a major principle. Culturalism became a strong commitment to a new culture of nationalism.[40] Largely under the leadership of the *Tonga ilbo*, together with Yi Kwangsu's articles in *Kaebyŏk*, many new intellectuals were assembled under the Korean news media and formed the cultural nationalist mainstream.[41] This cultural nationalism was, in fact, a revival of the progressive "patriotic enlightenment movement" of the first decade of the twentieth century.

The *Tonga ilbo* also launched an attack on the conservative literati, to which the literati in the countryside made a bitter counterattack. An editorial column on May 9, 1920 entitled "A Baton to the Head for Ming Poseurs" (*Ka-myŏngin tusang e ilbong*) provoked a strong response from the provincial literati. Kim Myŏngsik's series of editorials, which were published in the same period, also triggered controversy between the literati and the *Tonga ilbo*.[42] In September, a polemical series of editorials criticized Confucian rites. The *Tonga ilbo* initiated public debate on Neo-Confucianism and did not hesitate to reveal its progressive zeal to reform the conservative mind. The progressive tone of the *Tonga ilbo* was met with vengeance from traditionalists, and the colonial authorities capitalized on strong conservative criticism to legitimize the first suspension of the *Tonga ilbo* publication in late September 1920.[43] The official reason for the punitive action was the violation of the sanctity of Japanese Shintoism and the sacred position of the Emperor, but this was also a calculated paternalistic gesture to show off the colonial government's favor of the conservative literati class.[44]

In the early years, nationalist discourse readily challenged the colonial government even if this discourse officially focused on nonpolitical activities. In its first year of publication alone, in less than two months (late May to July), editorials of the *Chosŏn ilbo* were suspended from being published four times. The editorials exhorted a nationalist inspiration of the youth and sought to awaken the national identity of the people.

The *Tonga ilbo* proposed in the first issue that its principle was nationalism, implying that it was the legitimate heir of the March First movement.[45] Its journalists also proclaimed that democracy and culturalism were their other core principles. The basic overtone of the *Tonga ilbo* represented a typically bourgeois enlightenment perspective. Nationalists thought that working on progressive social reforms would prepare the nation for the long-term, gradual movement toward independence.[46] This "culturalism" embodied the enlightenment tradition of the progressive nationalist movements of the 1900s,[47] as well as the gradualism of An Ch'angho. Culturalism was also a strategy of the cultural rule policy (*bunka seiji*) which forbade political activities but allowed cultural activities.[48]

The cultural nationalists were self-proclaimed moderates, who focused their attention on nonpolitical issues, such as education and industry. According to Yi Kwangsu, political movements were more a source of trouble than a solution at the current level of societal development in the colony. Yi argued in his controversial article in *Kaebyŏk*, "The Theory of National Reconstruction" (*Minjok kaejoron*), that the failure of the progressive reform movement in the late 1890s was caused by the movement's premature politicization without first forming any strong foundation in the society. Yi suggested that nationalists "reform themselves first" before launching radical movements. Without the ethical and moral renewal of colonial intelligentsia, initiated by Yi's own individual determination, political movements were doomed to fail, he claimed. Thus, Yi proposed gradualism and pacifism, denying the utility of political independence movements. In a way this was reminiscent of An Ch'angho's program of fostering education and developing industry as prerequisites for Korean independence.

Barely before five months had passed in the first year of publishing, the nationalist press was subject to suspension measures. The *Chosŏn ilbo* experienced suspension twice in its first year, and the *Tonga ilbo* suffered from a four-month suspension. Due to oppressive colonial regulations, the bulk of public debates and public communication remained in the area of nonpolitical issues. Colonial newspapers lacked rights as well as the leverage to be selective about censorship items in the regulations. After this four month break, the *Chosŏn ilbo* and the *Tonga ilbo* resumed their publications in late December 1920 and in late February 1921 respectively. In an editorial on March 5, 1921, the *Tonga ilbo* declared that cultural rule was not free due to the absence of the press and the absence of freedom of assembly. As for the issue of the freedom of the press, the government-run *Maeil sinbo*, as early as April 30, 1920, wrote condescendingly about nationalist newspapers. It claimed that even civilized nations (i.e., the West) would not allow the negation of a state's sovereignty nor seditious activities, particularly in newly acquired territory.

In the early years of 1920 and 1921, Korean nationalists initially began to challenge colonial powers by addressing nonpolitical issues such as education, the economy, and laws. The fact that of 1,920 confiscated editorials almost half were on the issue of education indicates that education was not uncontroversial. The cultural nationalists, who needed to counter the ultrastatist ruling ideology, selected the notion of *minjung* (the people) as a new national symbol instead of *kungmin*,[49] a term tied to the Japanese notion of *kokutai* or national polity. The *minjung* were regarded as a basic unit of political action in a modern state. As the colonial government banned political usage of the term nation

(K. minjok, J. minzoku), the authority of the minjung came to be frequently mentioned. Yet the discussion of the minjung could not develop into political discourse corresponding to a Western concept of a political nation, because
political organizations were not permitted in colonial Korea.

Enlightenment of the minjung was a common theme of the Tonga ilbo journalists. The bourgeois nature of these writers was expressed in editorials that
recognized the inherent value of the minjung but recommended the constant
guidance of enlightened leaders. Yet the discovery of the concept of the minjung signified the intellectuals' recognition of the importance of the popular
class in the nationalist movement.

The Government-General of Korea did not attempt to officially oppose
nationalist culturalism but did so clandestinely. Realizing the strength of the
nationalist cultural movement, Saitō's advisory staff recommended capital-
izing on the rising tide of the Practical Education movement (Sillyŏk Yangsŏng
Undong) of the colony. The colonial government recognized the utility of the
cultural movement in moderating national movements and suggested the
active dissemination of the ruling ideas of the cultural movement.[50] In a serial
of editorial columns published in July 1921, the Maeil sinbo presented the view
of the colonial government as: "the cultural movement, in a nutshell, is a
reform movement which aims at reforming political organizations, social
institutions, industrial organizations, and educational institutions of modern
times."[51] The editorials of the Maeil sinbo offered the official version of the
cultural movement as the elite-led enlightenment movement aimed at the
cultivation of individual personalities.

The nationalist journalists of the Tonga ilbo realized the need to differentiate culturalism from the cultural rule of the colonial government. As early as
November 1921, the Tonga ilbo criticized cultural rule by referring to it as "gray
politics." The colonial authorities confiscated the article, which the Tonga ilbo
attempted to publish again after two months. The Tonga ilbo criticized colonial
rule as autocratic and demanded freedom of political organization.

Governor Saitō's colonial ruling policy was ultimately aimed at building
hegemonic order in Korea. It was hegemonic in the sense that the colonial
government anchored its rule at the institutional level as well as obtained
consent at a psychological level. Many Japanese leaders and cultural elites
expressed views that the Japanese colonial empire should reform and lead
Asian nations. The Japanese intelligentsia emulated the French notion of mis-

sion civilisatrice, which justified imperial expansion and colonial rule. Yet, as Peattie notes, the conditions of the East Asian context of Japanese colonialism were more akin to the assimilative continental colonialism of Prussia than the new imperialism of the French.[52] There were, moreover, some critics who opposed the idea of replicating the French model of *mission civilisatrice* in Korea. Professor Yamamoto of Kyōto University opposed Prime Minister Hara's assimilation policy and suggested home rule as an alternative. Yamamoto explained that for a country with a long history of autonomous culture, assimilation was almost impossible.[53] Yanaihara and other liberal or socialist-oriented Japanese scholars also criticized those who argued for the "civilizing mission" of Japanese imperialism.

International Relations during the Colonial Era

International relations among the great powers in Northeast Asia were a salient issue that attracted intellectuals throughout the colonial era. Nationalist newspapers devoted much space to news about international political relations. Items that frequently appeared on the *Tonga ilbo* editorial pages in the early 1920s related to the Washington Conference of 1921, India's anti-colonial movements, and Irish liberation movements. The *Maeil sinbo*, the official colonial gazette, also produced articles and editorials on the same topics, yet in a contrasting, critical tone. The nationalist writers and journalists attempted to insert news articles concerning incidents about anti-colonial independence movements, or opinions that were favorable to Korea's independence or liberation. The colonial police, for their part, prohibited the publication of Sun Yat-sen's letter that requested Japan discard expansionism and allow independence of Korea.[54] The colonial authorities argued that it was not Japan but the Western imperialists who had been threatening world peace.[55] But the report of various national independence struggles and activities of the overseas provisional government contributed to forming a favorable atmosphere and spreading hope for independence movements.[56]

The fact that numerous government reports on international relations and Japanese foreign policy were confiscated indicates that to publish criticism on the negative side of imperialist policy was out of the question. In the series of English editorials titled "Union of the Asiatic Peoples" published in the second week of June 1924, the *Tonga ilbo* reiterated its critical view on the issue, which it had earlier declared on May 2, and which had been silenced by government confiscation. The editorials demonstrated in a rather lengthy analysis that the imperialist deeds of Japan in recent history demonstrated that the cause of Asian unrest lay in the Japanese "imperialistic designs and militaristic spirit." In general, however, international news could only contribute indirectly to public opinion in the colonial public space because of censorship of this issue.

Issue of Politics

Cultural nationalists from the early years of the *Tonga ilbo* gradually turned their focus toward political issues that conflicted with the colonial government. In the first year of its publication, except for a few occasions, the *Tonga ilbo* only indirectly touched upon the ideas of modern state and modern politics in commenting on the nature of the governing of the Government-General. The *Tonga ilbo*'s more immediate concerns were focused on Korean society in general. However, it soon became clear that there was no such thing as a purely nonpolitical issue in colonial society. On many occasions, when dealing with either an economic or an educational issue, the nationalist writer of the *Tonga ilbo* reached for a political conclusion and reasoned that colonial rule should be based upon the interest and will of the people.

What was peculiar for the *Tonga ilbo* during its initial year of publication in 1920 was a paucity of political news. The absence of reporting on politics was a result of colonial repression that had dissolved all political organizations. The military rule of the Terauchi administration, which had entirely suppressed any political freedom and relevant activities in the colonial Korea, created a society without political rights, or political mechanism, and thus without political life. Although there was no such thing as institutional politics, precisely for this reason, politics permeated every dimension of individual and collective life in colonial Korea. The colonial authorities used the term "political" only for those pro-Japanese groups that openly proclaimed an attitude of collaboration. The *Tonga ilbo*, on the other hand, claimed that popular understanding of the political movements was necessary and believed the movements must involve resistance because of the autocratic nature of the ruling power from which the politics originated.[57] Thus, what were officially regarded as political movements were negatively received among the populace as something similar to pro-Japanese or collaboration.[58] Political activities of the radical nationalists, on the other hand, were usually called rebellious activities by the government and considered an intrinsically negative phenomenon "inimical to social order or public peace." The suppression of the basic freedom of Koreans to express their will and their demands, be they political or not, led to a state of utter dissatisfaction and frustration among the colonial population. And the colonial effect on the political language noted above became a serious obstacle to the autonomous development of political identity in the postcolonial era.[59]

Many colonial press reports criticized police brutality, wrongdoing, corruption, and oppressive measures. Among the press reports and opinion pieces confiscated by the colonial authorities, criticism of administrative practices was the dominant theme. Sexual abuse was only one of the heinous practices commonly found in colonial police investigations. The *Tonga ilbo* reported the case of Mrs. O of Maebong-ni, North Ch'ungch'ŏng Province as a typical example. The editorial of the *Tonga ilbo* reported that the young pregnant woman, who had been stripped by force while undergoing police interrogations, "out of shame and indignation" committed suicide on the way home.[60] The "Uroe myŏn affair" was a more deliberate and arbitrary attempt to cross the legal limit of investigations. During the brief time period of May and June 1924, at Uroe myŏn in North P'yŏngan Province, eight cases of offensive sexual harassment, which included rape, were committed by Japanese policemen.[61]

While Governor-General Saitō maintained an official commitment to Japan's assimilation policy by "geographic extension," a policy to which his mentor Prime Minister Hara firmly adhered, Saitō sometimes revealed a more flexible and open attitude toward colonial policy.[62] When cultural rule was proclaimed as a governing principle, the basic core of Japanese colonial rule changed from physical coercion to more subtle manipulation. As a vital means to settle immediate unrest and to ensure long-term colonial rule, a viable system of collaboration became the core element of Saitō's governance. Throughout his career as a governor-general of Korea, Saitō supported and mobilized many pro-Japanese groups for the purpose of disseminating assimilation propaganda. The concept of "the political" in this colonial situation was so influenced by the semiofficial activities of pro-Japanese political groups that most of the colonial population acquired an anti-political attitude and negative view of politics in general.

CAUGHT BETWEEN REBELLION AND REPRESSION

The Early Suppression of Socialism

Public discourse and argument posed by the nationalist media agitated colonial society up through the mid-1920s and left a long-term mark. Colonial nationalists were unable to overwhelm the new media milieu at will when public communication and the critical discourse of newspapers and political journals buttressed the colonial public sphere. Selective treatment of newspapers in accordance with their ideological standpoint became a tactic of colonial governance. There were times when aspects of socialism appealed to colonial opinion leaders, but as early as 1922 the severe repression by the colonial administration blocked publishing statements to this effect. The cancellation of the two major socialist journals in 1922–23 was an apt example.[63] Despite that the selective mechanism of exclusion worked against the leftist media, the socialists were already in vogue in 1923 and were growing stronger. It was on the basis of strong appeals to colonial intellectuals that leftist organizations posed a strong challenge to both nationalists and colonial authorities.

Sin *saenghwal* (New life) and Sin *ch'ŏnji* (New heaven and earth) were two early socialist magazines, along with other socio-political groups, activated in the early cultural rule era. Class struggle, the principle of socialism, was publicly identified at the inaugural meeting of the Comrade Association (Tongjihoe) in January 1922, when socialists attacked the nationalists' liberal premises and presented an alternative vision of national liberation through socialist movements and class struggles.

Socialist journalism could not have had a secure base in daily newspapers because extant laws of the colonial authorities forbade it. But in 1924, two of the strong socialist organizations made their appearance: the Federation of Workers and Peasants in Korea (Chosŏn Nonong Ch'ongdongmaeng) and the Federation of Youth in Korea (Chosŏn Ch'ŏngnyŏn Ch'ongdongmaeng). In November, the North Wind Society (Pukp'unghoe) and The Tuesday Society (Hwayohoe), two important leftist ideological groups, were formed. The former was organized as a branch of the North Star Society (Puksŏnghoe), a Korean socialist study group, and the latter was initiated as the New Thought Research Association (Sin Sasang Yŏn'guhoe).[64] Although socialist or communist thought was attractive to certain groups of the intelligentsia, Japanese repression prevented the permanent establishment of a socialist or communist party within Korea.

The Failure of Mass Movements and the Cultural Nationalist Crisis, 1923–1924[65]

On February 6, 1922, an editorial that asserted the necessity of building a private university in Korea was published in the *Tonga ilbo*. The next year saw the *Tonga ilbo* proposing another mass campaign, the Promote Korean Products movement, which was influenced by Gandhi's Swaraj's movement. Cho Mansik initiated the movement in P'yŏngyang in 1920, but it was the *Tonga ilbo* that transformed the movement to a nationwide scale in spring 1923. By October 1923, the perception regarding the growth of nationalist movements reached a crisis. Urgency for action redoubled when the two major national campaign movements supported by the *Tonga ilbo* failed in clear contrast to the rapid diffusion of socialist ideas and movements.

The cultural nationalists of the *Tonga ilbo* gave priority to strengthening the economic power of colonial Korea by increasing the production of nationalist business, rather than the distribution of wealth. Socialists attacked the nationalists' supply theory of economics criticizing it as an "egoistic exploitative movement of the middle class."[66] The cultural nationalists could not make the Promote Korean Products movement into a movement to boycott Japanese merchandise because of the repression of the Government-General of Korea. However, the colonial authorities did not want the cultural nationalists to gain influence and build unnecessary power. The Government-General's decision to reduce the tax on foreign products struck a critical blow to the movement.[67] As a cumulative result of socialist attacks, the cultural nationalists increasingly lost their influence on the colonial public. The mainstream discourses of the public sphere were by and large decided by the Korean nationalists, but socialists increasingly challenged this as in the case of the Promote Korean Products movement.

The major tactic of cultural rule was to weaken the most dangerous groups within the colonial population—socialists, anarchists, and communists—and to endorse various non-confrontational activities in order to prevent radical political movements from spreading rapidly. To further this aim, various measures were undertaken to reconstitute religious organizations or to implant pro-Japanese factions in various levels of the colonial society.[68]

However, the socialist ideas that did get out were potent enough to damage the cultural nationalists from the left. At the same time, the nationalists were being squeezed by the colonial authorities from the right.

In the fall of 1923, the colonial climate became increasingly volatile as news of Japanese atrocities in the wake of the Kantō earthquake, reached Korea. The initial Korean newspaper reports were quickly repressed, but the Korean public, in a few weeks, began to show signs of unrest when they heard the rumors of the Tokyo massacre. By the fall of 1923, the colonial government had to find some solution to (1) stop the trend of the rapid spread of socialist groups and (2) regain some favor from the nationalist elites in order to tranquilize the unsettled public. By contrast, the cultural nationalists had to devise a special plan to reverse the decline of the Association for the Promotion of Korean Products (Chosŏn Mulsan Changnyŏhoe) and to overcome the increasingly fierce challenges of socialists and left-wing nationalists.

The Cultural Nationalists' Failure to Move into the Political Arena

In early January 1924, the *Tonga ilbo* confronted another crisis when it published a series of headline editorials, "National Statecraft" (*Minjokchŏk kyŏngnyun*) (hereafter, the "Statecraft" editorial). When the series of editorials by Yi Kwangsu were published in early January 1924, it was as if the *Tonga ilbo* had opened Pandora's box. Concerning the editorial's proposal to build "a major political organization within the permitted limit in Chosŏn," many believed that Yi was alluding to a home-rule collaboration movement as an alternative to the radical national movements for independence. The editorial arguments, which were published under the author's name, were reminiscent of the "Theory of National Reconstruction" that had appeared in *Creation* in May 1922 and had ignited controversy. Yi Kwangsu could not overcome the alleged stigma of collaboration.

The Statecraft editorial represented a new approach to cultural nationalism. The editorial in question proposed the nationalist movement take a political turn to get out of the clutches of the colonial government and the socialists. The necessity for a political movement had been emphatically expressed in the previous year's confiscated editorial that stated "In the political sense, we need to form an organization that can represent the political will of the Korean nation."[69] The editors moved the location of the section for political news from page two to the front page, reflecting the changed emphasis of the *Tonga ilbo's* editorial board. The nature of the movement was deliberately vague, argued the author, so that the nature of the movement could be decided as the movement progressed. These editorials from the early 1920s were the culmination of discontent that even included attempts of moderate national leaders to transform national movements from nonpolitical to political ones.[70]

The editorials argued for the new nationalist political organization to be called the Association for the Research of Governance (Yŏnjŏnghoe). It was initially devised as a grand nationalist movement coalition which consciously emulated India's National Congress. For this, a political organization needed to be formed within the bounds of the law.[71]

At this suggestion, the socialistic General Federation of Workers and Peasants (Chosŏn Nonong Ch'ongdongmaeng) attacked the cultural nationalists claiming that the "Statecraft" editorial represented a collaborative home-rule movement. The socialist critics proposed a boycott of the *Tonga ilbo* as punitive action for collaboration, citing Yi's phrase "to form a major political organization within the permitted limit."[72] It was not clearly discernable whether the article was actually proclaiming a home-rule movement or simply a restating of Yi's previously argued gradualist method. The editorial was an attempt to seek a self-imposed doctrine of cultural nationalism rather than a confirmation of the previous nonpolitical stance of national movements. This position was reiterated in a condensed English editorial entitled "Political Organization needed in Korea" as follows: "But now they (Koreans) must break fresh ground by forming an open political organization within the limit of the present law . . . to lay down a foundation for further national movements."[73]

The editorial and the unrest it caused were interpreted differently by different factions. A secret report of the Government-General classified this as a case of a non-compromising movement and plainly stated that the editorial represented the view of the Association for the Research of Governance, an abortive political organization of former cultural nationalists. The colonial police did not classify it as a collaboration movement as they did such pro-Japanese groups as the National Society and Comrades of Greater East Asia.[74] From their perspective, the cultural nationalist leaders commonly felt a sense of crisis manifested by the failure of two major mass movements combined with a rapid upsurge of socialist movements.

THE BATTLE FOR DISCURSIVE HEGEMONY: THE PROJECT OF NAESŎN YUNGHWA

The failure of the cultural nationalists' attempt to lead had far reaching resonance in Korean society and weakened the *Tonga ilbo*'s influence on nationalist movements in particular. To diminish the increasing power of the socialist influence on communication and organization activities, the colonial government organized the All Faction Leaders League (Kakp'a Yuji Yŏnmaeng), a grand coalition of eleven pro-Japanese groups in March 1924.[75] Saitō and his close aids seemed to have oscillated between a plan for cultural hegemony and sheer coercive power. Whether a true assimilation policy believer or not, Saitō did not believe in the utility of force alone but considered hegemony as having considerable value. Home rule was one of the key issues often raised in times of crisis in colonial Korea. Governor-General Saitō furtively endorsed nationalists of the *Tonga ilbo* and other cultural nationalists to form a self-governing movement and upon his return from Japan in 1928, he considered home rule, or self-government as an alternative political option to keep his policy of co-optation alive.

The *Tonga ilbo* faced a developing crisis in April 1924. A group of young and able journalists moved to the *Chosŏn ilbo*, and the editing director, Yi Sanghyŏp, joined the *Chosŏn ilbo* in late April. Yi was followed by other journalists like Hong Chŭngsik, Kim Tongsŏng, and Min T'aewŏn.[76] It seems there had been contacts between Yi and Government-General high officials before the resignations. The common interests arising from the strong ascendance of the socialist groups may have drawn moderate nationalists and the colonial government closer. But an unexpected attack by leftist radicals dramatically changed the political situation of colonial Korea in early 1924. The incident caused the Government-General of Korea to renounce the plan to use the *Tonga ilbo* as a potential ally for a hegemonic project. By integrating more reliable pro-Japanese groups, the colonial government quickly launched the pro-Japanese political association, the All Faction Leaders League. Thus, the Government-General's official Japanese-Korean Reconciliation movement (Naesŏn Yunghwa Undong) strongly and openly contested the moderate nationalist movement throughout 1924.

The *Tonga ilbo* launched an attack on the colonial government's hegemonic project proclaiming it an attempt to sponsor and support pro-Japanese collaboration movements. The attack began with *Tonga ilbo* critiques of the All Faction Leaders League. On March 30, 1924, the *Tonga ilbo*'s editorial revealed that the All Faction Leaders League was the official mouthpiece of the Government-General of Korea, since the declared movement objectives were nothing more than the basic ideas of the official assimilation policy doctrine.[77]

The Convention of Public Officials (Kongjikcha Taehoe) convened in 1924 and was another major result of Japan's hegemonic project. It was an official attempt to spur the pace of assimilation by devising a Korean-Japanese integrated political organization. The official gazette *Maeil sinbo* repeatedly published editorial advertisements on various pro-Japanese political organizations such as the One People Society (Tongminhoe), the Mutual Admiration Society (Sangaehoe), Sŏnjoktan, and so forth.[78] The nationalist press unanimously criticized the pro-Japanese collaboration movements, and their editorials were banned.

A rare exception that escaped censorship was a *Tonga ilbo* editorial on June 18, 1924. The editorial calmly stated that "the Convention of Public Officials was not representing the true will of the people but the will of the colonial government, especially its geographical expansionism (*naeji yŏnjangjuŭi*) policy." Moreover, it argued that the movement was deceptive in nature because it faked Korean and Japanese consensus by co-opting pro-Japanese Korean officials in lieu of seeking the true public opinion of the Korean people. On June 30, 1924, the *Tonga ilbo* continued to control its tone and clarified that the petition of National Association, a pro-Japanese organization, reminiscent of another pro-Japanese organization, the Ilchinhoe (Association for Common Progress), on the eve of annexation, could not represent the true public opinion of the Korean people.[79] The author asserted further that the *Tonga ilbo* decisively concluded that neither home rule nor suffrage would be a solution for the Korean people's aspirations.

Saitō's colonial government continually put great efforts towards dividing and weakening nationalist movements. The bipolar division of nationalists into right and left factions in 1924–25, and the mutual mistrust and battle amongst nationalists and socialists was a "golden moment" for the hegemonic ruling of Korea. The idea of home rule was one of the most effective means to pursue the colonial government's hegemonic project. By continually maintaining close contact and thereby securing implicit cooperation from influential nationalists such as Yi Kwangsu, Ch'oe Namsŏn, and Ch'oe Rin, the colonial government could manipulate and weaken the positions of moderate nationalists. As was shown by the fatal Statecraft incident, by antagonizing the radical element of nationalists and socialists, Saitō could check the moderate nationalists of the *Tonga ilbo*. The scandal had caused an immediate crisis for the *Tonga ilbo* in 1924, but more importantly, its lingering effect resulted in the long-term overall weakening of the moderate national movement. Socialists' repeated allegations about the *Tonga ilbo's* alleged collaboration was, regardless of its verity, the most effective means to weaken the *Tonga ilbo's* influence on the general public. The ensuing turbulent era of 1924–25 was one of intense struggle for the Korean nationalist press. Communication to the public had been compromised, and the press was no longer as powerful as in the early 1920s.

In the 1920s, there was a fine line between moderate nationalists and collaborators. The *Tonga ilbo* and cultural nationalists maintained a stance of non-cooperation. The strategy of non-confrontation was distinctively different from the collaboration phenomenon. The clearly stated, official goal of the *Tonga ilbo* and moderate nationalists was invariably independence. The *Tonga ilbo* editorialists and other moderate nationalists never conceded to the colonial propaganda of annexation. The Government-General of Korea in the 1920s relied largely on pro-Japanese forces in forging the collaborative mechanism. Cultural nationalists were considered to be an enemy rather than an ally of Japanese colonialism. It was, therefore, in the strategically calculated interests of socialists or communists to blame cultural nationalists as collaborators or traitors. However, the non-confrontation strategy of moderate nationalists should not be misunderstood as collaboration. The significance of discursive practices in the nationalist battle against colonial power was that it effectively criticized the colonial ruling ideology and revealed its deceptive intent.

Socialist ideas could not have a forum accepted in the established public sphere, so the socialist views were expressed in a diffused way through diverse media, relatively small-scale leftist journals and magazines. However, some had privileged access for a limited period of time in major nationalist organs. In the early part of the 1920s, major newspapers and journals had many reporters who secretly became socialists. Many prominent socialists such as Kim Chunyŏn, Sin Iryong, and Cho Pongam were journalists for the *Chosŏn ilbo* and the *Tonga ilbo*. The *Chosŏn ilbo*, since mid-1924, published opinions which became increasingly lenient to socialist views. The *Chosŏn ilbo* did not hide its positive perspective on the rise of socialist organizations such as the Federal Alliance of Workers and Peasants and the North Wind Society.[80]

RETURN TO OPPRESSION: DECAY OF THE PUBLIC SPHERE

Exclusion and Repression: Decay of the Public Sphere

After the Peace Preservation Law was promulgated in Korea in May 1925, the Korean colonial public sphere began to weaken and decline.[81] Already by 1924, the increasing trend of repressive control had manifested in that the number of "seizure" orders had nearly quadrupled from the previous years' average of fifteen to fifty-six.[82]

Reflecting on the rapidly growing numbers of peasants and workers organizations, socialist discourse became very well received by the mid-1920s in colonial Korea. However, after 1925, activities of socialist journalists were severely restricted, and consequently socialist discourses were increasingly barred from participating in the colonial public sphere. The introduction of the Peace Preservation Law stopped radicalization of national movements and the spread of secret communist organizations in colonial Korea.

The waves of arrests of communists struck the colonial society hard after late 1926 and socialists, out of sense of urgency, sought cooperation with nationalists. In January 1927, socialists, in concerted efforts with nationalists, formed the Sin'ganhoe, a grand political movement of legal organization.

Once the era of Administrative Superintendent Shimōka (1924–25) began, the nature of Governor-General Saitō's cultural politics rapidly changed into the Industry First movement.[83] The development of popular opinion (*minŭi ch'angdal*) as an important part of cultural politics was clearly withdrawn by this time. Since mid-1925, the critical political issues such as criticisms of official colonial policy and protests of repression were raised occasionally, but the brutal repressive measures of colonial censor officials, such as seizure, suspension of newspapers, arrests of writers, or in the worst case, closing of the media, effectively defused ascendance of many critical opinions.

The repressive control of the colonial police was noticeably strengthened during the suspension of *Kaebyŏk* and the *Chosŏn ilbo* in August and September of 1925. The symbolic meaning of the closure of *Kaebyŏk* in 1926 was that the colonial public sphere was now extremely repressed and under the full control of the High Police. The intensified censorship activities of the colonial government on vernacular newspapers and magazines since mid-1925 continued until Saitō's rule was replaced by the more oppressive war period of the 1930s. The repressive policy of Saitō's colonial rule from the mid-20s significantly changed the nature of the colonial presses. No longer could the press satisfy the expectation of colonial residents that the press would serve to formulate public opinion.

The Tonga Ilbo's Decline and the Chosŏn Ilbo's Progressive Tone

Beginning in September 1924, when the number of able journalists moved from the *Tonga ilbo* to the *Chosŏn ilbo*, the level of the *Chosŏn ilbo*'s critical tone gradually increased and the leading role of the *Tonga ilbo* within nationalist movements weakened conspicuously. During the mid-1920s, as Saitō's colonial rule policy gradually reverted from a tentative ensemble of persuasion and manipulation back to the previous policy of brutal oppression, the utility of the *Tonga ilbo* role—to pacify the restive colonial population—rapidly decreased.[84]

The large number of confiscated newspaper articles in 1924 (183) and 1925 (177) should not be over interpreted as evidence of the nationalist presses. On the contrary, after 1925, freedom of expression began to shrink rapidly, but the troika of the three newspapers—*Tonga ilbo*, *Chosŏn ilbo*, and *Sidae*—temporarily caused a multiplication of the activities of the nationalist presses. A trend toward commercialization competition among the nationalist presses began to appear during this era. Meanwhile, the repressive measures of censorship effectively checked the critical function of nationalist presses and exacerbated the process of weakening the *Tonga ilbo*'s critical journalism during this period. The critical editorials about colonial policy were intensively repressed during the first half of 1925. After July 1925, *Tonga ilbo* writers could no longer raise critical political issues.[85] The major political task of the national movements was to question the way to overcome the division of the movements and reunite them, but the *Tonga ilbo* could not find a solution for this task.[86] After 1925, the editorials that directly provoked current political affairs gradually diminished.

Continual Manipulation of the Colonial Government

After 1925, the moderate nationalists of the *Tonga ilbo* could no longer produce discourses as persuasive and powerful as before. To the open suggestion
of home rule made by Chairman Soejima of the *Maeil sinbo* in late 1925, the
Tonga ilbo remained in total silence. Considering its nature of unprecedented
and controversial proposals, the *Tonga ilbo*'s no comment policy might have
been considered an expression of no objection or of positive opinion to the
home-rule proposal. The issue of home rule was obviously an effective "invisible" tool that continually manipulated the moderate nationalists. Preemptive
usage of both suffrage and home-rule petitions by pro-Japanese groups since
the early 1920s and particularly petitions by the National Association made it
almost impossible for the moderate nationalists to present their views about
a political solution because they seemed quite similar to extant collaboration
movements. Throughout his career, Governor-General Saitō never abandoned
his hegemonic project of forming a grand collaboration network that could
include moderate nationalists. For this reason, the idea of home rule reappeared in the colonial governance agenda during Saitō's last few years of rule.
Although the governmental party of Japan presented a proposal or resolution
for home rule in Korea several times, these top, military-dominated leaders
could neither allow Koreans the political rights of participation in the
Japanese Diet nor consent to devolve significant political autonomy onto the
Koreans. From 1928 to 1930, in his abortive attempt, Governor-General Saitō
cautiously and secretly searched for the feasibility of home rule in Korea.[87]

The Dialectic of Colonial Publicity and Repression

Because of censorship, the communication activities of moderate nationalists
were weakened as the socialist radicals critically distorted nationalist discourse. The tarnished image of collaborators as a result of the Statecraft
incident, and the inability to create a major alternative plan to deliver to the
nationalist movement, crippled the moderate nationalists in their attempts to
form public opinion. Radicalization and the resulting polarization of opinion
had no public forum.

It is difficult to determine whether cultural rule could have halted the
general trend of colonial public opinion radicalization. The cultural national-

ists carried out their socio-political activities in the political context of manipulation and control. Colonial publications could not overstep the basic limits imposed by the colonial authorities. But the colonial public sphere was much more than an encapsulated space of total control. The formative process of public opinion in the colonial public sphere was rather impressive considering the many pressures and interventions by the colonial power. Although the voices of cultural nationalists were drowned out in critical moments either by censorship or by the more radical socialist critiques, the undercurrent of dialogue among nationalists and the cultural elite was often underrated and misunderstood.

CONCLUSION

Korea's colonial public sphere was unique. The non-democratic nature of the colonial political system, devoid of any parliamentary mechanism for mediating political interests, made this quasi-liberal sphere from the early years highly unstable. However, in an attempt to channel the explosive potential of the latent grievances of Koreans into moderate nonpolitical movements, Governor-General Saitō decided, under the cultural rule doctrine, to allow freedom of communication and the appearance of a nationalist press, which in turn constituted the phenomenon of the colonial public sphere.

Korea's colonial public sphere was not an example of a straight-line development of modernity brought about through colonialism. Rather, it was a contingent phenomenon created by an equilibrium of forces created by the post-March First movement situation between nationalists and colonial authorities and discursive struggle. Cultural rule, publicized both in and outside colonial Korea, gives the logical though misleading impression of 1920's Chosŏn as a society that guaranteed a certain kind of free public realm, one which allowed the population social and political activities. However the colonial public sphere in Korea was actually based on the fragile relationship between the governing power and the power of indigenous groups. Until late 1923, the policy of appeasement of the nationalist press was a salient principle of Governor-General Saitō. But as soon as the repercussions of the editorial on statecraft played out, the feasibility of a compromise with the *Tonga ilbo* as a potential partner for the ruling coalition evaporated.

Koreans were allowed to have a public sphere for a time in the 1920s, but it was neither a Confucian type nor a liberal type of sphere. It was a clearly a colonial type. Cultural rule acted as a model case for the exercise of the ideology of assimilation. However, the tradition of public communication and nationalism created a colony with a paradoxical public sphere where critical public communication of the nationalist elites unveiled the colonial ruler's hidden agenda of perpetuating the status quo.

Even though the period of the colonial public sphere era was short compared to the rest of the colonial period, the public sphere experiment performed the important function of checking the arbitrary power of the colonial government and revealing the falsity of the ruling hegemonic discourses. The public sphere in colonial Korea was not an accidental phenomenon nor a mere phantom, but both a valuable achievement in the history of nationalist movements and a significant contribution to the formation of Korean national identity. The demise of this public sphere in the last fifteen years of colonial rule inhibited the development of political consensus and contributed to the chaos on the Korean peninsula when liberation suddenly came.

NOTES

1. Gi-Wook Shin and Michael Robinson, *Colonial Modernity in Korea*, 11.

2. The public sphere can be defined as a social realm where a critical debate can emerge. The condition for the public sphere at the individual level is a special type of action, either public political action or public debate. Seyla Benhabib, "Models of Public Space," 80. The condition of the public sphere for a society in general is the existence of a public organ, the critical press or media. Jürgen Habermas, *The Structural Transformation of the Public Sphere*, 60. In his recent work, Habermas defined a public sphere as a "network for communicating information and points of view," featured in "the social space generated in communicative action" Jürgen Habermas, *Between Facts and Norms*, 360. For public spheres in Asian contexts, see Mary B. Rankin, "The Origins of a Chinese Public Sphere"; Mary Elizabeth Berry, "Public Life"; and Yongjik Kim, "The Political Tradition."

3. Jürgen Habermas, *Between Facts and Norms*, 362.

4. Lucian Pye, *Communication and Political Development*, 26.

5. A good example of such works was Kang Tongjin, *Ilche ŭi Han'guk*, on the Japanese colonial ruling policy. By laying too much emphasis on the hegemonic aspect of the various tactics and strategies of colonial government, Kang unknowingly underestimated activities of the national elites.

6. For modern mass media that appeared in the last years of the Chosŏn Dynasty, see O Chuhwan, "Ilche ŭi tae-Han"; and Chŏng Chinsŏk, et al., "Han'guk kŭndae ŏllon."

7. Korea had a strong tradition of the public debate and the publicity since the fifteenth century. For this, see Kim Yongjik, "Han'guk minjokchuŭi kiwŏn"; Kim Yŏngjik, "Han'guk chongch'i wa kongnonsŏng," and the second section of this chapter.

8. Kim Yongjik, "Han'guk chongch'i wa kongnonsŏng."

9. Andrew Grajdanzev, *Modern Korea*, 56; Dae-yeol Ku, *Korea under Colonialism*, 142–43.

10. For the communication policy of Japanese colonialist rule in Korea, see Michael Robinson, "Colonial Publication Policy"; Kim Kyuhwan, *Ilche ŭi tae-Han ŏllon*; and Chŏng Chinsŏk, *Han'guk ŏllon sa*.

11. The colonial authorities proclaimed the establishment of "a liberal and righteous administration" and its principles as "stabilization of peace and order, deference to public opinion, abatement of officialism, reform in administration, improvement of general living, and advancement of popular culture and welfare." Andrew Grajdanzev, *Modern Korea*, 57.

12. On September 3, 1919 Saitō stated: "The rights of the people should be respected and the freedom of press and speech should not be interfered with unless it is distinctly calculated to be inimical to the preservation of peace" Seoul Press, *Administrative Reforms in Korea*, 12.

13. Kim Kyuhwan, *Ilche ŭi tae-Han ŏllon*, 169. Cultural politics were devised as a part of a defensive scheme to handle the crisis situation created by the March First movement. Hence, it is important to understand how the sense of colonial crisis affected Governor-General Saitō's rule in the 1920s. For the 1919 crisis, see Kang Tongjin, "Munhwajuŭi ŭi kibon sŏngkyŏk," 166–67.

14. Namei Aoyagi, *Sōtoku seiji shiron* 1928(b), 4.

15. Pak Ch'ansŭng, *Han'guk kŭndae chŏngch'i sasangsa yŏn'gu*, 317; Han Paeho, "Samil undong chikhue Chosŏn," 82–83.

16. The covert strategy of cultural politics was a hegemony building project. An important aspect of hegemony is that its intellectual and moral leadership is "objectified in and exercised through" civil society and not led directly by the state. Joseph Femia, *Gramsci's Political Thought*, 24.

17. Those who assert the importance of the "divide and rule" strategy of Governor-General Saitō understand some aspect of "hegemony building" of Saitō's cultural rule. But hegemony building is a distinct phenomenon constituted by complicated and systematic efforts to form a network of diverse social allies. Collaboration is one element of the grand project, but cannot be identified with the whole project.

18. Kim Kyuhwan, *Ilche ŭi tae-Han ŏllon*, 189.

19. Kang Tongin, *Ilche ŭi Han'guk ch'imnyak*, 26.

20. Ibid, 36–37.

21. Civilians who were appointed to the staff were Kikuchi Kenzō, Ōkaki Takeo, and

Ayugai Husanoshin. Yi Yŏn, *Ilcheha ŭi Chosŏn chungang*, 25.

22. For information on the *jōhō iumkai* (*Chosŏn Chŏngbo Wiwŏnhoe*), see Kang Tongjin *Ilche ŭi Han'guk ch'imnyak*, 29–31; and Yi Yŏn, *Ilcheha ŭi Chosŏn chungang*.

23. Itinerant peddlers (*pobusang*) were organized on a national basis and used by conservative forces from the late nineteenth century to break up "progressive" political movements.

24. Kang Tongjin, *Ilche ŭi Han'guk ch'imnyak*, 221.

25. Chŏng Chinsŏk, *Han'guk ŏllon sa*, 553.

26. The first four year span of the 1920s can be categorized as a model public sphere even if it was under colonial rule. The legal underpinnings of colonial rule did not change at all, in fact, it was aggravated by the seventh verdict promulgated in response to the March First movement in April 1919. But it was the political responsibility of the new governor-general and his staff to carry favor to moderate nationalists.

27. Michael E. Robinson, "Colonial Publication Policy and the Korean Nationalist Movement."

28. The *Sin saenghwal* incident was an early case of oppression on socialist journalism. The colonial court authorities applied the most severe measures, a permanent ban on publishing, setting early a tone for socialist media. The editorial chief and president were sentenced to more than two years in prison.

29. Michael E. Robinson, "Colonial Publication Policy," 332.

30. *Tonga ilbo*, July 22, 1920. The editorial criticized Saitō's cultural politics claiming that it would be no different from Terauchi's former assimilation policy given that the lecturing tour was dispersed. The *Tonga ilbo* published the same content later on August 3, 1920.

31. Among the sixty-nine confiscated items twenty-one were editorials. Most of the articles on international relations were simple reports. The numbers were calculated by the author based on author's own categories. The basic sources were drawn from Chŏng Chinsok, *Ilche sidae minjokchi*.

32. Ibid., 16.

33. Jürgen Habermas, *Structural Transformation*, 33, 52.

34. Chŏng Chinsŏk, *Han'guk ŏllon sa*, 473.

35. Ch'oe Chun, *Han'guk sinmun sa*, 205.

36. We will put Habermas' notion of communication in the wider tradition of the critical theoretical notion of discourse. Raymond Geuss, *The Idea of Critical Thinking*; Craig Calhoun, *Habermas and the Public Sphere*. Many have argued the importance of hegemony in colonial context. Gi-Wook Shin and Michael Robinson, *Colonial Modernity in Korea*; Ania Loomba, *Colonialism / Postcolonialism*; and Kang Sanjung, *Orient'allijŭm ŭl nŏmŏsŏ*. The only problem is that 1920s Korea was still in the relatively early period of hegemonic ruling, which since the late 1930s came closer to Gramscian model of hegemony. For Gramsci's notion of hegemony, see Joseph Femia, *Gramsci's Political Thought*.

37. The educational ordinances of the colonial administration promulgated in 1911, proclaimed the assimilation policy which established "separate and unequal" dual school systems for Koreans and Japanese. Wonmo Dong, "Assimilation and Social Mobilization," 156. This dual system, which perpetuated an unequal system, obstructed integration between the two nations, and lasted until the liberation of Koreans was achieved in 1945.

38. Kang Tongjin, *Ilche ŭi Han'guk*, 43–45; Kim Kyuhwan, *Ilche ŭi tae Han ŏllon*, 214–15.

39. While the campaign to establish a "people's university" (*millip taehak*) failed in Korea, the Government-General did establish Keijō Imperial University in Seoul in 1924, which was the predecessor to present-day Seoul National University. It is important to note, however, that ethnic Japanese were always the majority of students at this institution during the colonial period.

40. Kenneth Wells, *New God, New Nation*, 106.

41. For cultural nationalism see Michael Robinson, *Cultural Nationalism in Colonial Korea*; Pak Ch'ansŭng, *Han'guk kŭndae chŏngch'i*; and Ch'oe Chun, *Han'guk sinmun sa*.

42. The publishing of the serial editorial entitled "Address to the Fathers and Elders of Choson" (*Chosŏn puro ege koham*) continued for about a week. Because of the serious criticisms and the potential boycott movement by the literati, the *Tonga ilbo* had to publish apologies several times and the chairman Pak Yŏnghyo resigned. Tonga Ilbosa, *Tonga ilbosa sa*, 134–37.

43. The official reason for the suspension of the *Tonga ilbo* was its editorial on the reconsideration of the rite issue (September 25, 1920).

44. Ch'oe Chun, *Han'guk sinmun sa*, 194–95.

45. It is noteworthy that on the first issue the *Tonga ilbo* declared an ideology of nationalism and committed that it would represent the will of the nation. It further proclaimed that democratic liberalism and cultural enlightenment would be the newspaper's other key doctrines.

46. Kim Chunyŏp and Kim Changsun, *Han'guk kongsanjuŭi*, 7.

47. Pak Ch'ansŭng, *Han'guk kŭndae chŏngch'i*.

48. The *Tonga ilbo* editorial on April 7, 1920 started, "Since I have no freedom to discuss political method (of nationalist movements) . . . "

49. *Kungmin* (J. *kokumin*) means literally "people of the nation" a concept that implied dutiful subject hood without the participatory rights of true citizens.

50. The controversial phrase, "the cultural movement accompanied by prestige," does not necessarily mean the movement of cultural nationalists as Kang Tongin claimed. Moreover, it cannot mean that the cultural nationalist movement was creation of the Government-General of Korea. For this see Kang Tongjin, *Ilche ŭi Han'guk ch'imnyak chŏngch'aek sa*, 385–86; and Pak C., *Han'guk kŭndae chŏngch'i*, 290.

51. *Maeil sinbo*, July 16 and 17, 1921.

52. Ramon H. Myers, Mark Peattie, and Jingzhi Zhen, *The Japanese Colonial Empire*, 14.

53. Ono Ichiro, "Che ilch'a taejŏn hu ŭi singmin chŏngch'aek non," 49, 83.

54. The letter was banned from publication in the *Tonga ilbo* on Aug. 11, 1922. Tonga Ilbosa, *Tonga ilbosa sa*, 143.

55. *Maeil sinbo*, July 14, 1920.

56. Ch'oe Chun, *Han'guk sinmun sa*, 194.

57. The editorials proposed the use of political movements as analytical concepts. There were two types of political movements in Korea, i.e. (1) nationalist movements and (2) socialist movements, whereas home-rule movements were reactionary movements. See *Tonga ilbo* editorials, October 25 and 30, 1924.

58. In the police reports of the government-general of Korea, only five organizations were classified as political organizations. They were the National Society, the People's Aid Association (Yuminhoe), the Common Light Society (Tonggwanghoe), Friends of the People (Minuhoe), and Comrades of Greater East Asia. Chōsen Sōtokufu Keimukyoku, *Chōsen chian chōgyo*, 151.

59. The *Tonga ilbo* in a serial editorial reasserted the importance of the political movements with "its organization and training," a familiar expression of the Statecraft editorial published earlier that year. Yet, the *Tonga ilbo*'s attempt to revitalize the political movements of moderate nationalists could not materialize in subsequent years until the Singanhoe movement was proposed by initiative of the *Chosŏn ilbo*. See editorials of the *Tonga ilbo*, December 26–27, 1924.

60. For the English editorial, see *Tonga ilbo*, August 17, 1924. Both Korean and English editorials on the incidents were confiscated. For the Korean editorial, see *Tonga ilbo*, August 14, 1924.

61. See the series of English editorials in *Tonga ilbo*, September 11–13, 1924.

62. Somewhat unexpectedly, Governor-General Saitō presented his negative view of the cultural assimilation policy in his article in *Tonga ilbo*, April 1, 1920.

63. Michael Robinson, "Colonial Publication Policy," 326.

64. Kim Chunyŏp and Kim Changsun, *Han'guk kongsanchuŭi*, 38–42.

65. For cultural nationalism and promote Korean products movement, see Robinsŭn M. *Ilcheha munhwajŏk*, 147–158 and Pak Ch'angsung, *Han'guk kŭndae chŏngch'i*, 264–89.

66. See Yi Sŏngt'ae's article in *Tonga ilbo*, March 20, 1923.

67. The colonial police authorities prohibited mass campaign of the Promote Korea Product movement in Seoul. See editorials in *Tonga ilbo*, February 15, 1923. Robinsŭn, *Ilcheha munhwajŏk*, 156.

68. Kim Unt'ae, *Ilbon chegukchuŭi ŭi Han'guk t'ongch'i*, 301–3.

69. Editorial of the *Tonga ilbo*, November 3, 1923.

70. A biography of the *Tonga ilbo* president Kim Sŏngu explained, "The editorial written by Yi Kwangsu signified a major turn of the independence movement of our

nation. . . . It clarified that in a (colonial) Korea under the influence of the enemy, the method of legal political movement was inevitable in staging systematic and long-run protest movements." Inch'on Kinyŏmhoe, *Inch'on Kim Sŏngsu chŏn*, 265.

71. Inch'on Kinyŏmhoe, *Inch'on Kim Sŏngsu chŏn*, 260–65.

72. Japanese police sources reported that this was not done so much by accident as by deliberate decision by the cultural nationalists chief of staff, such as Song Chinu. See Chōsen Sōtokufu, Keishō hokudo keisatsusho, *Kōtōkesiatsu yoshi*, 45; Chōsen Sōtokufu, *Saitō makoto bunsho*, 225–34; Chōsen Sōtokufu, *Chosŏn ŭi ch'ian sanghwang*, 63.

73. *Tonga ilbo*, January 10, 1924.

74. The colonial police reports suggested that the ultimate goal implied by the movement was independence. Chōsen Sōtokufu, *Saitō makoto bunsho*, 230.

75. Kim Chunyŏp and Kim Changsun, *Han'guk kongsanjuŭi undong sa*, 21–24.

76. Tonga Ilbosa. *Tonga ilbosa sa*, 233–35.

77. The editorial was continued to the editorial of April 2 and English version editorials were published on April 3 and 4, 1924.

78. See editorials of the *Maeil sinbo* on April 20, 27, and May 11, 1924.

79. The editorial was moderate reiteration of its previous confiscated version on June 28, 1924.

80. See Chosŏn's editorials on April 21 and November 29, 1924.

81. Yŏngmok Kyŏngbu, *Pŏb ŭl t'onghan Chosŏn singminji*; and Richard Michell, *Thought Control in Prewar Japan*.

82. Tonga Ilbosa, *Tonga ilbosa sa*, 232.

83. *Maeil sinbo*, January 15, 1925.

84. For this reason, some of Korean scholars have argued that real intention of legalizing "cultural groups" was to countervail radical independence movements and domesticate nationalist movements Kim Unt'ae, *Ilbon chegukchuŭi*, 301.

85. The *Tonga ilbo* could not even question the validity of the Government-General decision or present any standard level protest at all. *Tonga ilbo*, August 4, 1925.

86. *Tonga ilbo*, June 22, 1925.

87. Kim Tongmyŏng recently suggested reevaluating question of home rule as expressing more than mere propaganda. He argues that the potential change of the paradigm of colonial rule from assimilation to self-governing was secretly sounded by the order of the governor-general in 1926–27. See Kim Tongmyŏng, "1920-nyŏndae chosŏn esŏ ŭi ilbon chegukchuŭi."

3

Expansion of Elementary Schooling under Colonialism: Top Down or Bottom up?[1]

SEONG-CHEOL OH AND KI-SEOK KIM

Prior studies of the process of structuring elementary education under colonial rule have mostly focused on the analysis of how colonizers handled education policies in the colonized country. While in the case of Korea it is important to identify the elements of Japanese education policy that were adopted, we will focus here on the even more important question of the reaction of the Korean people to colonial education policy. In African and Asian nations that were colonized by Western European powers, "while some colonized reacted favorably to colonial schools, others did not. Apathy was probably a more pervasive response than anything else."[2] Koreans, by contrast, were anything but apathetic.[3] Unlike the Taiwanese who were also under Japanese rule, Koreans defied the system rather than be neutralized or brainwashed by it.[4] Considering these facts, we can infer that Koreans' expectations for and recognition of the education policy were not synonymous with those of the Japanese government. Moreover, we might hypothesize that the Japanese imperialists did not attain their intended goals and created inadvert problems through their education policy. Thus in this chapter we intend to reevaluate Japanese colonial education policy from the point of view of the Koreans.

While we will not overlook the intent of the Japanese colonizers, and their educational policies, we expect to see the facts as "contested terrain" in which both nations' expectations and recognition diverge either through policy collision or interaction. The main focus of this chapter is primary education. Analyzing the process, size, and function of colonial education expansion and the educational curriculum will produce both ironies and unintended consequences.

CHARACTERISTICS OF THE EXPANSION OF COLONIAL EDUCATION

Shortly after colonizing Korea in 1911, the Japanese colonial empire announced the Korean Educational Ordinance (Chōsen Kyoikurei) a law that established a Japanese-medium, colonial educational system in Korea. Primary education consisted of a mandated four years of primary school (futsu gakkō). Secondary education included four years of middle school for boys (koto futsu gakko) and three years for girls (joshi koto futsu gakko) or two to three years of vocational school (jitsugyo gakkō). In 1915, the Japanese announced the Regulations for Technical Schools (Senmon gakko kisoku), which legalized technical schools (senmon gakko) as post-secondary educational institutions. Through the second decade of the twentieth century, a university did not exist in Korea and primary or secondary education for Koreans was not as extensive as it was for Japanese students in either Japan or Korea. During the same period, primary school (shogakko) for Japanese students was a six-year course, middle school (chūgakkō) or girls' middle school (koto jogakkō) for Japanese students offered five years for boys and four years for girls. After the outbreak of the March First movement for Korean independence in 1919, the Japanese partially changed their colonial education policy. Through the Korean Educational Ordinance of 1922, the primary school course was extended to six years for both boys and girls.[5]

The Japanese government also extended the boys middle school course to five years, the girls' middle school course to four years, and vocational school to three to five years. In addition, the Japanese established the first university, Keijō Imperial University, in 1924. Through such procedures, the colonial education system for Koreans became equal to that of Japan and that for Japanese in Korea. But the coeducation of Japanese and Koreans was not established on a full-scale basis. Primary schools and middle schools were divided in terms of ethnic groups; vocational schools, normal schools for primary school teachers, technical schools, and the university were coeducational for both ethnic groups. After the Korean Educational Ordinance of 1938, there were slight changes in these systems. For example, the names of primary or middle schools, which had been different for Koreans and Japanese, were unified and the rate of coeducation in those schools increased. Until 1945, the two systems were maintained without significant changes.

Separate from the schools initiated and controlled by the Japanese colonial government, however, other modern, educational institutions existed in Korea; modern private schools institutionally excluded from the colonial educational system. These schools had roots in the voluntary educational efforts of Koreans or Western missionaries before colonization. At that time, the Korean imperial government had been planning the modern educational system through the Kabo Educational Reformation in 1894. The content of this reformation included such things as an all-out opening up of educational opportunities, publishing new textbooks, training primary school teachers, and establishing the structure of primary, secondary, and higher education.[6] Because of other internal problems, including financial factors, the government could not accomplish good results in a short period of time. Despite these setbacks, Koreans actively developed these modern schools on their own and endorsed many private schools built by Western missionaries.

In the early 1900s, apart from private schools built by the Christian missionaries, there were more than one thousand private schools built by Koreans. These efforts were the result of the Patriotic Awakening movement (Aeguk Kyemong Undong) carried out by Korean citizens in opposition to Japanese aggression in the early part of the twentieth century. These schools, however, were destroyed or suppressed by the Japanese. The Regulations for Private Schools (Shiritsu gakko kisoku) in 1911 were edicts issued to restrict or suppress the educational facilities established by Koreans or Western missionaries. Simultaneously the Japanese Government-General of Korea began to change these schools into facilities for colonial education or, failing that, to delegitimize them. Labeling them "various private schools," (shiritsu kakushu gakko) the Japanese did not acknowledge the credentials of these schools. In the meantime, the Government-General kept a close eye on the curricula and teachers.

Pre-modern educational institutions, called sŏdang, also continued during the colonial period. Sŏdang were primary-level educational institutions teaching the rudiments of Chinese characters, arithmetic, Confucian ethics, and the classics. Koreans had a long tradition of running sŏdang in local districts using their own funds. During the colonial period, the sŏdang were not as severely oppressed by the colonial government as the modern private schools were, since their credentials were not officially recognized. They were also marginal institutions outside the colonial educational system.

If we look only at the surface of the colonial educational system, it seems to show the characteristics of a modern educational system. It consisted of primary, secondary, and post-secondary levels of education, and these educational opportunities were legally open to all Koreans regardless of class or social background. Looking more closely, we can see that colonial characteristics were strongly systemized inside the structure of educational institutions.

To begin with, we can examine the expansion of education during the colonial period. The increasing number of schools at each level during colonial domination is shown in Table 3.1. What kinds of progress in expansion do colonial educational facilities show? In 1912, there were 343 primary schools for Koreans; these numbers increased to 3,263 by 1942. For secondary education (middle schools for Koreans and vocational or normal schools for both ethnic groups), the number increased from sixty-four to 400 and for post-secondary education (one university and other technical schools for both ethnic groups), from two to twenty-one. In the case of the primary level, most colonial educational institutions were public schools, and the proportion of private educational institutions was less than 5 percent. For the secondary level, it was about 15 percent, for the post-secondary level, it was nearly 50 percent.

The number of so-called various private schools excluded from the colonial educational system had diminished dramatically during the colonial

Table 3.1 **Schools for Koreans by Level and Foundation, 1912–42**

Year	Primary[a]			Secondary[b]			Postsecondary[c]			Private[d]	Sŏdang[e]
	Total	Pub[f]	Prv[g]	Total	Pub	Prv	Total	Pub	Prv		
1912	343	343	0	64	63	1	2	2	0	1,323	18,238
1913	368	368	0	92	91	1	2	2	0	1,285	20,268
1914	404	384	20	99	94	5	2	2	0	1,214	21,358
1915	429	412	17	107	102	5	2	2	0	1,090	23,441
1916	447	428	19	121	114	7	5	5	0	973	25,486
1917	461	437	24	127	118	9	7	5	2	827	24,294
1918	507	471	36	130	119	11	7	5	2	780	23,369
1919	570	537	33	131	119	12	7	5	2	698	24,030
1920	681	643	38	115	99	16	7	5	2	661	25,482
1921	794	758	36	110	93	17	7	5	2	625	24,193
1922	947	903	44	111	96	15	8	5	3	653	21,057

Table 3.1 Schools for Koreans by Level and Foundation, 1912–42 (continued)

Year	Primary[a]			Secondary[b]			Postsecondary[c]			Private[d]	Sŏdang[e]
	Total	Pub[f]	Prv[g]	Total	Pub	Prv	Total	Pub	Prv		
1923	1,099	1,043	56	134	118	16	8	5	3	637	19,613
1924	1,141	1,090	51	138	122	16	9	6	3	645	18,510
1925	1,254	1,189	65	145	127	18	10	6	4	615	16,873
1926	1,342	1,266	76	160	138	22	11	6	5	600	16,089
1927	1,425	1,345	80	182	159	23	11	6	5	566	15,069
1928	1,510	1,430	80	200	176	24	11	6	5	549	14,957
1929	1,589	1,507	82	205	181	24	12	6	6	528	11,469
1930	1,727	1,646	81	214	188	26	14	6	8	513	10,036
1931	1,861	1,781	80	221	193	28	14	6	8	497	9,208
1932	1,978	1,898	80	230	200	30	14	6	8	471	8,630
1933	2,105	2,022	83	234	203	31	16	8	8	457	7,529
1934	2,221	2,135	86	234	202	32	16	8	8	430	6,807
1935	2,363	2,276	87	251	217	34	16	8	8	412	6,209
1936	2,504	2,419	85	277	237	40	16	8	8	394	5,944
1937	2,601	2,509	92	297	255	42	16	8	8	393	5,681
1938	2,707	2,607	100	317	273	44	16	8	8	357	5,293
1939	2,853	2,736	117	339	298	41	19	9	10	335	4,686
1940	2,995	2,861	134	360	309	51	19	9	10	300	4,105
1941	3,129	2,984	145	378	322	56	20	10	10	284	3,504
1942	3,263	3,122	141	400	336	64	21	10	11	252	3,052

Source: Chōsen Sōtokufu, Chōsen Sōtokufu tokei nenpo [Statistical yearbooks of the Government-General of Korea]. Keijō: Chōsen Sōtokufu, 1932–38, 1942.

Note:

[a] Primary school

[b] Secondary level: boys' middle school, girls' middle school, industrial school, normal school

[c] Post-secondary level: technical school, university

[d] Private school: various private schools outside colonial educational system

[e] Sŏdang: traditional primary school for Koreans

[f] Pub: public school

[g] Prv: private school within colonial educational system

period. From 1912 to 1942, the number had decreased from 1,323 to 252. The *sŏdang* had a similar destiny. In the early part of the century, Koreans generally preferred the *sŏdang* to colonial primary schools (*futsu gakko*). From 1912 to 1920, the number of *sŏdang* increased from 18,283 to 25,482. After that year, however, they began to decrease; in 1942, they numbered only 3,052.

By looking only at the increasing number of schools, it seems that the Japanese established a well-systemized, modern educational structure. These figures might also indicate that the Japanese were very positive and active in the education of their colonized pupils. But the actual expansion of Korean education should be clarified more specifically through the increase in the number of Korean students enrolled in school, rather than through the increase in number of schools.

How many Koreans were actually allowed to attend the modern schools? To address this question, we must examine closely some of the key educational statistics, such as school enrollment rates by nationality. It is very difficult, however, to estimate the school enrollment rate for colonial education. There is no data to show the age composition of the total population each year, and because it is impossible to identify the exact school age population for each level every year, we estimated the number of students per ten thousand inhabitants each year. Table 3.2 and figures 3.1, 3.2, and 3.3 show the actual number of students and the estimated number of Japanese and Korean students per ten thousand inhabitants in each educational level.

The opportunities for Koreans to obtain a secondary or post-secondary education were severely restricted. In 1942, the number of students enrolled in Korean secondary schools was only thirty-four out of ten thousand, but the number of Japanese was 520. In the case of post-secondary schools, there were two Koreans to forty-six Japanese in 1942. Although the number of secondary and post-secondary educational institutions increased during the period of Japanese domination, actual opportunities were open almost exclusively to the very small percentage of Koreans who could afford the large tuition and pass a highly competitive application procedure. Secondary schooling and post-secondary education in the so-called modern colonial education system constituted a rather nominal entity of little benefit to Koreans.

In the case of primary education, however, there was a rapid expansion of educational opportunity, even though there was a noticeable difference between Koreans and Japanese when it came to accessibility. Let us examine

Table 3.2 Students by Level and Ethnicity, 1912–41

Year	Primary education Korean	Primary education Japanese	Secondary education Korean	Secondary education Japanese	Postsecondary education Korean	Postsecondary education Japanese
1912	41,509 (28.5)	21,882 (897.8)	2,597 (1.8)	1,572 (64.5)	67 (0.0)	15 (0.6)
1913	47,451 (31.3)	24,915 (917.4)	3,136 (2.1)	1,918 (70.6)	113 (0.1)	28 (1.0)
1914	53,019 (33.9)	28,173 (967.4)	3,762 (2.4)	2,195 (75.4)	143(0.1)	35(1.2)
1915	60,690 (38.0)	31,256 (1029.3)	4,440 (2.8)	2,678 (88.2)	141 (0.1)	13 (0.4)
1916	67,628 (41.5)	34,100 (1062.5)	5,372 (3.3)	3,270 (101.9)	464 (0.3)	74 (2.3)
1917	75,688 (45.5)	36,183 (1088.4)	6,106 (3.7)	3,833 (115.3)	559 (0.3)	125 (3.8)
1918	80,113 (48.0)	38,447 (1141.3)	6,535 (3.9)	4,290 (127.3)	567 (0.3)	187 (5.6)
1919	80,632 (48.0)	41,447 (1195.8)	5,064 (3.0)	4,920 (141.9)	392 (0.2)	256 (7.4)
1920	107,365 (63.5)	44,007 (1265.1)	6,507 (3.8)	5,862 (168.5)	454 (0.3)	250 (7.2)
1921	159,361 (93.4)	47,279 (1286.1)	9,826 (5.8)	6,790 (184.7)	532 (0.3)	362 (9.8)
1922	238,058 (138.3)	50,322 (1302.0)	12,411 (7.2)	8,394 (217.2)	806 (0.5)	468 (12.1)
1923	306,358 (175.6)	52,686 (1307.3)	15,557 (8.9)	10,189 (252.8)	890 (0.5)	566 (14.0)
1924	374,347 (212.5)	56,478 (1372.2)	19,169 (10.9)	12,650 (307.3)	1,080 (0.6)	785 (19.1)
1925	407,541 (219.8)	56,105 (1320.9)	20,427 (11.0)	13,949 (328.4)	1,144 (0.6)	921 (21.7)
1926	441,872 (237.4)	56,987 (1288.3)	23,004 (12.4)	15,354 (347.1)	1,347 (0.7)	1,024 (23.2)
1927	453,943 (243.6)	59,091 (1299.0)	25,727 (13.8)	16,402 (360.6)	1,338 (0.7)	1,144 (25.1)
1928	465,314 (249.3)	62,130 (1324.6)	28,184 (15.1)	16,998 (362.4)	1,434 (0.8)	1,276 (27.2)
1929	474,117 (252.4)	64,963 (1329.9)	29,105 (15.5)	17,662 (361.6)	1,564 (0.8)	1,553 (31.8)
1930	492,613 (250.2)	68,253 (1360.0)	30,341 (15.4)	18,708 (372.8)	1,710 (0.9)	1,767 (35.2)
1931	502,107 (254.7)	71,925 (1397.5)	31,872 (16.2)	19,416 (377.3)	1,854 (0.9)	1,823 (35.4)
1932	517,091 (258.1)	76,052 (1452.9)	32,828 (16.4)	20,215 (386.2)	2,056 (1.0)	1,954 (37.3)
1933	564,901 (279.6)	79,397 (1461.9)	34,312 (17.0)	21,414 (394.3)	2,345 (1.2)	2,365 (43.5)
1934	640,140 (312.1)	81,523 (1452.2)	36,719 (17.9)	22,172 (395.0)	2,502 (1.2)	2,410 (42.9)
1935	720,757 (339.2)	84,395 (1446.5)	39,238 (18.5)	23,300 (399.4)	3,044 (1.4)	2,441 (41.8)
1936	802,976 (375.7)	86,775 (1424.9)	42,748 (20.0)	24,864 (408.3)	2,834 (1.3)	2,406 (39.5)
1937	901,182 (415.6)	89,811 (1426.7)	45,583 (21.0)	27,202 (432.1)	2,847 (1.3)	2,382 (37.8)
1938	1,050,371 (478.5)	92,991 (1468.3)	51,420 (23.4)	29,353 (463.5)	2,980 (1.4)	2,408 (38.0)
1939	1,215,340 (550.0)	96,156 (1479.1)	57,555 (26.0)	31,564 (485.5)	3,443 (1.6)	2,572 (39.6)
1940	1,385,944 (603.8)	97,794 (1417.7)	68,281 (29.7)	33,075 (479.5)	3,865 (1.7)	2,766 (40.1)
1941	1,571,990 (657.4)	99,316 (1385.1)	76,031 (31.8)	35,328 (492.7)	4,166 (1.7)	3,124 (43.6)
1942	1,779,661 (697.2)	103,831 (1379.2)	86,110 (33.7)	39,147 (520.0)	4,505 (1.8)	3,502 (46.5)

Source: Chōsen Sōtokufu, Chōsen Sōtokufu tokei nenpo [Statistical yearbooks of the Government-General of Korea]. Keijō: Chōsen Sōtokufu, 1932–38, 1942.

Note: ( ): Number of students per 10,000 inhabitants

more specifically the expansion of colonial education through the rate of enrollment. Figure 3.4 shows the estimated rate of enrollment for Koreans in primary education. The enrollment rate was estimated in the following way: to begin with, it was necessary to confirm what proportion of the population was of primary school age. There was, however, no age population data for each year of the colonial period. The only proper data available for population by age were census reports collected in 1930 and 1935. According to the census data for 1930, the proportion of the population from ages six to eleven was 14.4 percent of the total population. This figure was used to estimate the proportion of primary school age students.[7] Private schools outside the colonial educational system or traditional *sŏdang* are excluded from this figure.

The enrollment rate for primary school can be divided into four phases. The first phase starts from 1910. During this time, the enrollment rate was less than 10 percent. Koreans preferred the *sŏdang* to the primary school during this period.[8] But after 1920, the situation was reversed. It was around this

Figure 3.1 Number of Students in Primary Education per 10,000 inhabitants, 1912–42

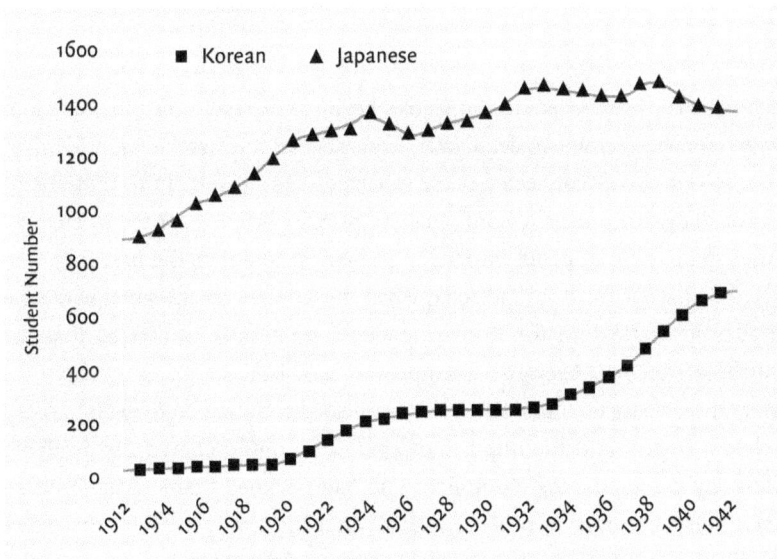

Source: Chōsen Sōtokufu, *Chōsen Sōtokufu tokei nenpo* [Statistical yearbooks of the Government-General of Korea]. Keijō: Chōsen Sōtokufu, 1932–38, 1942.

Figure 3.2 Number of Students in Secondary Education
per 10,000 Inhabitants, 1912–42

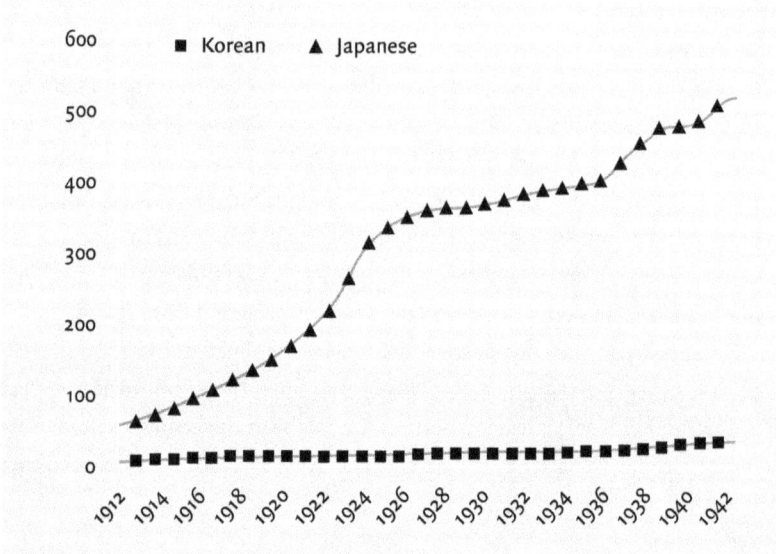

Source: Chōsen Sōtokufu, Chōsen Sōtokufu tokei nenpo [Statistical yearbooks of the Government-General of Korea]. Keijō: Chōsen Sōtokufu, 1932–38, 1942.

time that the primary education system began to expand. This phenomenon, which we will examine in detail later, suggests that the March First movement in 1919 was closely connected to the expansion. As a result of this movement, the attitude of Koreans toward Japanese primary schools started to change. After 1920, more students enrolled in primary school than did in sŏdang. The second phase is from 1919 to 1924, when the Government-General made the academic curriculum for Korean students nominally similar to that for Japanese students. They also attempted to establish one primary school for every three districts. Immediately, an overheated competition to get into these schools began, and the number of applicants outnumbered the available slots. By the 1930s, the enrollment rate had declined temporarily, because there was a shortage of primary schools after the "one school for three districts" plan and competition decreased because of the Great Depression of the early 1930s. However, after the last phase, beginning in 1933, the rate of enrollment dramatically increased again.

Figure 3.3 Number of Students in Postsecondary Education
per 10,000 Inhabitants, 1912–42

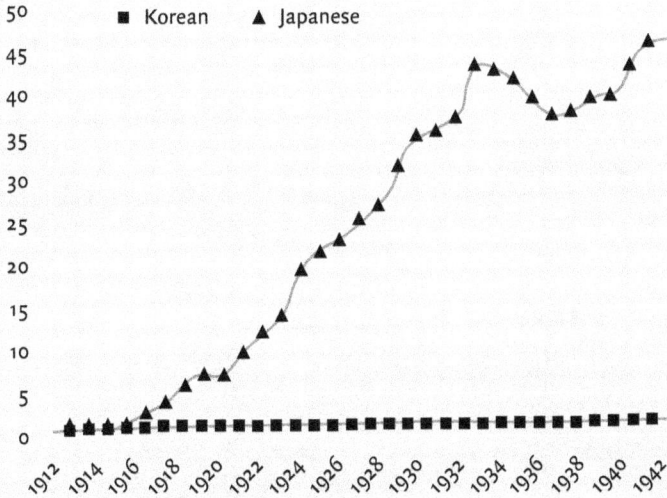

Source: Chōsen Sōtokufu, *Chōsen Sōtokufu tokei nenpo* [Statistical yearbooks of the
Government-General of Korea]. Keijō: Chōsen Sōtokufu, 1932–38, 1942.

During the 1930s, the Government-General continued its expansion policy
and more educational opportunities became available. This policy of expansion
continued until the end of colonization. In 1942, the enrollment rate for all
Korean students climbed to over 50 percent. Yet there was a distinct difference
in primary school enrollments with regards to sex ratios; the enrollment rate
of Korean boys was double that of girls. In 1942, the enrollment rate of Korean
boys was nearly 70 percent. This shows that primary education for male students was almost universalized during the late period of colonization. For
girls, the case was different; the ratio between the sexes was still uneven.

At the primary level, the expansion policy was carried out in practice, but did
not satisfy the educational desires of Koreans at the time. After the 1920s, the
demand for education always surpassed the supply. Figure 3.5 shows the number of Korean student applicants and actual admittance in primary schools.

Until 1932, both the number of openings and the number of applicants
increased at a similar rate. In 1933, both numbers increased rapidly, but this

Figure 3.4 Primary School Enrollment Rate (%) for Koreans, 1912–41

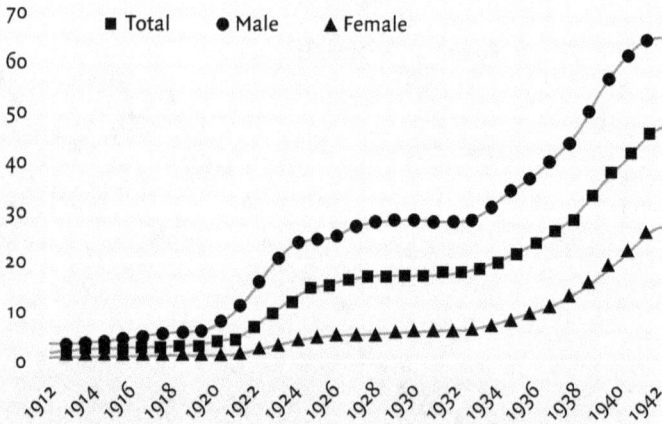

Sources: Chōsen Sōtokufu, *Chōsen Sōtokufu tokei nenpo* [Statistical yearbooks of the Government-General of Korea]. Keijō: Chōsen Sōtokufu, 1932–38, 1942; Chōsen Sōtokufu. Gakumukyoku [Ministry of education]. *Chōsen shogakko ichiran* [Prospectus of schools in Korea]. Keijō: Chōsen Sotokufu, 1912–1942.

time the number of applicants greatly surpassed supply. Such conditions did not diminish until the end of Japanese colonization.

After the 1920s, the competition to enter elementary school became chronic. The entrance examination for primary school, called the "mental test," was a basic intelligence test that also reflected the financial status of Korean children. For example, in the mental tests, teachers asked applicants questions like these: "If you add three to two, what's the result?" or "What's the price of this bill?" showing a 100 yen bill, or "What's wrong with this picture?" showing a picture of a horse with horns.[9] This entrance examination soon became a serious social issue. After the 1920s, Korean newspapers cited the entrance examination as a social problem and criticized the restrictive education policy of the Government-General. The major point of criticism was that, unlike any other citizens on earth, Koreans had to pass a qualification exam for primary school, while nearly all Japanese children in Korea went to school with test waivers.

The extreme difficulty of getting into school was not just a problem in primary education. The demand for secondary education had increased as rapidly as that for primary education. However, because the same expansion did not take place in secondary education as it did in primary education, entrance competition for secondary education became even more intense. Figure 3.6 shows the number of applicants and the actual number of students admitted into secondary educational institutions.

Competition temporarily decreased in the early 1930s when the number of applicants decreased as a result of the economic depression. It did not disappear altogether, however. Competitive situations became more serious as time passed. In 1939, the entrance rate dropped to 20 percent. For example in 1939, among the 4,041 technical school applicants, only 1,027 entered the school (24 percent); for Keijō Imperial University, among 588 applicants, only seventy-four entered (12.6 percent). Insufficient opportunities for secondary and post-secondary education had become a serious social problem.

DYNAMICS OF THE EXPANSION OF PRIMARY EDUCATION

As we have seen above, even though it was limited to primary education, an expansion of educational opportunities did take place under colonial rule. Does this mean that the Japanese actively carried out the expansion of primary education? To find the answer, we must first look at the historical facts. The schools that the Japanese expanded were almost all public primary schools. Because they were called "public" rather than "private," it could be said that the colonial government established the primary schools. But the situation is more complex than this. It is necessary to find out who initiated the expansion of the public primary school system, especially after the 1920s. A phenomenon shown in the expansion of these schools is that most Koreans were exceptionally interested in the expansion process. In other colonized countries under Western imperialism most people were generally indifferent to colonial education, other than the elites or those groups related to the market economy.[10]

Initially, of course, this interest was not present, and it fluctuated from period to period. From 1910–19, when Japan carried out a strictly oppressive policy in ruling Korea, most Koreans refused to enter the public primary schools; as mentioned above, they preferred the *sŏdang*, and some went to nationalistic private schools. As a colonial educational facility, the primary school was not entrenched in Korean society during this decade. After the March First movement in 1919, however, the direction of Korean educational

Figure 3.5 Primary School Entrance Competition, 1927–40

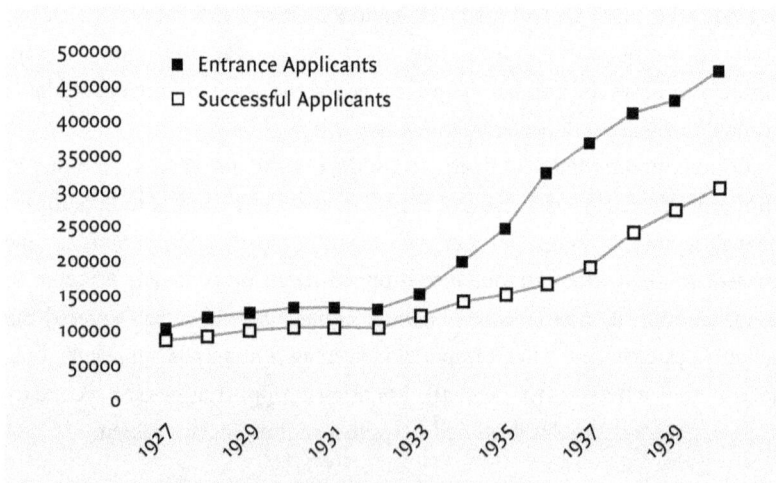

Source: Chōsen Sōtokufu. Gakumukyoku Gakumuka [Bureau of education, education branch]. *Gakuji sango shiryo* [Reference data for educational policy]. Keijō: Chōsen Sōtokufu, 1937, 1941.

action abruptly turned toward the primary schools. After that, entrance examinations were adopted and, as we have seen, entrance competition became a chronic social problem. Among other factors, many Koreans strongly resisted the Japanese policy of restricting educational opportunities.

In the 1920s and afterwards nearly all Koreans: nationalists, socialists, intellectuals, and the common people, urged the expansion of educational opportunities. Their main emphases were: to reflect the national interest in the purpose and content of education, to increase the number of public primary schools, to reduce tuition fees, to ultimately institute free, compulsory primary education, and to expand opportunities for secondary and post-secondary education.

The Government-General was skeptical toward this expansion plan being especially cautious about Koreans' enthusiasm for education. In 1929, for example, the superintendent's office in the Government-General reported: "There potentially exist impure elements in such an overheated desire for education."[11] In the mid-1930s, a similar political policy dominated, as expressed by Governor-General Ugaki during a provincial governors' meeting:

Figure 3.6 Secondary Education Entrance Competition, 1927–39

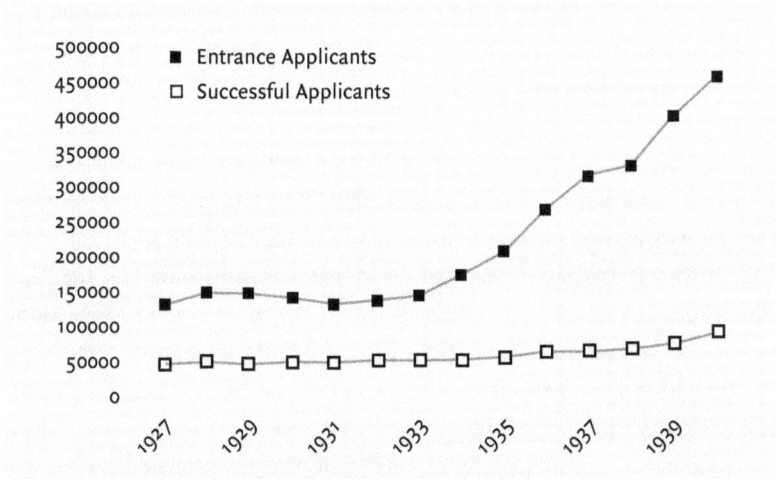

Source: Chōsen Sōtokufu. Gakumukyoku Gakumuka [Bureau of education, education branch]. *Gakuji sango shiryo* [Reference data for educational policy]. Keijō: Chōsen Sōtokufu, 1937, 1941.

> Considering the facts that there are so many who are eager to quench their own greed and desire or those who just provoke competitiveness, there is a strong possibility of producing unemployed people who are highly educated or hopeless[ly] lazy who do not conform to social standards, if we allow them to take advantage of the opportunity for education.[12]

In short, the Government-General of Korea must have had no option but to be skeptical about accepting Korean demands for education, but on the other hand it was impossible to suppress the desire for education. This discrimination toward the indigenous population in educational opportunity was something that clearly showed the contradictory character of Japan's colonial ideology of "treating with same charity" (*ichidōjin*) or "the oneness of Japan and Korea" (*naisen ittai*). Therefore, the Government-General of Korea could not but regard the problem of insufficient educational opportunity as a political issue. This passage from *Shisei shanjunenshi* (The history of thirty years of government in Korea) shows their position clearly:

> Recently, as educational aspirations suddenly rose, demand for schooling became more intense, even in the remote corners of the country. The impact of this phenomenon on public sentiment of Koreans should be regarded as a very serious situation.[13]

The Government-General found itself in a political dilemma about whether to agree to expand the public primary schools. After the 1920s, Japan activated a series of expansion policies in primary education: the "one school for every three districts" (sammyŏn ilgyo che) policy from 1919 to 1922 and the "one school for every district" (ilmyŏn ilgyo che) policy from 1929 to 1936. Along with this a "sub-school" (kanigakko)—a two-year primary education facility—was built after 1934. Despite this expansion of primary education, competition for entry did not subside, rather it became even worse. From 1938, consequently, a "second plan for expansion of primary education" policy was activated. This series of expansion policies was put into effect under the condition that Koreans would raise the funds for establishing the school. Thus, the Government-General only allowed and supported school expansion when Koreans provided a large portion of the cost.

The Korean people initiated a massive movement to establish public primary schools of their own. If there were no primary schools in their district, people organized to build one. After it was built, the Japanese government expanded the number of classes and extended the education period from four to six years. Thus, the Japanese expansion policies for primary education could not have been carried out without the foundational support of the Korean education movement. Expansion was not imposed from the top, but initiated from the bottom, by the colonized people. What was the specific procedure for founding a public primary school? A typical case was that of a village in Ch'ungch'ŏng Province.

> Yanggang district, Ch'ungch'ŏng Province, is a relatively big area where 1500 houses are located. There is a shortage of schools as the only school is temporary. Many children do go to school more than ten miles away, but only those who can afford to. Many cannot go to school. Those concerned about the youngsters' future, Pae Sŏgyong and Kim Yongnae, founded an organization called "Hŭnghakhoe" and collected money, as much as 7,000 yen, but to gain approval from the Government-General they need an extra 3,000 yen.

They have decided to get a loan. They also plan to raise funds to pay back
the loan as soon as the economy recovers. When they raise 10,000 yen, they
will submit the approval form for founding a school.[14]

The establishment of schools was the result of the active efforts of
Koreans. First, people in a certain district agreed on the need for a primary
school, and then they started a movement to collect the necessary amount of
money. Once the money was raised, they had to obtain permission from the
government. At that point, it was determined how much money would be
spent by the provincial government and Korean civilians, respectively. After
gaining permission, the Korean people combined their own money with the
provincial government's support fund and built a school. Expanding the number of classes and extending the length of study went through the same procedure. In raising funds for the construction of primary schools, almost
everyone in the district participated. Most raised money by collecting crops
after the harvest. This method was similar to a traditional practice used for
managing sŏdang, and it was broadly adopted in establishing primary schools,
especially in rural communities.[15] In cities, where major colonial administrative organizations were located, many primary schools were built before 1919.
Schools built after 1920 were partly funded by Korean civilians, but this proportion was relatively smaller compared to that of rural communities.

What was the ratio of Koreans' expenses in the overall primary education
expansion process? This figure is very important in establishing who oversaw
the procedure throughout the country. Table 3.3 shows the rate of expenses
assumed by Koreans in establishing public primary schools after 1920.

Table 3.3 shows that among the overall construction fees, about 42 percent came from money raised by Koreans. Other portions of the construction
fees that were not supported by the Japanese fund or the Government-General
were paid by the provincial local finance fund. And major portions of these
local funds were composed of taxes paid by Koreans.

Ordinary expenditures, mostly used for the salary of schoolteachers,
came from grants from the Government-General of Korea and from school
budget dues (gakkohi hukkakin), which were semi-taxes similar to the educational budget tax paid by Korean inhabitants and from school fees. For
example the proportions of revenue sources were 48.5 percent, 22.5 percent,
and 20.8 percent in 1930.[16]

Table 3.3   Local Education Finance for
Public Primary School Construction, 1924–38 (unit=*yen*)

Year	Male	Female	Female
1924	3,251,885	1,179,063	36.2
1926	2,427,976	928,198	38.2
1928	2,031,403	941,407	46.3
1929	1,949,350	754,873	38.7
1930	1,582,184	751,238	47.4
1931	1,441,766	574,807	39.8
1932	1,491,574	511,673	34.3
1933	1,262,408	503,672	39.8
1934	1,607,350	758,342	47.1
1935	2,137,496	927,160	43.3
1936	2,521,298	1,161,990	46
1937	4,697,902	2,170,684	46.2
1938	6,371,674	2,497,160	39.1
1924–38	32,774,266	13,660,267	41.6

Source: Naimu Kyoku [Bureau of interior]. *Chōsen chihan jaisei yoran* [A summary of regional finance in Korea]. Keijō: Chōsen Sōtokufu, 1924–38.

Primary education expanded through this procedure but was still dissatisfying to most Koreans. Educational opportunities available to Koreans in the 1940s were even less than the opportunities given to Japanese from 1910–19. In 1942, for example, Korean primary school students numbered approximately 700 among a population of ten thousand; in 1912, Japanese primary school students in Korea numbered almost 900 among ten thousand. But because of continuous Korean educational movements and pleas for educational opportunities, expansion of primary education became a reality. An important factor is that Korean civilians initiated and drove forward the expansion of colonial primary education.

We cannot however, overlook Japan's expansion policy. Why did the Japanese government put a series of expansion policies, albeit restricted ones, into operation? The answer to this question is undoubtedly found in a contradiction of the ideology of Japanese imperialism. The "treatment with the same charity" ideology declared by the Emperor of Japan, which stated that there would be no discrimination between the two nations, is a fine example of the contradiction within the ideology of Japanese imperialism. As shown in that motto, if equalization between the nations is actualized, then colonization itself must come to an end. In reality, however, inequalities in everyday life became chronic and the colonial situation worsened; colonial ideology contradicted itself and became a target for criticism. The inequality of educational opportunity was one of the most distinct social issues. This disparity permitted the discrimination of Koreans in everyday life and encouraged the spuriousness of colonial ideology. As a result, in order to secure from the Korean population the minimum consent necessary for the continuation of colonial rule, the Japanese were obliged to heed some of the Koreans' demands.

The Government-General expansion policy had another target other than those just declared: the hidden purpose of intensifying colonization via education. The one school per every district policy of 1929 complemented the practical education policy, which emphasized low-quality manual labor training in schools. Such training would inhibit any sort of national movement that might spring up through modern education. The sub-school policy in 1934 complemented the farm development movement policy, which reorganized the farm economy, which had gone bankrupt under the colonial economic system. The Second Plan in 1938 complemented the volunteer army policy of extracting military resources from Korea to invade China, and the plan of compulsory education in 1942 was directly related to the introduction of the conscription system in Korea. In short, the colonial government partly accepted the educational demands of Koreans under the condition that the Koreans meet the specific needs of colonial policy.

CHARACTERISTICS OF THE PRIMARY SCHOOL CURRICULUM

School curriculum

Initially, Japan's colonial policies focused on assimilation, turning Koreans into Japanese culturally and spiritually and eradicating the idea of a Korean nation. Along with the policy of assimilation, the Japanese government never omitted a simultaneous discrimination policy of appropriating the major social and political rights of Korean citizens. In other words, cultural assimilation via imposition of the Japanese language and social political discrimination by blood were two sides of the same coin.[17] Fundamentally, the policies could only contradict each other. In theory, the colonizer wants to treat the colonized as equals; at the same time, they do not allow the colonized access to the privileged-life system of the colonizers. These self-contradictions did not diminish throughout colonization; instead they became more serious, especially after the 1930s, when Japan decided to use the Korean people as a means of achieving imperialistic goals. Despite the self-contradiction, or rather because of it, Japan emphasized a strange policy as a way of concealing the problem, which was to make the Korean people "subjects of the Emperor (tennō)." This designation, which suggested Japanese ideology, was forced upon Koreans. Despite a delicate difference of expression in historical usage and Japanese courses between the Korean primary schools and Japanese primary schools, the fundamental principle was the same as in Japan. Teaching ideology through colonial education seemed no different than in Japan. In both countries, the Imperial Edict on Education (Kyoiku ni kansuru chokugo: kyoiku chokugo) was a source for Korean educational goals and curriculum content.

Primary school teachers taught students with textbooks written and edited by the Government-General. The official teaching language was Japanese, and a larger portion of the curriculum was devoted to learning Japanese than to algebra. In the 1920s, the ratio was 39.7 to 18.6 percent; 37.6 to 17.6 percent in the early 1930s; and 35.2 to 16.5 percent in the late 1930s. The Japanese Emperor's ideology was reflected not only in such subjects as Japanese language, history, and geography, but also in Korean language instruction, for which the number of credits was getting smaller and smaller. From 1910-1919, the four-year primary school course provided twenty-two hours (including Chinese character lessons) of Korean lessons out of a total 106 hours per week. In the 1920s, the percentage of Korean lesson hours dropped to 12.4 percent (22hrs/161hrs). In the early 1930s, it became 11.7 percent (20hrs/182hrs). After 1938, it dropped dramatically to 8.8 percent (16hrs/182hrs). Eventually, Korean became an optional subject and after 1941 disappeared altogether from the primary school curriculum.[18]

School Discipline

Emphasis on school discipline became ever stricter in the early 1930s, when different types of ceremonies celebrating the Japanese Emperor and imperialism became increasingly frequent. Pseudo-religious rituals such as bowing to the Imperial Palace (Tohō yohai), visiting the Shinto shrine (jinga shanbai) on ceremonial and national occasions, and idol worship including cultish rituals related to the document of the Imperial Edict on Education, the Imperial Portrait (gojinei), and the Divine Box (kamidana),[19] were also frequently compulsory for Korean pupils, especially after 1930.[20] The content and form of school discipline all displayed militaristic, totalitarian, and pseudo-religious characteristics.

The schools also provided a new course for physical training similar to military drills and ceremonies. Tennō ideology was not the only feature of Japanese colonial education in Korea; another typically colonial characteristic of education was that courses were not focused on academic subjects such as science and literature, but mainly on lower-level job training, the so-called practical education policy of the 1930s.[21] In 1929, the Government-General of Korea amended the regulations for primary schools and introduced a mandatory new course called Vocation into the primary school curriculum. From that year on, the expansion policy of primary education, called "one school for every district" (ilmyŏn ilgyo che), began to operate.

Additionally, the Guiding Primary School Graduates policy (Futsu gakkō sotsugyosei shido) was introduced to reinforce vocational training in primary education. This policy aimed to train graduates of primary schools to become efficient farmers two or three years after graduation. In most cases, teachers of the primary school took charge of training.[22] Under the practical education policy, knowledge-oriented education was strongly criticized. Vocation courses consisted of manual agricultural labor, such as weeding, sowing seeds, plowing, weaving straw ropes, feeding cattle, rearing silkworms, harvesting, selling vegetables at the market, and building barns.[23] These activities were basically the same as those enacted in the traditional sector of Korean agriculture. Hours in the curriculum were allocated to this course, 320 hours for six years, but actual hours devoted to the course in the school usually amounted to more. For example, in 1933, some primary schools located in Kyŏnggi Province forced their pupils to take 418 hours of vocation courses in six years. The Government-General of Korea also fostered rivalry among vocational education programs by giving funds to schools according to the outcome.[24] The goal of the course was to decrease Koreans' desire to move toward more modern vocations and to force them to remain in the agricultural sector. Through this policy, the Japanese hoped to suppress any sort of socialist, labor, or peasant movement from educated Koreans. Their motto was: "The lazy brain is the factory that produces the devil."[25]

Of course, the Japanese had carried out a similar policy in Japan a few years back in pursuit of the goal known as "adapting education to real everyday life." The policy, however, was implemented differently in the colonial education system in Korea. First, the Japanese intended to run vocation-oriented middle schools in Japan as they had run vocation-oriented primary schools in Korea. In Korea, they intended to transform primary education into so called terminal education. Second, vocation-oriented education in Japan focused on industrial labor training related to the industrial sector of economy. In Korea, as we have seen, this focused on low-level manual labor that was related to the traditional agricultural economy. This fact shows the clear intention on the part of the Japanese to degrade the quality of Korean education, as compared to that of Japan.[26]

The important point to realize is that the dual policies of assimilation and discrimination were enacted in colonial education even though on the surface Japanese and Korean education during this era appeared to be the same. This education policy, rarely seen in other colonized regions of Asia or Africa, deprived the colonized of their past and future at the same time, as Albert Memmi has indicated, and never contradicted the Japanese goal of keeping the Korean colony a colony.[27]

THE UNINTENDED CONSEQUENCES OF JAPAN'S COLONIAL EDUCATION POLICY

Colonial education in Korea was used as an ideological device to perpetuate the colonization of Korea. Koreans, however, consistently resisted the policy. Not just a small number of pro-Japanese people, but the majority of Koreans irrespective of social class demanded the expansion of primary education and even started to raise funds for it. Here one must realize that the unspoken aspirations of the Koreans were not synonymous with Japanese intent.

Koreans and Japanese had different ideologies and expectations for the establishment of the primary schools.

The expectations underlying their active interest manifested in the following ways. First, Koreans intended to strengthen their political power through education. The fact that the main forces of the March First movement in 1919 were students was something that changed Koreans' conceptions of modern education in particular. The idea that modern education could develop knowledge had already existed long before colonization. In the decade after 1900, civilian groups carried out both an education movement to establish private schools and the Patriotic Awakening movement. But these movements were almost completely suppressed. In response, the Japanese continued to carry out a policy that was intended to oppress any nationalistic educational activities. Under these circumstances, there was no other choice but to use the ongoing colonial education system. After the 1920s, most Koreans chose to enter colonial primary schools rather than remain illiterate.

Second, Koreans wanted and expected social upward mobility through education. Of course, the chances for such mobility were rare under the colonial social structure. But, in fact, it was the only avenue that provided the opportunity of social upward mobility to Koreans. Especially after the year 1920, most Korean farmers began to experience serious financial problems. Because of various irrational farm policies and regulations set by the Japanese, the farm economy rapidly began to go bankrupt.[28] In 1938, among 3 million Korean farming households, the proportion of upper-level farmers was about 3 percent; middle-level farmers, 20 percent; and of low-level farmers, 73 percent. Among low-level farmers, 74 percent were extremely poor, cultivating fewer than 2.5 acres.[29] It can be said that Korean reactions to the colonial education policy indicated the characteristics of a survival strategy under the extremely hard living conditions of a colonized country. Thus, it is evident that education became the only means for those Koreans who had no other option but to repeat the farmers' hardship. Because they could only count on hope and possibility, many Koreans began to participate positively and actively in educational activities. The pursuit of education, however, did not entirely ensure upward social mobility or improved living conditions.

The Koreans' hidden aspirations and expectations inevitably clashed with the Japanese goals for colonial education. Would not the perception of such clashes by the Japanese authorities have an influence on actual education? In respect to the unintended consequences of colonial education in Korea, the admonition of Japanese Vice Governor-General Ikegami in 1928 is significant. While explaining the reasoning for introducing the practical education policy, he pointed out several problems of colonial education in Korea:

> It should be pointed out that these days some students are reading wrongful materials full of false ideology and are eager to receive higher education only for the purpose of getting a good paying job, disregarding the Great Empire's need for building its abilities and future. They are not willing to work hard, and thus are having trouble getting a job, are accustomed to using "radical" language and even "polluting" the main idea of the people's commonwealth. It is very important to intensify the education of loyal citizens and the work force, not only to meet the purpose of establishing the principle of education but also to correct the people's wrong ideas toward education.[30]

In his speech, Ikegami criticized colonial education for being a "reading education" and pointed out "false ideology," "the unemployment rate," "overheated competition for higher education," and "radical language" as bad consequences. Could these four points be the unintended consequences or unexpected ironies of colonial education? First of all, "false ideology" seems to point to the student movements based on nationalism and socialism. Students became literate through their courses in the Japanese and Korean language in primary schools. To become literate not only implies that students had a greater possibility of becoming institutionalized to Japanese imperialism, but it also implies that Koreans had built a foundation for obtaining knowledge and judging certain matters independently. Tsurumi pointed out that in Korea, unlike Taiwan, education allowed Korean nationalism to spread in profound ways.[31]

Second, what Ikegami referred to as "overheated competition for higher education" signifies the ironies inherent between a people's desire to change their social status and the goals of colonial education. As Foster pointed out, colonial education will stir up the people's desire to change their social status; an outcome never intended by the colonizing country.[32] The Government-General of Korea intended to allow Koreans to obtain only limited educational opportunities at the primary school level, with no advancement to the secondary school level. However, Koreans' desire for higher education became stronger as they received education, and as a result the so-called overheated competition phenomenon arose. The Government-General established a new policy to cool down competition and finalize education for Koreans at the level of primary school, but this policy failed. Koreans' desire for higher education became even stronger than before, again generating the social problem of competition. Under these circumstances, the education provided in primary schools took on the features of preparing students to take the primary entrance exam. Teachers praised by Korean students and parents were the so-called good instructors who knew how to guide students in passing the entrance exam. Sometimes parents called for the dismissal of teachers who failed to help enough students pass the exam.[33]

Third, the unemployment rate signaled the ironies inherent in the Koreans' need to upgrade their social status versus the Government-General's dilemma, which arose from not recognizing Korean desires. Educated Koreans were eager to get jobs in the second and third industry sectors, in which no slots were available for them. Even though colonial industrialization took place in Korea after the 1930s, it did not generate enough jobs.[34] Consequently, the unemployment rate worsened, and people who had received a higher education could not find employment. Among the Koreans an insightful idea spread about the source of the unemployment, namely, that it was inherent in the colonial system; the Japanese workforce had higher priority for second and third industry sector positions.

The fourth irony of Ikegami's speech is his mention of "radical" language. Here he was referring to the complaints from qualified people who failed to get careers. Social crises inevitably arise when the primary people's ordinary desires are not met, and this problem could not be solved, even when the Government-General set a policy that Koreans could receive a rudimentary level of education or tried to adjust people's thoughts towards education. That was not a problem of ideology but of existence, to be precise, the unintended outcome for Koreans which had originated from the Japanese practice of educating the younger Korean generation under Japanese rule. For these reasons, Japanese colonial education in Korea could only be evaluated from a perspective of "contested terrain."

NOTES

1. This chapter is a slightly revised version of Seong-Cheol Oh and Ki-Seok Kim, "Japanese Colonial Education as a Contested Terrain: What Part did Koreans Play in the Expansion of Elementary Schooling," *Asia Pacific Education Review* 1, no. 1 (December 2000): 75–89.

2. Gail P. Kelly and Philip G. Altbach, "Introduction," 18.

3. O Sŏngch'ŏl, "1930-nyŏndae Han'guk."

4. Patricia E. Tsurumi, *Japanese Colonial Education*; Patricia E. Tsurumi, "Colonial Education in Korea and Taiwan."

5. Along with the six-year-course common school, the four-year-course common school lasted through the late 1930s.

6. Yu Pangnan, "Han'guk kŭndae kyoyuk," 1–3.

7. Chōsen Sōtokufu, *Showa go nen Chōsen*, 14.

8. From 1910–19, some Japanese common school teachers and military policemen of the region tried to capture *sŏdang* children and force them to enter common schools, which had had difficulty gathering enough Korean pupils. Among the Korean people, rumors circulated that the Japanese were plotting to make Korean pupils into soldiers. O Sŏngch'ŏl, *Singminji ch'odŭng kyoyuk*, 23.

9. O Sŏng-cheol, "1930-nyŏndae Han'guk," 150.

10. Gail P. Kelly and Philip G. Altbach, "Introduction," 18.

11. Chōsen Sōtokufu keimukyoku, *Chōsen ni okeru domeikyokyo*, 5.

12. Ugaki Kazusige, "Dotsishikaigi ni okeru," 144.

13. Chōsen Sōtokufu, *Shisei Shanjunenshi*, 796.

14. *Tonga ilbo*, January 27, 1930.

15. O Sŏngch'ŏl, *Singminji ch'odŭng kyoyuk*, 101–10.

16. Ibid., 103.

17. Komagome Takeshi, *Shokuminchi teikoku Nihon*.

18. The sum of all study course hours for all grades was 182 hours in a week.

19. The Imperial Portrait was a portrait of the Japanese Emperor; the Divine Box was a small wooden box in which the so-called spirit of Amaterasu-ōmikami, the founder of the Japanese Empire, was deified. In every school, both symbols of *tennō* ideology were located inside a small shrine called *hoanden*. All pupils had to bow to the shrine when they entered and left the school. O Sŏngch'ŏl, *Singminji ch'odŭng kyoyuk*, 349.

20. O Sŏngch'ŏl, *Singminji ch'odŭng kyoyuk*, 325–68.

21. Ibid, 277–323.

22. Ibid, 309–10.

23. Ibid, 299–310.

24. Ibid., 304.

25. Kamasuka Dasuku, "Genkon kyoiku no hei o joshi," 26.

26. Kokuritsu Kyoiku Kenkyujo, Nihon kindai kyoiku hyakunenji 1-kyoiku seisaku, 350–58; O Sŏngch'ŏl, Singminji ch'odŭng kyoyuk, 310–14.

27. Albert Memmi, The Colonizer and the Colonized.

28. Yi Hongnak, "Singminji ŭi sahoe kujo,"139–99.

29. Ibid., 163.

30. Ikegami Shiro, "Doshigakukaigi ni okeru," 455.

31. Patricia E. Tsurumi, Japanese Colonial Education in Taiwan.

32. Phillip Foster, Education and Social Change in Ghana.

33. O Sŏngch'ŏl, Singminji ch'odŭng kyoyuk.

34. From 1933 to 1938, the proportion of factory workers in secondary industry decreased from 46.5 percent to 30.5 percent and the actual number of factory workers in 1938 was just 182,771. Chŏng Chinsŏng, "Iljeha Chosŏn e issŏsŏ," 31–38. From 1930 to 1940, the proportion of unemployed in the total population increased from 53.6 percent to 62.1 percent. Chōsen Sōtokufu, Showa jugonen Chōsen.

4

National Identity and Class Interest in the Peasant Movements of the Colonial Period[1]

DONG-NO KIM

Understanding Japanese colonialism in Korea is essential not only for reconstructing Korea's historical experience, but also for understanding the current functioning of contemporary Korean society, which has been considerably conditioned by its colonial legacy. Social distortions in the everyday life of Korean people today are often attributed to the malicious heritage of the Japanese colonial rule that ended more than half a century ago. The impact of colonial rule has thus been grave and everlasting on Korean society.

Despite the great significance attached to colonial rule, which lasted for over three decades, we have yet to possess a comprehensive and unbiased picture of the period. On one hand, the negative attitude of Korean people toward colonial rule, especially when linked to their strong feeling of nationalism, has often hindered an objective analysis of the events and structural changes that occurred during the period. On the other hand, an excessive concern with the modern institutions established during the period has prevented some scholars from understanding the nature of colonialism underlying these institutions. These two approaches constitute the mainstream of Korean historiography in the analyses of the Japanese colonial period. Two key words that represent the current understanding of Korea's colonial experience are exploitation and modernization, each being placed in the center of the two approaches, the nationalist and the modernist.

Significant contributions that current studies have made to the understanding of the colonial period in Korea should not hide their common fallacy of overreliance on a normative evaluation of the period, whether they emphasize exploitation or modernization. To counter the normative orientation of the two approaches, I offer an alternative approach that will attempt to objectively analyze the empirical reality, as it existed, without being descriptive or morally judgmental. The group I am concerned with is the peasantry that composed the main body (approximately 80 percent) of the population at that time. In particular, I am interested in studying issues of national identity and class membership. My intention is to investigate the extent to which nationalist antagonism and class interests dictated the everyday life of the peasants during the colonial period.

Nationalist historiography has depicted the Korean peasants as victims of Japanese exploitation and consequently portrays them as warriors in the nationalist struggles against a foreign exploiter. Alongside this view a completely different picture also exists that presents the peasants as the carriers or even the beneficiaries of modernization as pursued by Japanese imperialism, though this view does not completely negate the fact that Japanese colonial rule and landlords exploited the peasants. Confronting these two contradictory views, I think a more accurate picture can be determined through an empirical investigation of how the peasants' perception of their national identity interacted with their class interest. I intend to examine this interaction between political ideology and economic interest by looking into the peasants' behavior patterns revealed in the collective manifestation of their grievances.

In this chapter, I argue that peasant uprisings in the colonial period exhibited some peculiar characteristics that were absent in peasant protests before the period of colonization. Unlike peasant movements during the Chosŏn Dynasty when protests against the state or state bureaucrats dominated, after Japan colonized Korea peasants waged class struggles against landlords. This fact shows an interesting distortion of the peasants' identity, since it contradicts one's expectation that the peasants' struggles against the state, rather than landlords, would intensify after colonization, because the state they faced was not theirs but a colonial one imposed from outside. This transition from nationalist to class identity in the peasantry was not natural, but resulted from the establishment of the modern institutions introduced by Japanese colonialism.

To determine the peculiar nature of the peasants' identity as reflected in their social movements during the colonial period, we first need to examine peasant uprisings before the colonial period. Before taking on this task, however, a discussion of methodological problems is in order to avoid the error of excessive reliance on normative evaluations of the period.

METHODOLOGICAL PROBLEMS IN
EXAMINING THE COLONIAL PERIOD

As outlined above, we find two contrasting approaches to the colonial period in Korean historiography: the nationalist approach, emphasizing exploitation by the Japanese and the revisionist or modernist approach, accentuating the construction of modern institutional establishments during the period. Since the issues have already been discussed in several works,[2] I will not explore, in any detail, the debates of these two factions, which center on the main themes of cadastral surveys in the 1910s and industrial development in the 1930s.

Whatever features each faction may emphasize to identify the nature of colonial rule, the two approaches evince a common tendency toward a teleological interpretation of Korean history. The nationalist perspective tries to link the disruption in Korea's historical development with Japanese imperialism, which obstructed indigenous progress toward the establishment of modern political and economic systems. Thus, the primary objective of this approach is to show how the Japanese aggression destroyed the internal dynamics and the progress of traditional Korean society, as well as how the Korean people resisted the invasion. The modernist approach, however, finds a new starting point in Korean history during the colonial period and views modernity as beginning in the colonial period and accelerating after liberation, particularly during the industrial development of the 1960s. The modernist perspective has a strong inclination to find continuity between colonial economic development and postliberation industrial development.

Interesting polarities of continuity and discontinuity are evident in these interpretations of Korean history. Nationalist historiography assumes a polarity between the continuous internal developments during the Chosŏn Dynasty and the sudden disruption by Japanese invasion. The modernist approach argues that social development since the introduction of modern institutions during the colonial period continued to mature until this development reached its apex in contemporary Korean society. This development is then contrasted with the stagnation of traditional Korea before colonization. These two different trajectories of historical teleology dramatically demonstrate the influence of normative values on empirical investigations. Many specific instances of the impact of a normative orientation on the study of colonial history are also cited.

It is clear, then, that without deconstructing this normative orientation and replacing it with a more analytical approach to empirical reality, we will never reach an objective picture of the colonial period. One serious problem arising from excessive adherence to a normative orientation is that the strict dichotomy between exploitation and modernization—the polarity that stems from the teleological interpretation of colonial history—will hinder our recognition of the possibility that the two can exist simultaneously and even interact with each other to constitute a complex whole.

One effective way to replace the normative approach with an analytical one is to detach normative meanings from the key terms used in colonial studies, especially modern, colonial, and nation. Of the various terms with normative connotations, I will focus on the term *modern* since debates in colonial studies center around it. In current historical writing in Korea the term, modern, has had the normative connotation of something good, a virtue, especially when it is contrasted with tradition. Because of this normative evaluation of the term, nationalist historians naturally deny the possibility that this good thing could have been brought by foreign aggressors; rather it came about through the Korean people establishing their own nation-state after liberation. Historians of modernity, on the other hand, regard the colonial period as the beginning of a new era and consequently believe that the presence of any internal tendencies toward the modern before the colonial period can be dismissed. To legitimate its way of perceiving Korean history, each perspective has selected a particular part of the whole and attached normative meanings to it. Such a partial truth, however, can never be a solid foundation upon which we can build a comprehensive understanding of the colonial period.

It has long been a tradition of mainstream social science, as inheritor of the legacy of evolutionism, to believe that the modern period has progressed as compared to previous eras. This belief in historical progress is not as empirically grounded as the great works of Kant, Hegel, and Marx would have us believe. To provide the term modern with a more solid empirical foundation, we should consider it as a strictly chronological term, not as a normative term carrying the implication of progress. Chronologically speaking, modern denotes the time that comes after the feudal period in European history or the premodern era in a more general sense and is characterized by features that were absent in the premodern period. This usage allows us to discern some characteristics of the modern period in its institutional arrangements.

The ways of developing this political structure are diverse,[3] and a state anywhere in the world must now have certain features if it is to be called modern. Some scholars attending to this point have suggested various institutional features of the modern period.[4] We can classify various aspects of the establishment of modern institutions into four categories: political and economic systems and cultural and social relationships. In the political realm, the most noteworthy feature of the modern period is the establishment of a national state that has a centralized power structure, clearly demarcated boundaries, institutional separation between politics and other realms of everyday life (especially the economy), and the monopoly on the legitimate use of violence.[5]

Modernity in an economic system certainly implies the establishment of capitalism, especially industrial capitalism, in which mass production and mass consumption for the maximization of profit prevail as opposed to the precapitalist society dominated by the principle of subsistence. A modern economic system requires everything be sold and purchased in the market, including human labor. The value of human labor as a commodity cannot be determined until the laborers are liberated from the traditional bonds that have hindered the formalization of this arrangement and have dominated human beings through personal rule. In this sense, the creation of formally free labor or the formal freedom of each individual was a prerequisite step towards a modern, capitalist economy.[6]

In terms of social relationships, we expect a new type of human being in the modern political and economic systems, since the traditional individual is unsuitable for a modern system. The most prominent feature of social relationships in this respect is the detachment of an individual from traditional collectivities. The centralized national state demands subjects to be exclusively faithful to it, to the exclusion of other alternatives, while the capitalist economy assumes that an individual commodified his labor under his own will without interference from any supra-individual entity. This new type of individual who secured individuality vis-à-vis the collectivities created individualized social space in the public sphere or civil society.[7]

Culturally, the most serious problem modern society faces is to find an ideological adhesive that will integrate individuals into one social body. All the institutional features of modern society and its political, economic, and social spheres accentuate solipsistic individuals separated from the collectivities and from each other, and this separation ultimately poses a problem of social integration. In this sense, it is no surprise to see that nationalism appears in the wake of the modern period in order to incorporate individuals within an entity that is more comprehensive than the family, the tribe, and the community. Nationalism in modern society is, above all, an ideological force that enables the horizontal integration of individuals by cross-cutting various political, economic, and social interests, thereby replacing the outdated vertical hierarchy of the traditional society.[8]

These institutional characteristics of modernity that first appeared in Europe during the eighteenth century are almost universal nowadays because of their tendency toward globalization.[9] Nevertheless, the response of Third World countries to the process of modernity was diverse. In some places modernity bred the positive consequences of societal development, while in others the results were negative. These different outcomes show that modern institutional arrangements are neither good nor bad in and of themselves. Thus, the effects of modern institutions should be determined empirically by analyzing them solely in the social contexts in which they functioned.

Understanding modernity in this way, we do not need to negate the possibility that it was introduced in the colonial period from outside, nor do we necessarily need to consider the colonial period as a dark age. We instead must analyze the effects modernity produced in the colonial social structure and the everyday lives of ordinary people. This is certainly an empirical question unrelated to moral judgment, which should be postponed until all the factual investigations are completed. Now we can turn our attention to the empirical question of how peasant identities were reflected in the peasant movements. We will start from the question of how the peasants tried to manifest themselves through their collective precolonial behavior and how their identities were altered during the colonial period.

PEASANT IDENTITIES AND
SOCIAL MOVEMENTS IN THE PRECOLONIAL PERIOD

It is not easy to ascertain how Korean peasants perceived themselves, especially when we lack direct evidence testifying to their identity. One appropriate way to accomplish this task is to check how Korean peasants tried to manifest themselves to others. The phenomenon of the peasant movement is certainly such an occasion and the best place to analyze the goals of peasant struggle.

Until the year 1862, the rural segment of Korean society was relatively stable. Although peasants had been under enormous economic strain, they only thought about staging a rebellion and fell short of putting their ideas into practice. The sudden eruption of peasant grievances in the Chinju area in 1862, however, had great repercussions. During this year, thirty-seven rebellions erupted across the country. The majority took place in the three southern provinces of Chŏlla, Kyŏngsang, and Ch'ungch'ŏng.[10] Although the number of peasant uprisings after 1862 fluctuated, rebellions became routine and the number of protests increased over the years. This trend became more evident after the opening of the country in 1876 and culminated in one monumental uprising, the Tonghak Peasant movement, in 1894. For example, in 1893 alone at least sixty-five rebellions occurred in fifty-five regions.[11] This trend shows that the flames of peasant protest, sparked in 1862 by the three southern provinces, had now swept the country.

In terms of the causes of peasant rebellions from 1862 to 1894, we find a certain consistency; many peasants protested against excessive tax burdens and bureaucratic corruption of taxation processes. As Table 4.1 shows, peasant uprisings were directed mostly against corrupt officials who practiced extortion through the taxation and land survey process. Contrary to the general belief in the study of the agrarian economy held by some ahistorical Marxists, the main target of the peasant rebellions was not the landlords, as the tenancy dispute had only secondary significance to peasants. This fact indicates the underdevelopment of class conflict on an economic basis in precolonial agrarian society. It demonstrates how an active intervention by the state in the distribution of the economic surplus can affect the relationships among social classes.

Table 4.1 does not include all peasant rebellions in the period, since it relies on governmental records, such as the Veritable Records of the Chosŏn Dynasty, which may have over represented large-scale rebellions, because only large rebellions were reported to the central government. The figures, however, certainly indicate that rebellions mainly resulted from the corruption of local bureaucrats and petty functionaries in the process of taxation, accounting for about 85 percent of all major rebellions since 1862. From this trend we realize that the peasants opposed and protested against the state and state bureaucrats, not the economic ruling class. Taking this into account, we can say that their primary identity was not based on belonging to a certain eco-

Table 4.1 Peasant Rebellions in the Late Nineteenth Century

Year	Directed Against				
	Local Officials	Petty Functionaries	Landlords	Status System	Etc.
1862–80	4	2	1	1	1
1881–90	13	12	2	1	·
1891–93	16	8	2	·	2
Total (%)	33 (50)	23 (35)	5 (8)	2 (3)	3 (5)

Source: Chosŏn Wangjo Sillok; Han Ugŭn. Tonghangnan kiin e kwanhan yŏn'gu
[A study of the causes of the Tonghak Rebellion]. Sŏul: Sŏul Taehakkyo Ch'ulp'anbu, 1971.

nomic class. Rather, they espoused anti-state struggles and fought against the malfunctions of the political system. This peasant identity is also well confirmed by the Tonghak Peasant movement in 1894, considered the epitome of peasant movements in the traditional period.

Unlike previous rebellions, which were mostly short lived and regional, the Tonghak Peasant movement was the first popular national protest in Korean history. The movement broke out in March 1894 and lasted about eight months. The primary goal of the Tonghak movement before this uprising was to demand religious tolerance from the state for the sect and the posthumous recognition of its martyred founder, Ch'oe Cheu who had been executed as a criminal in 1864. The religious nature of the movement, however, began to change during the Poŭn gathering of 1893, which lifted the movement to a new level of political struggle against foreign invasion.

The Tonghak Peasant movement gained new momentum in March 1894, when thousands of peasants gathered in Paeksan and delivered their call to arms of their uprising, the Call to Righteousness (ch'angŭi mun), which was endorsed by three leaders of the movement: Chŏn Pongjun, Son Hwajung, and Kim Kaenam. Under the manifesto to "inwardly punish corrupt officials and outwardly drive away foreign barbarians,"[12] they launched their struggle against the corrupt government and fanned the flames of popular protest all over the country. In several critical battles against government forces, the peasants effectively demonstrated their superior military power and outstanding morale, reinforced by the religious ideology of the Tonghak sect. In this advantageous situation, fearing the movement was about to develop into an international war on the Korean peninsula after military intervention by foreign countries, such as China and Japan, the peasant army negotiated peace with the government.

The compromise provided the peasant army with an opportunity to perform local administrative duties in Chŏlla Province.[13] This event marked the ruling period of the Tonghak movement, which did not last long. The swift victory of Japan over China in the Sino-Japanese War was a serious threat to the peasant army since the Japanese Army marched to the southern part of Korea after its victory over China. In preparation for the attack by the Japanese Army, Chŏn asked the peasants to mobilize, and the response to the call to mobilize was so favorable that approximately 167,000 gathered to fight. The large size of the peasant army, however, was not sufficient to face the more formidable Japanese Army equipped with powerful, modern weapons and technology. The defeat of the peasant army in the decisive battle of Kongju nullified the dream of the peasants to take care of their grievances through violent protest.

It is not easy to identify the nature of the movement since it was preceded by several steps that involved the participation of various heterogeneous elements. By acknowledging that diverse interests were involved in the outbreak and maintenance of the movement, we can detect the peasantry's intent in their collective struggle by classifying some of their prominent demands. It is relatively clear that the second uprising was motivated by the necessity to wage an anti-imperial struggle against the Japanese Army. Official documents describing this event are filled with rhetoric emphasizing the nationalist feeling of the Korean people. For example, just before and after the Kongju battle, the most critical struggle the peasant army waged against the Japanese forces, Chŏn vainly sent appeals to local magistrates asking them to participate in a nationalist coalition.

In contrast to the second uprising, the main motivating factors for the peasants during the first uprising and their period of self-rule government were complex and do not allow for easy identification of the nature of the movement. From reliable historical sources, however, we can verify that the primary feature of the movement was the confrontation between poor peasants and the state. In the Call to Righteousness, the leaders of the movement revealed how the political corruption of bureaucrats was related to the aggravation of the peasant economy and social unease. Consequently, the peasant army exclusively attacked corrupt local bureaucrats and petty functionaries and plundered government storage only during the initial period of the movement.

This tendency continued throughout the movement, as revealed by the peasants' demands of the government in the Chŏnju compromise. Politically, they demanded, above all, the punishment of corrupt bureaucrats and the abolishment of some governmental apparatuses that had been the source of administrative malpractice. Economically, the majority of the demands focused on the tax systems and the commercialization of agriculture. These demands included keeping the rules of taxation without raising any additional tax rates, prohibiting the re-collection of taxes peasants had already paid, and not collecting tax from uncultivated lands. The social demands of the peasant army centered on the inequalities of the rigid social status system and included abolishing the slavery system and discrimination against outcasts, allowing widows to remarry, and appointing governmental officials on their merits, not on their ascriptive standards.

Viewed comprehensively, it is clear that the peasants participating in the Tonghak Peasant movement and other protests struggled against the state and state bureaucrats, not against the economic ruling class.[14] This finding demonstrates the underdeveloped formation of an economic landlord class system, which is believed to have resulted from an extreme fusion of political power with economic wealth. This system signifies that the primary identity of peasants lay with membership in a national and political entity, not in association with an economic class.

PEASANT IDENTITIES AND PEASANT MOVEMENTS IN THE COLONIAL PERIOD

Colonization unquestionably brought about fundamental changes in various aspects of Korean society, and the agrarian economy was no exception. Among the various aspects of the agrarian economy, I will specifically focus on peasant identities as they were reflected in peasant movements. In looking at the peasant movements of the colonial period, we find a definite change in pattern compared with precolonial movements. To understand this transformation, we must first determine what changes occurred and then investigate the influence these changes had on peasant identities.

At the risk of oversimplification the peasant movements during the colonial period can be divided into four stages: (1) calm, 1910–19, (2) tenant disputes, 1920s–30s, (3) Red Peasant Union movement, 1930s, and (4) calm 1940–45. The peasants were relatively subdued in the early and very late period of Japanese colonial rule mainly because the colonial government controlled them strictly and harshly. Even admitting the physical forces the Japanese wielded after 1910, however, it is surprising that the first decade of Japanese rule passed without serious attacks from below, except for some sporadic, violent protests held against the land survey.[15] In explaining this unexpected trend of peasant protests in the 1910s, we also need to pay attention to the possibility that the confiscation of land during the land survey was not substantial.[16] The silence of peasants in the 1940s resulted from the extreme suppression exerted by Japan during the Japanese war against Western powers.

Aside from the relative silence in the early and late period of colonial rule, the majority of agitations and violent manifestations of peasant grievances took place during the 1920s and 1930s. Though the Red Peasant Union movement was more radical, tenant disputes were a more representative form of peasant protests. Not only did more peasants participate in various regions across the Korean peninsula, but their voices were also more clearly heard in the tenant disputes than in the Red Union Peasant movement, which was ideologically organized and regionally restricted. Therefore, tenant disputes are the most appropriate subject for investigation if we are to see how ordinary peasants lived and struggled during most of the colonial period.[17]

Various historical data provides us with a sense of the general tendencies of the peasant movements. One index is, of course, the frequency and number of participants in protests, which are summarized in Table 4.2.

Table 4.2 shows the frequency of tenant disputes in the colonial period. In fact, the disputes were so widespread that they constituted the most representative peasant movement of that period. In other words, the most acute antipathy the peasants showed was directed against the landlords, both Japanese and Korean,[18] and not against the state as in the precolonial period. As we have noted, this fact seems quite contradictory to our expectation that the peasants struggled against the state more fiercely than before now that the state they faced was colonial, not their own nation-state.

Some other general features can be extracted from Table 4.2. First, the significance of tenant disputes increased over time, as revealed in the increase in

Table 4.2 General Trend of Tenant Disputes in the Colonial Period

Year	Disputes (D)	Participants (P)	Participants per Dispute (D/P)
1920	15	4,040	269.3
1921	27	2,967	109.9
1922	24	2,539	105.8
1923	176	9,063	51.5
1924	164	6,929	42.3
1925	204	4,002	19.6
1926	198	2,745	13.9
1927	275	3,973	14.4
1928	1,590	4,863	3.1
1929	423	5,419	12.8
1930	726	13,012	17.9
1931	667	10,282	15.4
1932	300	4,687	15.6
1933	1,975	10,337	5.3
1934	7,544	22,454	2.9
1935	25,834	59,019	2
1936	29,975	72,453	2.4

Source: Chōsen Sōtokufu, Nōrinkyoku [Bureau of agriculture and forestry]. Chōsen nōchi nenpō [Annual reports on Korean agricultural lands]. Keijō: Chōsen Sōtokufu, 1940: 5, 6, 26–27.

the number of occurrences and participants. However, we may also notice that the number of participants in each dispute dwindled after the middle of the 1920s and especially after 1934.[19] Second, the colonial government introduced some laws to try to resolve the conflict between the landlords and peasants in the early 1930s, such as the Tenancy Arbitration Ordinance (sojak chojŏngnyŏng) in 1932 and the Agricultural Land Ordinance (nongjiryŏng) in 1934.

Besides these general features, some other factors account for the fluctuations in the number of protests. The increase during the 1920s can be explained by the peasants' enhanced organizational capacity and the mush-rooming of peasant organizations that were mainly initiated by outside nationalist or socialist groups. The unexpected sudden increase of protests in 1928 is attributed to the unprecedented dismal harvest caused by natural disasters, which elicited widespread disputes over rent. Sudden increases in rent in 1933 and afterwards, however, had different meanings. The introduction of the Tenancy Arbitration Ordinance in 1932 furnished a new way to orderly and peacefully resolve conflicts between landlords and tenants. This new institutional outlet to mitigate the grievances over the tenancy system significantly reduced the patience of both peasants and landlords.[20] Consequently, distinctive features of the disputes after 1932 included an increased participation of landlords wanting to safeguard their economic interests while milder disputes became the norm and direct physical demonstrations virtually disappeared.[21]

Though this general outline of peasant protests shows how the peasants behaved at the apex of the colonial period, it does not reveal why the peasants participated in the movements. In fact, it is more important to know what upset peasants and what they strove for in their collective protests if we are to identify the real nature of the peasant identities and protests. The answers to these questions can be obtained by quantifying the causes of peasant protests, presented in Table 4.3.

The data in Table 4.3 is not all-inclusive and may over-represent the large-scale disputes, since it was collected by the Bureau of Police, not by the Bureau of Agriculture. The table, however, sufficiently testifies that the disputes were primarily concerned with tenancy rights and secondarily with rent. In the 1930s tenancy rights were the dominant cause of disputes, except for 1930–31, while the problem of rent was more important in the early 1920s. Besides these fluctuations over the years, there were also vacillations within years. Generally, since tenancy contracts were made in the winter and early spring and the rent was collected after the estimation of harvest in the fall, disputes over tenancy rights were concentrated in the winter and spring, while the disputes over rent occurred in the fall.[22]

What implications do the two different causes of tenant disputes have? It is certainly not a logical problem but rather an empirical one, since the same cause may have different meanings in different social contexts. However, we may notice some general implications based on these diverse empirical stud-

Table 4.3 Causes of Tenant Disputes

Year	Tenant Disputes (%)				
	Tenancy	Rent	Miscellaneous Expenses[1]	Etc.	Total
1920	1 (6.7)	8 (53.3)	4 (26.7)	2 (13.3)	15 (100)
1921	4 (14.8)	16 (59.3)	2 (7.4)	5 (18.5)	27 (100)
1922	9 (37.5)	6 (25.0)	2 (8.3)	7 (29.2)	24 (100)
1923	117 (66.5)	37 (21.0)	15 (8.5)	7 (4.0)	176 (100)
1924	126 (76.8)	26 (15.9)	5 (3.0)	7 (4.3)	164 (100)
1925	1 (9.1)	5 (45.5)	—	5 (45.5)	11 (100.1)
1926	4 (23.5)	10 (58.8)	1 (5.9)	2 (11.8)	17 (100)
1927	11 (50.0)	6 (27.3)	3 (13.6)	2 (9.1)	22 (100)
1928	21 (70.0)	4 (13.3)	1 (3.3)	4 (13.3)	30 (99.9)
1929	17 (47.2)	7 (19.4)	1 (2.8)	11 (30.6)	36 (100)
1930	30 (32.3)	42 (45.2)	5 (5.4)	16 (17.2)	93 (100.1)
1931	17 (29.8)	27 (47.4)	2 (3.5)	11 (19.3)	57 (100)
1932	26 (51.0)	12 (23.5)	6 (11.8)	7 (13.7)	51 (100)

Source: Chōsen Sōtokufu, Keimukyoku [Police administration bureau]. *Saikin ni okeru Chōsen chian jōkyō* [Recent conditions of public security in Korea]. Keijō: Chōsen Sōtokufu, 1933, 1938: 158–59.

[1]Miscellaneous expenses include transportation of rent in kind, transfer of land taxes, and water fees.

ies. First of all, it is clear that the disputes over tenancy rights were more directly related to subsistence, since the confiscation of tenancy rights represented the most critical threat to peasants' survival in the agrarian economy, where other subsidiary employment opportunities were quite rare. On the other hand, disputes over rent were more likely related to the pursuit of profits by peasants if the disputes did not result from an excessively high rent. Another implication is that the disputes over tenancy rights tended to initiate conflict among peasants. Since the change of tenants played on the assumption of a zero-sum game, competition for land increased among them. In contrast, the disputes over rent were prone to bring about cooperation and unity among the peasants since the collective reduction of rent was a common good to be shared among participants.

With this general theoretical guidance, we may draw some conclusions from the given data. First, the shift in the dominant cause of the disputes from rent to tenancy rights shows that the economic conditions of the peasants worsened as time passed. In the early 1920s, the peasants still possessed some space to struggle for economic profits. This space significantly decreased as their subsistence became threatened starting in the mid-1920s. On the surface, this represents a good example of offensive mobilization by the peasant movement in the early 1920s as opposed to defensive mobilization after the mid-1920s. This point was picked up by a new approach repudiating the traditional argument that the peasants were poverty driven and their social movements were subsistence oriented.[23]

Despite the outstanding contributions of this new approach, however, the issue is still inconclusive when determining how much the peasants were motivated by a desire to maximize economic interests in the process of the ever-expanding commercialization of agriculture in the early 1920s. The main reason it is difficult to validate the new approach thesis is that the struggles over rent in the early 1920s and afterward were mostly motivated by the urgent need to survive during a terrible harvest caused by natural disasters,[24] not by the desire to reduce rent for maximization of profit.[25] On the whole, then, even admitting some possibilities of tenant disputes originating from offensive motives, the general motive of collective peasant behavior was to sustain their subsistence in the face of harsh exploitation by landlords.

Another important point to be derived from this data is that a large increase in the disputes over tenancy rights instead of rent obliged the peasants to compete among themselves for land to cultivate. This acute mutual confrontation among the peasants resulted from the landlords' desire to control their tenants more strictly than before. Whenever a tenant could not fulfill his duties or protested against the landlord, the latter did not hesitate to replace him with a new tenant who would be willing and able to pay rent and be more docile to exploitation. Because of this the data just before 1925 shows the rate of tenant changes reaching almost 40 percent per year. This change accounts for about 80 percent of the total disputes in South Chŏlla Province at that time.[26] Against the divide and conquer strategy employed by the landlords, the peasants fiercely protested to the extent that the economic condition drove them to a subsistence crisis. After all, the frequent turnover of tenants incurred the ubiquity of peasant strife and peasants struggled not only against the landlords but also among themselves.

From this explanation, we learn that the peasants struggled against landlord exploitation that threatened their subsistence. This is a dramatic shift from the precolonial period. As we have already seen, the peasants in the late Chosŏn Dynasty fought against the state and state officials as well as foreign invaders, and thus their primary identity centered on membership with the nation-state. Their descendants in the colonial period, however, waged their most desperate struggles against the landlords, not against the colonial government. To the great dismay of the nationalist historians who anticipated that all Koreans who lived in the colonial period would be warriors against foreign imperialism, this fact implies that peasants identified more with class interests than national interests.

Of course, this interpretation may face opposition from the traditional viewpoint that emphasizes the political and anti-imperial nature of tenant disputes,[27] an argument that certainly possesses its own empirical foundation. The peasants' struggle against the landlords naturally included an element of anti-imperial political protest since a significant number of Japanese landlords in Korea concentrated their land ownership in prosperous areas and the Japanese Government-General assisted Korean landlords in the process of their accumulation of wealth. Nonetheless, this polarization of the nationalist peasants and the pro-Japanese landlords provides a very simple thesis that is hard to acknowledge. The homogeneity of each class was never empirically proven and the confrontation between the classes was never straightforward; peasants attacked both the Japanese and Korean landlords in their struggle for economic interest. Besides, some Korean landlords, albeit nationalist, were the target of furious peasant protest since they achieved economic gain at the expense of peasant subsistence.[28] Moreover, as we will see, the Japanese Government-General was not always on the side of landlords, but sometimes sided with tenants when it was in the government's best interest and necessary to enhance agricultural productivity.

Insofar as we try to perceive the nature of the peasant movement, however, it is evident that the peasants were not so much concerned with the grand cause of political ideology as with the economic prerequisites for survival.

Most demands the peasants made in their disputes were economic: guarantee of tenancy rights, reduction of rent, and the elimination of the transfer of land taxes and water fees. This is not to say that they were born profit seekers and so egoistic as to be ignorant of their ethnic identity. It rather implies that their economic conditions were desperate, as we will see later, and their social condition was constructed in such a way as to require them to behave primarily as a member of an economic class, not as a member of a colonized nation. For a better understanding of how the colonial modernity introduced by Japanese imperialism distorted the everyday life of the peasants, it is important to find out the social conditions that made them behave in this way and to reveal how this kind of distortion was possible.

ESTABLISHMENT OF MODERN INSTITUTIONS IN THE COLONIAL PERIOD

The shift in the direction of colonial period peasant movements from the struggle against the state and foreign invaders to one against the landlords can be attributed to the establishment of new institutions. What kind of new institutional arrangements brought about this change in peasant movements and identities? Since the peasant movements mainly erupted in the 1920s, we need to focus on institutions introduced by the colonial government in the 1910s, of which the most important were the cadastral survey and the new tax system.

Regarding the cadastral survey, no agreement has been reached on how much land ownership exploitation occurred because of it. Its purposes, however, were clear. In the planning stage, the Government-General made it clear that the survey was to provide legal authorization of land ownership and the establishment of a new land tax system: "Politically, the survey intended to reform the land tax system by authorizing land owners and economically, to transform land into agricultural capital by clarifying the rights attached to it."[29] That is, the Japanese intended to achieve two goals simultaneously: the (1) fiscal goal to institutionalize modern land ownership and land tax for the consolidation of their colonial rule in Korea by securing the resources for the management of the colony; and the (2) economic goal of introducing a capitalist market economy to maximize profits from agricultural investment.

To accomplish these two goals, the Government-General required all landowners to register their lands. By doing so, landowners would be given legal authorization of land ownership unless there were disputes over registered lands. By adopting this principle of land registration, rather than directly investigating land ownership, the Government-General endeavored to control all individual properties while minimizing the cost of the survey. The registration seemed to have met some resistance, but not enough to halt the survey completely. Some scholars[30] have argued that the completion of land ownership registration marked the beginning of a modern property system. This is partly true, since in most periods of the Chosŏn Dynasty the central government never authorized individual land ownership under the pretext that all land belonged to the king. This argument is also partly false, however, since there was an attempt to start a land ownership survey in the last phase of the dynasty.

What was completely new about the land survey of 1910–18 was that it legally authorized only one type of right to the land—land ownership—to the exclusion of the various rights customarily attached. Unlike the Kwangmu land survey (1894–1904), which intended to protect the cultivation rights of peasants as well as landownership, the new survey negated any kind of rights peasants possessed to the land.[31] This was a great threat to the peasants' interest. The peasants customarily retained cultivation rights for the land they reclaimed by putting their labor and money on the line.[32] Called by various names, including *hwari*, this right was so firmly rooted in Korean agrarian society that it was sold, subleased, and even inherited. Denial of multiple rights attached to the land not only deprived the peasants of the economic basis for their subsistence, but also detached them from their former complementary relationship with the landlords, in which both parties prospered by admitting the other's right to the land.

A deeper implication of this new type of property right was that it satisfied an essential condition for the development of a capitalist economy. Without establishing exclusive property rights to the land, a capitalist economy could not prosper because multiple rights to the land might hinder the mobility of agricultural capital and reduce the attractiveness of land as a marketable commodity. By eliminating this obstacle, Korea finally entered into a market economy, in which human relationships were made formal and contractual. We find one vestige of this change in a new form of tenancy contract. In the precolonial period, tenancy contracts were the least formal arrangement and were mostly made orally. Even when a written document was used, its contents were very rudimentary, lacking the detailed terms of most written contracts, such as duties of tenants, conditions for the contract's termination, and even its duration.[33] Around 1930, even though written documents did not yet prevail, a new form of document became available to a wider circle of landlords and peasants. In the southern regions, for example, where most of the agricultural crops were produced, almost 30 percent of tenancy contracts were bound through a written document and the renewal of tenancy rights was not automatic at the end of the term. These contracts, however, lasted on average about three years.[34]

Together with the introduction of a capitalist economy, the most immediate goal of the land survey was to institutionalize a new tax system. In order to secure a strong financial basis for colonial rule, it became an urgent task for the colonial government to clearly identify taxpayers and to broaden the tax base. It is still uncertain how much revenue the colonial government reaped from the enlarged tax base, since the tax rate was initially set at a relatively low level and the subsequent increases were not phenomenal when adjusted to the inflation rate. Therefore, the colonial government had to ask for financial assistance from the Japanese government. As a result, throughout most parts of the colonial period there was a continuous flow of capital to the colony from the Japanese government.[35] Viewed from a long-term perspective, however, the expansion of the tax base certainly provided a solid foundation for the stabilization of the financial structure of the colony, since a modest increase in the tax rate would result in a large sum.[36] In this sense, it is no accident that the first task the Government-General launched after colonizing Korea was the land cadastral survey.

The survey's identification of landowners was to have more far-reaching consequences. The survey dissolved the crux of the land tax systems of the Chosŏn Dynasty, such as the kyŏlbuje system and the corporate taxation system, and paved the way to introduce modern ones. The basic principle of the kyŏlbuje system was to determine the tax burden of a given parcel of land by the amount of crop it produced, not by its value in the market. Under this system, one kyŏl referred to the amount of land required to produce the same amount (one kyŏl) of crop.[37] Since the kyŏl was proportional to the productivity of land, the actual size of one kyŏl differed depending on the quality of land; the higher the fertility of the land, the smaller the area of the kyŏl. Strictly speaking, the kyŏlbuje system in this sense was not a land tax but a crop tax, since the same parcel of land could have a different tax rate, depending on its productivity.[38]

In fact, the kyŏlbuje system was a good source for taxation corruption. The evaluation of land quality, which was quite arbitrary, reaped great fortunes for tax officials and petty functionaries, since bribery was rampant to under evaluate the grade of land for tax purposes. Moreover, where the land survey had not been conducted for over a hundred years, tax officials and petty functionaries could illegitimately benefit from increased land productivity that had not been reflected in the old land register. As a result, corrupt officials benefited from this inefficient tax system by draining state finances and taking advantage of the economic adversities of peasants.

The introduction of a new system helped to resolve the major problems of the land tax system. Based on the market value of the land, which was assessed during the land survey, the Government-General decided to fix the land tax at the rate of 13/1000 of the land price, which was roughly equivalent to 5 percent of total agricultural products.[39] By equating the real value of land with its value for tax purposes and by eliminating all rights to the land other than land ownership, profit predictability for agricultural investment could be enhanced. This is an essential element in the rational organization of production factors and as Max Weber[40] emphasized, this process is the central characteristic of modern capitalism.

Another important aspect in the alteration of the land tax was to dissolve the corporate taxation system and replace it with a modern individual system. In the face of rampant corruption among tax officials and attempts at tax evasion by poor peasants, the central government of the Chosŏn Dynasty introduced the corporate taxation system, which secured a certain amount of money by attaching taxes to a collective whole, such as a village. Once the tax burden was fixed at the village level, the government cared very little about how taxpaying was divided among villagers. The dynasty was only concerned with the collection of the total amount from the corporate body. The actual distribution of the tax burden among villagers and its collection was managed by intermediaries called hosu, sŏwŏn, and chakpu. This taxation system, coupled with the central government's lack of control at the village level, provided the local villages with opportunities to self-govern. Consequently, village leaders seized a considerable degree of autonomy in local affairs, including judiciary decisions.[41] The local yangban associations (hyanghoe), not the local government, became the actual governing organ in the local village, which was controlled by local elites, including the old gentry from the prestigious yangban families and the new gentry who took charge of the corporate tax system.

This collective responsibility taxation system encouraged the cooperation of village members since they could establish a community of common destiny when the government tried to raise taxes for the corporate body. A tax increase under this system was a threat to the subsistence of everyone in the village, including both peasants and landlords. Thus, when the government attempted to increase tax rates, it faced resistance from all village members. Instead of specific village members, all members mobilized resources for rebellion throughout the village society, as was the case in the Chinju uprising of 1862. Here we can ascertain the coalition between peasants and landlords in their protests against the state and the state's attempt to collect more taxes from the peasant community.

This should not, however, suggest a romantic picture of the peasant community in which its members mutually aided each other and wholeheartedly cooperated with one another. More often than not, villages contained many elements of internal conflict. However, during critical junctures when the destiny of the village as a whole was in danger, the members of the peasant community, regardless of their class background, formed a united front to fight against the outside force. To a large extent, this type of solidarity arose during confrontations with the state over taxes.

Once landowners had been clearly identified, the Government-General replaced the corporate taxation system with an individual one. This change reflected the enhanced infrastructural power of the colonial government,[42] especially in its capacity to collect information, since the individual taxation system could not have been instituted without very detailed and updated information about land ownership.

The new individual tax system had great repercussions in local politics. In order to institutionalize the individual taxation system, the colonial government reorganized the local administrative system. First, it annihilated the power of intermediaries who illegitimately benefited from their involvement in the distribution and collection of taxes in the village. Elimination of intermediaries had long been the unfulfilled goal of state reform movements in the Chosŏn Dynasty. Relying upon its superior despotic and enhanced infrastructural power, which reduced the necessity to depend upon the supplementary role of the local leaders, the Government-General succeeded in replacing intermediaries with governmental officials. For this purpose the colonial government established a new basic unit of local administration, the myŏn, which superseded the old administrative units of tong and ri.[43] Alongside the changes in local administration, the tax system also converted to an individual landlord direct tax payment system where landlord payments were made directly to the myŏn office.

DISINTEGRATION OF THE PEASANT COMMUNITY
AND THE PEASANTS' NEW SURVIVAL STRATEGY

The ultimate social impact of the modern tax system, especially the new individual taxation system, was to be the demise of the traditional peasant community. Centralizing the state structure by introducing a new tax system and local administrative apparatuses, the government sharply curtailed the autonomy of self-government found in local villages. Replacing the self-governing village with a new, official local administration unit meant an ever more thorough penetration of the state into the village. Furthermore, the abolition of the corporate taxation system dissolved the harmony among villagers and pitted them against each other. Through this process individual subjectivity was created. Individuals then became detached from the old community and integrated into a system that featured a higher unit of political control—the colonial government.

With the separation of individuals from their communities, the relationship between landlords, peasants, and the state naturally began to change. The collapse of the peasant community and the creation of an individual were related to the demise of homogeneity among the village members. One of the most direct symptoms of this divergence among villagers was class division. This does not, of course, argue that the precolonial Korean economy was characterized by the absence of class division. Rather, the economic distance between landlords and peasants widened even more, and this cleavage could not be compensated by the now obsolete cooperative relationship between them.

The shaping of the new economic separation between the classes was assisted by the agricultural policies of the Government-General. It has been generally agreed upon in Korean historiography that the colonial government devised various measures to facilitate the economic interests of landlords.[44] The colonial government not only protected the interests of large landlords in the land survey and in the estimation of land tax, but also provided many subsidies to those landlords who faithfully followed government agricultural policies. The Government-General fortified the economic position of the landlords who eagerly introduced new rice hybrids, organized water irrigation associations, and tried to enhance agricultural productivity.

As a result, landlords were in a position to accumulate a large amount of capital, which was reinvested in land ownership. This continued until the 1930s, when the conversion of agricultural to industrial capital became feasible with the inception of industrialization in Korea.

At the other extreme, we find the dire poverty of peasants. Not only did the number of tenants increase over time, reaching approximately 53 percent of total households in 1932,[45] but also the economic conditions of most peasants worsened. For instance, even in 1925, when economic conditions were relatively more affluent than in later years, nearly 40 percent of agricultural households showed a deficit in their agricultural management.[46]

The increased economic distance between the landlords and the peasants can be explained by various mechanisms, the most representative of which were the commercialization of agriculture and the Program to Increase Rice Production (J. Sanmai zoshoku keikaku, K. Sanmi chŭngsik kyehoek). Some classic works[47] on agrarian politics have already emphasized that the most critical impetus for social change in agrarian societies came from the commercialization of agriculture. Facing the development of this new mechanism of the market economy,[48] landlords, in order to maximize their profit, generally tried to control their tenants much more strictly than before. Most frequently landlords raised the rent—not only fixed rents (tojije) that were increased to account for about half of the agricultural production, but also share rent (pyŏngjak pansuje) by raising the proportion of the crop that had to be remitted to landlords well above 50 percent—thus surpassing the limit of peasants' tolerance.[49] When the tenants could not meet the increased rent, the landlords did not hesitate to replace them with new tenants. In addition, the landlords actively intervened in the labor process of tenants by selecting seeds and demanding the use of new agricultural tools, fertilizers, and technology to increase land productivity. Sometimes landlords even loaned money to their tenants at usurious rates that eventually deprived peasants of any profits or land.[50]

The aggravated relationship between the two classes worsened through the intervention of the colonial government. The most appropriate example of this intervention was the Program to Increase Rice Production. The common thread running through the agricultural policies of the colonial government, from the beginning to the end of the colonial period, was to increase agricultural productivity to meet the demands for food in Japan. This intention was most actively pursued through the rice production improvement project. The Government-General encouraged landlords and peasants to participate in the project by giving substantial incentives to those who were qualified, including direct financial support. The development of irrigation systems, the introduction of new seeds and agricultural technology, and the increasing application of commercial fertilizers, however, caused peasants enormous economic distress, since the costs were too high for most peasants and financial subsidies were given only to wealthy landlords and peasants.

The peasants' ardent desire to enhance agricultural productivity was not matched by their capacity to participate in the project, unless they dared to go into debt to meet the enormous cost. Perceiving that the project might significantly increase total output, however, the landlords who were under the aegis of the colonial government eagerly forced their tenants to participate in the project despite the high costs.[51] Both the colonial government and the landlords gladly witnessed the successful completion of the project, realizing more wealth from increased productivity, while strong economic pressures were exerted on the peasants to compensate for the increased expenses of production. This represents an instance of how the agricultural policies of the Government-General helped extend the economic distance between the two classes.

Because there was no social mechanism to mitigate the aggravation of class relationships, the divergence between the classes led to acute and escalating social conflicts. Individuals, separated from the traditional peasant community and from each other, were required to form new relationships that were more legal and formal than personal and communitarian. Most of all, the landlords saw their relationships with tenants as economic, which could be easily nullified when economic terms were not satisfied. Those tenants who failed to pay rent on time with good quality rice lost their tenancy rights. This resulted in an extremely high tenancy turnover rate and widespread protests.

In addition, with the introduction of a formal tenancy contract, personal considerations, traditionally allowed between landlords and tenants, lost their usefulness. Intensified agricultural commercialization, which provided more chances for economic profit, motivated landlords to be more calculating in their decision making and to disregard the economic difficulties of tenants.[52] Under the pretext of using a modern contract, the landlords rejected tenants' demands to reduce rent during natural disasters, such as severe droughts and floods, which reduced the normal harvest.[53] Tenants' grievances increased not only because the actions of landlords critically threatened subsistence, but also because these actions signaled the end of the paternalistic care the land-lords had formerly bestowed upon tenants in the most desperate situations.[54] The modern formal relationship between these two classes was achieved only with the dissolution of the peasant community and the threat to the subsis-tence of a large section of the peasant class.

Annihilation of the minimal benevolence allowed by custom and the ter-mination of a moral economy that had already waned made the old survival tactics of the peasants obsolete. This situation demanded that the peasants find a new means to their survival in the unsympathetic world of the market economy, without relying upon personal considerations of the landlords and the peasant community as a whole. To the extent that the peasants' member-ship with the community no longer assisted their subsistence, the peasants aimed to form a new type of collaboration through which they could stand against the harsh exploitation of the landlords. This problem led peasants to seek partnership with political groups, both nationalist and socialist, that could organize peasants and urban workers around political goals.

The peasants created their own survival tactics by setting up a new horizon-tal alliance among themselves with the help of outside leadership, which replaced the traditional vertical integration across social classes. The socialists were most active and effective in organizing peasants. They first established the United Coalition of Peasants and Workers of Korea (Chosŏn Nonong Ch'ongdongmaeng) in 1924, which was followed by the formation of the Korean Communist Party the next year. Around 1927, the United Coalition of Korean Peasants (Chosŏn Nongmin Ch'ongdongmaeng), which was separate from the umbrella organization, became a more comprehensive peasant orga-nization that included owner-cultivators as well as tenants.[55] Following this pioneering venture of the peasants, new organizations mushroomed: in the period 1926–8, the number of peasant organizations increased almost three-fold from 119 to 307; by 1931, there were over 1,700 such organizations.[56]

The political ideology of these organizations was so influential that it worked cogently in the mobilization of peasants.[57] When the influence was not strong enough to induce the voluntary participation of peasants, the organizations initiated more compulsory measures. Not surprisingly, the carriers of peasant movements at this time were not so much individual peasants as various types of peasant organizations.[58] This does not mean, however, that the peasants faithfully followed the political ideologies of these organizations without reservation. The peasants developed their own demands to alleviate their economic distress and did not necessarily advocate the total transformation of colonial society, as demanded by socialist and other nationalist forces.

Nevertheless, it is hard to deny that the outside leadership of political groups decisively boosted the organizational capacity of isolated peasants and that the marriage of convenience between the two forces was quite forceful in pushing the peasant movements forward. This incomplete articulation of social forces lasted until the 1930s when the radical political organizations shifted their attention toward the Red Peasant Union movements, while most peasants waged individual battles against the landlords within the rules stipulated by the new agricultural policies such as the Tenancy Arbitration Ordinance (sojak chojongnyŏng) and the Agricultural Land Ordinance (nongjiryŏng).

Concomitant with the change in the peasants' strategy for class struggle in the age of a market economy, the landlords also organized themselves to maximize their economic interests. The Japanese initiated the landlord association even before they colonized Korea. In the early 1910s, the colonial government established a para-governmental agricultural organization, which the local magistrate chaired and all landlords owning medium-sized or larger holdings were qualified to participate.[59] The primary objective of the landlord association was to promote the introduction of new seeds and agricultural technology to enhance land productivity. An active trend of organizing landlords continued, so that in the late 1910s more than one hundred organizations existed in each province. In the 1920s, when the project for the improvement of rice production was the main goal of agricultural policy, the colonial government again established a tight partnership with the landlord associations. Though this alliance did not result in satisfactory outcomes, the colonial government seemed quite happy to find helpful collaborators in achieving its economic and political goals.[60] The landlord associations' inability to deal with the violent and collective protests of the tenants eventually moved the Government-General to find new ways to directly control the peasants—the carrot-and-stick strategy—which was reflected in the change of tenant laws in the 1930s.

In this manner, the division between peasants and landlords was completed. Both parties had to build new foundations along class lines. Separated from each other and the peasant community, both landlords and peasants experienced conflicts in economic interests. Unlike the precolonial agrarian society, in which the peasant community was a unitary body in its protests against excessive taxation by the state and state bureaucrats, now the disintegration of the peasant community and its division across class lines during the colonial period critically hampered the development of a nationalist coalition. This situation was certainly much more favorable for the development of class conflicts than the formation of the nationalist coalition, which required cooperative relationships across class divisions. Through this analysis we can explain how international struggles between the colonizer and the colonized were transformed into intranational class struggles between landlords and peasants.

CONCLUSION

We know from this analysis of social change in Korea's colonial period, especially the analysis of peasant movements and identities, that the members of the peasant community were divided into new groups along class lines during the colonial period. Compared with the precolonial period, when the peasants and landlords sometimes joined forces to protest against the state and foreign invaders, this was a new phenomenon developed as modern agricultural institutions were transplanted from the other side of the world. Now that the old survival tactics had lost their effectiveness, peasants needed to develop new strategies without relying on the traditional community rules. This situation required peasants to find unity among one another in order to face ever-increasing exploitation from landlords and more generally the ruthless operation of the market economy. Focusing on survival tactics caused the peasants to pay much less attention to the nationalist struggle against foreign invaders.

The distorted transformation of an international struggle against foreign imperialism into class struggle gained its impetus from the separation of

Figure 4.1 Relationship between the State and the Korea Peasant Community in the Chosŏn Dynasty and Colonial Period

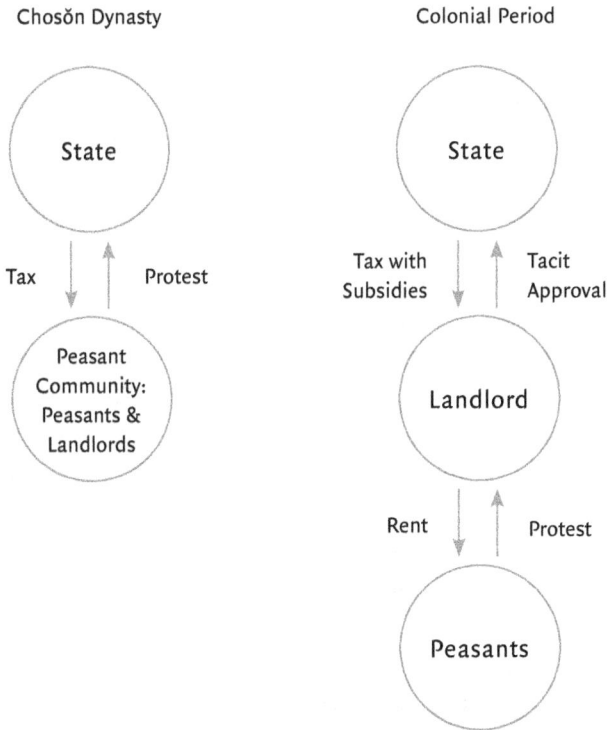

Chosŏn Dynasty   Colonial Period

State   State

Tax ↓   ↑ Protest   Tax with ↓   ↑ Tacit
                                          Subsidies   Approval

Peasant
Community: Landlord
Peasants &
Landlords

                                          Rent ↓   ↑ Protest

                                                    Peasants

individual peasants from their communities, which in turn resulted from the introduction of modern institutions by the Japanese colonial government. The cadastral survey was the starting point of this movement, and the subsequent land tax law critically damaged the traditional peasant community. The change in land tax from a corporate tax to an individual tax dissolved the binding force of community members that had been expressed in anti-state protests. The transformation of social relationships from the corporate taxation system to the individual tax system is diagramed in Figure 4.1.

The social impact of this change was striking. Not only was the peasant community internally divided because of the disharmony of economic interests among its members, but more importantly its relationship with the state acquired a new dimension. With this change, the state now did not need to directly face the violent protest of peasants, but rather acted as a mediator between the two classes and arbitrated their conflicts.[61] The state stood above and beyond class structure itself and could pretend to take the economic interests of all classes into account. It is no wonder, therefore, that the colonial government did not always side with the landlords, but rather sided with the peasants if they could be used as a vehicle to achieve the government's agenda. When it pointed at the improvement of agricultural productivity, the Government-General believed that the tenants would be the real authors of this improvement and that their economic condition could be ameliorated if that goal was attained. This was one of the reasons why the Government-General sometimes allied with peasants in arbitrating tenant disputes and later employed some measures to soothe peasant grievances at the expense of losing the more beneficial partnerships with the landlords.

It is pointless to deny that modern institutions were introduced during the colonial period. It is equally pointless, however, to deny that social distortions were introduced by this change. Even without morally condemning colonial rule in Korea, I hope we might verify that the modern institutions implemented by the colonial government during this period constituted a large threat to the survival of the majority of Koreans. The large peasant population was separated from their community and hurled into the vortex of rapid social changes that required new strategies for survival. They could not help but wage class struggles for their subsistence and pay less heed to the nationalist call for resistance against the colonial government. This distortion of the national spirit into the narrow confines of class antagonism was the serious price the Korean people paid for the introduction of modern institutions into the agrarian economy of the colonial period.

NOTES

1. The Korean version of this chapter has been published in the Han'guk Sahoehak. Kim, Dong-No, "Ilche sidae Singminji Kŭndaehwa wa Nongmin Undong ŭi Chŏnhwan," Han'guk Sahoehak (Korean journal of sociology) 41, no. 1 (2007): 194–220.

2. Kim Tongno, "Singminji sidae ŭi kŭndaejŏk"; An Pyŏngjik, "Han'guk kŭn-hyŏndaesa yŏn'gu"; Sin Yongha, "'Singminji kŭndaehwaron' chaejŏngnip."

3. For instance, Charles Tilly, Coercion, Capital, and European States argues that the nation-state as a modern phenomenon resulted from the preparation or waging of war

in a competitive state system, while Theda Skocpol, *States and Social Revolutions*, maintains that the nation-state came from the social revolutions arising from the crises of an old political system.

4. Anthony Giddens, *The Consequences of Modernity*; Jürgen Habermas, *The Structural Transformation*.

5. Michael Mann, "The Autonomous Power of the State"; Gianfranco Poggi, *The State*.

6. It is interesting to note that Karl Marx and Max Weber both pointed out "formally free labor" as an essential feature of modern capitalism, although their theoretical orientations were strikingly different. Karl Marx, *Capital: A Critique of Political Economy*; Max Weber, *The Protestant Ethic*.

7. Jürgen Habermas, *The Structural Transformation*.

8. Tom Nairn, *The Break-up of Britain*; Patricia Crone, *Pre-Industrial Societies*, 18.

9. Anthony Giddens, *The Consequences of Modernity*, 63–64.

10. Ch'oe Chinok, "1860-nyŏndae ŭi millan," 386–88.

11. Kim Yangsik, "Kojongjo millan yŏn'gu," 671.

12. O Chiyŏng, *Tonghaksa*, 112.

13. The peasant army was officially supposed to act in an advisory capacity by establishing a corrective office (*chipkangso*) to each district magistrate in order to prevent extortion and to protect peasant interests. In effect, however, the office worked as an administrative apparatus: supervising the administrative procedures of the local government, handling judiciary proceedings and controlling the army and weapons in the provinces. Sometimes it even expelled magistrates and other local officials from governmental offices. *Kabo yangnyyŏk*, 65.

14. Despite some evidence supporting the existence of class struggle during the movement, it is still doubtful whether this can be conceptualized as a genuine class struggle. Even when the peasant army attacked landlords and wealthy peasants, it did so mainly to gather resources for the wars against the government and the Japanese Army. *Chŏn Pongjun kongch'o*, 1894/1974: 149.

15. Im Kyŏngsŏk, "1910-nyŏndae kyegŭp," 222.

16. It is difficult to determine what proportion of land was confiscated and illegally transferred in the land survey. Unlike the time-honored argument that the Government-General confiscated almost 40 percent of the total land in Korea. Sin Yongha, *Chosŏn t'oji chosa*. Recent studies have revealed that the proportion is almost negligible. Cho Sŏkkon, "T'oji chosa saŏp kwa." Though the validity of each standpoint requires further investigation, it seems that if the confiscation took place on such a phenomenal scale, we would naturally expect general uprisings by the peasantry and landlords. This expectation was not in actuality fulfilled. Edwin H. Gragert, *Landownership under Colonial Rule*.

17. Gi-Wook Shin, *Peasant Protest and Social Change in Colonial Korea*.

18. Asada Kyoji, "Hang-Il nongmin undong," 52.

19. The decline in the number of participants per tenancy dispute in the mid-1920s is somewhat deceptive and requires careful interpretation. Most studies on the subject utilize statistical data published by the Government-General Bureau of Agriculture and Forestry and argue for the decline in the occurrence of peasant protests. Data from the Bureau of Police, however, suggested that the number did not decrease substantively until the 1930s. Chōsen Sōtokufu Keimukyoku, *Saikin ni okeru Chōsen chian jōkyō*, 1933 and 1938: 157–58. One possible explanation for this divergence between the two sets of data is that the latter mainly included the larger disputes while the former encompassed almost all disputes no matter the size. If this is the case, we can guess that the scale of the large disputes did not decrease until the 1930s.

20. Chōsen Sōtokufu, Nōrinkyoku, *Chōsen nōchi nenpō*, 1940: 6.

21. Ibid., 26, 33.

22. Ōwa Kazuaki, "1920-nendai," 22.

23. Gi-Wook Shin, *Peasant Protest and Social Change*.

24. Chōsen Sōtokufu, *Chōsen no gunshū*, 1926: 21–24.

25. Another piece of evidence that seemingly testifies to the peasant movement's adoption of an offensive stance is the case of Amt'aedo, where peasants refused to accept the 40 percent rent reduction offered by the landlords while asking for a further reduction to 30 percent of the total. Chōsen sōtokufu, *Chōsen no gunshū*, 1926: 33–35. The crop both sides were feuding about was, however, barley, not rice, which was considered the secondary cereal necessary for the subsistence of poor peasants. This dispute shows that the demand for rent reduction was not always related to the offensive stance taken by wealthy peasants.

26. Chōsen Sōtokufu, *Chōsen no gunshū*, 1926: 8, 19.

27. Abundant studies maintain this standpoint, the most representative of which are Cho Tonggŏl, *Ilcheha Han'guk nongmin*; Chu Ponggyu, *Ilcheha nongmin kyŏngjesa*; and Asada Kyoji "Hangil nongmin undong."

28. Ōwa Kazuaki, "1920-nendai," 19–22.

29. T'akchibu, *Toji chosa ch'amgosŏ*, 1–3.

30. Yi Yŏnghun, "T'oji chosa saŏp ŭi sut'alsŏng kŏmt'o."

31. Ch'oe Wŏn'gyu, "Hanmal Ilche ch'ogi," 362

32. Peasants sometimes dared to falsely register as tenants of royal palaces to avoid excessively high land taxes, while trying to keep their own land ownership. In this case, the peasants were burdened only with the duty of paying rent to the palaces, since the latter were exempt from the government taxes.

33. Chōsen Sōtokufu, *Chōsen no kosaku kankō*, 1930, vol. 1: 117–21.

34. This does not mean, however, that the tenancy contract had a fully modern form, since most rent was still paid in kind, not in cash, and more contracts were conducted orally than by written document. Chōsen Sōtokufu, *Chōsen no kosaku kankō*, 1930, vol. 1: 117, 405–6.

35. Cho Sŏkkon, "Sut'allon kwa kŭndaehwaron ŭl nŏmŏsŏ."

36. The tax base increase was substantial. In 1918, after the land survey had been completed, the taxable land size reached 4.23 million *chŏngbo*, an almost 80 percent increase over that of 1910 when Korea was colonized. Wada Ichiro, *Chōsen tochi chizei seido*.

37. One *kyŏl* as a unit of the amount of crop is equivalent to 100 *bu*, which is literally translated into the amount of rice 100 adult males could carry on their back. One *kyŏl* as a unit of land size differed according to the quality of the land. In the case of the highest-quality lands, one *kyŏl* of land was about 100 *are*, or 4,047 acres in Western measurement.

38. Dong-no Kim, "Peasants, States, and Landlords," 82.

39. Pae Yŏngsun, "Hanmal Ilche ch'ogi," 210.

40. Max Weber, *The Protestant Ethic*, Introduction.

41. The tendency to share power between the local officials and *sajok* was strengthened when the latter solidified their power base by forming consanguineous villages (*tongjok purak*) as an extension of their estates. Ko Sŭngje, "Kŭnse hyangch'on chedo," 10.

42. Michael Mann, "The Autonomous Power of the State," 113, distinguishes two dimensions of state power: despotic and infrastructural. The despotic power of the state concerns the range of actions that the state elite is empowered to undertake without routine and institutionalized negotiation with civil society, while infrastructural power is defined as the state's capacity to penetrate civil society, and implement logistically political decisions throughout the realm. Modern states mainly rely upon infrastructural power through their enhanced capacity to control social infrastructures, especially information gathering and processing capability.

43. Ch'oe Wŏn'gyu, "Hanmal Ilche ch'ogi t'oji chosa," 359. One unfortunate consequence of this change in local administration was that it terminated the mutual relationships of the village. In the past, the common property of the village had been used for the village events, such as village festivals, and to help the poorest village members. Dong-no Kim, "Peasants, States, and Landlords," 73. The confiscation of the village rice paddy by the official administrative apparatus critically weakened these projects.

44. Yi Yŏnghun, "T'oji chosa saŏp ŭi sut'alsŏng kŏmt'o"; Cho Sŏkkon, "Sut'allon kwa kŭndaehwaron ŭl nŏmŏsŏ"; and Enuma Jiroy, "Ilcheha Chosŏn ŭi nongŏp hyŏngmyŏng."

45. Chōsen Sōtokufu, Nōrinkyoku, *Chōsen nōchi nenpō*, 1940: 149.

46. Chōsen Sōtokufu, *Chōsen no kosaku kanshū*, 1929: 32, 38.

47. Barrington Moore Jr., *Social Origins of Dictatorship and Democracy*; Eric Wolf, *Peasant Wars of Twentieth Century*.

48. The exports of crops and the subsequent commercialization of agriculture began before Korea was colonized. This tendency, however, accelerated at a much higher rate after colonization. For instance, in 1910, only 4.7 percent of the total rice produced in Korea was exported to Japan; the rate had reached nearly 20 percent a decade later. Im Kyŏng sŏk, "1910 nyŏndae kyegŭp kusŏng," 186–87.

49. Hori Kazuo, "Ilbon chegukchuŭi ŭi Chosŏn," 248.

50. Chōsen Sōtokufu, *Chōsen no gunshū*, 1926: 10.

51. Kim Tohyŏng, "Ilche ŭi nongŏp kisul pogŭp," 445, 453.

52. Landlords became so sensitive to economic interests that one report on the customs of the tenancy system of the time termed them the "utilitarian type of land-lord." Chōsen Sōtokufu, *Chōsen no kosaku kankō*, 1930 vol. 1: 86; vol. 2: 21.

53. Chōsen Sōtokufu, Keimukyoku, *Saikin ni okeru Chōsen chian jōkyō*, 1933, 1938: 156.

54. Chōsen Sōtokufu, *Chōsen no kosaku kankō*, 1930, vol. 2: 113.

55. Asada Kyoyi, "Hang-Il nongmin undong," 19.

56. Chōsen Sōtokufu, Keimukyoku, *Saikin ni okeru Chōsen chian jōkyō*, 1933, 1938: 168.

57. Chōsen Sōtokufu, Keimukyoku, *Saikin ni okeru Chōsen chian jōkyō*, 1933, 1938: 6, 49.

58. Chōsen Sōtokufu, *Chōsen no gunshū*, 1926: 26–30.

59. Hori Kazuo, "Ilbon chegukchuŭi ŭi Chosŏn," 212.

60. The usefulness of the landlord associations to the colonial government was predominantly economic, since the latter utilized the former for the increase of agricultural productivity by obliging it to disseminate new technologies. This does not negate the possibility that the state also kept in mind the political motive of indirect control of the colonized people through these organizations. See Chōsen Sōtokufu, *Chōsen no gunshū*, 1926: 15.

61. Pae Yŏngsun, "Hanmal Ilche ch'ogi ŭi," 198.

5

The 1920 Colonial Reforms
and the June 10 (1926) Movement:
A Korean Search for Ethnic Space[1]

MARK E. CAPRIO

On April 26, 1926 Sunjong (1873–1926), the last emperor of the long Chosŏn Dynasty (1392–1910), quietly passed away at the age of fifty-three. He had served three years as emperor (1907–10) and sixteen years as "king" following his demotion by the Japanese colonial authorities in 1910. The Japanese colonial government quickly announced June 10 as the day that the ex-monarch would receive his state funeral. The Korean peninsula entered into a state of mourning and began preparing for what many anticipated would be Korea's last opportunity to host such an event. Sunjong's death presented opportunities, as well. Anti-Japanese elements saw the funeral as another opportunity to rally the Korean people and to demonstrate their aversion to Japanese colonial rule. Japanese colonial officials viewed the occasion as an opportunity to assess the progress made by Japan's colonial administration, particularly the state of Korean national sentiment.

June 10 arrived, and Sunjong received a sendoff that befitted his royal status. But little else of note occurred on this day. Compared to the events that surrounded his father's funeral seven years previous, far fewer Koreans managed to get arrested, much less tortured or killed by Japanese authorities. Efficient control of organized leftist groups left the student groups with the task of carrying out Korean independence activities on June 10. Consequently, students comprised the greater part of those arrested on that day. The colonial police released the majority of these Koreans by the end of the day, many without receiving indictments. Compared to the attention that the 1919 March First Independence movement received, June 10, 1926 passed into history relatively unnoticed.

The significance of the June 10 movement (*yuk sip manse undong*) grows when examined as a part of the larger interaction between the Japanese administration and the Korean nationalist movement over the 1920s. The period between Sunjong's death and funeral provided both sides with the opportunity to test the new colonial spatial lines drawn in the aftermath of the 1919 March First Independence movement. Administrative reforms established in the wake of the Japanese mishandling of the demonstrations sought to co-opt the Korean nationalist movement by extending the space in which it could operate. Members of this movement used the opportunity to spread cultural awareness among the Korean people. Sunjong's death offered both sides the chance to assess, challenge, and possibly redraw the spatial boundaries that the reforms set.

COLONIAL SPACE AND KOREAN INDEPENDENCE MOVEMENTS

The legacies of independence movements and insurrections are primarily remembered by numbers: the greater the number of participants, the more forceful the reaction by the oppressor; the bloodier the result, the greater the legacy. A strong counterforce demonstrated by the hegemonic power generally is a response to the subjugated people crossing "red lines" that challenge its legitimacy. Once ended, both sides reassess their use of this space and make adjustments.

Korea's first organized declaration of its dissatisfaction over Japanese rule, the 1919 March First Independence movement, demonstrated a clash in colonial space: the Korean people attempted to extend their limited space by drafting a peaceful statement of independence. Later, they challenged Japanese space by first refusing to disburse and then by violently confronting the Japanese gendarmerie and police units. The Japanese, for their part, tried to contain this threat to their space but also attempted to roll it back by use of excessive force directed at what they perceived to be its roots. The needless casualties that this force produced brought unwanted international criticism of Japanese administration of the Korean peninsula. It gained the Korean independence movement a brief windfall of international attention to their plight.[2]

These unfortunate results forced both sides to renegotiate their colonial space. The Japanese learned that use of violent confrontation against their colonial charges encouraged criticism from colonial contemporaries and strengthened Korean resistance. Redefining its colonial mission in cultural terms, with emphasis placed on control through education rather than military force, appeased overseas critics and co-opted colonial opposition. By offering the Korean people the opportunity to experience culture on their own terms—that is, as Koreans through their indigenous language—the colonial government first revealed its understanding of the limits of assimilation. At the same time the Japanese government suggested arrogant confidence that the Korean people would eventually choose the Japanese culture once they realized its superiority over the weaker Korean culture.

The domestic Korean independence movement recognized that direct confrontation would neither drive the Japanese from the peninsula nor encourage foreign governments to come to the colonized people's aid. Korean survival demanded a much more prudent exploitation of colonial space: using it to strengthen the people's sense of Korean-ness rather than confront the Japanese physically. It soon became evident that extending colonial space beyond these parameters would only be possible through subtle and gradual efforts. More radical efforts could only thrive abroad.

Sunjong's death and state funeral tested the commitment of both sides to maintain this space and exercise restraint should their space be infringed upon. Their success contributed to the relatively peaceful sendoff that the former emperor received, and consequently to the relative inattention that history has afforded the June 10 Independence movement. What little attention it does receive generally emphasizes the repressive efforts by colonial authorities to block planned anti-Japanese demonstrations, or its role in encouraging student and communist resistance movements.

One of the first "histories" to cover Sunjong's state funeral, the *Secret History of the Yi Royal Palace* (*Yi ōkyū hishi*), was published just over two months after the event. The short passage devoted to this day credited lessons learned by the Japanese from the previous state funeral as a way to nurture the "relative satisfaction felt in the [Korean] people's hearts."[3] Japanese authorities later considered the funeral in a different light. A 1932 Government-General police report included the June 10 incident on its short list of "significant disturbance incidents" (*jūdai sōjō jiken*) that followed the 1919 March First movement. It undervalued Korean participation, noting that but one hundred Koreans participated (as opposed to 500,000 Koreans in the 1919 disturbance). A scribbled four-line summary of the incident charged students with "distributing a disturbance agitation manifesto" (*sōjō sendō gekibun*) and occasionally shouting "Independence forever!" (*tongnip manse*).[4]

Post-liberation histories of the Korean independence movement have provided more depth into the movement's plan and added more detail to the events that transpired on the day. The volume of information, however, hardly approaches that available for other movements. Commentary on the 6–10 movement considers who to blame for the event's relative insignificance and argues the event's place in the Korean people's anti-Japanese resistance movement.

Ki-baik Lee credits Japanese vigilance for the movement's relative insignificance. The Japanese were "mindful of their earlier [1919] experience . . . [and] maintained the strictest vigilance and discovered what was underway before the funeral."[5] Woo-keun Han deems the efforts a "failure" because the Japanese were able to stop it from spreading.[6] One recent account contained in a document titled "Kim Il Sung Memoirs" accuses "factionalists within the Korean Communist Party" for disrupting Korean efforts by leaking plans for the mass demonstrations to the Japanese police.[7]

More useful accounts attempt to place the June 10 movement within the context of the Korean anti-Japanese resistance movement. Kim Hoil considers the role that the Korean student movement played, linking their participation in the movement to the two most popular uprisings of this period, the 1919 March First Independence movement and the 1929 Kwangju student uprising. For this reason he considers the 1920s the "student's decade."[8] The influence that student participation had on future anti-Japanese activity is also noted in a contemporary Korean history association (Han'guk Kǔnhyǒndae Sahakhoe) publication, which noted that the 6–10 movement gave the students valuable organizational experience.[9] Yun Sǒksu acknowledges the students' contribution but laments that efforts put forth by Korean communist groups have not been given due credit. Party shortcomings and Japanese oppression limited the scope of the movement, yet at the same time the "revolutionary fever demonstrated by Koreans at this time fertilized subsequent people's liberation movements."[10] One discussion on independence movement history notes that the efforts of participating groups to unify right- and left-winged ideological factions proved useful in forming the Sin'ganhoe (New Shoot Society), a united front organization that emerged in February 1927.[11]

The efforts put forth by leftist elements have encouraged North Korean interpretations that acknowledge the incident's contribution to development of the Korean Communist movement. One North Korean history text places the event within the context of the liberation struggles being organized by oppressed peoples throughout the world. Korean participation took the form of labor strikes, sharecropper disputes, and other forms of civil disobedience. It was within this context that the 6–10 *manse* demonstration struggle erupted.[12] The *Nodong sinmun* in June 2001 used the occasion of the seventy-fifth anniversary of the "June 10 anti-Japanese demonstration" to remind its readers of the role that the Japanese reactionaries, along with the United States imperialists, and South Korean "military warmongers play in preventing the "aspiration of the . . . demonstrators" from being "realized on a nation-wide scale."[13]

The June 10 Manse Movement

Newspaper articles and government reports help us piece together the events that occurred between Sunjong's April 26 death and his June 10 funeral. The ex-emperor's health, which had never been good, began to seriously deteriorate on January 11, 1926. Three months later, on April 6, newspapers announced that his health had taken a decisive turn for the worse (*goyōtai kyūhen*). The *Tōkyō asahi shinbun* began to report, in detail, the changes in the ex-monarch's vital signs—his body temperature, his pulse and breathing rates, and his urine output. Sunjong, the daily continued, suffered from inflammation in his legs and irregular sleeping patterns. Anasarca (*mukumi*) had also spread through his body.[14] At this time the Government-General thought his condition to be serious enough to summon his brother, Prince Ŭn, then residing in Japan.[15]

Sunjong's condition fluctuated over the next few days. On April 7, the media reported that the previous day had seen his condition improve slightly, enough for him to enjoy a mid-day meal. Three days later, however, his condition again took a turn for the worse. After a few days, as the former monarch fell into a coma, the Japanese emperor and empress displayed their concern by sending an imperial grant of plum wine as a statement of their sympathy (*omimai toshite umeshū wo gokashi araserareta*).[16] The next day his condition was pronounced "hopeless" (*gozetsubō*) and even his physician, Dr. Ikeda, prepared to return to Japan.[17] Sunjong lingered for another two weeks before he finally succumbed on April 26, 1926.

Preparations for Sunjong's funeral and succession began almost immediately. Short articles that straddled the former emperor's death notice and picture (in full military regalia) in the Tōkyō asahi shinbun reported that the Japanese emperor had sent a telegram of condolences. It also announced that a special cabinet meeting had been called to decide the funeral procedures. Just below this announcement rested a third headline that proclaimed Prince Ŭn, Sunjong's crown prince, as his brother's successor (gokeishō).[18]

The Japanese cabinet convened the next day and decided that Sunjong would be given a state funeral (kokusō), and that Vice Governor-General Yuasa Kurahei would head the funeral committee.[19] Also on this day the prince regent (the future Showa Emperor) announced that he had cancelled his birthday celebrations planned for the next day. Newspapers also reported that the Japanese government planned to convey Sunjong with the insignia of field marshal posthumously.[20] Finally, on April 29, 1926, the media relayed the news that the Japanese government would contribute 140,000 yen and an Imperial Guard of Honor to Sunjong's state funeral.[21]

The Japanese media also noted signs for concern. Directly below the Tōkyō asahi shinbun's reportage of the cabinet's decisions, the newspaper reported an increasing number of Koreans assembling in front of Ch'angdŏk Palace, and that their wailing, "Aigo!" was growing increasingly louder. This same newspaper afforded valuable front-page space to a story titled "Koreatown at Night" (Yoru no senjin machi), which reported that despite the presence of over 300 police and firemen, Japanese residents were still being harassed along Bell Street (Chŏngno). One man was even ordered to "take off his glasses" by confrontational Koreans.[22] The Japan Times noted that the Japanese police were finding it "difficult keeping order as a number of unruly Koreans attempted to agitate the crowd."[23]

The relationship between the Japanese and Koreans, normally distant, endured a heightened tension over the forty-five days that separated Sunjong's death and state funeral. A report issued by the Japanese Police Bureau's library division (Keimukyoku toshoka) later that year outlined numerous incidents of confrontation initiated by Koreans angered over Japanese insensitivities to their grief. Many Koreans complained of the strict tactics employed by Japanese police to control the crowds. Other complaints centered on the business-as-usual attitude adopted by Japanese entrepreneurs. In schools, disputes arose among faculty members over the actions they should take—whether to allow time for prayer or even to close the school in the deceased ex-emperor's honor. Korean newspapers, this report concluded, took advantage of these incidents to raise the national consciousness of the Korean people.[24]

Incidents of civil disobedience by Korean students occurred in schools throughout the peninsula over the period leading up to the state funeral. The report detailed one of the disturbances that took place at Unggi Public Common (elementary) School (*Kōritsu futsū gakkō*). Here a confrontation between faculty and students broke out on April 30 when fifth and sixth grade students, angered over the school's neglect to even mention the former monarch's death, refused to sing at the regular morning assembly. The teacher's unsympathetic response to their insubordination only exasperated the problem. One group of students confronted a teacher in class for insulting them. They were promptly marched before the school principal who apologized to the students for his oversight. His confession only agitated the "naiveté emotions" (*junshin nara kanjō*) of these "infantile" (*osanai*) students who proceeded to interrogate the school head. They reminded him that he had surely remembered to announce the birth of the crown prince's first child and had even honored the occasion by canceling classes for the day.[25]

Incidents also took place in places where Koreans gathered to mourn. The report described an altercation between police and mourners that took place in the vicinity of the Gate of Kindness (*Tonhwamun*) and the Golden Tiger Gate (*Kŭmbŏmmun*) in detail. Drawing from the Korean language *Sidae ilbo* (Times daily) report, it provided as backdrop for this incident, the scene of tens of thousands of Koreans gathered to mourn Sunjong's death. The sight of so many people laying prostrate on the ground and shedding tears caused even soldiers stationed at this post to "cry into their uniform sleeves." Suddenly, horseback and foot patrolmen arrived to drive the people off, horses kicking at them as they scattered. The police answered any resistance with violence, the newspaper reported.

Another incident involved a Japanese expatriate, Nakai Kamekichi, who ran a camera store. Angered at the proprietor's apparent lack of respect, a group of Koreans surrounded him and trampled on his cameras. The mob called for the disrespectful man's head. The police, however, made no attempts to arrest those who assaulted the cameraman. They simply dispersed the crowd so as not to cause further agitation.[26]

These events demonstrate the Japanese authorities exercising select cau-
tion in their handling of the situation. Their actions toward the Korean
people generally remained prudent, and on occasion (such as the Nakai
incident) temporarily expanded Korean space to allow them to express their
grief. This space was by no means infinite; the authorities often moved to
contain crowds that they felt to be out of hand. Thus, while the administration allowed Korean students extra space to confront school officials or
proprietors; it drew the line when Korean activities threatened to physically
harm Japanese nationals.

The Government-General began to tighten this space as the day of the
state funeral drew near. On June 7, 1926, just days before the funeral was to
take place, Japanese police uncovered a "communist plot" planning to launch
a "revolution" on June 10. Newspapers implicated the Women's Labor Union
as an accomplice. In Seoul alone 300 Koreans were arrested. The Japan Times
crowed, "authorities had nipped in the bud a revolutionary plot to overthrow
the government and establish communist rule in Chŏsen." This newspaper
also reported a police raid on a Ch'ŏndogyo (heavenly way) meeting.[27] It
continued to report on this crackdown the next day adding that police had
spread their investigations into the Korean schools where they maintained
strict vigilance over the students and searched their dormitories.[28]

The Government-General took additional precautions to ensure against
Korean unrest on the day of the funeral. It dispatched seven thousand military
(both army and naval) personnel to Seoul and situated others in Pusan,
Inch'ŏn, and the northern cities of P'yŏngyang, Hamhŭng, and Wŏnsan. The
administration also limited Korean access to the capital. Kim Hoil estimates
that twenty-eight thousand Koreans had their movements restricted by
Japanese authorities.[29] Police and soldiers mobilized throughout Seoul from
the morning of the funeral's eve, particularly concentrating their efforts along
the route that the procession carrying Sunjong was to pass.[30]

The Japanese matched their visible displays of force with soft demonstrations of respectful condolence appropriate for this solemn occasion. The
Government-General authorizing that Sunjong would receive a Korean-style
funeral reflected a lesson learned from the time of Kojong's death, whom they
buried Japanese style. Directives drawn up for the ceremony designated it
appropriate for the Korean people to dress in their traditional white garb and
the Japanese in their customary black clothing. The Japanese administration

used its media to publicize its sympathy. The June issue of the government monthly journal *Chōsen*, distributed to both Japanese and Korean governmental employees, opened with a series of pictures depicting Governor-General Saitō Makoto in proper attire making his way to the palace to pay his respects. Three more pictures displayed different angles of the "Korean bell" that was to be displayed at Toshōkan in Nikko, the burial grounds of Tokugawa shoguns.

Sunjong's death and funeral also provided the media with the opportunity to advertise Japan's assimilation ambitions. The Japanese government established Zojoji Temple in Tokyo as the place for Japanese and expatriate Koreans to pay their respects to Korea's last emperor from afar.[31] A picture of people climbing the temple steps, with a caption informing readers that Japanese and Koreans were joining together in prayer, appeared in the *Japan Times*.[32] The *Tōkyō asahi shinbun* bannered its coverage of Sunjong's funeral with the headline "Japanese and Koreans united in grief" (*Naisen hitoshiku awareshimi wo wakatsu*). The newspaper emphasized this union by arranging pictures of Koreans and Japanese participating in ceremonies held both in the homeland and colonial capital. These reports were silent on the disturbances that took place over this time. Yun Sŏksu, whose work details the communist role in this movement, describes Sunjong's funeral procession as a series of "struggles" that passed through Chŏngno and into other parts of the city. One struggle became so intense that a wall of one school collapsed, killing and injuring a number of Koreans. Yun calculates that over 160 people were seriously hurt "by violent acts of the barbarous Japanese," and hundreds more were detained or arrested by the Japanese police.[33] The *Hanminjok tongnip undongsa* (History of the Independence movement of the Korean nation) provides a timetable of the events of this day beginning with fifty students who yelled, "*manse!*" at 8:25 a.m. in the vicinity of Kwansu Common School. This history text estimates that the Japanese arrested over one thousand two hundred Koreans, the majority of which one thousand were outside the capital.[34]

The trial records of thirteen Koreans are instructive as to the anti-Japanese activities that took place on June 10, but also of the control measures that the Japanese installed after 1919 to deal with social disturbance. The charges that Japanese authorities levied against these Koreans fell into three categories: secretly printing and distributing inflammatory pamphlets, distributing Korean national flags, and yelling Korean independence slogans. The court found ten of the defendants guilty of violating Government Ordinance Seven (*seirei*), enacted in 1919, and the Government-General's Publication Act (*insatsuhō*). One participant, Yu Myŏnhŭi, was found in violation of only Government Ordinance Seven. He and the nine others received five-year sentences. One student, Pak Hagyŭn, was sentenced to sixty days in jail and released for time spent awaiting trial. The others received suspended sentences, although the courts ordered the pamphlets, equipment used to print the pamphlets, and the Korean flags confiscated, as required by the Peace Preservation Law (*chian iji hō*) enacted in 1925.[35]

The numbers of Korean participants, Koreans arrested, and Korean casualties during the June 10 Independence movement paled in the shadows of those incurred during the March First movement. During the March First movement, close to twenty thousand Koreans were arrested, an event which saw (according to police estimates) 1,962 Koreans either injured or killed.[36] The Japanese refrained from attacking perceived nerve centers of anti-Japanese groups such as churches. Their relatively prudent response helped contain the duration of this movement to a few days. This containment may have perhaps been due also to a more vigilant and prepared Japanese police force, but also to the fact that the leftist elements who assumed control over the preparations had long been on the Japanese radar, particularly after the Government-General enacted peace preservation legislation the previous year. The Korean people, aware of the limited chance of success, from the March First movement experience, were more reluctant to take to the streets to demand their independence from a Japanese administration that was not ready to retreat any time soon.

Instead, Koreans searched for alternative means to disseminate and strengthen a sense of national cultural consciousness among the people. These efforts fragmented over the question of intensity and means: should Koreans demand immediate independence or prepare for future sovereignty? Should they fight for this privilege or seek assistance abroad? A gradual nationalist movement believed that Koreans could gain their independence and maintain their sovereignty only by strengthening their consciousness of Korean culture, by proving themselves worthy of these rights. Efforts that it made to strengthen Korean cultural awareness were assisted by a growing print culture that devoted its pages to advertising Korean history, championing its heroes, and advising efforts made to improve the quality and health of people's livelihoods. In this sense, this cultural nationalist movement exploited to a greater extent than other national movements, the post-March First cultural rule advances made by the Japanese administration.[37]

SUNJONG, KOREA'S LAST EMPEROR

One of the characteristics that united the Korean reform movements of the late nineteenth century was the determination to reform the throne, rather than form a new dynasty. The Independence Club, Korea's most ambitious reform movement, never put forth reform proposals demanding that King Kojong relinquish his throne. To the contrary, they joined others in urging the monarch to strengthen the throne by declaring himself emperor.[38] In doing so he became the Kwangmu Emperor. This is not to say that the king/emperor was popular among Independence Club members. Indeed, many came to loathe him. Yet, unlike the Japanese who could "restore" their emperor and focus the reforms needed to modernize their country, the Korean government had no legitimate figure to replace their king. The Japanese resident-general attempted to rally the Korean people behind Kojong's feeble-minded son, Sunjong, who succeeded his father as the Yunghŭi Emperor. The failure of this experiment expedited Japan's absorption of the Korean peninsula.[39]

Part of the reason for the less than enthusiastic response to efforts by the June 10 movement's participants may have been the Korean people's less than enthusiastic impression of Sunjong himself. Those who attended his funeral felt greater pity than reverence toward the former emperor. For many, the royal remains that passed along the parade route represented the end of the Chosŏn Dynasty rather than the end of a man's life.[40] Sunjong was, after all, the only surviving son of King Kojong and Queen Min. His younger brother, Prince Ŭn, whom the Japanese initially named as his successor, was the son of one of Queen Min's former ladies-in-waiting, Lady Ŏm. This would not have prevented Ŭn from assuming the Korean throne.[41] More likely, the Japanese government believed they had little to gain by handing Sunjong's position to someone who spent more time among the Japanese—he was also married to a Japanese princess—than his fellow Koreans.

Sunjong's enthronement by the Japanese and his suspected ties with the colonial administration would later cause some Koreans to see him as a traitor.[42] The Japanese placed him on the throne after the Resident-General Itō Hirobumi forced his father to abdicate in 1907—after Itō learned that Kojong had organized a secret mission to The Hague to enlist international sympathy for Korea's plight. The resident-general exploited this opportunity to force upon the Korean government yet another treaty that extended Japanese administrative control over Korea's domestic affairs.[43]

Sunjong's short life was neither happy nor healthy. In 1895 he witnessed the Japanese murder his mother, Queen Min. His sister-in-law, Nashimoto Masako (Korean name Yi Pangja), who was married to his half-brother Prince Ŭn, wrote that during Sunjong's childhood an attempt was made to poison the young prince. This left the boy physically and mentally challenged. His weak physical state also left him impotent and thus unable to produce an heir to the throne.[44]

Soon after his father's abdication, the Japanese authorities began using Sunjong as a symbol of the new Korea and of Japanese-Korean integration. They first displayed him as a modern monarch by cutting his traditional Korean topknot as a symbol of his modern transformation. His alleged compliance set an example for his subjects to follow. F. A. McKenzie, a British reporter in Seoul, recalled:

> On the abdication of the old Emperor, the Cabinet—who were enthusiastic haircutters—saw their opportunity. The new Emperor was informed that his hair must be cut. He did not like it. He thought that the operation would be painful, and he was quite satisfied with his hair as it was. Then his Cabinet showed him a brilliant uniform, covered with gold lace. He was henceforth to wear this on ceremonial occasions, and not his old Korean dress. How could he put on the plumed hat of the Generalissimo with a topknot in the way? . . . A few hours later a proclamation was spread through the land informing all dutiful subjects that the Emperor's topknot was coming off and urging them to imitate him.[45]

Sunjong's coronation began soon after he parted with his topknot. This ceremony also was choreographed to symbolize Korea's transition from tradition to modernity. The new emperor first entered the hall in imperial court dress accompanied by Korean court music; after a brief intermission he returned dressed in modern military uniform to the tune of European marching music. McKenzie described Sunjong's expression as vacant, rather than bored.[46]

The Japanese display of the Korean emperor was intended both for Western observers and his Korean subjects. Their displaying the power to replace Korean emperors demonstrated to other colonizing powers the extent of their authority on the peninsula, a litmus test for the degree to which Japanese civilization had developed. Itō would discover later the extent to which this message failed to gain Korean attention. Many Koreans were not prepared to accept as legitimate this attempt by the Japanese to exercise their authority over Korean royalty.

In early 1909, Itō Hirobumi escorted Sunjong on two imperial processions that brought the emperor first through southern Korea and then up into northern Korea. By leading Sunjong around his empire, the resident-general hoped to demonstrate Japan-Korea goodwill and to tame the righteous army attacks.[47] Hamada Kenji has suggested that Itō's positive experiences during the southern trip encouraged him to plan the northern trip. The disappointing trip to the north convinced the resident-general that only annexation could save Korea.[48] Soon after he resigned his post and finally agreed to support annexation.

Recent research casts doubt on this interpretation. Christine Kim demonstrates that Itō experienced anti-Japanese behavior during both trips. In the south, rumors that the Japanese planned to kidnap the emperor caused Koreans to surround the Japanese warship that the emperor had boarded with a flotilla of fishing vessels. Similarly, in Mokp'o, Koreans laid themselves on the railroad tracks to impede the train's departure. These fears were no doubt fueled by past Japanese behavior. After all, it had been Itō who had taken Crown Prince Ŭn to Japan as a child to attend Japanese schools. In the north, Koreans greeted the procession by waving Korean national flags, while they trampled over Japanese hi no maru (rising sun) flags that lay scattered on the ground. In Ŭiju, Koreans attacked one of the factories that produced Japanese flags.[49] A number of Korean men did emulate their emperor by cutting off their topknots, a point frequently mentioned in the official reports of the trip.[50] Yet there was little room for pride in seeing their feeble monarch escorted by the Japanese resident-general as he made his way around the Korean peninsula.

The Japanese government finalized their decision to annex Korea soon after Itō returned to Tokyo.[51] On August 22, 1910, the Japanese imposed the Treaty of Korea-Japan Annexation (Nikkan heigō jōyaku) on the Korean government. Again the Japanese government required Sunjong's display of acquiescence to demonstrate Korea's acceptance of this development. Issues of Korean, English, and Japanese newspapers that announced annexation carried Sunjong's last imperial edict (J. *shōchoku*, K. *choch'ik*). Here the deposed monarch explained his decision to place Korea's future in Japan's hands.

> We have done all in Our power to improve the system of government and to promote the welfare of the people since We succeeded to the throne. We have long been in delicate health, and Our condition has now become incurable to Our great sorrow. We are afraid that We may not be able to discharge Our great task. We thought it better therefore to entrust the great task to other hands with a view to perfect the system of government and to carry out reforms. We have, therefore, decided to cede the sovereignty of Korea to H. M. the Emperor of Japan, whose cordial friendship We have long enjoyed, in the hope that the peace in the Extreme East will be assured and that the masses of the country will be fully protected.[52]

He then called upon his subjects, both "high and low," to "solely depend upon the civilization and the new government of the Japanese Empire, which is fully realizing the conditions of things and the world progress."[53]

The Japanese enlisted Sunjong's cooperation even after annexation. His name continued to find its way into the Seoul newspapers, particularly over the first few months following annexation. These newspapers carried updates on how Sunjong and his wife coped with the new circumstances. The reoccurring theme that these stories emphasized was that the royal couple had made the transition to Japanese lifestyle rather smoothly. Both Korean and Japanese newspapers depicted the couple as enjoying congenial relations with Governor-General Terauchi Masatake and his wife. Sunjong made courtesy calls on the Government-General offices to thank the governor-general for his efforts; the ladies got together for tea parties.[54] Depictions of the Meiji Emperor's relationship with Korea often took the form of his imperial friendship with Sunjong, as advertised by letters and gifts that the emperor sent to the Korean court. One postcard featured the Japanese emperor gazing down upon Sunjong.[55] Sunjong, for his part, was depicted as displaying the utmost respect toward the Meiji Emperor. During the Meiji Emperor's last days in July 1912, the *Maeil sinbo* used Sunjong's appropriate behavior as an example for all Koreans to follow. On July 25, the newspaper announced that Sunjong had decided to voluntarily abstain from unspecified Korean and Western leisure activities that he normally enjoyed. Five days later the newspaper reported that Sunjong passed the time waiting for the latest reports on the emperor's condition; at times he angrily demanded information when it was not forthcoming. The former monarch, the *Maeil sinbo* informed, spent every waking hour praying for the emperor's recovery.

Newspaper reports on Sunjong's daily life described him and his wife as cooperative. The media also wrote on the positive attitudes that the royal couple held toward making the transition to Japanese culture. These articles appeared in the English *Seoul Press* and targeted the peninsula's Western population. One such article, titled "Daily Life of Prince and Princess Yi,"[56] described the royal couple's life as one in transition. Both had adopted the custom of bathing daily and maintained frugal lifestyles. It also noted that "Prince Yi generally wears informal Korean clothes . . . Princess Yi devotes herself very diligently to the study of Japanese [and] is now able to speak Japanese very fluently."[57]

As in the case of the Japanese imperial family, Sunjong also had decisions made and monies donated in his name. This was the case of the heavily reported Korea aristocrat tour that left for Japan in October 1910 and arrived in Tokyo just in time to celebrate the Japanese emperor's birthday on November 3. Sunjong first approved the tour's list of participants. Min Chŏngsik's participation required special handling due to his having participated in anti-Japanese insurrections. But Sunjong gave him his blessing upon hearing of Min's desire to "see the land of his erstwhile enemies," the newspaper reported.[58] The *Maeil sinbo* noted that Sunjong also helped finance the tour by making a 5,000 yen donation.[59]

The Japanese continued to exploit the Korean royal family as Sunjong's health turned for the worst. At this time Prince Ŭn reentered the spotlight.[60] The May 1926 issue of the Government-General magazine, *Chōsen*, reported on the former crown prince's visit to his ailing brother by listing the other activities on his busy schedule: After arriving from Tokyo on April 12 at 9:00 a.m. the prince first went to pray at Chōsen jinja, the shrine that the Japanese dedicated to their most revered goddess, Amaterasu. He then had an audience with the governor-general and vice governor-general. It was not until after he had taken his midday meal in the governor-general's residence that he found time to visit Sunjong. The next day, Ŭn's busy schedule brought him to two women's schools (one Japanese and one Korean), a central testing center, and a number of other stops before he caught the 14:40 train for Inch'ŏn.[61] His next appearance in the news was a few days after the funeral when he presented himself before the Japanese emperor to thank him on behalf of the Korean people for Japan's assistance in burying his brother.

Sunjong's death also provided Governor-General Saitō Makoto with an opportunity to promote Japanese-Korean assimilation. In his eulogy Saitō emphasized his administration's efforts to unite the eighty million Japanese and Koreans who had joined together to pray for Sunjong's recovery. He then reviewed the prince's contribution to the two countries at the time of annexation. Saitō recalled:

> The Prince ascended the Korean throne in Meiji 45 [1912 (sic 1907)]. He administered benevolent rule and maintained fraternity [shinwa] with Imperial Japan for a long time. Finally, in Meiji 43 [1910], in light of the domestic and foreign situation, he arranged the tremendous plan [kobo] for Japan-Korea annexation before stepping down from the throne. His sacrifice preserved the divine millet [shinshoku], and strengthened the peaceful environment [kōhei] of the people's lives. His action also established Oriental peace [tōyō heiwa].[62]

The Japanese official's message inaccurately credited Sunjong with providing the guidance that led to his country's union with Japan.

The composite picture of Sunjong depicts a man more appropriately pitied than revered. He was hardly a figure that could rally the Korean people to demonstrate for their independence. The Japanese role in forcing Kojong's abdication and choreographing Sunjong's ascension to the throne, along with his alleged cooperation following annexation, also drew black marks against him. Rather than fight Japanese rule, he appeared to accept it. He joined the resident-general on tours across the peninsula; he wrote letters of regret and reception to departing and incoming Japanese officials; and he received a fair amount of press suggesting his eagerness to cooperate with the colonial administration. This reportage left the Korean people with little reason to consider whether Sunjong protested, or even objected to, Japanese rule, much less to judge whether he may have taken his own life (as many suspected his

father had in 1919) as a sign of protest over Japan's subjugation of his country. Thus, to many Koreans, Sunjong's death drew pity and sorrow over the
loss of an era rather than anger at the loss of their last ruler.

The Japanese administration's interest in promoting Korea's royal family
as imperial subjects apparently waned early in the period of colonial rule. Up
to his death it frequently used the media to depict Sunjong as an exemplar of
proper behavior during times of mourning or celebration. His brother Ŭn's
marriage into the Japanese imperial family personified the Japanese-Korean
relationship that the imperial government hoped to forge. The administration, while offering this family the respect they believed it was due, apparently
preferred to minimize the exposure family members received in the public
eye. Although rumors circulated toward the end of the war that the Japanese
planned to revive the Korean monarchy, Sunjong's heir apparent, Ŭn, never
received his coronation.[63]

KOREAN PREPARATION
FOR A SECOND INDEPENDENCE MOVEMENT

Koreans determined to rally the people to demonstrate their independence
focused on the opportunity presented by the event—Sunjong's state funeral—
rather than the former monarch's appropriateness as a symbol of Korean
nationalism. Original plans for the demonstrations targeted June 10 as a day
to inform the Korean people of future demonstrations, rather than the actual
day in which these activities would be carried out.[64] Organizers emphasized
two points: first, their success required coordination among a wider range of
like-minded groups, and second, the movement would have to extend its
space and incorporate more forceful measures than simply yelling "manse!" as
characterized in the previous bourgeois-directed 1919 movement.

The reforms enacted in the aftermath of the 1919 Independence movement
provided demonstration organizers in 1926 with more tools to inform the
people of the significance of Sunjong's death and to rally support. Throughout
the first half of the 1920s the Korean press developed a number of techniques
to broadcast appeals for Korean independence. They informed their readers
of contemporary independence movements, such as the activities of the Irish
and Indian liberation groups. They retold the stories of successful independence groups, such as the American efforts in the late eighteenth century.

Finally, these newspapers instructed the Korean people on ways in which they should upgrade their level of civilization to prepare for their eventual liberation. On occasion, the press boldly called for its readers to take to the streets and demand their independence. Even the Japanese recognized the effect that these newspapers had on strengthening Korean national identity, as noted in several reports that examined Korean sentiment around the time of Sunjong's death and burial. By this time the Japanese control had tightened following the enactment of peace preservation legislation in 1925. From this time Government-General censorship became more stringent.[65] In 1940, it ordered all private Korean newspapers to cease publication.

Historiography on the Korean preparation for the June 10 movement has focused attention on two groups: communists and students. Korean communists first came together outside of Korea in 1918 under the direction of Yi Tonghwi, the founder of the Korean Socialist Party. This group reorganized in August 1919 and became the Korean Communist Party (KCP) after abandoning efforts to join the Korean Provisional Government in Shanghai.[66] The Japanese administration under Saitō Makoto initially attempted to co-opt this political body following the March First movement. Through the 1925 peace preservation legislation though, the Government-General greatly curtailed KCP activities. Eventually, Japanese harassment drove KCP members from the peninsula and forced them to draw closer to Soviet and Chinese communist groups.

Soon after Sunjong's death, the KCP quickly formed a special guidance committee to plan for the June 10 movement (6–10 undong t'ujaeng chido t'ŭkpyŏlhoe). This committee, headed by Kwŏn Taehyŏng, aimed to print and distribute fifty thousand copies of their manifesto to people in fifty-eight cities throughout the peninsula.[67] This committee also aspired to organize the revolutionary elements of Korea's socialist, democratic, and religious youth groups into the Greater Korean Independence Party (Taehan Tongniptang).

The KCP completed their manifesto, Chosŏn tongnip kyŏnggo mun, on May 17, 1926 and began printing copies on machinery purchased from Japan. The contents of this document resembled similar statements made by the KCP.[68] It started with a brief statement that declared Korea's right to independence and an appeal for Koreans to join the party and participate in the efforts toward organizing a united front. The manifesto also appended a list of nineteen slogans that emphasized two sets of goals. Most immediate was Korean sovereignty—"Korea for the Koreans" and "Korean Language in Korean Schools." Prerequisite to this was the departure of the Japanese administration—"Expel the Japanese from Korean Soil" and "Abolish Japanese Colonialism." A second purpose incorporated labor reform demands—"Equal Pay for Equal Work," an "Eight-hour Work Day," and "Factory Worker Strikes."[69] These latter demands risked dissuading potential allies from participation. Not only did they stray from the primary objective—Korean independence—but these items also conflicted unnecessarily with the interests of a potential ally, Korea's entrepreneurs.

The KCP ultimately failed to create this united front. First, it developed breaks within its own ranks as one faction argued for even more violent anti-Japanese displays than had been envisioned by the organizers. Their efforts also wrought regional schisms as Seoul-based communist groups refused to join with like-minded groups in Korea's interior. Communist members of the Seoul Youth Association (Ch'ŏngnyŏnhoe), for example, refused overtures by Yi Chit'ak, an influential member of Kwŏn's guidance committee, for this very reason.[70] KCP members also failed in their efforts to enlist assistance from the more moderate nationalist groups. Kang Taryŏng, chairman of the second Communist Party, met with An Chaehong, Pak Tongwŏn, Yi Chongnon, and other cultural nationalists only to have his hopes dashed by the downfall of the reformists (kaeryangjuŭija). Yun Sŏksu notes that the KCP had better luck with religious groups: it obtained support from Ch'ŏndogyo, while other religious organizations passed information on KCP activities to the masses in the countryside.[71] However, this support fell far short of the united independence party that the KCP had hoped to establish.

Bad fortune also contributed to the failure of Kwŏn's efforts. Just days before the funeral, the Japanese police discovered copies of the KCP manifesto during a raid conducted on a Chinese currency counterfeiting organization. The uncovered document clearly revealed Kwŏn as the organization's ringleader.[72] The ensuing crackdown netted the core of the movement, including Kwŏn, who was arrested three days before the funeral was scheduled to take place. The authorities were probably well prepared to act even without this discovery. The lists of facilities to raid and the Koreans to detain had no doubt been compiled long in advance. The pamphlet provided evidence to allow Japanese authorities to justify their detainment through peace preservation legislation.

Difficulties with monitoring student groups perhaps provided Koreans with better opportunities to strategize plans made for the funeral day. Thus students comprised the majority of those arrested for activities that took place on the day of the funeral. Their efforts to galvanize Korean sentiment by distributing leaflets and yelling "*manse!*" became all the more important in light of the success that Japanese police had in suppressing adult-organized, anti-Japanese activities in advance. Without the student efforts there would have been no June 10 movement to speak of. Student political involvement had been growing from the early years of the decade: it would continue to grow to the end of the decade, exploding once again in November 1929 in Kwangju when Korean students were punished after coming to the rescue of Korean girls being harassed by Japanese students.[73]

The June 10 movement acted as a bridge to organize sporadic acts of civil disobedience into a unified effort. Plans to organize for the funeral began at the time when students heard the news of the former monarch's demise. One of the central organizing groups, the Korean Students' Scientific Research Association (Chosŏn Haksaeng Kwahak Yŏn'guhoe) learned of his death while on a spring outing. Upon returning to Seoul, forty of them met in one student's boarding house to discuss strategy. The group managed to print out ten thousand leaflets to distribute along the funeral parade route. Private school students also participated in a similar way. On the day of the funeral they distributed leaflets, yelled an occasional *manse*, and waved the forbidden Korean flag—all crimes under various acts legislated since 1919. Even though many of the students had their prison sentences suspended, they still faced disciplinary action by their schools including: suspensions, expulsions, and university admittance rejections.[74]

This short inquiry into the Korean preparation for the June 10 independence movement is informative on Korea's post-March First independence movement activity. First, the failure of the KCP to organize like-minded groups demonstrates a common fragmented characteristic of colonized societies. The Japanese authorities drew potential participants away from anti-Japanese activity by suggesting that the Japanese colonial reforms demonstrated improvement, offering hope that the Korean situation could improve even more. The colonial authorities also created splits in the Korean anti-Japanese movement by driving the more radical groups off the Korean peninsula. Providing those who stayed with a means for legal organization and publication created divisions within the anti-Japanese movement. Disagreement arose, for example, over the extent and means in which Koreans should display their anti-Japanese sentiment. These factors, along with a better-informed and more prominent police force, complicated any large-scale efforts to organize around a common cause.

The shadow of the March First movement also lingered in the attitudes of the general Korean population. The failure of the masses to take to the streets and demand their independence, as they did seven years earlier, could have reflected the failure of the KCP to organize Korea's anti-Japanese groups. It more likely resulted from the people realizing what Yun Ch'iho concluded in 1919 when he refused to join the March First Independence movement. In an interview with the Japanese *Mainichi shinbun*, Yun listed the following reasons for his non-cooperation:

(1) The question of Korean independence will have no occasion to appear in the Peace Conference. (2) There is no power in Europe or America which will be so foolish as to offend Japan by espousing the course of Korea. (3) If independence were given to us, we are not ready to be profited thereby. Japan gave us independence in 1894. What did we do with it? (4) When a weak race has to live with a strong one, the former must win the good will of the latter as a matter of self-preservation. (5) This foolish agitation of the students only prolongs the military administration of Korea. If shouting *Mansais* through the students will win a national independence there can be no subject, nation, or race in the world. (6) Don't be deceived by schemers like Ch'ŏngdogyo [heavenly way] people.[75]

The 1920 Reforms: Preparation for June 10?

The Japanese administration began its preparation for the 1926 state funeral soon after the dust cleared from the disturbances caused by Koreans from March 1919. It did not take much foresight on the Government-General's part to anticipate that Sunjong's eventual death would provide the Korean people with another opportunity—perhaps their last—to rally patriotic sentiments. A repeat of the Japanese police's brutal suppression of this demonstration risked Japan further tarnishing its international image.[76] Japan answered this challenge with "cultural rule" (*bunka seiji*). The Japanese government appeased its international critics by advancing an administration that vowed to nurture the Korean people's cultural awareness. It also co-opted members of the Korean opposition by inviting them to join the process. They could write for the Korean newspapers and even, in the case of Yŏ Unhyŏng, meet with Japanese officials to discuss Japan's colonial policies.[77]

The newly instituted reforms that took effect in 1920 reflected Japan's ambition to cultivate cultural understanding among the Korean people. They promised Koreans more schools for their children and increased the duration of this education from four to six years.[78] The reforms allowed Korean children with sufficient Japanese language ability to attend schools that hitherto catered exclusively to the expatriate Japanese students. The Government-General even promised the Korean people local self-governing rights should they demonstrate cultural advancement.

Other reforms sought to bridge the gap that separated the Japanese and Korean people. The police force shed their military uniforms and swords in an effort to adopt a more congenial appearance to the Korean people. The Government-General also promoted Korean language study among Japanese residents to encourage communication between the Japanese and Koreans. In an effort to promote mutual understanding between the two peoples, it arranged tours to the Japanese islands for the Koreans and visits to the Korean peninsula for the Japanese.[79] It also brought Korean exiles back to their homeland to demonstrate to them the advances that their country had made under Japanese rule.

The Government-General's decision to relax its publishing legislation had the most immediate, and explosive, effect on Korean society. Korean language publication up to this time had been restricted to the government-friendly *Maeil sinbo*[80] and a few minor periodicals. In 1920 the Japanese administration issued permits that allowed three additional newspapers—the *Tonga ilbo*, *Chosŏn ilbo*, and the *Sidae ilbo*—to commence publication. The appearance of a number of magazines at this time also contributed to the burgeoning print culture boom within Korean society. The Japanese reasoned that allowing the Korean people greater freedom of speech would first rectify an injustice. It had become harder to justify prohibiting from the Korean people that which it permitted Japanese residents, an indigenous press. The administration also agreed that more lenient publication privileges would contribute to the Korean people's cultural development.[81]

In many ways the Korean newspapers did contribute directly to promoting modern culture among the Korean people. Newspapers kept their readers informed of the latest developments, of the opinions and accomplishments of prominent Koreans, as well as their arrests. The *Tonga ilbo*, for example, sponsored annual literary and sports contests that encouraged Koreans to develop in these areas. The newspaper also used its pages to promote women's rights and challenged men to live by the same standards that they expected of their women. It argued that Korean civilization could not progress if society expected women to remain faithful to unfaithful men. The newspaper regularly encouraged Koreans to raise their standards of living to meet the standards of the civilized world in terms of health and hygiene.

The Japanese administrators applauded these efforts, but it frowned upon other efforts made by the newspaper to promote what they perceived as anti-Japanese sentiment and Korean nationalism. The *Tonga ilbo* did not shy from criticizing Japanese administrational shortcomings, particularly its Japanese-centered school system and its colonial infrastructural projects. This newspaper also promoted Korean nationalist sentiment: it advertised the efforts of Korean language associations, as well as the accomplishments of Korean heroes, and publicized the developments of Koreans in police custody.[82] As one Japanese report would later conclude, institutions such as the Korean newspapers served as lifelines that perpetuated Koreanness rather than transformation points to a greater appreciation of the superior Japanese culture.[83]

The Government-General listed, in less public forums, the control benefits that reforms in publication provided. First, allowing Koreans legal publication rights was seen as a way for the administration to co-opt the numerous illegal publications that had been distributed over the first decade of Japanese rule.[84] More frequently mentioned was the greater understanding of Korean sentiment that these publications allowed the Japanese. Saitō's predecessor, Hasegawa Yoshimichi, reflected on this advantage as follows: "Restrictions on speech and assembly [have been] overly severe." It is "in keeping with the times to relax these restraints and allow people to say openly what they want to say. Thereby we can know what they are thinking and point out where they are wrong."[85] Vice Governor-General Mizuno Rentarō's reasoning focused more heavily on the control factor. He later recalled:

> Due to the articles and editorials that appeared in Korea's vernacular news-
> papers, we were able to know the Korean people's trend of thought.
> [Previously] we were not able to transmit out opinions to the people. The
> Government-General's organs and newspapers included only the adminis-
> trative side and thus we lacked the means to listen to the common voice.
> We thus could not govern them with justice. As for the Koreans, by allowing
> them the means to extend their voice through vernacular newspapers, we
> gained for the first time access to the voice of the commoner. It was like we
> finally built a chimney for the kitchen stove. Because we did not have this
> chimney earlier the smoke from the stove had no escape route and simply
> smoldered and darkened the room. [The chimney provided this outlet and]
> made the room much brighter and the moods fresher. This is good. If there
> is no chimney the logs do not enflame properly causing the fire to break
> out. It is safe to say that because we did not have this chimney erected in
> [1919] the "*banzai undō*" [Manse movement] turned into a disastrous fire.[86]

Mizuno's tenure in Korea ended in June 1922 but this "chimney" provided the
Japanese administration with the window it needed to monitor Korean activity
during the critical forty-five days that separated Sunjong's death and his funeral.

The Government-General's encouragement of Korean-language study
potentially brought the Japanese into greater contact with the Korean people. Discussion on the role that the Korean language would play began soon
after annexation. Some Japanese argued that Japanese expatriates should
learn the Korean language; others contended that since Korean was the
inferior language it should mercifully be allowed to disappear.[87] The March
1919 demonstrations informed the Government-General of the need to
actively encourage Japanese to study the Korean language. It instituted a
Korean proficiency exam and provided salary incentives to government
employees (primarily teachers and members of the police force) who successfully sat for the exams. The Government-General listed three benefits to
Japanese acquisition of the Korean language: administrative efficiency,
Japanese-Korean unity, and peace maintenance.[88] In addition, other Japanese
studied the language to enhance their genuine interest in the Korean culture
and to strengthen their ties with the Korean people.[89]

That members of the Government-General Police Bureau consistently performed best on the Korean proficiency exams suggests a more central con-

cern supporting this reform. In 1925, for example, of the 246 successful sitters for the exam, 199 worked for the Japanese police bureau.[90] Their responsibilities would suggest their needs for language proficiency to be among the greatest. The ability for them to make personal contact with the Korean people facilitated their capacity to help Koreans in need, but also to interrogate Koreans who violated the law. Their ability to read and understand the Korean language was vital for their ability to censor Korean publications. Fluency in the Korean language also increased the Japanese ability to infiltrate subversive Korean groups and collect information.

The period between Sunjong's death and funeral provided the Japanese administration an opportunity to test the effectiveness of these policy reforms. A 120 page report, the "Ri denka no shikyo ni saishi 'shinbunshi wo tōshite mitaru' Chōsenjin no shisō keikō" (Tendencies in the Korean people's thought 'as seen through newspapers' at the time of the death of the Yi monarch), was a product of these efforts. This top-secret report, completed sometime after the state funeral, collected, translated, and offered analysis on articles that appeared in the Korean vernacular press regarding the Korean people's reaction to the former emperor's death. Japanese translation of the Korean press was not in itself unique—the Japanese government did this quite often. In this case, however, their ambition was more focused: to take advantage of the "golden opportunity" (kokikai) that Sunjong's death provided to gain an acute understanding of the thoughts and emotions of the Korean people.[91]

The most valuable information that this report offers is the Japanese interpretation of the Korean people's behavior over this short period within the greater framework of Japanese rule in Korea. Regarding the Korean people's attitude toward Sunjong, the report noted the newspapers' mixed criticism of the deceased monarch and sympathetic commentaries that "shook the human spirit." It also noted that not one newspaper called for "convalescence prayers" to be offered on Sunjong's behalf. Instead, Korean language newspapers seemed more interested in publicizing events such as the Golden Tiger Gate incident to rally the people's participation in independence-directed activities.

The report's impressions regarding the Korean people's behavior during the funeral noted a lack of any sense of unrest among the participants. Students distributed inflammatory leaflets and shouted, "*Manse!*" However, the average spectator was disciplined and "did not show much reaction" to these agitators. Rather than interpret this as a success of the assimilation policy, it concluded simply that Koreans "now realized that no good could come from their participation in these activities."[92]

The report acknowledged that Japanese surveillance of these newspapers yielded little in the way of new information about the Korean people. The report's compilers did, however, feel confident in putting forth a number of observations. First, they complemented the Korean people on their maturity. Whereas in 1919 the people adopted a rebellious ambition without reflecting on their personal capacity to induce change, by 1926 they had come to realize not only that they lacked the capacity and preparedness for anti-Japanese rebellion, but also the futility of such a reaction. On the surface, the report continued, it appeared that a sense of tranquility had set in over the people. This, however, was deceiving; the Korean sense of national consciousness had advanced strongly as they developed capabilities in areas such as education and industry. The report observed that Koreans reflected on their so-called power of national solidarity and sought to establish national culture standards when given the opportunity. Sunjong's death and funeral provided the people with one such opportunity.[93]

A second report issued in January 1927 corroborated these findings and suggested a reason why Korean national sentiment endured despite Japanese efforts to assimilate the people. The failure of overseas Koreans to gain support for the independence efforts at the 1921 Washington Conference forced some Koreans to rethink the means they employed to reach this goal. Rather than demand immediate independence, they now supported gradual efforts to foster national consciousness and to develop the intellectual and industrial abilities of the Korean people. This new approach also advanced Korean economic independence by organizing Korean boycotts of Japanese products. Rather than the Korean people scripting impractical slogans demanding Japan's departure and Korea's independence, this movement focused on more practical demands, such as calls for improvements in education.[94] This trend was evident in the demands presented by students at Korea's next demonstration, the Kwangju student movement that broke out in November 1929.[95]

The two reports shared the view that Korean participation in institutions that stimulated Korean nationalist consciousness hampered the Japanese administration from reaching its goals of assimilation. This observation worked in two opposite ways. On the one hand the vernacular media provided an outlet for nationalist instruction that provided the Korean people with the knowledge they needed to maintain their culture. By acknowledging this important role of the media these two reports also acknowledged mistakes in the Japanese belief that the Korean people would naturally gravitate toward the Japanese culture once they recognized its superiority over their own. Likewise, enrolling the Korean people in institutions designed to promote favorable Japanese sentiment among its constituents (such as education) had an opposite effect. Rather than strengthen Korean affinity toward Japanese culture, it encouraged students to demand that more attention be given to their native Korean heritage. The insensitivity of Japanese officials and instructors fanned these flames, as witnessed on several occasions during the period between Sunjong's death and funeral.

CONCLUSION

As the Korean people prepared to bid adieu to the last legitimate symbol of the long Chosŏn period, the Government-General had reason to feel confident that it could bury Sunjong while controlling attempts by Korean groups to use his death to rally popular nationalist sentiment. Sunjong's having less prestige than his father Kojong worked in Japan's favor. More importantly, the colonial administration had embedded measures to control such disturbances in the reforms it enacted after the 1919 Independence movement. Signs of this confidence began to appear even before Sunjong took to his sickbed, as the Government-General began to tighten censorship standards over the indigenous media and curtail incentives for Japanese to study the Korean language. Finally, its enactment of peace preservation legislation in 1925 armed the police with a legal preemptive tool to control potential disturbances before they got out of hand.

The Korean people's relative inaction, at least when compared to the March First demonstrations, resulted from a number of factors. Initiatives by the major left-wing Korean groups proved ineffective, in part, because they failed to organize a united front against Japanese colonial rule, but also because the Government-General's preventive measures proved so effective. Whether Koreans would have been more active had these measures failed is the primary question that the reports introduced above sought to answer. The reports' conclusion—that Korean reaction would have been much the same—explained changes in Korean tactics and reasoning rather than revealing an indication that cultural rule policies were leading the Korean people to Japan's colonial goal: assimilation. Indeed, both reports remarked that exposing Koreans to their culture through the indigenous media was having the opposite effect—stronger Korean sentiment.

Time, at least in June 1926, was on Japan's side. Koreans having lost their last legitimate figure to rally nationalist sentiment, and with the international community virtually indifferent toward Korea's plight, Japan could afford to prudently cut into Korean ethnic space by gradually curtailing the reforms that it enacted six years previous. Attacking this space directly by ending the reforms—as some recommended—would have risked arousing civil strife. However, the Japanese government could risk targeting the peripheral elements of this space—the more radical political elements and media contributions—without sacrificing much social stability. Whether planned or otherwise, Sunjong's death offered the Government-General a forum to observe Korean reactions to the initial attempt to tighten their ethnic space. The lessons that the Japanese learned proved invaluable in the late 1930s when wartime circumstances allowed Japan to radically curtail Korean ethnic space.

NOTES

1. This chapter benefited from comments received during presentations given at the Chōsenshi Kenkyūkai in Tokyo and the Korea Studies seminar at the University of Washington. I am particularly indebted for suggestions received from Clark W. Sorensen, Yong chool Ha, and Wonmo Dong.

2. For example, the Suwŏn massacre, where twenty-nine Koreans were herded into a church that the Japanese later set on fire, gained the attention of the United States Senate. "Valor Medal for Root—National Arts Club will Honor Head of Mission to Russia," 4182–86. Thomas E. Watson, a senator from Georgia, used Japan's mishandling of the March First movement in March 1920 to argue against the appropriateness of Elihu Root being honored with a valor medal by the National Arts Club. See also Frank Baldwin, "The March First Movement: Korean Challenge," chap. 5 for a review of Japanese and Korean confrontations during this independence movement.

3. Gondō Yorōsuke, Yi ōkyū, 268–70.

4. This list appears in the secret periodical Shisō geppō (September 15, 1932): 4–6.

5. Ki-baik Lee, *A New History of Korea*, 363.

6. Woo-keun Han, *The History of Korea*, 487.

7. This document, with its author listed as Kim Il Sung and titled "With the Century," can be found at Internet Archive, http://www.archive.org/stream/WithTheCentury/202_djvu.txt (accessed May 3, 2011).

8. Kim Hoil, "Ilcheha '6–10 haksaeng undong' ko," 595.

9. Han'guk Kŭnhyŏndae Sahakhoe, *Han'guk tongnip undongsa kangŭi*, 136–37.

10. Yun Sŏksu, "Chosŏn kongsandang kwa 6–10 pan-Il siwi undong," 96–118.

11. See *Hanminjok tongnip undongsa*, vol. 8, chap. 2. The Sin'ganhoe lasted from 1927–31.

12. Kim Ch'angho and Kang Sŏkhŭi, *Chōsen tsūshi*, 100–101.

13. As summarized in the June 10, 2001 edition of the *Korean Central News Agency* http://www.kcna.co/jp/item/2001/200106/news06/10.htm (accessed May 3, 2011).

14. The *Tōkyō asahi shinbun* offered two reports in its April 6, 1926 edition. Its front page story simply announced that Sunjong's condition had suddenly deteriorated; a second story on page three provided a summary of changes in the monarch's condition since the previous January and listed Sunjong's vital details from the previous few days. The reportage of such details on a daily basis was a practice that Japanese newspapers offered their readers at times when the health of Japanese emperors turned critical.

15. Prince Ŭn, born in 1897, two years after the 1895 murder of Queen Min, was Sunjong's half-brother. He was taken to Japan as a young boy by then Resident-General Itō Hirobumi. After finishing his schooling at the prestigious Gakushuin (Peer school) he was married to the Japanese Princess Nashimoto in 1920.

16. *Tōkyō asahi shinbun*, April 10, 1926.

17. Ibid., April 11, 1926.

18. Ibid., April 27, 1926. Prince Ŭn never succeeded his brother to the Korean throne. Rumors, such as one spread by the Washington representative of the Sino-Korean People's League, warned that the Japanese wanted to place Prince Ŭn on the Korean throne as a puppet, the likes of Pu Yi of Manchukuo. "Japs Up to Her Old Trick Again," 309.

19. *Tōkyō asahi shinbun*, April 28, 1926, 1.

20. *Japan Times*, April 28, 1926.

21. Ibid., April 29, 1926.

22. *Tōkyō asahi shinbun*, April 29, 1926. It further reported that the individual was not harmed in any way.

23. *Japan Times*, April 29, 1926.

24. Chōsen Sōtokufu, Keimukyoku Toshoka, "Ri denka no shikyo ni saishi 'shinbunshi wo tōshite mitaru' Chōsenjin no shisō keikō."

25. Ibid., 301–5.

26. Ibid., 285–86. The two boys who directly assaulted the policemen were brought into custody.

27. *Japan Times*, June 8, 1926.

28. *Japan Times*, June 9, 1926.

29. Kim Hoil, "Ilcheha '6–10 haksaeng undong' ko," 600.

30. Yun Sŏksu, "Chosŏn kongsandang kwa 6–10 pan-Il siwi undong," 114.

31. *Chōsen*, June 1926.

32. *Japan Times*, June 10, 1926.

33. Yun Sŏksu, "Chosŏn kongsandang kwa 6–10 pan-Il siwi undong," 115.

34. See *Hanminjok tongnip undongsa*, 240–41.

35. The trial record, which gave precise details on the time and location of their crimes, the number of pamphlets they distributed, and the words used by the students' in their calls for Korean independence, is found in *Ilcheha sahoe undongsa charyo ch'ongsŏ*, 8: 33–76. This report is dated November 17, 1926.

36. This figure is higher than subsequent estimates that revised this number to total 1,199 Koreans. At the other end of the scale, Pak Ŭnsik estimated 53, 207 casualties. See Frank P. Baldwin, "The March First Movement," 233.

37. Michael E. Robinson, *Cultural Nationalism in Colonial Korea*. I consider the *Tonga ilbo's* contribution to this movement in my "Assimilation Rejected: The *Tonga ilbo's* Challenge to Japan's Colonial Policy in Korea."

38. Vipan Chandra, *Imperialism, Resistance, and Reform in Late Nineteenth-Century Korea*, 132–33.

39. Hilary Conroy, *The Japanese Seizure of Korea*, 380–82; Peter Duus, *The Abacus and the Sword*, 203–4; Unno Fukuju, *Itō Hirobumi to Kankoku Heigō*, 105–15. Yi Chonggak, *It'o Hirobumi*, 299–307.

40. After escorting his mother to view the funeral rehearsals, Yun Ch'iho entered in his diary on June 7, 1926 that because "this type of Regal procession will never be seen again in Korea . . . every Korean seems to manifest special interest in the event." *Yun Ch'iho ilgi*, 9: 67.

41. Pyong-Choon Hahm, *The Korean Political Tradition and Law*, 92.

42. Sunjong was considered a traitor following liberation. Chung Chul (Chŏng Ch'ŏl), a representative of the Marine Alliance, in a speech described him along with Lee Wanyong (Yi Wanyong) as Koreans who "sold Korea to the Japs." Chung's audience responded with applause and shouted, "That's right." For a summary of this speech see "Translation of a Part of the Police Report" (March 3, 1947) 1: 101.

43. Unno Fukuju, *Itō Hirobumi to Kankoku heigō*, 95–96; Peter Duus, *The Abacus and the Sword*, 207–8.

44. Yi Pangja, *The World is One*, 127.

45. F. A. McKenzie, *Korea's Fight for Freedom*, 127–28.

46. Ibid., 129–31.

47. Unno Fukushi, *Itō Hirobumi to Kankoku heigō*, 114–15; Christine Kim, "The King

is Dead," chap. 3. Reports of the tour are found in Kuksa P'yŏnch'an Wiwŏnhoe, ed., T'onggambu munsŏ, Vol. 9: 265–67, 341–42.

48. Hamada Kenji, Prince Itō, 207–8.

49. Christine Kim, "The King is Dead," 96–98.

50. Kuksa P'yŏnch'an Wiwŏnhoe, T'onggambu munsŏ , Vol. 9.

51. Peter Duus argues that Itō's resignation did not signal a change of heart regarding annexation by the residency-general. Indeed, on a number of occasions Itō demonstrated acceptance of this end. Peter Duus, The Abacus and the Sword, 135–36.

52. This English translation is taken from the Japan Times, August 31, 1910. It also appeared in the Seoul Press. Japanese and Korean versions appeared in the August 30, 1910, issues of the Keijō shinpo and the Maeil sinbo respectively. Sunjong's name was also found on letters of regret and welcome to outgoing and incoming resident-generals, which were published in the Seoul Press.

53. Ibid.

54. These visits were reported in the Maeil sinbo in the form of short four- to five-line announcements during the week of October 9–15, 1910.

55. A copy of this postcard is found in Kwŏn Hyŏnhŭi, Chosŏn esŏ on sajin yŏpsŏ, 124.

56. The Seoul Press referred to Sunjong as "prince," and his wife as "princess."

57. "Daily Life of Prince and Princess Yi," Seoul Press, December 20, 1910, 2. Ellen Salem offers a less glowing assessment of the Korean court's reaction to Japanese language policies. Ellen Salem, "Women Surviving: Palace Life in Seoul after the Annexation," 87.

58. Seoul Press, October 21, 1910.

59. Maeil sinbo, October 25, 1910.

60. Prince Ŭn's 1920 marriage to Nashimoto received a fair amount of publicity in the Japanese and Korean media.

61. "Ri gyokudenka no gobyōki goheiyu no kigansai," Chōsen (May 1926): 136.

62. Saitō Makoto, "Ri Gyokudenka wo itami tatemi tsurite," Chōsen (June 1926): 2. Saitō used Prince Ŭn's marriage to Princess Nashimoto in a similar way.

63. "Japs Up to Her Old Tricks Again."

64. March 3, 1919, the day of Kojong's funeral, was a quiet day in Seoul, but demonstrations in the northern half of the peninsula kept the movement alive, as reported in Frank Baldwin, "The March First Movement," 92.

65. For example, the Tonga ilbo, was closed for six months because it suggested that the three imperial treasures (the sword, the jewel, and the mirror) demonstrated Japanese religion to be idol worship. Michael E. Robinson notes that the number of erasures increased after 1925 in his "Colonial Publication Policy and the Korean Nationalist Movement," 326.

66. Dae-Sook Suh, Documents of Korean Communism, 8.

67. Information on the KCP preparation for the June 10 movement is taken primar-

ily from Yun Sŏksu, "Chosŏn kongsandang kwa 6–10 pan-Il siwi undong."

68. See for example, the 1925 slogans in Peter H. Lee, ed., "Slogans of the Korean Communist Party," 462.

69. This manifesto can be found in Kim Hoil, "Ilcheha 'haksaeng undong' ko," 601.

70. Regional disputes also appeared during the planning stages of the Hyŏngp'yŏng (Equity society) movement that took place in the early 1920s. Organized in South Kyŏngsang Province to liberate the *paekchŏng* outcast group, members from Taegu and Seoul formed splinter groups and initially refused to participate in activities organized by the southern Korean group. See Joong-Seop Kim, *The Korean Paekjŏng Under Japanese Rule*.

71. Yun Sŏksu, "Chosŏn kongsandang kwa 6–10 pan'il siui undong," 103.

72. Kim Hoil, "Ilcheha 'haksaeng undong' ko," 602. It should be noted that the Japanese police experienced a similar stroke of luck just before the 1919 independence movement began, when police found copies of the Declaration of Independence to be distributed on March first. Insufficient details, however, prevented them from acting in time. See Frank Baldwin, "The March First Movement," 78.

73. Kim Hoil counted 224 incidents of school boycotts between 1920–26, with forty-eight incidents occurring in 1925 alone. See his "Ilcheha 'haksaeng undong' ko," 599. The Kwangju incident resulted from Korean students being punished for coming to the aid of a Korean female student being harassed by Japanese male students. The school authorities admonishing the Korean students while refusing to punish the Japanese students set off demonstrations in Kwangju that spread throughout the entire peninsula.

74. Ibid., 603–7.

75. *Yun Ch'iho ilgi*, vol VII, March 2, 1919, 261–62.

76. For the foreign reaction to Japan's handling of the 1919 Independence movement see Dae-yeol Ku, *Koreans Under Colonialism*; and Nakata Akifumi, *Nihon no Chōsen tōchi to kokusai kankei*.

77. For the dialogue of these meetings see Kang Dŏksan's *Ro Unkyō* [Yŏ Unhyŏng] *hyōten* 1, chap. 7.

78. See Patricia Tsurumi, "Colonial Education in Korea and Taiwan," for a discussion on the effect of education under Japanese rule on Korean nationalism.

79. The text for these reforms is found in "Chōsen shisei no kaizen," 73–141. Saitō advertised these reforms in English in the article "A Message from the Imperial Japanese Government to the American People: Home Rule in Korea?" *The Independent* (January 31, 1920): 167–69, 191.

80. A report titled "Chian jōkyō [Security situation] compiled in March 1935 lists Kim Charhŭm as the publisher of the *Maeil sinbo*. See *Nitteika shakai undoshi shiryō sōsho*, 308.

81. The Japanese administration expressed this aspiration in a letter sent to the *Tonga ilbo* offices to announce the Government-General's intention to indefinitely suspend its

publication rights over the newspaper's frequent violations of publication regulations. This letter is found in Kim Sangman, *Tonga ilbosa*, 151.

82. See Mark E. Caprio, "Assimilation Rejected," 129–45.

83. This aspiration that the Korean people would eventually choose Japanese over Korean culture was based on the idea that as a people matured they would realize the benefits of the superior culture and adopt it as their own. In this sense the Government-General mistakenly believed that the Korean culture could be used as an avenue to this end. Michael E. Robinson's work on media during the colonial period demonstrates that the Japanese introduction of Korean newspapers and radio programs helped maintain the Korean culture. See Michael E. Robinson, "Colonial Publication Policy and the Korean Nationalist Movement," and "Broadcasting in Korea, 1924–1937: Colonial Modernity and Cultural Hegemony."

84. Kim Sangman counted at least twenty-nine underground newspapers circulating at this time. See Kim Sangman, *Tonga ilbosa*, 66.

85. Hasegawa's reform suggestions are found in *Saitō Makoto monjo* 1: 325–402. Richard Devine's English translation of this reform proposal appears in "Japanese Rule in Korea after the March First Uprising: General Hasegawa's Recommendations," 523–40.

86. Mizuno Rentarō, *Mizuno Rentarō kaisōroku, kankei bunsho*, 52.

87. Within days following annexation the Japanese language newspaper *Keijō Shinpō* (Keijō [Seoul] daily) argued that it was necessity for Japanese to study the Korean language because it would take the Korean people decades to learn Japanese and forget Korean. See "Chōsengo to Nihongo" [Korean and Japanese], *Keijō shinpō* (September 1, 1910). This argument is also found in the discussion on education policy that preceded the administration's enactment of Korea's First Education Act of 1911. I cover this in my *Japanese Assimilation Policies in Colonial Korea*, 92–100. Yamada Kanto provides an overview of Korean language study by Japanese in his *Shokuminchi Chosen ni okeru Chosengo shorei seisaku: Chosengo wo mananda Nihonjin*.

88. Ibid., 69.

89. Iwashita Takeki notes that his father enjoyed speaking Korean when he had Korean guests at his house. See his *Shonen no hi no haisen nikki: Chōsen hantō kara no kikan*, 114.

90. *Chōsen*, November 1925, 136–41. See also Yamada Kanto, "Nihonjin keisatsuka ni tai suru Chōsengo shōrei seisaku," 123–50.

91. "Ri denka no shikyo," 244.

92. Ibid., 249–50.

93. Ibid., 250.

94. Chōsen Sōtokufu, "Dokuritsu undō ni okeru minzoku undo no kōgai" (January 1927).

95. As listed in Kashima Setsuko, "Kaisetsu: Kōshū [Kwangju] gakusei undō," 12.

6

Japanese Assimilation Policy and Thought Conversion in Colonial Korea

KEONGIL KIM

INTRODUCTION

An early definition of thought conversion (K. *chŏnhyang*; J. *tenkō* 轉向)[1] was framed through the collective studies of thought conversion in 1959. At that time, thought conversion was defined as "the change of thought as a result of power forcibly exerted."[2] This definition is too broad to indicate if thought conversion is specific to any specific time period or geographic region, for instance, Japan in the 1930s. Various types of forcible conversion, such as the Tokugawa suppression of Christianity in the seventeenth century, the purging of opponents by the Bolsheviks in the establishment of the Soviet regime, and the communist witch hunts of McCarthyism after World War II can be subsumed under this definition.

However, thought conversion originated in Japan from around the 1930s to the end of World War II and was later applied to colonial Korea. Under this process, recalcitrant Koreans, whether leftists, nationalists, or Christians, had "impure" ideas winnowed out of their heads by totalitarian methods of interrogation until they were ready to confess their political "sins" in writing, and after the late 1930s they had to join local branch groups for those who had "reformed" their thoughts.[3] Seen from the perspective of an individual, it had meant succumbing to physical force, such as torture, which was sanctioned by the state. The state in turn officially recognized conversion by converts who openly confessed in public, which implied that the change in their thoughts was an official statement.

Modern laws are applied to the behavior of people, not to their thoughts or beliefs. In contrast, thought conversion was designed to punish not only a prohibited act but also the thought underlying the act. Through open confession and official criticism of the thought or belief that motivated the act, the Japanese state sought to make its mark—largely a negative or counter one—on individual minds. This meant that individuals had to place their thoughts beyond the reach of state power.

Thought conversion has generally been regarded as reflecting the peculiarities of Japan. Far beyond the narrow but generally understood meaning of thought suppression by anti-government activists, especially orthodox Marxists, Japanese thought conversion reflects the modernization strategy in Japan after the Meiji Restoration. In this respect, Tsurumi Shunsuke asserted that the term tenkō was formed in the political atmosphere of the fifteen interwar years in Japan and that the word depicted the intellectual and cultural inclinations of this period.[4]

This concept succinctly reveals the inherent dilemmas of modernity as pursued by the Japanese state. These dilemmas are, for instance, those of the East versus the West, of tradition versus modernity, of the self versus the other, or further, of the particular versus the universal. The case of thought conversion would typify how the Japanese state molded its own identity. It left, in turn, an indelible stigma on the Japanese national identity that has persisted even to this day.

Major works on thought conversion have often explained this phenomenon in relation to traditional features of Japanese society. For instance, thought conversion was either linked to the concept of rehabilitation, which has a long tradition in Japanese society, or, as Tsurumi mentioned,[5] it was contrived as a mild punishment for thought criminals since traditional village customs did not physically punish people who held eccentric beliefs. Within a broader perspective, Bellah asserts that the Japanese converts, being Japanese, tended to return to the primordial loyalties of family and nation.[6]

This peculiarity was also reflected in studies of thought conversion after World War II. According to these studies a sense of frustration, indignation, shame, or feeblemindedness was followed by the act of thought conversion. Thought conversion meant discarding and negating one's cherished beliefs or ideologies, which implied one betraying one's loyalty to a committed group. Thought conversion in this context was, in principle, considered to be undesirable, and converts deserved to be blamed. What would happen, however, if the so-called betrayers were to become the majority within a society?

This phenomenon partially explains why mainstream Japanese scholars after World War II hardly reproached the wartime converts,[7] in sharp contrast to the case of Korea, where the convert was criticized as much as those who imposed the thought conversion. Since conversion, for example, was understood as the transformation of collective ideology, oriented toward the emperor (tennō) system and based upon national unity,[8] Japanese scholars tended to delve into the convert's motives, attitudes, or responses instead of emphasizing external factors or pressures from external sources related to the conversion, which was usually the case in Korea.

Generally speaking, thought conversion has been understood as having two aspects: it is both forceful and repressive, for it accompanies the compulsion of force. At the same time it is paternalistic and conciliatory, for the offender is not punished; instead, he is absorbed into the system. The "love and affection" side of conversion based on Japan's culture has tended to be emphasized in Japan, although the oppressive side of conversion has sometimes been alluded to.[9] Although arrest, torture, and the fear of death are said to play as important a role as traditional sociocultural factors,[10] substantial analysis tended to emphasize the converts' own will and determination and the change in their thinking.[11]

Understanding conversion in both countries reveals subtle but crucial differences of opinion. If we were to summarize these two aspects of thought conversion as oppression and paternalism, it could be said that the latter manifested in Japan whereas the former was emphasized in Korea. This implies that in Japan the converts or offenders and the scholarly interpreters, who had suffered from the conversion policy during the war years and after the end of the World War II, understood conversion within the same context. In Korea, in contrast, there was a disjunction between converts and interpreters, with the former being harshly reprimanded morally and politically. Here conversion has been enumerated as another manifestation of brutality perpetuated by Japanese imperialism. The sharp contrast of opinion in understanding thought conversion as practiced in the two countries seems to reflect differences both countries have faced in numerous respects today.[12]

The purpose of this chapter is to examine the concrete context of the social conditions that generated these differences. By applying the conversion policy to a case other than its original site in Japan, it is possible to touch issues and to derive implications different from the mainstream discussions. At the heart of this difference lies the question of national identity. In this context, the various responses of Korean converts are examined in an attempt to confront the contradictions caused by the assimilation policy of Japanese imperialism. It would, however, be better to examine the Japanese experience in thought conversion before addressing the main issues.

THE JAPANESE EXPERIENCE WITH THOUGHT CONVERSION

The following questions will be discussed in this chapter: Why did mass conversion operations emerge in this period; what were the motives and intentions of those who proffered conversion; and how did thought conversion impact the formation of modern thought and national identity in Japan? As mentioned earlier, Japanese imperialists launched into the conversion project in the 1930s and carried it out through the end of World War II in 1945. In a broad perspective, however, thought conversion can be interpreted through the traditions of pre-Meiji Restoration Japan. Although the responses of East Asian countries to Western penetration in the late nineteenth century were rather diverse,[13] such responses required accommodating the Western culture on the basis of each country's traditions. The countries differed only in the way each response was interpreted and realized in each nation. Nevertheless, all of these countries were soon swayed by the religion-like worship of Western science, technology, and industry. Accordingly, Korea, Japan, and China have each adopted contrasting strategies for achieving modernization ever since.

The earlier passion for Western culture and enlightenment (bunmei kaika) was soon replaced by an attempt to preserve Japan's own tradition and culture. Japanese bureaucrats and intellectuals believed that imprudent acceptance of Western civilization was not desirable, and they expressed anxiety over the possibility that Japanese traditions, which had been developed over thousands of years, would be destroyed. A skeptical approach toward Western civilization and an interest in finding the virtues of Japan's tradition and culture had set in as a major characteristic of Japan during the late 1880s and 1890s[14]; this view was mainstreamed during the twentieth century.

Japanese bureaucrats and intellectuals tried to achieve modernization through a top-down approach by maintaining Japanese values based on traditional family and village life. Most people in Japan had been dominated by the traditional social order and were accustomed to group solidarity and parochialism. Modern civil society as defined in Western terms was alien to them, and individualism was not a familiar concept. These conditions made it easy to substantiate the will of dominant power rather than the interest of the people in the problem of integrating alien thought to the indigenous system, which had become the major task of Japan in the twentieth century.

The Imperial Rescript of 1879 on Education (教育勅諭), issued by the Japanese emperor, emphasized "grand principles dominating the relations between king and subject, father and son," and condemned "the indiscriminate emulation of the Western ways" in the education of people.[15] Three years later, the Imperial Rescript on the Military (1882, 軍人勅諭) stressed the same points. The Imperial Rescript on Education (1890, 教育勅語) proclaimed the principle of loyalty and filial piety as "infallible for all ages and true in all places."[16] Finally, the Japanese government declared that national loyalty and filial piety were one and the same and the 1910 revision of Japan's ethics textbooks.[17]

These were not promulgated as laws, or measures, to be applied to the arena of civil society as defined in Western terms. Rather, they were arranged by the state to stamp its will on the people without the buffer of civil society. In primary school and through the conscription system, children and soldiers respectively were castigated if they could not eloquently memorize the whole content of the edicts, and if they could not write the Chinese characters within them.[18] Individuals drifted into the modern system through harsh discipline, the process deeply impacted on being modern Japanese.

This system, emphasizing traditional values and morals instead of Western formal democracy, was once called the "family state" or the "theocratic state."[19] Its purpose was to attain social integration by providing for the equality of all people under the emperor and through the values of family and community rather than through the election of representative bodies, as was the case in Western countries. Central to the system were beliefs relating to the emperor.[20] The ideals of the emperor were based on the belief that the imperial line had remained unbroken throughout eternity. One problem with this belief was that it did not remain a simple mythology; instead, it had become the rationale for the "theocratic state." In this context, the so-called kokutai 國體 is "the driving force peculiar to the Japanese nation, or the tradition inherited by them."[21] Whatever its abstruse definition, the expression kokutai represented the social system managed by the untainted Japanese spirit.

The passage of the Peace Preservation Law in 1925 (治安維持法) and successive amendments vindicated and supported the *kokutai* social system. Though vague, the law stipulated which ideas were foreign. "Un-Japanese" ideas of "abnormal alien thought" were regarded as a threat to national solidarity and violated *kokutai*.[22] As a result, from 1934–35, the liberal interpretation of the Japanese emperor, who had dominated Japan since the period of the Taisho Democracy, was refuted and attacks on this theory were mounted on a large scale.[23] The Japanese government denounced this theory as a "non-Japanese, blasphemous, Europe-worshipping" ideology that ignored the nation's own traditions. Behind this denouncement was the idea that Western thought—whether liberal or socialist—was dangerous and harmful.

> We have imported too many Western ideas, some of them incompatible with the Japanese spirit, and the result has been the ideological unrest so characteristic of our times. What we have to do now is to turn to our traditional culture which kept us an ideologically homogeneous nation in the past and can make us such again.[24]

For the purpose of "enriching genuine Japanese culture," as was once remarked, "the Japanese public was taught to make foreign nations the scapegoat. The West was hauled before the court-martial and found guilty."[25] The manipulation of the West's image reached its apex near the end of World War II. One episode of this period was the campaign to forbid the curling of hair, launched in the 1940s by ultra-nationalists on the grounds that using electric power to curl hair was unpatriotic conduct and, as a result, offended *kokutai*.[26] In sum, Japanese modernization had departed from "Japanese spirit, Western talent" (和魂洋才) and moved toward being obsessed with the "Japanese spirit." The Japanese emphasis on their own tradition blinded its people to the fact that their achievement actually was grounded in "Western talent."

In this context, it was no wonder that modern Western values were vulgarized or ran to extremes. Western thought was denounced and lessons from the past were stressed. For instance, modern liberal and socialist ideas were interpreted as emphasizing only individualistic and materialistic values that were thought to be in opposition to traditional concepts such as loyalty, harmony, or social equality.[27] Tradition and modernity, the East and the West, and the self and the Other were recognized as mutually exclusive categories, and each pair was presented as irreconcilable.

It was in this context that thought conversion policy gained relevance, since conversion meant surrendering "strange foreign thought" and returning to "pure Japanese spirit." It was "the phenomenon of conflict occasioned in the indigenization of imported thoughts."[28] The conversion policy was applied only to a portion of the population; most ordinary people were not the objects of government policy because they could easily accept the state ideology of Japanese mythology through their primary school and military education. Rather, intellectuals and university students were the victims of the policy, for they had been influenced by Western thought largely through universities, which were modeled after academic institutions in Europe. Although the conversion policy was applied mainly to intellectuals, its influence was felt throughout the entire society nonetheless.

The influence of radicalism among intellectuals had expanded on a worldwide scale during the 1920s and 1930s, and Japan was no exception. Reflecting that the Japanese socialist movement was largely dependent upon intellectuals,[29] socialism, communism, and sometimes anarchism were enumerated as the most dangerous foreign ideas threatening Japanese society in the earlier days of the conversion policy. This perception resulted in socialists and communists becoming its major targets. However, after the 1930s, the criteria for judging conversion widened to "un-Japanese thought" in general and anything having a tinge of the Western. A great many liberals and Christians were affected by the policy.

This ideological shift was related to the criteria for judging conversion, that is, the problem of its definition. In the earlier days of the conversion policy, the government was merely satisfied with the suspect's declaration of abandoning his or her heretical thought. The best example would be a memorandum written by Manabu Sano and Sadachika Nabeyama, the top leaders of the communist movement in Japan, near the end of May 1933. Their proclamations describing how they had abandoned their communist beliefs were based on renouncing communist internationalism. They stated that each country must carry out its own unique revolution by considering its national characteristics and historical conditions. After their statements, hundreds of other imprisoned communists soon followed their lead. Conversion thus became a social phenomenon rather than the product of decisions by individuals.

The next stage of conversion was motivated by a revision in conversion policy between 1936 and 1937. During this stage, state power was not merely satisfied with the offenders forsaking beliefs or retreating from social movements, but demanded that these individuals demonstrate that they had improved after accepting the Japanese spirit. In arriving at this stage, as Sano himself redefined later, conversion "means that those who have repented their own evil sins and have committed painful self-denial obtain new faith by the power of purification and are reborn into completely new Japanese."[30] A Japanese writer similarly confessed that conversion at this stage became "the resuscitation of the human being, not merely the turnover."[31] This stage extended the conversion target from radicals to liberals and Christians.

It now seemed apparent that the attempt to integrate traditional thoughts to foreign ideologies after the Meiji Restoration had changed to the principle of expelling "useless Western thought" and returning to "pure Japanese thought." The Japanese tradition was idealized as the universal principle that had sufficient power to confront ideologies of Western origin.[32] Moreover, the imposition of such "universalism" spread over East Asian countries by what was referred to as the "Greater East Asia Co-Prosperity Sphere."

THE COLONIAL COUNTERPART IN THOUGHT CONVERSION

It was the common rule that policies and promulgations in colonial Korea were the extension and the later application of policies already enforced in Japan. The thought conversion policy was no exception. Nevertheless, there was a sharp difference in motives for adopting the system as an instrument of control. The themes of return to tradition and rejection of Western modernity were internalized in the minds of converts in Japan, and the Japanese government could justify the process. Imprisonment or torture by the political power was considered subsidiary in this respect.

In contrast, the Japanese authorities introduced thought conversion into colonial Korea as a means to maintain colonial public security. There was evidence that the colonial power was reluctant to introduce the conversion policy to the colony.[33] However, it was obliged to adopt the policy since harsh punishment and repression had not had any positive results in preserving public peace.[34] Though the colonial government adopted the thought conversion policy from the later part of 1933, shortly after its application in Japan, it is significant that there were no similar repercussions in Korea. It did not invoke the massive implementation that took place in Japan.[35] Large-scale thought conversion occurred later, when Japan declared war with Northern China in 1937.

More concretely, shortly after Manabu Sano and Sadachika Nabeyama issued their conversion proclamations in 1933, 30 percent of those not convicted (those under detention between the time of arrest and final sentencing) and 36 percent of the convicted followed this example in Japan.[36] Moreover, 74 percent of the convicted converted, whereas only 26 percent of the convicted stood pat on their belief in Japan.[37] In the case of colonial Korea,[38] a report stated that 732 offenders among a total of 2,021 cases had converted (Table 6.1).

The ratio of these offenders to the total is 36 percent, higher than that for Japan. It comes down to 25 percent, if we exclude Category A (hangdongjŏk 行動 的, people defined as those not willing to abandon their cherished beliefs), which can hardly be seen as a case of genuine conversion. What needs to be emphasized is the ratio of offenders by category of those not convicted and convicted. The latter accounted for 50.7 percent of total offenders, nearly double the former (26.2 percent). This figure contrasts Japan, where there was no significant difference between the two categories. Considering that it was easier to control the convicted in prison, it implies that the conversion policy was engendered by force in the colony, rather than by the spontaneity of individuals.

Table 6.2 shows the conversion trend of convicted offenders from 1934 to 1938. There is a sharp rise in the ratio of converts to the total convicted recorded in the two periods. The first upturn was from June 1936 to March 1937, when the growth rate was approximately 7 percent. In December 1936, the Korean Thought Criminals' Protection and Supervision Law (Chosŏn Sasangbŏm Poho Kwanch'allyŏng) was enacted. The next upturn was from March to September 1938, when an approximately 14 percent increase was recorded within only six months. In May 1938, the National Mobilization Act (Kukka Ch'ongdongwŏn pŏb) was enforced, and the Wartime National Thought Service Federation (Sikuk Taeŭng Chŏnsŏn Sasang Pokok Yŏnmaeng) was organized to control thought criminals under the auspices of the colonial authorities in July of the same year.

The abrupt increase in the number of the coverts during the enactment of such laws cannot be explained without the intervention of colonial power. Another fact to be emphasized was that the number of non-converts increased proportionately with the number of converts. Although this

Table 6.1 Survey on the Conversion of Korean Offenders, November 1, 1933

		Converts/Categories (%)			
	Total	A[1]	B[2]	C[3]	Total
Unconvicted	1197	94 (7.8)	206 (17.2)	14 (1.2)	314 (26.2)
Convicted	824	127 (15.4)	259 (31.4)	32 (3.9)	418 (50.7)
Total	2021	221 (10.9)	465 (23.0)	46 (2.3)	732 (36.2)

Sources: Chōsen Sōtokufu, Sisōkeppō [Monthly report of thought]1933: 36–37; Germaine A. Hoston, "Ikkoku Shakai-shugi: Sano Manabu and the Limits of Marxism as Cultural Criticism," 99–100.

Note:

[1]Category A, conversion of action (haengdongjŏk), was defined as not abandoning one's thought but promising not to commit oneself to social movements.

[2]Category B, conversion of theory (ironjŏk) was the case of abandoning one's thought.

[3]Category C, conversion of religion (chonggyojŏk), meant abandoning one's thought for the sake of religion.

These definitions roughly corresponded with the Japanese authorities' own classification in Japan; political (seiji-teki) conversion was the case based on political differences of opinion with the Communist Party. Citizen (shimin-teki) conversion involved a desire to return to normal life as a good Japanese citizen. In religious (shūkyō-teki) conversion one gave up communist ideology because of a new belief in something else, though not necessarily an organized religion.

increase was largely due to the decrease in quasi-converts or unknown categories, it is notable that, notwithstanding the persistent conversion offensive by the colonial power, a considerable number of people refused to convert until the end of the 1930s. This period of massive conversion from late 1937 through 1938 coincides with the change in conversion policy mentioned above—that is, from merely abandoning one's thoughts to that of "perfect conversion." In this respect, we could raise the question of whether conversion in Korea was the result of an individual's spontaneous decision or that of imposition by coercion and force.

Table 6.2 Conversion Trends of Korean Convicted Offenders, 1934–38

Category (%) Years	Converts	Quasi-converts	Unconverted	Unknown	Total
End of 1934	266 (30.1)	275 (31.1)	141 (15.9)	203 (22.9)	885
Feb. 1935	267 (27.5)	300 (30.9)	157 (16.2)	246 (25.3)	970
June 1936	253 (29.6)	200 (23.4)	176 (20.6)	225 (26.3)	854
March 1937	289 (36.8)	210 (26.7)	154 (19.6)	133 (16.9)	786
June 1937	256 (37.2)	190 (27.6)	120 (17.4)	122 (17.7)	688
March 1938	273 (40.9)	130 (19.5)	128 (18.9)	136 (20.6)	667
Sep. 1938	320 (54.9)	68 (11.6)	128 (22.1)	66 (11.4)	582
End of 1938	305 (55.7)	61 (11.1)	113 (20.6)	69 (12.6)	548

Sources: Chōsen Sōtokufu. Sisōihō [Assorted report on thought] 3 (1935): 179; 12 (1937): 182–84; 15 (1938): 217–19; Chikei kyōkai [Association of rule for criminals]. Chikei [Rule for criminals] 15 (1937): 16; 17 no.1 (1939): 11; 17 no. 4 (1939): 3.

In answering this question, it must first be remembered that Koreans were supposed to be motivated by external constraints, not by their own will. If one result of conversion was the indoctrination of national ideology epitomized by the "Japanese Spirit," this hardly was the case in colonial Korea. For instance, as Table 6.3 shows, the case of "national" self-awakening influenced a meager proportion, 1 percent to 3 percent.[39] In contrast, family affection or repentance by arrest influenced a large proportion, over 30 percent in either category.

The categories of repentance by arrest and education were vaguely defined. These categories could be seen as another expression of the intrusion of colonial power upon the convicted. As such, the category with the highest percentage turned out to be family affection. The same was true in Japan, where family and love of home were the most important factors in the decision to convert.[40] The only difference was that the consideration of family, directly or indirectly, was related to a national self-awakening in Japan,[41] whereas the consideration of family endured for its own sake in colonial Korea. Once one confessed, one had to abandon one's own thoughts for the

Table 6.3 Conversion Motives of Convicted Offenders

Motives	Number of Convicted Offenders (%)		
	Feb. 1935	June 1937	March 1938
Religion	11 (1.9)	10 (2.2)	3 (0.7)
Family Affection	181 (32.0)	141 (31.6)	137(34.1)
National Self-awakening	11 (1.9)	6 (1.3)	15 (3.7)
Negation of Ideology	14 (2.5)	14 (3.1)	15 (3.7)
Personal	15 (2.6)	9 (2.0)	7 (1.7)
Result of Education	119 (21.0)	95 (21.4)	92 (22.9)
Repentance by Arrest	204 (36.0)	166 (37.2)	131 (32.6)
Miscellaneous	12 (2.1)	5 (1.1)	3 (0.7)
Total	567 (100.0)	446 (100.0)	403(100.0)

Source: Chōsen Sōtokufu, Sisōihō [Assorted report on thought], 3 (1935): 178; 12 (1937): 185; 15 (1938): 219–20.

sake of one's mother or wife rather than maintain "public questions such as social concerns or attitudes."[42]

NATIONAL IDENTITY AND POLITICS OF CONVERSION

Although most Korean converts interpreted the imposition of forceful conversion in purely private terms, this did not mean that they were not interested in political issues or social concerns. Even though the Japanese writer Fusao Hayashi mentioned during the Pacific War that "Korean writers had no nation, or country to return to even though they converted,"[43] Korean intellectuals, as the conversion policy moved to its second stage starting at the end of 1930s, endeavored to justify their conversion by whatever form of commitment and motivation they felt especially urgent.

The national question lay at the heart of this process, just as in the Japanese case. This was evident from the fact that the original Sano-Nabeyama proclamation repeatedly mentioned the peculiarities of Japan's kokutai.[44] It should, however, be remembered that the problems the conversion policy had invoked were much more complicated and contradictory to the Korean people than to the Japanese. The assimilation policy that Japanese imperialism had officially emphasized from the beginning of the forcible annexation of Korea was the origin of this contradiction.

The theory emphasized that the Korean and Japanese people had the same origins, the same ancestors, a common culture, and a common history. According to this theory, Korea was to become Japan's extension, not its colony. The Japanese seizure of Korea in 1910 was therefore regarded as a national reintegration, not an imperialist invasion of Korea. Koreans were labeled as the "newly attached nation" and the Korean peninsula was designated as the "new territory" or the "outer land" rather than the colony.[45] The similarity between the Koreans and the Japanese implied that segregation of both nations was unnatural and their "amalgamation" was inevitable.

From the perspective of the colonizer, this meant that the issue of who dominated whom was avoided and colonial conquest thereby was justified. At the same time, however, it also carried the implication that the colonized did not have their own identity or history, an implication that deprived them of their right to claim their independence. Whatever the implications and effects of the assimilation policy, it was true that the policy itself was hampered by the impact of the March First movement in 1919. With the adoption in the ensuing decade of the conciliation policy, usually referred as the Cultural Policy (Bunka seiji), the Korean Self-Rule movement (chach'i undong) prospered during the 1920s. However, the movement drifted into strong currents of backlash initiated by the colonial people.

Meanwhile, in 1932, the establishment of the puppet regime in Manchuria (Manchukuo) revealed the subtle but crucial issues behind the assimilation policy of Japanese imperialism. As is well known, the Manchukuo puppet state proposed the minzoku kyōwa (racial harmony 民族協和) movement which supported a multiracial polity in which Chinese, Manchus, Mongols, Koreans, and Japanese would cooperate as equal citizens in a self-governing unit.[46] Though controlled by the Japanese, the Manchukuo regime officially proclaimed itself an independent state, unlike Korea which was a colony of the Japanese imperialism.[47] This situation—Koreans as citizens of an independent state on the one hand and Koreans as colonial subjects on the other hand—seemed to be contradictory and deluding. Koreans living in Manchukuo could identify themselves as a Korean nation (*Chosen minzoku*), which was strictly forbidden in Korea and in Japan.

It was in this context that the self-rule movement, which lost its influence as a result of blatant attacks from the Korean people, took a second upturn during the early 1930s. Though its resuscitation could not be sustained any longer, it was in this context that the colonized converts glimpsed a glimmer of hope in acquiring Korea's national independence. They were doubtful about eradicating national consciousness from the minds of the colonized; "it was impossible to erase the idea of nation from the brains of Korean[s]," and although the converts "abandoned their communist thoughts" they nonetheless "did not forget the concern for their nation."[48] In this respect, they contended that the Japanese assimilation policy in Korea was false. One convert's opposition to colonial policy was grounded on the motto of "*Ilsŏn yunghwa*" (Japanese-Korean fusion and harmony 日鮮融和):

> It was a near miracle for one to believe it possible to assimilate twenty million people having four thousand years of history. Regarding the advocacy of Japanese-Korean fusion and harmony, the adoption of a policy that did not permit the Koreans' right to speak was doomed to failure.[49]

As such, Kang Munsu emphasized that the right of self-government should be given to the Korean people within certain limits. It was, as he asserted, necessary to have "the organization to respect the opinions of Koreans in colonial domination, that is, a self-government system to speak on Korean politics." The movement for the achievement of that purpose was the "movement of self-rule based on sane and legal grounds." He added that heretofore the nationalists' self-rule movement was actually for the Korean people and his communist movement was nothing but a "hollow, unreal disturbance at the expense of severe sacrifice."[50]

It was not only Kang Munsu who found the new "path for the future" through the self-government movement. Wang Sunbong also asserted that the communists' conversion was a kind of "political phenomenon," not "social fashion." He reasoned that the alternative form of political movement had to be pursued to save the colonized people if the revolutionary movement of the past turned out to be a failure. To him, "political" and "alternative" referred to "the main currents of the political-cultural movement for the attainment of self-government."[51] In this way, the converted communists turned toward the self-government movement because they believed it was attainable and based on legal and modest means.

Viewed from the colonial politics perspective, these communists' occasional support for the self-government movement could hardly be distinguished from the self-rule movement initiated by nationalist rights. Moreover, converted communists had no proponents or organizations of their own that would represent and implement their assertions. Considering the fact that the pro-Japanese organizations of the self-rule movement boldly launched a petition to enfranchise Koreans in the Japanese Diet under the blatant campaign of the forced assimilation *naisen ittai* policy (Japan and Korea one body 內鮮一體), we can cast a doubtful eye on the communist converts' ideas of national identity. It is not difficult to find misunderstandings of the self-rule movement, as was the case with the author Kang Munsu.

However, there was a crucial difference between these two sides. Proponents of the self-rule movement were true believers in the attainment, however impossible, of the eradication of all differences between Japanese citizens and the population of colonial Korea. The fragile dream of the communist converts, however, cannot be ignored, even though these dreams only survived as a form of desire. Even though they had a dream, they could not make public their opinion. One of the means for the realization of their dreams was the slogan of Asianism, proposed by Ishiwara Kanji and the East Asian League (Tōa renmei).[52]

Established in 1939, the East Asian League mounted slogans, such as "Independence of East Asian countries" and "League of China and Japan" (which was diametrically opposed to the official Japanese policy of retaliation against China). However, it should quickly be pointed out that the movement of the League had the same purpose that the mainstream Japanese military did, that of confronting the rising Chinese Nationalism. Only the method of achieving the goal was different. The League emphasized the adoption of a gradualist and conciliatory approach rather than the direct use of force adopted by the Japanese military.

Despite the inclusion of the word "independence," the slogans of the East Asia League were directed at China, first and foremost. However, some

Koreans also wanted to be the League's benevolent beneficiary. The official response was that the League endeavored to allow the Koreans the "highest form of self-rule." This soon became a mere allusion about future independence.[53] Concurrent with the launching of what has been referred to as the Greater East Asia Co-Prosperity Sphere, the movement of the League gradually subsumed into a campaign for the Pacific War. In this respect, the dreams of the converted communists ended in illusion.

Japanism, Asianism, and the Assimilation Policy

It is no wonder, then, that almost all Koreans had gradually been driven to negate the concept of Korean nationalist thought in the colony until this mentality became the general gist of the times by the end of the 1930s. Imposition of the forced assimilation policy by the Japanese imperialists left hardly any room for the Koreans to preserve even a vestige of their own national identity. In the attempts to convert the "thought criminals" into faithful subjects worshipping the emperor as a personal god, Japanese authorities relentlessly drove Koreans toward total assimilation; the Koreans should have become identical to the Japanese. For the adoption of such a conciliatory policy to work, as conversion was originally based upon the belief that its targets were all-Japanese,[54] the ultimate doctrines to which all offenders would come around were supposed to be the same for both the Japanese and Korean people.

This belief partly explained why the Japanese authorities pushed the assimilation policy of *naisen ittai* to the utmost. It also explained why Taedong Minuhoe proclaimed in its charter that "a strong combination of *naisen ittai*" was essential to realize the goal of the "conversion of Korea" and the ideal of the construction of "tomorrow's Korea."[55] The well-known novelist Yi Kwangsu mentioned after his conversion that "those intellectuals who do not recognize the general trend of the time will become like Rip Van Winkle." He further asserted that "Koreans should become Japanese in their blood, flesh, and bone obliterating their being Koreans, that really is the only path leading to the eternal life of the Korean people."[56]

Whatever the case, it was obvious that Korean converts were urged to express the Japanese spirit, imposed upon their minds through their activities, more explicitly than the Japanese did. Just as support for the battlefront was Japan's "lifeline," borrowing an expression of the time, was it not true that becoming an "incarnation of the whole Japanese being" was also the lifeline for the Koreans? In this sense, the Japanese spirit should be represented and carried by the Korean converts in a more Japanese-like manner than among the Japanese themselves. It seemed almost impossible for Korean converts to escape from this expectation except through the imposition of another reality, say, the liberation in 1945.

The Korean case of conversion entailed a kind of abdication of self and identification with the Other. Colonial converts were extremely skeptical of the concept of the nation's independence and national pride alike. They insisted that it was impossible for a small nation such as Korea to compete with the great powers, therefore her independence was not realizable.[57] They further asserted that nationalist ideas of liberation or independence were parochial and unrealistic, for the stern reality was that colonial Korea could not be sustained in isolation from Japan.[58] If it was true that central to the Japanese conversion experience was a sharp sense of defeat,[59] Korean converts' sense of defeat was far more serious and desperate. The optimistic vision of national liberation that prevailed in the 1920s disappeared soon after the 1930s. The movement for enhancing Korean tradition during the 1930s barely survived.[60] It goes without saying that a sense of despair and skepticism was widely diffused in this situation, a circumstance that easily led to the negation of one's own identity.

Conversion was a procedure that officially approved this turnaround of negating their own national identity. If the modern Japanese intellectuals were to emulate their Western counterparts, the Korean converts were to resemble the Japanese as "sub-Westerners." If the latter did this, however, they were forced to abandon their stand against the Japanese. With the return to their original community blocked, converted communists arrived at a state theory (kokka shugi) centered on Japan. The Taedong Minuhoe listed the realization of the "great-state" theory as the first principle in its platform. It declared that the age of national agony was over and tomorrow's world would be "a great state, a great nation, and a great culture." It asserted that concern for national liberation was both out of date and useless:

Today [. . .] one nation and one state is [sic] meaningless. To organize the great state for the purpose of co-existence and co-prosperity of the nations on the basis of common traditions, lineage and resources together with geographical conditions will solve the modern national problem and improve the innate ability of the nations.[61]

According to this opinion, the leading role for the realization of the great-state theory should be attributed to the nation that had the most developed culture and ability. A great state could be realized through the enhancement of the Japanese spirit or by simply employing Japanism. In this sense, conversion itself had a double meaning for some of the Korean converts, largely the Marxists. Japanese converts went from Marxism to nationalist identification within a harmonious and unique national body (kokutai). Converted communists in Korea went from Marxism to nationalist thought to Japanese-centered Asianism.[62] In other words, Japanese converts inclined to support nationalism or its avatar, Asianism, without having to abandon the class cause. Koreans, in contrast, were forced to accept Japanism or Asianism instead of renouncing their own thoughts.

Accepting conversion entailed finding a new ideology to replace the one that had been lost. Nabeyama recalled that it took him seven years to fully stamp out his doubts after his public conversion.[63] If Korean converts had desperately tried to find an ideology to fill the emotional void after discarding their beliefs, Asianism would have been a possible candidate. Hence colonial intellectuals eagerly embraced this notion and were deeply involved in constructing the ideology of the Greater East Asia Co-Prosperity Sphere.[64] A typical example would be Kim Tujŏng, who proposed "Neo-Japanism." Against the position of self-government, which some converts had taken, Kim claimed that colonial Korea was merely the extension of Japan proper. Asserting that ultimately the Korean nation would be incorporated as a province of Japan, he envisaged that Greater Asianism would be realized through the naisen ittai policy.[65]

Another example can be found in the conversion novel, Barley (Maek 麥), by Korean writer, Kim Namch'ŏn. O Sihyŏng, an intellectual who had once been active in the social movement, explained his conversion as that "from a monistic to a pluralistic perspective of history." After conversion, his effort to achieve a theoretical understanding of his act led him to the effort for the establishment of Oriental Studies. O realized a "self-awakening of being Eastern" in the face of the international political crisis in Korea.[66] Here is his court statement.

I thought Western people had one belief about history. They believe, for example, that history is a thing like flowing water or a ladder with stairs. It is the idea that Western nations stand at the forefront, the Asian nations following their tracks in the middle, and barbarian nations are at the rear. It is said that history flows from antiquity through the Middle Ages to modern and contemporary eras, just like a stream of water. [. . .] This probably would be a monistic perspective on history. Beyond this perspective, however, *an illusion about history like this will be crushed when world history seen from [a] pluralistic perspective is established by our own efforts.* Historical reality shows this as we see it in the present.[67]

O realized that the renewed awareness of the identity of the East had been based on a pluralistic perspective of history through "the spiritual resuscitation of building a new system of thought," that is, conversion.[68] Putting aside how deeply O sympathized with the Japanese spirit, it is obvious that it was Asianism rather than Japanism to which Korean converts, including O, adhered. They believed that Asianism reflected an attempt to establish something unique to the East in opposition to the West, and that not only Japan but also Korea were included in this category.

At the heart of so-called Asianism, however, was the idea that the Japanese community was based upon the unity of Japan as a nation. Though the community was said to be representative of Asian nations, it refused to recognize each of the other members. The aim of the Japanese assimilation policy lay in the obliteration of individual identity and the extermination of national consciousness. Asianism had sustained successive Japanese invasions of other Asian nations. Japanese intellectuals endorsed or kept silent about their military invasions and the cruel repression tactics used in her colonies.[69] The conversion system itself was an effective means of inducing their consent.

Asianism and the idea of the Greater East Asia Co-Prosperity Sphere could not attain the status of universalism, however much it pretended to. It was an imaginary ideal and a false ideology. It ignored the fact that universalism depends on the uniqueness of each part which become, in turn, indispensable components of the whole. If the uniqueness of each part were to be eradicated, the basis of universalism itself would be in jeopardy. Moreover, the above-mentioned pluralist histories, together with the so-called negation of the West or "overcoming of the modern" were nothing but rhetoric. For it was not the denial of the modern, but the pursuit of it, that provided Japanese imperialism with the success of modernization.

From this perspective, even if thought conversion has been evaluated as a success by current studies on Japan, a different conclusion can be derived when we move to the case of colonial Korea and East Asia. By attempting to establish unitary self-identity through a system pretending to be universal, the Japanese authorities precipitated its eventual demise.

RESISTANCE TO CONVERSION POLICY

A discussion of thought conversion would not complete without an examination of the case of non-conversion or false conversion (gisō tenkō 偽装轉向). As we have already seen in Table 6.2, the number of non-converts in Korea remained constant, over 20 percent, until the end of the 1930s. Although it was true that non-converts or false converts were not a serious threat to the implementation of the policy in Japan, Korean converts obstinately resisted, to the point of impairing the policy.

This partly explains why the massive response in Japan caused by the memorandum from Sano and Nabeyama had few repercussions in colonial Korea. The reaction of colonized Marxists was cold and hostile in general.[70] Moreover, there was a report that thought criminals in Korea were harshly maltreated if any such offender decided to convert.[71] In this situation, it had been nearly impossible for Korean converts to perceive arrest, imprisonment, and interrogation as instruments of benevolence and feel gratitude, as in the case of Japanese converts.[72]

However, the number of non-converts in Korea gradually approached that of those in Japan by the end of World War II. For instance, among the 2,794 thought offenders out of a total of 5,290 repeaters placed under protection and supervision (hogo kansatsu) during the years 1936–1941, the ratio of non-converts to the 2,794 offenders was 5.5 percent in 1937, which dropped slightly to 3.4 percent in 1941.[73] In Japan, statistics published by the Justice Ministry in March 1943, showed only thirty-seven (1.5 percent) were unreformed out of the 2,440 communists prosecuted.[74] Though comparison of both cases seems to be inadequate, it can be said that Korea recorded a lower rate of success for its conversion policy than Japan. Moreover, a commentator estimates that approximately thirty thousand thought criminals were jailed in

1945 from both the southern and northern regions of Korea, though exact numbers were not available.[75]

Whatever the trend of the non-converts had been, it was interesting that Korean offenders in prison actively organized so-called false conversion tactics as an extension of their movement. An activist in prison analyzed three types of non-converts: the ones who persistently struggled against Japanese imperialism; the ones who took care of themselves and prepared for their release from prison; and finally the ones who chose the path of false conversion.[76] The non-converted communists residing in jail carefully examined and selected the candidates for false conversion. These individuals were expected to be released from prison earlier than non-converts and could pursue communist activities after release. The candidates were instructed to show a conciliatory attitude toward prison officers and were exempt from participation in prison struggles. These types of false conversions were frequently organized toward the end of the 1930s.[77]

There are several other reasons why non-conversion could be interpreted as a form of resistance to colonial rule. It was indicated that the first motive of conversion in Japan was a sense of isolation from the masses, that is, the fear of being segregated from an ordinary life.[78] Korean converts also found a pretext for justifying the act of apostasy in the name of the nation. Nevertheless, there existed radical differences between the situation in Japan and Korea. In Japan, where conversion had become a mass phenomenon, the attitude of the people toward the converts was warm and hospitable in general. It was as if they had returned from being a "fallen" people "contaminated" by Western thoughts; they had transformed themselves and had rejoined the "sane" Japanese nation. In this way, individuals could overcome the experience of severe isolation, after they had been converted, through identification with their family, friends, society, and nation.

This experience contrasts greatly with the responses of jailed activists toward Korean people who had converted. Usually negative terms were used to describe converts. They were stigmatized as "dogs" or were totally ignored. The communists, for example, called them "manure pails" and "patients."[79] The attitude of people in general toward the converts also was not positive; Korean converts were accused of betraying the Korean nation and the Korean people. Most of the colonial people suffered under colonial rule and war mobilization. To many, the insistence upon the disintegration of the nation seemed absurd, and the only way to escape colonialization seemed to be through supporting Korean national independence.

Lastly, there was the sharply contrasting situation that non-converts of both nations were faced with while under the control of U.S. occupation forces. Several Japanese communist leaders who had not converted until the end of World War II experienced difficulties after their release from prison. The major reason for their difficulties was that their thoughts and language had been severed from that of ordinary people after the end of the war. Tsurumi Shunsuke told the story of a thought procurator, once a liberal, who, after urging other thought offenders to convert, converted.[80] The fifteen years of this conversion policy had led the entire nation to a "genuine Japanese position." The conversion of intellectuals was, as it were, the conversion of Japan. In a similar vein, nearly all of the studies on conversion after the end of the war were negative: non-converts were said to be "fools devoid of adaptive capacity to everyday life" or "uncritical of defeated thought and obstinately adhering to it."[81]

The situation was totally different for Korean non-converts. Despite the long twenty-year vacuum in their activities, activists had little difficulty adapting to everyday life and relating to the common sentiments of the people, on whom they had exerted a major influence for several years after liberation. The seemingly well-established Japanese "identity" of the Korean people was totally negated at once.

CONCLUSION

This chapter has examined the issue of thought conversion in colonial Korea together with the related topics of national identity, the Japanese assimilation policy, Asianism, and what was once referred to as the Greater East Asia Co-Prosperity Sphere. Analyzing thought conversion in the Korean context revealed several discrepancies with thought conversion in Japan, though both policies shared common features. This also explains why the implications relating to thought conversion in the case of Korea, significantly diverges from mainstream studies on Japan.

The three types of Korean intellectuals discussed above exemplify these differences. If the major motives for justifying conversion could be summarized as a concern for the nation and the people, a significant few adhered to the cause of national identity in the name of the people. The precarious balance, however, soon skewed in one direction. Most of the Korean intellectuals obliged, reluctantly or voluntarily, to accept the impossible goal of the colonial policy, that of seeking to obliterate their own Korean identities. Desperate efforts were made to reconcile the contradictions engendered by the forced assimilation policy.

The demarcation between the political integrity of national independence and collaboration with imperialism soon became blurred since everyone had been urged to engage with the war effort in one way or another. Death or imprisonment, or occasionally seclusion from everyday life, awaited those who were reluctant to collaborate. As was frequently mentioned,[82] the great tragedy of the colonial period was that so many Korean intellectuals were compromised. Through forced conversion, the Japanese not only turned Koreans against Koreans, but also succeeded in compromising the emergence of modern intellectuals, though this was not their real intention.

The irony of this fact was that the conversion policy survived after colonization and was applied by the Korean victims. The enactment of the notorious National Security Law after liberation (1948) and the fact that "unconverted" political prisoners still remained in prison were two of the negative legacies Japanese imperialism bequeathed to Korean society. This fact, along with the provision of what has frequently been referred as the "Comfort Corps"[83] for the Japanese war effort, is surely one of the issues that will continue to cast a shadow upon the peaceful co-existence of East Asian countries in general as well as on the nations concerned.

NOTES

1. *Tenkō* has usually been understood as "change of direction" or "change of heart," and indicates that, although the term is often translated as "conversion" or "defection," neither English word adequately conveys the full range of meaning. Patricia Golden Steinhoff, "Tenkō," 5.

2. Sisō no Kagaku Kenkyūkai, *Kyōdō Kenkyū–Tenkō*, 5.

3. Bruce Cumings, *Korea's Place in the Sun*, 177.

4. Tsurumi Shunsuke, *Senjiki Nihon no seishinshi*, 8.

5. Richard Mitchell, *Thought Control in Prewar Japan*; Tsurumi Shunsuke, *Senjiki Nihon no seishinshi*, 169.

6. Robert N. Bellah, "Continuity and Change," 399.

7. Norma Field once described the atmosphere of Japanese intellectuals from the end of World War II to the mid-1950s as follows: intellectuals, especially writers, were engaged in their own battles to cleanse their ambivalent records and to exchange charges and countercharges of apostasy. This was the context within which studies of thought conversion could have been situated. Norma Field, "War and Apology," 14.

8. Itō Akira, Tenkō to tennōsai, 2, 319.

9. Richard Mitchell, Thought Control in Prewar Japan, 100–102; Tsurumi Shunsuke, Senjiki Nihon no seishinshi, 33.

10. Richard Mitchell, Thought Control in Prewar Japan, 13, 146, 186.

11. Tsurumi Shunsuke, Senjiki Nihon no seishinshi, 23.

12. It is not my intention to insist that conversions in both countries did not show any resemblance. The aims and effects anticipated from the implementation of the conversion policy was basically the same in both cases. Further, few in either country had officially apologized for their apostasy and betrayal after 1945. Be they communists or liberals, it was very hard for them to have even the thought of responsibility for the war in Japan. Fleeing from responsibility is tacitly approved. The same is true in Korea. Although a special act for punishment of pro-Japanese, including the converts, was established at the end of 1948, this act was abrogated within a year. Thus the question of punishing pro-Japanese has remained an unsolved problem in Korean society. Itō Aikra, Tenkō to tennōsai, 5.

13. In Korea, this is represented by the term "Eastern Ways, Western Machines" (tongdo sŏgi). In China, it was "Chinese Learning, Western Technology" (Chung-t'i hsi-yung). The Japanese understand it as "Japanese Spirit, Western Talent" (Wakōn yousai).

14. W. G. Beasley, The Rise of Modern Japan, 99.

15. Ibid., 96.

16. A. F. Thomas, "Japan's National Education," 51–52.

17. Richard Mitchell, Thought Control in Prewar Japan, 184–85.

18. Tsurumi Shunsuke, Senjiki Nihon no seishinshi, 44.

19. Ibid., 40, 44.

20. W. G. Beasley, The Rise of Modern Japan, 127.

21. See Tsurumi Shunsuke, Senjiki Nihon no seishinshi, 38. Its meaning combines koku (country) and tai (body, basis, or essence), which makes Japan different from other countries. Bruce Cumings, Korea's Place in the Sun, 181. Direct translation of kokutai as "national polity" is awkward, as Steinhoff suggests, for it includes both the legal and constitutional structure of the nation and its spiritual and cultural structure centering on the emperor and the family. Patricia Golden Steinhoff, "Tenkō," 3. Article I of the Meiji Constitution proclaimed the imperial line as unbroken throughout eternity. In May 1929, kokutai became an actual legal term. The Japanese Supreme Court decided that it

meant that the, "unbroken line of emperors held the supreme power." Richard Mitchell, *Thought Control in Prewar Japan*, 95.

22. Richard Mitchell, *Thought Control in Prewar Japan*, 30–31.

23. Richard J. Smethurst, "The Military Reserve Association." The legal theorist Tatsukichi Minobe insisted that the emperor was less than the state and subordinate to its laws, whereas Tatsuka Hozumi emphasized traditional attitudes toward the divinity of the emperor, who represented an ethical imperative in his theory of the state. The Japanese government, as Mitchell asserted, had decided to maintain the comforting Japanese tradition in which politics and ethics were intertwined. See Richard Mitchell, *Thought Control in Prewar Japan*, 66–67.

24. A. F. Thomas, "Japan's National Education," 50.

25. Galen M. Fisher, "Revisiting Japan," 220–21.

26. Tsurumi Shunsuke, *Senjiki Nihon no seishinshi*, 50.

27. Ministry of Education. "Fundamentals of Our National Polity," 286.

28. Honda Shuōko, "Tenkō bugakuron," 209.

29. W. G. Beasley, *The Rise of Modern Japan*, 173.

30. Germaine A. Hoston, "Tenkō: Marxism and the National Question," 111.

31. Hayashi Fusao, "Tenkō ni tsuite." After 1945, he became a forerunner of the revival of positive appraisal of Japanese imperialism, asserting that the Pacific War was the finale of the Hundred Year War with the West.

32. Tsurumi Shunsuke, *Senjiki Nihon no seishinshi*, 172.

33. Chi Sŭngjun, "1930-yŏndae sahoejuŭi," 27–29.

34. For instance, 572 out of 974 thought criminals who served their full sentences recommitted their crime and went to jail in 1931. *Chungang ilbo*, December 20, 1932.

35. One reason was that there was no Communist party initiative that led to massive conversion as in Japan. The Korean communist movement almost starved to death around the middle of the 1930s, though there were numerous efforts for reconstructing the communist party after the issue of the December theses in 1928 by the Communist International. Kim Minch'ŏl, "Ilcheha sahoejuŭijadŭl ŭl chŏnhyang nolli," 238.

36. Richard Mitchell, *Thought Control in Prewar Japan*, 111.

37. Tsurumi Shunsuke, *Senjiki Nihon no seishinshi*, 21.

38. The strict comparison of the term was almost impossible, for the criteria for classification was different in both cases.

39. The original expression of the word "national" is *kungminjŏk* in Korean and *kokuminteki* in Japanese.

40. Richard Mitchell, *Thought Control in Prewar Japan*, 133, 143.

41. Among the conversion motives of the Japanese convicted in 1942, the highest was national self-awakening (31.9 percent), followed by consideration of family (26.9 percent), repentance by arrest (14.4 percent), finding theoretical contradiction (11.7 percent), and

religion (2.2 percent). The percentage of national self-awakening among Japanese sharply contrasted with that of Koreans, although the Japanese percentage was for later years.

42. Ch'oe Yongdal, "Kansōroku," 305.

43. Hayashi Fusao, "Tenkō ni tsuite"; Kim Yunsik, "Chŏnhyangnon," 183.

44. Sano wrote in his prison diary, "(I) felt painfully the negation of being a Japanese who had forgotten about being a Japanese. . . . That it was necessary to open up a unique path to socialism with the strength of our own national people was the first reason for my *tenkō*." Germaine A. Hoston, "*Ikkoku Shakai shugi: Sono Monabu* and the Limits of Marxism," 181.

45. Peter Duus, "Chōsenhan no keisei," 65–67.

46. Louise Young, *Japan's Total Empire*, 287.

47. The expansion of Japanese imperialism at the turn of the twentieth century coincided with the triumphant days of Western imperialism. This explains why Japan annexed Korea as a colony during this stage. The atmosphere, however, changed abruptly after World War I. Faced with the critique of colonial management within European countries, whether for reasons of efficiency or for humanity, and challenges of the rising anti-colonialism and anti-imperialism within the colonies, negative attitudes towards colonialism and imperialism prevailed on a world scale.

48. Ch'oe P'anok, "Hikōhō undo kara kōhō seikatsu heno sakebi," 27; Kang Munsu, "Senjin shisōhan," 101.

49. Kang Munsu, "Zōshinsho," 49.

50. Ibid., 48–49.

51. Wang Sunbong, "Senjinshisō han tenkō shawa," 98–99.

52. Ueda Tatsuō, *Chōsen no mondai to sono kaiketsu*, 11, 29, 60.

53. Kobayashi Hideo, "Tōarenmei undō," 240–41.

54. Patricia Golden Steinhoff, "Tenkō," 70.

55. The association was established in September 1936 by communist and nationalist converts such as An Chun, Ch'a Chaejŏng Cha, and Yi Sŭngwŏn. Contrary to *Taedong minhoe*'s predecessor, Paegakhoe, the aim of which was to protect and relieve the converts, this organization was apparently oriented toward pro-Japanese activities. Under the slogans "Withering Away of Communism," "Withering Away of National Self-determinism," and "Withering Away of the Popular Front," it aimed to achieve the complete unity of the Japanese and the Koreans, full support of the colonial government, and the establishment of a grand culture based on the emperor system (*hwangdo*). See Chōsen Sōtokufu, Shisōihō 12 (1937); Chi Sŭngjun, "1930-yŏndae sahoejuŭi," 44–54.

56. See Yi Kwangsu, "Shinteki shintaisei to Chōsen bunka no shinrō," 78, 85. Of course, the absurd exaggeration of this statement should not be interpreted as a direct statement of Yi's true beliefs. There was, however, every reason not to believe in his confession after the liberation of 1945 that Korean intellectuals, including Yi, faced the threat

of massacre if they did not cooperate with the war mobilization effort. Yi, Kwangsu, "Na ŭi kobaek," 333–35. His collaboration with the Japanese, he implied, was not spontaneous, and his cooperation with Japanese imperialism was the means of Korea's salvation.

57. This thought reminds us of the logic employed by the Korean proponents of Japan's annexation of Korea in 1910. Korea's independence, they asserted, was a "daydream" and, if realized, it meant her subjection to the domination of other countries. Kim Tujŏng, Bōkyō sensen syori no hitsuzensei, 93.

58. Chōsen Sōtokufu. Shisōihō 12 (1937): 41.

59. Richard Mitchell, Thought Control in Prewar Japan, 110

60. For a detailed discussion on this topic, see Keongil Kim, "Intellectual Context of Korean Studies."

61. Chōsen Sōtokufu. Shisōihō 12 (1937): 39.

62. Kim Sŏkpŏm, Tenkō to sinnitshiha, 53.

63. Patricia Golden Steinhoff, "Tenkō," 151, 153.

64. Numerous attempts have been made to define the exact meaning of Asianism. Its origin can be traced back to the late nineteenth century, when Western powers encroached on the East. Initiated by the Meiji state, this ideology was largely used to camouflage the Japanese invasion of Korea, China, and other Asian countries. Although not all Asianism was intended to support the Japanese military invasion of the continent, it served as the justification for the establishment of the Greater East Asia Co-Prosperity Sphere. See Kim Keongil, "Chŏnshigi Ibon ŭi Taedonga Kongyŏnggwŏn kusang kwa ch'eje."

65. Kim Tujŏng, Bōkyō sensen syori no hitsuzensei.

66. Kim Namch'ŏn, Maek, 139.

67. Ibid., 184, emphasis added by author.

68. This thought reflected the theory of the Kyōto School in the 1930s. Young philosophers of this school, such as Iwao Koyama, Masaki Kosaka, and others, broadly discussed "the age after modern." Sakai criticized their concept of a pluralistic world history as nothing more than "the rhetoric of anti-modernism" seen from the context of the 1930s' situation. He mentioned that their motive was to seek the path of modernization, not anti-Western determination. Therefore, he continued, their pluralist view of history was another modification of monistic history and nothing more than the ugly face of universalism. Sakai Naoki, "Modernity and Its Critiques," 105–14.

69. Itō Akira, Tenkō to tennōsai, 9.

70. There were several reasons for this hostility. Some believed that such a memorandum was the result of coercion by power rather than a voluntary act. Others hated former compatriots' betrayal of the communist movement. Still others insisted that the proclamation had little to do with colonial Korea, for the colonial communist movements had the task of national liberation as well as class struggle. See Chōsen Sōtokufu,

Keishō hokudo keisatsusho, *Kōtōkei satsu yōshi*, 8–9.

71. Chŏng Yondŏk, "Ilcheha (1932–5) chŏnhyang," 374.

72. Patricia Golden Steinhoff, "Tenkō," 173–74.

73. Kim Minch'ŏl, "Ilcheha sahoejuŭijadŭl ŭl," 240.

74. Richard Mitchell, *Thought Control in Prewar Japan*, 147.

75. Kim Sŏkpŏm, *Tenkō to shinitshiha*, 40.

76. Chŏng Yongdŏk, "Ilcheha (1932–35) chŏnhyang," 374.

77. Chŏng Yongdŏk, "Ilcheha (1932–35) chŏnhyang," 376; Kim Minch'ŏl, "Ilcheha sahoejuŭijadŭl ŭl," 239–40.

78. Kim Yunsik, "Sasang chŏnhyang kwa chŏnhyang sasang," 267–68.

79. Chŏng Yongdŏk, "Ilcheha (1932–35) chŏnhyang," 374, 376.

80. Tsurumi Shunsuke, *Senjiki Nihon no seishinshi*, 32, 78.

81. See Kim Sŏkpŏm, *Tenkō to shinnitsiha*, 5; Itō Akira, *Tenkō to tennōsai*, 2, 16, 343. This evaluation does not exclude the non-converts' virtue of rejecting the pressure to succumb to state power. After the end of World War II, the communist party reigned over other parties based on its moral superiority, for it contained significantly fewer non-converts.

82. Michael Robinson, "Forced Assimilation," 320; Bruce Cumings, *Korea's Place in the Sun*, 172–74.

83. Bruce Cumings, *Korea's Place in the Sun*, 179–80.

7

"Colonial Modernity" and the Hegemony of the Body Politic in Leprosy Relief Work

KEUNSIK JUNG

In recent studies of the colonial history of East Asia, the consensus that colonial reality cannot be understood as a simple, colonizer-colonized dichotomy, but only in more complex structures has made significant progress. Tani Barlow argues that the category of "colonial modernity"[1] is a useful innovation for grasping a complex reality and for historicizing "the detritus of the past ideology of colonial modernization."[2] Gi-Wook Shin and Michael Robinson suggested an interactive approach, such as considering "three interlocking and mutually influencing ideas: colonialism, modernity, and nationalism."[3] They insist the conception of "colonial modernity" is heuristic in explaining colonial Korea, but because the term is ambiguous and abstract it must be concretized and substantiated. For this task, we should focus on the "late" and "periphery" imperialism of Japan and the dynamic reaction of diverse social groups within the Korean colony.

Under Japanese political and military rule, in certain cultural fields such as religion, education, medicine, and social work, Western imperial forces competed for hegemony in Korea. The modern medical and social work systems especially showcased the power of Western modernity and Christian humanitarianism to the colonized countries. The Japanese rulers also used medical policy as an important colonial strategy in governing Korea and Taiwan. Using medical technology introduced from the West, the Japanese tried to govern patients and minority groups by constructing many hospitals and asylums.

The reaction of Koreans to the new institutions differed according to their position on the social spectrum and the different social effects of two imperial forces. When we consider hegemony during the colonial and postcolonial periods, it is important to grasp, as Joong-seop Kim points out, the double-edged nature of colonial modernity and its enabling and constraining effects on social minorities.[4] Their experiences are important empirical indices of the safety and continuity of social order in colonial and postcolonial periods.

In colonial Korea, the terrain of leprosy relief is where, compared to the modern project of Western forces, the double-edged nature of Japan's colonial project is manifest. The incidents of Hansen's disease (leprosy) revealed important social problems in numerous social minorities. Like the countries ruled by Western colonialism, colonial Korea suffered severely from this disease. Related to the Western Christian image of disease and the colonial policy of Japan, leprosy, was the symbol both of the damned and of people given special grace by God in the Bible.[5] Leprosy was, paradoxically, the "sacred malady" and the disease of the soul. The Japanese employed their leprosy policy strategically in ruling Korea, especially at the end of the colonial period. After the mid-1930s, they segregated "lepers" from society and advertised this deed publicly as a successful example of their colonial policy.

Japanese and Western leprosy control tactics and the experiences of Korean patients will thus provide examples or reference points for understanding colonial modernity in Korea. The leprosy control system in East Asia moved from a "leave them alone" policy to the modern asylum in the late nineteenth and early twentieth centuries. Even though some patients remained in their homes or on the street, many were segregated from society and confined to leprosy asylums. Modern medical treatment of leprosy in Japan was initiated by French missionary workers in 1889. After establishing public leprosaria through the enactment of the Leprosy Prevention Law of 1907, the Japanese government accepted a family style. In 1931, the act was revised and they were transformed into state-run leprosaria, which emphasized the absolute segregation of lepers. In the case of colonial Korea, medical treatment of leprosy started later than in Japan, and was, as in Japan, initiated by Western missionaries. There were three missionary leprosaria in Kwangju (1910–26, moved to Sunch'ŏn in 1926), Pusan (1909–40), and Taegu (1913–45). While the Japanese established and managed a state-run asylum (1916–45) on Sorokto, a small island off the southern coast of Korea. The leprosy policy of the Government-General of Korea changed in the mid-1930s. By this time, missionary leprosaria were more numerous than those run by the Japanese.

What did the Japanese leprosy policy initiate, and what made the Japanese change their policy? Are there any important differences in the management, control, and outcome between the two types of treatment? Because the establishment of the new asylums did not entail the reform of past irrationalities but rather only the establishment of hegemony over a new terrain, it is important to examine the social context.[6] Consequently, I will compare the social contexts of colonial, state-run leprosaria with that of the Western, missionary-run leprosaria in colonial Korea, to conceptualize these different regimes in colonial Korea.

The relationships between institutional powers, organizational management, and patients differed among the various leprosy asylums. The difference in management between an asylum run by the colonial state and one privately owned by missionaries had significant impacts on patients' daily lives and their states of mind. The system of control in state asylums became confused shortly after liberation from the Japanese in 1945, and it is necessary to focus on how this confusion highlighted differences between state and private asylums. While the state asylums experienced a serious breakdown of order and severe class struggles, private asylums did not. These outcomes clearly demonstrate how colonial power worked before liberation and what resulted from it as well. Not only did the political factors and the U.S. military government involvement during the post-liberation period play a role, different principles of control did so as well.

In this chapter, I will first discuss the construction of modern asylums and second, the similarities and differences between the Western and the colonial state-run asylums. To do this, it is necessary not to stop with a structural or institutional approach, but rather to grasp the dynamics of the interaction among the Japanese rulers, the asylum operators, and the patients. A middle-range study such as this needs to look not only at the formal documents of system managers, but also at the data gathered from the patient's perspective.[7]

Western missionaries wrote many reports.[8] Because there are few materials written by patients, in-depth interviews are a useful and necessary way to grasp patients' consciousness and life histories. Here the oral histories of elderly patients in the Sunch'ŏn asylum and the Sorokto hospital are useful sources.

THE HISTORY OF MODERN LEPROSY CONTROL IN KOREA

There is some evidence that leprosy existed in traditional Korea during the Chosŏn Dynasty prior to the seventeenth century,[9] but it is difficult to uncover any records after that time. We can identify only the mention of leprosy in the "Tal" (mask) play in Kyŏngsang Province. Even though leprosy existed during the late Chosŏn Dynasty, it was considered an ordinary problem by Koreans. Leprophobia had not been a concern in Korea.[10]

Leprosy patients were rediscovered in Korea by medical missionaries.[11] The American Northern Church began to show an interest in the problem in 1904, but it took time to establish institutions. Medical missionaries began to establish leprosaria in the main cities of the southern areas of Korea.[12] The first leprosarium, in Pusan in 1909, and the third, in Taegu in 1913 were established by the American Northern Presbyterian Church and were managed by Dr. A.G. Fletcher. The Pusan facility was handed over to the Australian Presbyterian Church and managed by Rev. J. N. Mackenzie.[13] The second leprosarium was established by the American Southern Presbyterian Church in Kwangju in 1910 and managed by Dr. R. M. Wilson. In the beginning, the international leprosy relief organization Mission To Lepers (MTL) played a crucial role by providing financial support.[14]

In the process of rediscovering leprosy patients and the establishment of asylums, we find the mythic element of missionary relief work. It is unclear whether or not leprophobia existed before the introduction of Christianity into Korea.[15]

Leprosy was rediscovered dramatically in Kwangju in 1909. Dr. W.H. Forsythe, who was known to Koreans as a good samaritan[16] accompanied one female patient to Kwangju on horseback. Dr. W. H. Forsythe's reputation was a strong motivation for missionaries to continue leprosy relief work and for Korean patients to trust the mission's vision. Mythic episodes about Jesus' blessing were to be enacted before the missionaries provided any relief aid. As in the Third World, leprosy took on a new meaning in Korea and became a means of manifesting God's blessing through the leper's disdained body. In fact, an extract from the Bible published in 1893 was given the title "On Leprosy." According to the Bible, leprosy was a sin and could not be cured without God's help. This conception of leprosy may have been spread until about 1907 by the first boom of Protestantism.

The rediscovery of lepers increased leprophobia. As Gussow said, "leprosy stigma had reappeared through the influence of modern forces and events."[17] Due to the proliferation of Protestantism, people increasingly considered leprosy as a manifestation of divine wrath. The three cities in which leprosaria were located were major cities of the southern part of Korea and played very important roles both in missionary work and the medical system.

Making the Leprosy Patient a Social Other

Before and after the Korean colonial period, imperial Japan changed its policies on administering leprosy patients. Patients confined to their homes or found wandering homeless on the streets were voluntarily or involuntarily admitted into modern, institutionalized asylums. During this process, leprosy patients were redefined as social strangers, and leprosy became a social issue; leprosy patients were now institutional captives of the state power. The leprosy asylum was based on the principle of isolation from society and depended on the concept of a logical justification for this isolation, such as improved hygiene, protection from social threats, the provision of modern medical technology, and treatment.

Western missionaries, not Japan, initiated these modern institutions. In the leprosy relief field, an international organization for leprosy was established in the 1870s and beginning in 1909 assisted Western missionaries working in Korea. As soon as news of the leprosaria spread, leprosy patients begged to enter the asylums.

The establishment of leprosaria was important not only in terms of the introduction of a new institution but also in terms of the formation of a new way of looking at leprosy. The patients' bodies belonged to Western medicine, and their souls belonged to the Christian world. Even though some had been banished from their homes before they were taken into the asylum, they were not treated as outcasts. After the establishment of the leprosaria, the bodies of patients were objectified as mere things that must be segregated from society, while patients' souls could be cured and relieved only by God. From the Christian point of view, leprosy was both the price paid for sin and a demonstration of the glory of God. As the Christian image of leprosy was reconstructed, the social division between patients and non-patients widened.

Not only missionaries, but also patients accepted the need for social segregation via the leprosaria.

In the 1920s, the social problems thought to be caused by leprosy patients became a public issue. Because of Japanese cultural politics disseminated mainly through public media such as Korean newspapers, leprosy patients were accused of criminal behavior. This popular belief was amplified and dramatized by various accusations; an analysis of news articles about baby kidnappings and infanticide, however, reveals most of them to have been attempted murder cases. Leprosy's reputation as a sign of God's wrath, influenced public discourse in the 1920s and reinforced the horror and aversion of the general population to leprosy patients.

This change in public attitude deepened the social "Otherness" of vagrant sufferers. Wandering from town to town, victims of Hansen's disease came to internalize the prejudice against them and often entered leprosaria voluntarily. The leprosaria provided shelter from social prejudice and the press. The asylums also controlled sufferers with regulations and consolidated their status as outcasts.

The numbers of patients in missionary leprosaria grew until they reached two thousand in the mid-1930s. Thereafter, the status of leprosy patients changed from social Other to social enemy to be eradicated. As the Japanese colonial regime became more totalitarian, eugenic thinking provided increasingly stronger support for a policy of absolute segregation. Oppression, discrimination, and even the murder of lepers were no longer considered illegal, because forcible isolation by the colonial authorities and the deep social prejudice against leprosy sufferers were legally accepted. Leprophobia spread in the name of maintaining social order and was not censored by the colonial authorities.

ESTABLISHMENT OF THE JAPANESE COLONIAL LEPROSARIUM

In 1916, the Japanese rulers established a state leprosarium with a capacity for 100 patients on Sorokto. Why did they begin the leprosy relief program at that time? Why did they select a small island as the place for a leprosy relief program? Was their program related to missionary activities in Korea?

The Japanese health bureaucrat, Nishigawa Yoshigata (1940) defined the significance of the leprosy prevention project in Korea as the image of the imperial state and a health, humanitarian, and an administrative problem.

Which were the most important factors? The context of Japan's own leprosy policy, the initiatory period of the leprosy project, and the scale of the first state leprosarium provide valuable clues. The Japanese started leprosy relief programs on a small scale in which the goal was not to heal patients, but rather to help create the image of a civilized state and to propagandize the legitimacy of colonizing Korea. During the decade of the 1910s, it was important to promote the image of a cultured state in the international context. During this first period, the Government-General reviewed the numbers of wandering leprosy patients and leprosy patients institutionalized in missionary asylums, the hazards of contagion, and the problems of spoiling the city landscape. They were especially anxious about the hegemony that medical missionaries had over the Korean people. In Japan at that time, two current views existed on the management of leprosy patients. Japan's leprosy control policy was influenced by Western missionaries, yet it was not consistent with missionary policy in terms of segregation. Most Japanese health bureaucrats insisted that leprosy patients should be completely segregated in an isolated place,[18] and Japanese rulers tried to transplant their policy of absolute segregation to Korea. Medical missionaries, in contrast, supported a moderate segregation policy. The Government-General accepted the absolute segregation policy and established the Charity Hospital (Sorokto Chahye Pyŏngwŏn), a small asylum on the southern island. The location was selected by calculating the cost of living and the labor productivity of patients.

After the March First movement, the Japanese rulers seriously pondered the causes of Korean estrangement and the effect of missionary social work, including leprosy relief. One medical officer, Murata[19] saw the leprosy relief project as a political issue and interpreted the colonial situation as one in which Japanese military power ruled the Korean body, and Western missionaries ruled the Korean soul. Because leprosy relief work became a possible battlefield for hegemony, he asked the colonial state for a more radical relief program and insisted on the importance of expanding the state leprosaria in order to wrest hegemony from Western missionaries. The most famous health bureaucrat, Kensuke Mitsuda, expressed the same opinion. Explaining the unbalanced ratio of institutionalized leprosy patients in the missionary and Japanese leprosaria, he suggested that it was a source of Korean Western toadyism.

From the mid-1930s onward, consequently, the Japanese colonial state took a more active role in delivering leprosy relief aid than did the Western missionaries. The Japanese colonial state instigated a new leprosy control program by establishing an agency called the Chosŏn Leprosy Protection Association (CLPA) in 1932. This move represented not only transplanting the Japanese Leprosy Protection Association to colonial Korea but also acted as a breakwater against the Korean civil movement for leprosy relief. Some leaders in the Korean nationalistic camp had begun to campaign to relieve leprosy in 1928. Hŭngjong Choi, first assistant to Dr. R.M. Wilson, had suggested they organize to eradicate leprosy in Korea. Yun Ch'iho, the chairman, and most of the members had Christian backgrounds. From the late 1920s to the early 1930s, the Korean campaign for leprosy relief was based on the harsh and desperate situation arising from the failure of the Japanese colonial government to expand patient facilities. But Korean leaders also agreed with the absolute segregation policy. However, because the Government-General suppressed their fundraising efforts both directly and indirectly, they were unable to continue their plan. After the Japanese authorities organized the CLPA, in 1932, they let it monopolize all of its funds.

The CLPA compelled Koreans to raise funds to establish a leprosarium[20] and to create a leprosarium on Sorokto in March 1933, where they remodeled old facilities and made the entire island a sanatorium. In September 1933, Masaki Suho became director of the Sorokto leprosarium and organized a council of patients to exploit the patients' labor in building the leprosarium. The colonial authorities legislated the Korean Leprosy Prevention Act in 1934,[21] expanded the state leprosarium, and legalized the forced detainment of leprosy patients.[22] In 1935, the first round of construction was completed. The leprosarium had a capacity of three thousand patients and included a main office building, a medical treatment house, a public hall, and a jail. The Japanese invasion of Manchuria in 1931 caused this aggressive policy change. From this period on, the Japanese empire realized that it needed to stabilize its established colonized countries socially and economically in order to successfully invade other countries. There was another consideration involved in expanding the state asylum after the invasion of North China. The complete segregation of colonial leprosy patients was a factor in imperialistic military stationing. The safeguarding of soldiers' bodies was viewed as a means to safeguard the imperial state;[23] the military needed the complete segregation of leprosy patients.

From this time on leprosy patients became the target of police manhunts. They were viewed as social enemies to be eradicated, not simply as social outcasts. By legislating forcible segregation in 1934, the Japanese accomplished the involuntary institutionalization policy more exhaustively. With this law, the provincial governor gained the right to control the jobs of people suffering from leprosy and to institutionalize them. In addition, the director of the asylum obtained the right to take lepers into custody and to determine disciplinary punishment. After 1934, the Japanese colonial leprosarium had grown larger than the missionary leprosaria,[24] and the Japanese changed the name from Charity Hospital to Rehabilitation Asylum. The CLPA started the second phase of construction at the end of 1936 and finished construction at the end of 1937. The asylum now had a total capacity of 4,770 patients. By 1939, the asylum had reached a total capacity of 5,770. From this year on, compulsory patient labor became a serious matter. By the end of 1940, the Rehabilitation asylum accommodated 6,136 patients and was the one of the largest leprosaria in the world.

With the outbreak of the Pacific War, most Western missionaries returned to their home countries. The management of the Sunch'ŏn and Taegu asylums was handed over to new Japanese managers who were retired policemen. The Pusan asylum was shut down and converted into a military camp.

As soon as the Pacific War broke out in 1941, Yoshinobu Hayashi, the manager of the Tama leprosarium in Japan, told the patients, "You are the frontline agents for leprosy relief," implying that the labor of patients with mild cases of leprosy would be exploited.[25] One medical officer at the Nagashima leprosarium in Japan estimated the number of Hansen's disease patients in the Philippines, East Asian islands, Burma, and Malay at two hundred thousand. To isolate these people, they promoted the construction of twenty asylums and planned to let three thousand patients with mild symptoms from Japan and Korea run these asylums.[26]

When Kenske Mizda released a condolence message about Masaki Suho's death in *Eisei*,[27] the journal of his leprosarium, he emphasized the need for the construction of leprosaria in Indonesia, India, South China, and Burma. These institutions would adopt the colonial Korean leprosarium model, built by Suho in Sorokto. Mizda insisted that his policy of absolute isolation should apply to Japan's newly occupied countries. This policy was set forth by "The Statement about the Extermination of Leprosy in Great East Asia" and written by the directors of fourteen leprosaria in Japan. The movement to establish networks among state leprosaria, free cities from leprosy, and exterminate leprosy in East Asia became part of the national ideology and extended beyond medical science; emphasis on removing lepers from society combined with eugenics created a Fascist-like policy. This plan was not implemented, but it reveals the contradictions in the isolation policy.

As we have seen, the policy on Hansen's disease in colonial Korea can be divided into three periods: the period of noninterference until 1909, the period of missionary leprosaria (1909–35), and the period of fascistic state leprosaria after 1935.[28] On the process of institutionalization, some differences between the colonial state asylum and missionary private asylums can be identified. The date and context of establishment, location and size, as well as the metaphoric significance of the asylum's name are significant for our analysis.

MANAGEMENT AND CONTROL OF LEPROSARIA

Admission and Discharge

In the mid-nineteenth century, two different policies on Hansen's disease existed in the West. One, which Norway implemented from 1857 to 1860, was a relative isolation policy that, in principle, admitted house treatment. The other was an isolation policy that the government of Hawai'i developed in 1865, in which the Hawaiian government examined the citizens, deported lepers to the island of Molokai, and allowed patients to govern themselves in 1888.

In the beginning of the twentieth century, various institutions and asylums were created in East Asia into which many vagabonds were incorporated. The Japanese empire began to establish state asylums for Hansen's disease patients in 1907 and adopted an isolation policy. After the establishment of the Leprosy Prevention Law of 1907, the policy permitting absolute isolation consolidated.[29] There were few, if any, cases in which patients' self-administration was allowed.

Even though the leprosarium, one of the more modern asylums, began to offer services in the 1910s, most lepers stayed in their own homes or led vagrant lives. At that time most asylum patients admitted themselves voluntarily. Around 1930, according to a colonial police report, the number of ordinary homeless beggars numbered over fifty thousand in Korea; a portion of which included leprosy patients. In 1938, under the forcible segregation policy, half of them had not been institutionalized. However, even after they recovered their health, most could not return home because their family and neighbors would no longer accept them.

In terms of admission and discharge, there were some differences between missionary asylums and state asylums. Generally, applicants lined up in front of the gate of missionary asylums to get permission to be admitted. The institutions were always crowded beyond proper capacity. Crowding became more serious in winter; the applicants called themselves "dead dogs" and begged the administration to save their lives.[30] In the case of the Kwangju leprosarium, lack of space caused those who could afford the cost to be given priority admission after 1925.[31] If a patient recovered his health, he would ask that another family member be institutionalized in his place.[32] Serious cases took priority over mild cases. In the early 1910s, the death ratio was as high as 25 percent. In the late 1930s, a few poor patients were admitted for free, but a larger group of patients were required to pay the admission fee. Many patients recovered their health and left the asylum, even though discharge from the asylum meant disciplinary action for most. Some of the discharged patients who were healthy worked as Christian evangelists or stayed in the asylum's satellite village. Discharged patients along with people who were waiting for admission formed free colonies of lepers.[33] These villages were recognized and supported by missionaries through treatment and church services.[34]

In the case of the colonial state asylum, admission was more compulsory. In the early 1930s, many patients, at the news of the expansion of the institution, asked their local provincial hall or police officers to be admitted.[35] After 1935, however, the situation changed radically. Under the CLPA, the police aggressively arrested wandering patients in the cities and looked for them in billeting areas. Hansen's disease sufferers were arrested for begging in the city, forced out of the province,[36] or sent to the Sorokto asylum.

In the 1920s, it was possible to leave the state asylum, but it became difficult to leave after 1935. From 1917 to 1941, only a few patients were allowed to leave, and the discharge ratio was below 10 percent. During this period, out of 2,997 cases, 1,770 patients died and 312 escaped.[37] This colonial state asylum was, in effect, a grand prison because it was impossible for patients to leave freely, and work was compulsory. Gradually it gained the image of being at the end of world. The difference in compulsory hospitalization and the possibility of discharge between the Sorokto leprosarium and the missionary leprosaria created a corresponding image in the public mind from the end of the 1930s to 1945.

Administration

The Sorokto leprosarium was a state asylum operated by bureaucratic order, and whose staff was composed of a principal, directors of departments, nurses, and security guards. Security guards kept a close watch over the patients' everyday activities to prevent their escape. Under the supervision of the guards the patient trustees were organized to control the patients. Patients were not allowed to organize themselves; instead, the institution carefully selected patient trustees and established control by means of a divide-and-rule system. Classifying the patients into three levels: light symptoms, heavy symptoms, and restricted movement; the establishment let mild case patients help patients with restricted movement. A patient was in charge of each house and village. He or she reported the condition of the patients twice a day; when trouble happened, all were punished together.

The island asylum was separated from the outside world by its natural border. Its spatial organization was carefully designed and the residential area for staff—off limits to patients—was quite different from the residential space for patients. Asylums included "contaminated" and "non-contaminated" zones respectively. When the staff entered the contaminated zone, they always put on masks and gloves and decontaminated everything they wore afterward. They also sterilized letters to and from patients, an action that allowed them to monitor patients' mail and to highlight patients' separation from society.

By contrast, the missionary asylums were operated by patient semi-autonomy. The director of the asylum made decisions through consultation with the patient in charge of facilities. The asylum director was a missionary and had a tendency to control the asylum indirectly through the church. In the case of the Kwangju asylum, the patients in charge were Korean church elders, except for the first general superintendent. A clerical secretary and a bookkeeper were in charge of furloughs under the general superintendent.

In the Sunch'ŏn asylum, an autonomous system was established in the late 1920s. Dr. Wilson tried to guide patients toward solving their own problems by teaching basic medical education and labor skills. However, the church

Table 7.1 Leprosarium Administration Styles

	Missionary Asylum	Colonial State Asylum
Administrative character	Religious hegemony	Oppressive Rule
Admission	Voluntary segregation	Involuntary segregation
Attitudes toward patients	Social Other to be tended	Social Other, enemy to be eradicated
Director	Missionary medical doctor	Medical army officer/Health bureaucrat
Discharge	Permitted	Not permitted. Escape only way out.
Division of space	Male/Female zones	Healthy zone/Infected zone
Finances	Semi self-sufficiency	Expense of the colonial state
Punishment	Discharge/Discretion	Five levels of punishment
Incarceration	No	Yes
Prison	No	Yes (1935)
Routine schedule	Vague/ Duty to attend chapel	Daily routine/ Roll-call twice daily
Self-government	Semi-self-government	Not permitted/ Control agency of patients

usually reprimanded violators. Most of the violations involved sexual relations, marriage outside the church, and violence.

The missionaries studied the ideal asylum model.[38] The Sunch'ŏn asylum, which Wilson established, was one such model. Learning from past experience, the doctor considered these factors: isolation from normal villages, separate residence areas for men and women, protection from wind and cold, ideal direction for receiving sunshine, and a coastal area nearby for ease of obtaining products from the sea. He also located church and treatment facilities directly in the center of the asylum.

What was the relationship between the missionary leprosaria and the colonial state government? Generally speaking, it was dualistic. At the official level, they acted in concert, at least before 1940. Because missionaries stuck to the principle of division of politics and religion, they did not criticize the

Japanese leprosy policy. From 1923, the colonial state gave regular financial aid to the missionary asylums based on number of patients. They also assisted by donating medicine. Sometimes the Japanese royal authorities honored missionaries for their humanitarian work. In 1932, the missionary asylums depended on the colonial state for about 37 percent of their funding; in 1940 about 47 percent. For official ceremonies the missionaries invited provincial bureaucrats and accepted Japanese "national" rituals. Medical missionaries also attended academic conferences held in Japan.

On a deeper level, however, the missionaries and the Japanese were competing for hegemony over the Korean people. According to his private and official letters, Wilson always endeavored to accept as many patients into his asylum as possible, for both humanistic and evangelistic reasons. He kept himself very busy fundraising while at the same time stressed the need for self-sufficiency. On the other side, the colonial authorities were sensitive to missionary activities, and these two factors held each other in check. After the outbreak of the Sino-Japanese War, the strain increased, especially with regards to the issue of shrine worship. The missionaries were finally forced to leave their asylums around 1941.

Discipline and Punishment

The human body is defined differently by religion and culture[39] and is a dynamic object of strategic differentiation. The modern power of discipline accomplished social Othering, taming, and normalizing. Power without normalization is unstable.[40] In the leprosarium, patients were forced to obey rules, learn new disciplines, and be reborn as "modern" beings. Modern power colonized patients' bodies by dividing the bodies and souls of Hansen's disease sufferers.

Patients had to obey the rules of the leprosy asylum, but the rules differed according to the type of asylum. In the colonial state asylum, under the first director's discipline all patients had to adapt to every aspect of the Japanese lifestyle. The second director, aware of the patients' discontent, modified patient lifestyles. The third director formulated even more specific discipline. The "Rules by Heart" were very complicated and composed of twenty-seven items.[41] The first was that patients must thank the "Emperor's grace," and the second item insisted that they must obey staff orders in every aspect of their lives. The seventeenth rule dictated that patients must observe the strictly defined schedule, and the nineteenth through twenty-third concerned patients' control by their trustees, which followed a rigid hierarchical order. The twenty-fifth rule concerned freedom of association and thought deprivation,[42] and the last rule stated that patients must agree to have autopsies for academic purposes. This last rule was solely a colonial condition and was not demanded in Japan.

In addition to these formal regulations, there were informal regulations controlling the patients' everyday activities, some of which were severe. If patients spoke to the staff, they should maintain distance and face in a certain direction, not face to face.[43] According to Shilling,[44] in the affluent West there is a tendency for the body to be seen as an entity that is in the process of becoming: a project to be worked at and accomplished as part of an individual's self-identity.[45] In other conditions, however, the concept of the body is different; in colonial societies, the body of the oppressed should be forged through norms of concrete action and disciplined rituals.

Restrictions imposed on the lepers became more rigid after the mid-1930's. Mizda's principle of absolute segregation was applied to the expansion and remodeling of the Sorokto asylum. As the number of patients grew because of the compulsory isolation requirement, criminals were included, and a facility for criminals was needed. A jail was established on Sorokto to control criminal patients. This jail for lepers on Sorokto was the first and only one among the Japanese colonial asylums.

Controlling the patients' observance of the laws was the priority of the director of the Sorokto leprosarium. Patients who violated the rules were severely beaten and locked in a special confinement room that had been built in 1935. The director had the right to punish patients without judicial proceedings. In Japan, this right had been granted to the directors of public asylums in 1916. Based on the CLPA of April 1935, this right was given to the director of Sorokto asylum. The CLPA allowed compulsory confinement of lepers, arbitrary examination by a police chief, and the director's right to administer punishment. The asylum director punished patients with thirty days of solitary confinement and food cutbacks for a week. In special cases, sixty days' confinement was possible. The patients were under continuous threat and were forced to obey the asylum regulations and the orders of the staff.[46] In the confinement room they could be beaten and tortured without judicial proceedings. Their ideology and thoughts were controlled as well as their bodies.[47] In the missionary leprosaria, staff did not allow socialistic ideology in the name of separation of politics and religion. Patients who presented an ideological grievance, whether nationalist or socialist, would be expelled at once. The Sorokto asylum also prohibited the introduction of social ideology of any kind. Patients who expressed the intention of doing so were put in solitary confinement. The confinement room controlled patients' bodies and minds alike. With the additional construction of asylum facilities in 1936, both the patient death rate and the number of escapes increased. Furthermore, to maintain order in the asylum, vasectomies were forced on male patients who violated rules, and this technique proved a most efficient punishment, since it was viewed with utmost horror by patients.

In missionary asylums, the rules were simpler. Exhibiting sexual behavior, visiting alternative sexuality, and damaging of facilities were not permitted. Patients who violated the rules were reprimanded by the managing committee of the church. In cases of severe transgressions, patients could be expelled. Though attending church was not a formal rule, patients were, in effect, obliged to attend church services. Non-Christian patients suffered from psychological pressure. Some beatings, criticism of harsh rules, and severe punishments took place in the evangelistic asylum as well, but according to witnesses interviewed with experience in both places, patients were definitely more comfortable in the evangelistic asylums than in the state-run ones.

The patient autonomy system established in the Sunch'ŏn leprosarium at the end of 1920 proved to be the most effective administrative method in running the missionary leprosaria. The authorities of the church formed the highest decision-making organization, held elections, and selected one executive manager in annual general meetings held at the end of the year. The leprosarium had eleven departments: discipline, materials, general affairs, sanitation, education, husbandry, farming, labor, carpentry, brick laying, and masonry. The steering committee consisted of twenty-two members, made up of two members from each department. The advisory committee consisted of doctors, steering committee members, and a general manager. Five standing committee members were selected from among the advisory committee members and managed the monthly budget and general affairs to deal with these matters.[48] Excluding doctors and accountants, all committee members were patients. An old patient told me that he felt he was treated like a human being because of this autonomy and he thought that this point contrasted with the conditions in the Sorokto leprosarium.[49] When a Japanese director replaced a missionary worker, the patient autonomy system collapsed. The administrational system of Sorokto affected the missionary asylums until 1945.

THE MECHANISM OF NORMALIZATION AND PATIENTS' RESPONSE

Medical Treatment

There were differences among missionary asylums in terms of treatment. The Kwangju asylum was a leader in treatment method development and in the training of medical assistants. In its annual report in 1916 and in the report by Dr. Fowler in 1921, we can see the early situation of treatment and prevention activities. Dr. Wilson tried to experiment and develop new treatments using chaulmoogra oil and camphor; he stressed regular injections, good nutrition, baths, active field labor, and psychological release. He also emphasized more medical treatment through religious education in church and in the local area rather than medical treatment in the hospital:

> We worked hard to let people know the method of prevention and hygiene. They didn't know the method at all. In the Bible study class we gave them books about various kinds of disease prevention methods and taught them preventive methods and hygiene. My chief assistant, Mr. Choi, gave lectures to the village residents about leprosy preventive methods for a month, traveling from village to village.[50]

In the early 1920s, Wilson anticipated that within twenty-five years leprosy could be eliminated if four conditions were fulfilled: mass education; segregation of all patients into villages, camps, and asylums; mass treatment; and the concerted effort of Christian associations in combination with the government.[51]

According to the Mackenzie Report on the Pusan leprosarium, patients "believed they could overcome their leprosy if they had medical treatment, so they wanted to enter an asylum, even though their disease developed into a serious stage."[52] In their early stage, missionary asylums were called leprosy hospitals. Even if a few treatments were provided, "hospital" was not really an accurate name. Patients generally believed in the possibility of a cure and were obsessed with seeking medicine; at that time many patients used traditional folk medicines before and after admission. From time to time, patients used a mercurial ointment as part of traditional treatment. After the early 1920s, the administrator of the Government-General Hospital, Dr. Shiga Kiyoshi, recommended and furnished an ethyl ester treatment to missionaries, but Wilson did not trust that treatment.[53] The effect of his chaulmoogra oil treatment caused a decline in the death ratio and a rush of patients into the asylums.

Wilson selected some young patients to educate medically. They became patient-doctors and nurses who took charge of simple treatments and injections:

I asked my Korean assistants to pick up six smart patients to help in medical treatment. They learned the method of giving prescriptions, medical examinations, and [sic] microscopes. I taught them how to operate. They could perform simple operations, general diagnosis, and normal prescriptions. They helped me a lot.[54]

In 1929, the Sunch'ŏn asylum had about thirty nurses and medical assistants. Some patient-nurses were sent to the Pusan asylum. Wilson was a theorist of leprosy asylum management and not just a simple medical missionary. According to his 1938 report, he thought medical treatment was only 25 percent of leprosy treatment. Other factors depended on mental, socio-economic, and physical conditions. Particularly, in cases where the patients suffered from a severe inferiority complex and deep frustration, spiritual and religious treatment was considered very important to overcome such traumas.

A team of doctors and nurses carried out treatment in the colonial state asylum. Because of the great number of patients, however, the number of treatment teams was not adequate. The ratio of patients per doctor at this asylum was higher than that in Japan; ethyl ester became the major medicine, and treatment was restricted to purely medical purposes. Because the supply of living commodities grew shorter and shorter by the end of 1930, medical treatment for patients worsened.

Education and Religion

The normalization of social Others is the most efficient tool of power for controlling them.[55] Because of a combination of the high illiteracy rate and the goals of the missionary leprosy asylums, education and religion were the most important means by which to normalize leprosy patients in missionary asylums. Once leprosy patients were admitted, they learned how to read and write, then proceeded to read the Bible—a process that took about six months. Wilson believed it was a real privilege and sign of grace that patients could be given shelter and escape from illiteracy at the same time.[56] Because the Bible was a major text, education was the first step towards Christianizing Hansen's disease patients. Christianity led them to adapt themselves to the anguish of their world by anticipating the outside world's happiness. The order of the church was the order of the asylum. Most of the patients attended church and internalized the Christian worldview. They could maintain order within their faith in spite of the change of power.

Other classes in vocational skills were offered, including medical work, carpentry, brickmaking, masonry, plastering, spinning, weaving, and so on. Foremen managed teams of skilled patient-workers who could construct new buildings[57] and teach patients in other missionary asylums. The function of education had developed into a school in the 1930s. In the case of the Sunch'ŏn asylum, Aeyangwŏn, in 1938, ten patient-teachers taught general education and technical education to the eighty patient-students. This kind of school was expected to be the fundamental self-sufficient base for patients when they returned to society. By contrast, education was very restricted in the colonial state asylum. This was a natural outcome given that the governing principle was permanent isolation. The education of Sorokto patients actively began only after Korean liberation.

Christianity is an important issue in studying the Sorokto case. There were different views on the relief of the lepers among missionary workers, the Government-General of Korea, and patients themselves. The history of Christianity on Sorokto reveals the strife over hegemony over patients' minds. In the 1910s, the Christian religion was not allowed on Sorokto; patients were forced to convert to Shinto. Patients who did not comply were beaten and tortured.[58] When the Government-General changed the ruling system into one of cultural control, a new director, Zenkichi Hanai, invited a priest to join the patients for the first time. Christianity spread in 1925. In the early 1930s, patients' cultural activities increased, affected by the literary movement of patients in the leprosaria in Japan. When compulsory isolation became serious, and a new chief, Suho, was assigned to Sorokto, Christian activity decreased. Worst of all, a Japanese Christian missionary and a priest were expelled in 1935 and 1936 in turn. Rituals of Japanese militarism such as shrine worship took the place of Christianity. Although the Japanese authorities suppressed the Christian faith of the patients, they could not extinguish it.

Labor and Industrial Therapy

In missionary asylums, physical activity was regarded as not only a means for reducing expenses, but also as a way to fulfill the need to be productive from a clinical perspective. To supply food for patients, managers bought and reclaimed as much agricultural land as possible. Patients were proud of their buildings, which they had constructed themselves. Work became a most efficient tool in nurturing self-affirmation in patients. In the long term, it was a kind of preparation for returning to society.

It was R.M. Wilson who first made the patients work. He planned patient autonomy and self-sufficiency from the early stages of the leprosarium's foundation. He gave meat to the patients in recompense for their labor, knowing that Koreans loved meat and this could provide good incentives for diligent labor.[59] Patients occupied farmland,[60] and a general director managed the farmland as a whole. The missionary asylum was an independent economic community, with special money set aside for wages and purchases.

Around 1921, Wilson began to refer to patient's working activities as industrial (occupational) therapy. Labor, he believed, encouraged the patients to think positively and to overcome their accumulated habits of self-denial. When he designed the new asylum in Sunch'ŏn in 1926, he endeavored to secure broader fields and distributed small vegetable gardens to every cottage. The small size of the vegetable gardens gave significant meaning to the asylum in terms of patient's work habits and the principle of self-sufficiency. While laboring for the asylum, patients were paid about 10 percent of the average wage in society and earned different wages according to the type of labor. After the Sunch'ŏn leprosarium completed construction in 1929, patients did the cooking, cultivating, sewing, and everyday

Table 7.2 Leprosarium Normalization Types

	Missionary Asylum	Colonial State Asylum
Approach	Comprehensive	Medical
Education	Comprehensive Christianization	Narrow
Marriage	Permitted from 1934	Permitted from 1936
Medicine	Chaulmoogra oil	Ethyl Ester
Patient labor rationale	Occupational therapy	Occupational therapy/ later forced labor
Personnel	Self-educated	Bureaucratic
Religion	Christianity	Shintoism, Buddhism, Christianity
Resistance	Church arson	Killing of deputy and director
Vasectomy	Mutual agreement	Forced

activities for free; they earned 4 *sen* for nursing, constructing, and making bricks; 8 *sen* for heavy labor; and 12 *sen* for technical labor. But patients were grateful for the small reward and expressed thanks that the leprosarium fed them and gave them money.

Missionaries indicated that gender differences in work habits affected treatment and mental outlook. Korean women were good patients from a clinical perspective because they had learned many diverse manual skills from a young age. The death ratio of women patients was also lower than that of men.[61]

In the colonial state asylum, industrial therapy was not introduced in the beginning, but by the late 1920s it was adopted. Like Aeyangwon, the Sorokto asylum paid a small wage for the patients' labor, about 10 percent of the average wage at that time. According to the type of work, patients earned different wages. From the mid-1930s, policy increasingly switched to forced or unpaid labor. The expansion of the state-run asylum depended mainly on the mobilization of patient labor. According to patients, village heads competed with each other to pick out patients who had a good work record from the time they had been admitted to the asylum. Patients who could not work were not welcomed.

An individualized work diary was written for each patient and tightly controlled. Work hours were assigned to the patients as a village unit and then distributed as a household unit. Work at Sorokto was divided into outdoor and indoor activities. Construction, driving, cultivating, and salvage operations were included in the outdoor category; indoor jobs included making shoes, making soy sauce, and basic maintenance. Brick manufacturing began in 1934, and the bricks were used in constructing the leprosarium. When brick production exceeded the demands of the leprosarium at the end of 1930s, they were sold to the outside community. During this period, patient laborers were exploited and frequently suffered work-related injuries and deaths.

Marriage and Vasectomy

Marriage between patients was a major issue in managing the leprosy asylums, as was patients' sexual desire. Because they suffered from the same disease and shared food and lodging, patients were prone to feel compassion for each other. Even though the Christian leprosaria had a relatively mild social policy, they severely separated men and women and church law prohibited sexual relations. This problem was discussed in Japan around 1910; at that time, the Western missionaries offered relatively moderate segregation, but the Japanese health bureaucrats insisted on absolute segregation. It is interesting that former camps insisted on banning marriage, but later camps would permit marriages on condition that a vasectomy was performed. Kenske Mizda, the director of a Japanese public leprosarium since 1915, permitted marriages with males who had undergone vasectomies as a measure to prevent the escape of patients. He justified this policy as needed not only for the protection of patients but also to protect outside people from the disease. Male patients were apt to be both mild-mannered and diligent in courting female patients in a situation where the proportion of males to females was three to one. Mizda argued that patients had the possibility of having infected babies, even though leprosy was not a hereditary disease. Dr. Kiyoshi Shiga, the director of the Government-General Hospital, said in 1926 that there was no way to eradicate leprosy without a vasectomy.[62]

In Korea, missionary workers first permitted marriage between patients under the condition of sterilization. R.M. Wilson had experimented with permitting patients to marry in 1934, when an incident brought on by the patients' resistance—arson—occurred at the asylum church. Realizing the importance of socio-cultural factors in the management of a leprosarium, Wilson believed that Koreans had three major dreams: to have a home, a family, and a son. The fulfillment of these dreams was both important for patients to comfortably adapt to their situation and for the asylum to maintain a stabilized order. Selecting eleven skilled patients, he received ten patients' agreements to enter into marriage after a vasectomy. When this first round of experiments proved successful, thereafter many patients married after sterilization.[63]

The colonial state asylum established this policy in 1936. One aspect was the same as with the missionaries; it was a tactic for diminishing patients' discontent. Marriage on condition of vasectomy was not accepted by patients in the first phase, but in the early 1940s, 840 couples accepted this condition. The other use of forced vasectomy in this asylum, however, was a kind of punishment.[64] Whenever male patients did not obey staff orders or asylum regulations, they were given vasectomies. Because they were conducted upon discharge from the incarceration room and before release, patients were seized with fear of them. For them the punishment of a vasectomy literally meant loss of life. In fact, vasectomy became a strategy for decreasing the number of patients; from the eugenics perspective, it was not only a way to eradicate the disease but also a way to ultimately eradicate the patient population itself.

Resistance by Patients

Though the diverse types of normalization had succeeded, patient resistance occurred sporadically in leprosy asylums. There was some resistance in missionary asylums, the main target of patient discontent being the Korean superintendent. In cases of unrest, participants were expelled. In the Taegu Asylum, fourteen patients went on strike in 1930. Fletcher wrote in his report that he thought that close observation and management were needed.[65] In the Sunch'ŏn Asylum, as mentioned, the asylum church was set on fire in 1934. The arsonists included some patients upset by the Christian-oriented management of the superintendent and patients who felt anxious about the asylum's discharge procedure.[66] They stayed in a patient community outside the asylum for a while until they were caught and punished. Some were sent to the jail on Sorokto, while two killed themselves.[67] These events indicate that Korean asylum patients did not agree with missionary control.

In the colonial state asylum, the first collective resistance by patients protested the mandating of the Japanese lifestyle in the late 1910s. After 1919, the second Japanese director permitted Korean lifestyles and religious freedom. Fundamentally, the rigid control system suppressed the occurrence of collective resistance. Occasionally, however, it failed, as illustrated by the murders of a senior patient who played the role of trustee in 1941 and the director of the Sorokto Asylum in 1942. In the latter case the patient insisted that his action was a protest against the inequality involved in the granting of permission for temporary return to hometowns, the cruelty of forced labor, the tyranny of the confinement room, inhuman treatment by the chief nurse, the curtailment of food, and so on. By this time the Japanese rulers had constructed their huge leprosaria and had sung the praises of their leprosy policy to the Japanese government and the Korean people alike, while the lepers showed their hostility by murdering key managers.

The patients in the two types of asylums showed different types of struggle because of the differing degrees and methods of suppression and the changing characteristics of the governing body. As the case of Sorokto indicated, severe suppression temporarily controlled the discontent of patients but caused strong resistance in the end. In the case of the missionary asylums, we need to study the meaning of religion, and how it relates to the social "Other" in the context of a ruling system: Christian belief as a form of resistance to colonial power is one thing; Christianity as an alternative controlling power is another.

CONCLUSION

Modern leprosaria were introduced to the Korean colony in the early twentieth century. The Western missionaries provided medical relief, while the Japanese asylums were used as a method of colonial control. Unlike Japan, the competition among Western and Japanese rulers and Korean nationalists was evident in Korean leprosy relief. The Korean nationalists lost power after the establishment of the Chosŏn Leprosy Protection Association, and Japanese forces and Western missionaries were left to compete for hegemony.

The missionary asylums adopted various approaches when dealing with patients and had different characteristics than the asylums controlled by the Japanese. In the case of Sorokto Asylum, absolute isolation, vasectomy based on eugenics, arbitrary punishment, and compulsory labor were all employed. In the missionary asylums, relatively mild isolation, patient autonomy, and Christianity were the predominant methods of social control. Based on these differences, the colonial state asylum run by the Japanese could be conceptualized as a "directory regime" and the asylum run by missionaries as a "tutelary regime."

The directory regime began in Japan and it was transplanted to the Korean colony where the Japanese rulers institutionalized patient autopsies and established solitary confinement rooms.[68] The leprosaria in colonized Korea permitted less freedom and autonomy to patients than leprosaria in Japan. This institution reflected the colonial policy of the Japanese: In the first period of colonization, the Japanese had a less strict policy towards leprosy patients because the Japanese government was concerned about their national image. By the end of colonization, the Japanese changed their focus and were exploiting patients for their labor to the benefit of the military and to keep society functioning normally. Compulsory mobilization of the asylum patients into forced labor and strict control characterized the directory regime. Although this kind of regime seemed to thoroughly control the colonized country, including leprosaria, it was clear that without compulsory control, the government was so unstable that it could not properly maintain the colonial system. During this period, the Japanese colonial government demanded extreme unity from its own people without admitting differences, a demand that was greatly increased in colonized Korea.

The tutelary regime of mission-led leprosaria, in contrast, meant to spread the Christian mission to the social minority. The church authorities governed the patients. Relatively mild medical treatment and isolation techniques, education, patient autonomy, and self-sufficiency were all employed. The missionaries regarded the patients both as social Others and as would-be-normal people. In this way the regime developed stability, but it gave patients who had already experienced social discrimination little dignity. Unlike the directory regime of the Japanese colonizers, the tutelary regime could be rooted in the minority mind. Even though the church authorities sometimes suppressed and over controlled their patients, the tutelary regime had socio-psychological benefits because it was not a political controlling power.

During the colonial period, patients were able to realize the differences between tutelary regimes and the directory regime; between the missionary asylums and the asylum controlled by the Japanese. This realization would bring about the reform of the Korean leprosy policy and the leprosaria after 1945. During the colonial period, however, the Sorokto Asylum was viewed as a place of despair, and the missionary asylums as hopeful places of rehabilitation. There was some criticism about the missionary asylums later, of course. During the 1960s, Han Haŭn, a famous leprosy poet and the leader in the rehabilitation of lepers, criticized the missionary asylums for their cruelty toward patients, in contrast to other Korean Christians.[69]

After 1945, Korea and Japan developed different attitudes toward discrimination against Hansen's disease patients. The compulsory isolation and sterilization operations imposed by the Japanese were serious violations of human rights, and some activists demanded compensation for victims. Until the mid-1990s, segregation was practiced in Japan.[70] Takeda said this was a result of extreme exclusion and was deeply rooted in modern Japan.[71]

From 1945 through to the 1950s, meanwhile, the Korean government kept the previous system and segregated people suffering from Hansen's disease from society. The negative image of leprosy patients during the colonial period led to some incidents where patients were murdered after liberation. Unlike Japan, however, the Korean leprosy policy was transformed from an asylum system to a rehabilitation village system. During this transformation, asylums adopted the tutelary regime style, which promoted patient autonomy, a self-sufficient system, and church-centered administration. The issue of patient compensation for those infringed and discriminated against by the Japanese colonialists has not been officially mentioned at the national level since Korean Independence, even though some criticism has been made and some former administrators have apologized for their past behavior.[72]

NOTES

1. See the inaugural issue of *Positions: East Asia Cultures Critique*, 1 no. 1 (Spring 1993) devoted to the concept of colonial modernity.

2. Tani Barlow, *Formations of Colonial Modernity*, 20.

3. Gi-Wook Shin and Michael Robinson, "Colonial Modernity," 5.

4. Joong-seop Kim, "In Search of Human Rights," 312.

5. Saul Nathaniel Brody, *The Disease of the Soul*, 101.

6. David J. Rothman, *The Discovery of the Asylum*, xix.

7. Gussow emphasized the importance of the patient's view in studying the social history of leprosy. Zachary Gussow, "Leprosy, Racism, and Public Health."

8. For example, Dr. R. M. Wilson, who was director of the Kwangju and Sunch'ŏn asylums, wrote personal letters and periodical reports in several magazines: *Without the Camp, The China Medical Journal, Leprosy Review,* and *Korean Mission Field*.

9. For a more detailed discussion of the history of leprosy in Korea, see Chŏng Kŭnsik, "Singminjijŏk kŭndae wa sinch'e ŭi chŏngch'i."

10. Gussow insisted that the stigma of leprosy disappeared at the end of the Middle Ages and reappeared in the nineteenth century through the influence of modern forces and events, and that the role played by the United States in maintaining a separatist leprosy tradition was significant as in Culion, Philippines and at Molokai, Hawai'i. Zachary Gussow, "Leprosy, Racism, and Public Health."

11. Although the Western missionary, Dr. H.N. Allen, first discovered leprosy patients in 1886, and M.B. Ingold in 1902, they did not offer relief programs to them. R. Wunsch, *Fremde Heimat Korea*, 43.

12. The relief work for leprosy was initiated in the same period as the establishment of dispensaries for the general population. The establishment of dispensaries by Western missionary doctors brought about a fundamental change in the medical system. The dispensary was the place where doctors saw patients and prescribed medicine for members of a community. It was a real house and a perceptual structure. David Armstrong, *Political Anatomy of the Body*, 8.

13. Helen Mackenzie, *Mackenzie—Man of Mission.*

14. L.M. Bechelli, "Advances in Leprosy Control."

15. This situation is very similar to that of Japan. When the first Infectious Disease Prevention Act was established in 1897, Hansen's disease was not included in this act, because people had very little interest in Hansen's disease. Shoji Takeda, *Segregation as Disease*, 26. However, after Western missionary workers started to establish leprosaria in 1889, the Japanese changed their attitude for the sake of their international position. The Diet stressed the importance and the necessity for leprosaria. The Ministry of Home Affairs investigated Hansen's disease for the first time in December 1900. According to the data—30,359 cases—199,075 family-line households and 999,300 family-line members were collected. Because the police executed this investigation, not medical doctors, it did not represent accurate reality but showed that the possibility of a contagion still remained. After their victory in the Russo-Japanese War in 1905, the Japanese people insisted that new laws be enacted to remove the state's disgrace. The Infectious Disease Prevention Act II was established in 1907, and five leprosaria with a capacity of 1,080 patients were built in Japan. Yamamoto Junichi, *Hansenbyo Nihon no rekishi*, 51.

16. R.M. Wilson, "In Heroic Mould," 10.

17. Gussow concluded that Western imperialism, germ theory, the activity of missionaries, and racism contributed to leprophobia. Zachary Gussow, *Leprosy, Racism, and Public Health*, 22, 201–9.

18. Mizda proposed using Iriomoteshima in Okinawa as a leprosarium site in 1915, but his proposal was not accepted. Instead, a leprosarium was built at Nagashima in Sedonaikai. Kenske Mizda, "Condolence for the Death of Chief Suho."

19. Murata was a Japanese health bureaucrat and the director of the public asylum in Japan in 1927.

20. At the end of 1935, 1,220,000 *yen* was raised.

21. In Japan, the people decided by consensus to establish the Korean Leprosy Prevention Act to purify the country. This act supported detention by legal force, the extension of the state leprosarium, and local movements for the prevention of leprosy. It developed a system to control lepers during wartime. Mizda's concept, emphasizing absolute isolation, spread from Japan to Asian countries. He insisted that the "No Leprosy in the Country" movement should arrive, through "sympathizing sufferers and mutual assistance," this occurred at the point of "No Leprosy in Japan, No Leprosy in China, No Leprosy in Asia." Kenske Mizda, "Condolence for the Death of Chief Suho."

22. In Japan, Act II, the "Leprosy Prevention Act," established in 1907 was the first act that dealt with the prevention of Hansen's disease. This act was revised in 1931 and 1953 and was not abolished until 1996. The Japanese leprosy policy called for compulsory examination, confinement, and isolation lasting ninety years. In other words, this policy would exterminate lepers and isolate lepers until their deaths.

23. Fujino Yutaka, *Kyōseisareta kenkō: Nihon fashizumu-ka no semei to shintai*.

24. The Sorokto leprosarium had 764 patients; the missionary leprosaria had 1,750 patients in 1932. After the first reconstruction, there were 3,773 patients in the Sorokto leprosarium; 1,800 patients in the missionary leprosaria; and 7,400 patients in Japanese society by the end of 1935. Yamamoto Junichi, *Hansenbyo Nihon no rekishi*.

25. Tama Zenshōen Kanja Jichikai, *Kue issho: Kanja ga tsuzuru Zenshōen no shichijūnen*.

26. Shoji Takeda, *Segregation as Disease*, 51.

27. Kenske Mizda, "Condolence for the Death of Chief Suho."

28. Otani divided the Japanese Hansen's disease policy into four periods: the period of vagrant lepers under the rule of the early Meiji, the period of public asylum for twenty-five years after Act II in 1907; the period of the state asylum, which supported the isolation policy, after the revision of Act II in 1931; and the last forty years after the Prevention Act of 1953. Fuzio Otani, *History of Abolition of Leprosy Protection Act in Japan*.

29. In the early Meiji period, leprosy, even though it was defined as a contagious disease, was generally considered a hereditary disease according to eugenics theory.

30. Dr. R. M. Wilson, *Without the Camp* 67 (1913).

31. *Tonga ilbo*, May 25, 1925.

32. Dr. R. M. Wilson, *Without the Camp* 140 (1931).

33. Ibid., 118 (1926).

34. Ibid., 128 (1928); 159, (1936).

35. *Tonga ilbo*, September 7 and October 1, 1933.

36. In Japan, unlike Korea, the "No leprosy in my town" movement spread and led to the compulsory isolation policy.

37. *Tonga ilbo*, August 3, 1923.

38. Dr. R. M. Wilson, *Without the Camp* 97 (1921); 126 (1928).

39. Jan Marie Law ed., *Religious Reflections on the Human Body*.

40. Martin Hewitt, *Bio-politics and Social Policy*.

41. Kungnip Sorokto Pyŏngwon. *Sorokto Pyŏngwon 80-yŏnsa* : 1916–1996.

42. By the end of the 1920's, secret patients associations, such as Susong Youth Association, Agriculture Promoting Association, and Patients' Solidarity, were organized, but Director Zenkichi Hanai exposed and dispersed them. Sim Chŏnhwang, *A 70 nyŏn—challanhan sŭlp'ŭm ŭi Sorokto*.

43. Sim Chŏnhwang, *A 70 nyŏn—challanhan sŭlp'ŭm ŭi Sorokto*.

44. Chris Shilling, *The Body and Social Theory*, 5

45. Ibid., 5.

46. Yun Chŏngmo wrote in her novel that the real motive for the establishment of confinement was to control political offenders. Yun Chŏngmo, *Kŭrigo hamsŏng i ttŭllyŏtta*, 92.

47. Confinement, nicknamed a "special sickroom," became common in Japan in 1938 and was used as a mechanism for slaughter. Shoji Takeda, *Segregation as Disease*, 55. Ninety-two patients were confined from 1939 to 1947. People fought for patients' rights and asked that the technique be abolished, which happened in 1947. Confinement at Sorokto, however, was harsher and more severe for patients; it might have been the severest such facility in the world, but no public attention was paid to it.

48. Dr. R.M. Wilson, *Korean Mission Field* (1929).

49. Interview by Keunsik Jung with former patient of the Sorokto leprosarium.

50. Kwangju Asylum, *Annual Report*, 1916.

51. Dr. R. M. Wilson, *Without the Camp* 97 (1921).

52. Kwangju Asylum, *Annual Report* 1916.

53. Dr. R. M. Wilson, *Without the Camp* 109 (1924).

54. Ibid.

55. Martin Hewitt, *Bio-politics and Social Policy*, 229.

56. Kwanju Asylum, *Annual Report*, 1916.

57. Dr. R. M. Wilson, *Without the Camp* 124 (1927).

58. Yi Kyŏnghyŏng, "Osun ŭi binnanŭn ch'ottae."

59. Dr. R. M. Wilson, *Without the Camp* 67 (1913).

60. Ibid., 70 (1914).

61. Helen Mackenzie, *Mackenzie-Man of Mission.*

62. Yamamoto and Fuzino have completed significant studies of the social history of leprosy in Japan. Yamamoto studies the origin of Japanese leprosy and the history of modern leprosy control. Fuzino is interested in the relationship between the segregation policy and Japanese eugenics. He indicates that Japanese Fascism was based on eugenic thinking and insists that the Japanese "super-medical management" policy included drastic measures such as vasectomies. Fuzino's study provides an important reference for the comparison of Japanese leprosy control policy in Korea and Japan. Junichi Yamamoto, *Hansenbyo Nihon no rekishi; Yutaka Fuzino, Japanese Fascism and Medical Problems.*

63. R.M. Wilson, Personal letter, 1954.

64. In 1915, compulsory sterilization operations began at the Jonsei Hospital for patients who wanted to marry. After World War II, the law authorized sterilization operations on lepers based on eugenics and consolidated the practice in 1948. Even though leprosy was proven contagious and not hereditary, Japanese Fascist eugenics enforced the sterilization procedures.

65. Fletcher A. G., "Country Clinics or Dispensaries for Treatment of Cases of Leprosy," 58–66.

66. Dr. R. M. Wilson, *Without the Camp* 150 (1934).

67. Ibid.

68. Otani mentions that the absolute isolation policy towards lepers developed into Fascism in the stage of premature democracy and modernity. Fuzio Otani, *History of Abolition of Leprosy Protection Act in Japan.*

69. Han Haŭn criticizes the relief activities for leprosy patients conducted by missionaries, arguing that these activities were intended to attract attention and interest from Koreans in the name of philanthropy. Han claims that the missionaries depended upon the aid from the Government-General of Korea for feeding patients, and that there were many cases of homicide, physical abuse, violence, confinement, forced discharge, and malnutrition in leprosy asylums. Han Haŭn, "Naja ŭi sahoe pokkwi esŏ ŭi silchejŏk munje."

70. The Academic Association for Leprosy in Japan officially apologized for their past errors in 1994.

71. Shoji Takeda, *Segregation as Disease*, 70.

72. Japanese specialists such as Hamano Kikuo (1965), a director of the Japanese Leprosy Association, regrets the fact that the misguided leprosy policies of colonial Japan hurt many people in Taiwan, Okinawa, and Korea. The policy included forced segregation of patients, the violation of human rights, and the negative view of patients as enemies to be eradicated.

8

Colonial Body and Indigenous Soul: Religion as a Contested Terrain of Culture

KWANG-OK KIM

Focusing on the experiences of a colonized people and their ways of remembering the past, this chapter aims to reconsider the issues of the colonization of consciousness and the consciousness of colonization among Koreans during the Japanese occupation. Through a reconstruction of the historical process in which the Japanese colonialists destroyed the cultural system of the colonized Koreans through the use of rhetoric, this chapter attempts to understand how the natives responded to and counter-manipulated this process of colonial modernization.[1] It is a study of the conflicting relationship between the secular power of the colonial state and the sacred authority of the colonized society.

Here, experiences in the indigenous religious communities attract our concern because religions quite often provide people with a cultural process to shape a counter-explanation of their life experiences opposed to the official discourse of the state. Especially in the colonial situation, in which a direct challenge to the state is impossible, religion and ritual provide the populace with a special space for manipulating their ideological stance in relation to sacred and supernatural beings. So, conflicts and confrontation on the question of the legitimacy of rule between the colonizers and the colonized were given voice through ritual or scriptural interpretation. The colonizers typically attempted to destroy the spiritual world of the colonized and to construct an image of power in the mind of the colonized,[2] while the colonized exploited their cultural resources in order to develop various kinds of strategies in dealing with the colonial power.

Keeping silent, marginalizing the self from the official arena, miming foolishness and adaptive inefficiency, or inviting stigmatization are other forms of resistance that a dominated people adopt in everyday life. In the same way, religious practitioners construct a space of vagueness, ambiguity, and mythic sacredness beyond the rationality and science officiated by secular authority. In this regard, we need to observe how the Korean people manipulated various arts of resistance, in their religious and ritual activities as well as their everyday life, to oppose the violence of colonial power.

The Japanese colonial authorities called the native tradition "*dozoku*" (native custom, K. *t'osok*) or *minzoku* (folk custom, K. *minsok*). "Native" (t'o) here suggests uncivilized, barbarous, and savage, while "folk" (min) in this context evokes backward, irrational, and emotional peasants. By labeling the Korean tradition with the words like *dozoku* or *minzoku* (folk, among the people) the Japanese colonialists constructed an image of Koreans as uncivilized and uncultured; Korean culture could be erased or destroyed and then replaced by the Japanese culture under the name of colonial modernity. The usage of these newly introduced academic terms in the name of scientific methodology led Koreans to regard their own tradition as inferior and childish and, therefore, studies of Korean culture became marginalized.

In this way, the Japanese excluded the native Korean belief systems and rituals from the category of religion and classified them as pseudo or fake religion (*ruiji shūkyō*) or even simply as folk customary religion (*minzoku shūkyō*). This colonial perspective on Korean-ness survived in the post-colonial education system and reiterated the denouncement of Korean traditional culture under the banner of modernization in the early 1970s. It has only been since the 1980s that the new post-colonial generation intellectuals began to reconsider Korean folk tradition as part of the popular culture movement.

The main observations here concern shamanism and Confucianism, although Christianity and other forms of folk religion are also considered. The Confucian tradition is embedded in the everyday life of the Korean people regardless of their class and religious background. Thus, it is the backbone of Korean culture and through the elaboration of Confucian ritual and ethics that the Korean people competed for their cultural superiority on the one hand and tried to construct a cultural community of their own to support or challenge the state authority on the other.[3]

Shamanism is another pillar of the Korean worldview. While Confucianism emphasizes state authority, a hierarchical social order, knowledge, and education, shamanism generates an ideology of egalitarianism and provides the symbolic experience of liberation from differentiation and the yoke of lived reality. The Confucian pursuit of solemnity, refined behavior and taste, and high-level knowledge stands in stark contrast with the vulgar, coarse, uncivilized language and drama of a shamanic ritual performance. Through the mediation of a shaman, a spirit and spectators communicate with each other and finally achieve psychological liberation from emotional agony and grievance.

Because religion is a cultural system,[4] it is posited in a power relationship between the state and society. In this regard, we may approach the colonial encounter in the field of religious life from the perspective of the politics of culture, as well as, the culture of politics by positing religion in the context of political and social life.[5]

This chapter is an anthropological approach to the process of colonial definition and construction of indigenous culture.[6] This chapter focuses on Koreans' memories of the period of colonial rule. These experiences were filled with hegemonic struggles between the official definition of "Korean culture" by the colonial authorities and the privatized discourse of the indigenous tradition. The Japanese colonialists tried to distort and manipulate the colonized Koreans' culture and history in order to prove "scientifically" the "national inferiority" of Koreans.[7] In this regard, the study of colonial cultural policy is particularly important.

Reconstruction of colonial experiences is, however, not an easy task because of the scarcity of available official records. Most documents and written materials were destroyed at the end of Japanese rule and subsequently during the Korean War. Also, the hidden intention behind the rhetoric cannot be easily explicated, because an articulated policy may hide multiple purposes: a governmental act on religious activities might have concealed a specific political intention, and a social campaign might have been organized for ideological control. Furthermore, the result, intended or not, of a particular policy usually did not follow immediately. Colonial projects were multifaceted, and hidden intentions would appear only after the lapse of a certain period of time. Therefore, studying the colonial experience by referring only to written materials and official documents is limited and carries with it a high possibility of distortion.

Anthropological fieldwork is required to overcome the methodological difficulties and to interweave pieces of personal and social experience into a holistic story. What is missing in the documents will be filled in by informants' memories of the past as presented in their narratives. Here the accuracy or objectivity of personal memories may be questioned because they can be selected, distorted, and even invented. Though it is arguable in a sense, I would maintain that a collective history might be constructed if people share their memories in everyday situations. By scrutinizing the families mentioned in the official record and conducting interviews with people in the villages concerned, we can examine the trustworthiness of the stories told. Fieldwork reveals that the colonial experiences were so deep and vivid that to this day Koreans remain haunted by these memories.[8] Since telling a tale is another form of conscious commitment to one's own history, anthropologists are concerned with the form, content, and meaning of the histories people are making. To overcome the limitation of the statistical and empirical approaches, we must adopt another method of memory analysis to penetrate historical reality as it is imprinted in the participants' minds.

For research convenience I have focused my observation on a local community in the Andong region, where I have been doing anthropological fieldwork for over twenty years. This community retains a strong Confucian tradition as well as its peasant folk culture. During the colonial period, not only the Confucian elites but also the peasants produced prominent leaders in the anti-Japanese resistance movement. Therefore, Andong provides examples of various forms of conflict and tension between the colonial power and the indigenous society.

EMBODYING COLONIAL POWER

Restructuring Physical and Social Space

Colonial power first became visible through the alteration and redefinition of physical and social spaces dedicated to the colonizers' everyday life. In the city of Andong, within two years of colonization, the Japanese colonizers built the local administrative office along with the new police headquarters, fire station, district court, military garrison, post office, and bank. Later, the Japanese erected the railroad station at the end of the street that originated at the colonial administrative office. These edifices sufficiently symbolized and embodied the colonial power in the Korean peoples' consciousness.[9]

The colonial government built a Japanese residential district, including an elementary school exclusively for Japanese children, in the vicinity of the city administration buildings. In 1938, the colonial authorities erected a municipal Shinto shrine on the mountain behind the Japanese residential compound. As a result, most parts of the city remained mainly Korean while the southeastern areas became Japanese, a situation that at first produced an interesting picture in that Japanese flags filled the southeastern district while the rest of the city appeared relatively quiet during official celebrations. The city center included banks, offices, Japanese shops, restaurants, and entertainment houses. As the commercial area expanded, the traditional Korean market moved from the city center to the southwestern part of the city.

In this way, Andong's living space became divided into an indigenous world and a foreign one, or a pre-modern and a modern world occupied by Koreans and Japanese, respectively. Out of their sense of cultural superiority, the Koreans in their district maintained their traditional attitude of despising the Japanese. For a taste of modernity, however, they had to come to the Japanese district, although some stern Confucian scholars of the old generation regarded the Japanese district solely as a place to indulge the vice of material greed and the amoral pleasures of alcohol and women.

In front of the police headquarters, a bell tower was erected that was high enough to have a bird's eye view of the whole city. Twenty-four hours a day a fireman stood watch and sounded a siren at noon. Whenever large groups of Koreans congregated in some corner of the city, the watcher rang the emergency bell and immediately dispatched a police unit. In this way, Koreans in public spaces remained under continuous watch and control. When the Japanese commemorated their national heroes by issuing bells or sirens, they ordered Koreans to stand still and bow. One day a deaf Korean man kept walking when the siren sounded to commemorate the souls of soldiers who sacrificed themselves for the Japanese Empire. The military police caught and severely beat the man. When the man's father protested this cruel treatment, a young military officer slapped him on the cheek and threatened him with a saber. After the incident, as many elderly people over eighty years of age still remember, Korean adults remained in their houses on such occasions while their children performed the ceremonies at school.

As the Japanese began to occupy the main social, administrative, and economic arenas, many Confucian intellectuals from prominent families went into exile in China to carry on the anti-Japanese independence movement. For example, Yi Sangyong, the primogeniture heir of the locally prominent Yi lineage, sold all of the properties allocated to his house, traveled to Manchuria, and established a military academy to produce officers to lead the fight against the Japanese.[10]

With a strong academic tradition, the people of Andong were enthusiastic about the opportunity of a modern education for their children. At the turn of the century, prior to the Japanese occupation, many prominent local lineages converted their traditional schools, *sŏdang*, into unofficial modern schools, invited young intellectuals to teach modern education courses (i.e., mathematics, physics, geography, and even some English), and provided meeting spaces for special public lectures on contemporary national issues. Ten years after colonization, the colonial government had incorporated nearly all of these private schools into the public school system. Among them, Hyŏptong Hakkyo, a school established by the Ŭisŏng Kim and Chŏnju Yu lineages, succumbed to arson, while military police shot two teachers because they emphasized Korean national consciousness.[11] Struck by this violent attack, people refused to send their children to public schools, because they were suspicious of the colonial education curriculum. Gradually they agreed with the theory that the Koreans had lost the nation because Korea failed to receive new knowledge before Japan did. Parents began to send their children to the public schools, saying that they had to "get into the tiger's den in order to catch the tiger."[12]

In the city of Andong, there was an elementary school for Korean children and one exclusively for Japanese children. After elementary school, Japanese children went to Seoul or Taegu or to their hometown in Japan for further education, while most Korean children could not continue their education. Only an exceptional few could afford to study at the middle schools in Taegu and Seoul. Later in the 1930s, a public school for agriculture and forestry opened and allowed Korean students from neighboring counties to study.

Some prominent local figures, albeit not all of them, left Andong, abandoning local society and the ordinary people to the colonial administration. The colonial government recruited people from lower strata of the traditional estate system to fill assistant positions in the official bureaucracy and police force. In this way, a radical change took place in the traditional, local society power structure and traditional local dignitaries came into continual conflict with the newly emerged Korean agents of the colonial power.

Death Space and Private History

The colonial government also attempted to put both "death space" and people's private history under its control by introducing a public cemetery system. Traditionally, the Koreans buried their dead in private graveyards following a geomantic analysis of an auspicious site in order to secure fortune for the family concerned. More significantly, a grave is a place where living descendants revive their memories of the person buried and transmit their private history generation after generation.

In fact, the Japanese government designed the new cemetery system to accommodate graves that were on land that the Japanese wanted to develop as farmland. The government also had to remove graves to carry out large construction projects. Burial of a family member in the public cemetery required the permission of the administrative authorities.[13] Poor people who could not afford private graves welcomed the cemetery system. Japanese residents had a corner of the cemetery specially allocated for them; however, the Japanese usually sent cremated remains back to Japan.

Koreans were horrified by the practice of cremation, which they understood as an act of killing the dead twice. Some protested that cremation would pollute the air and the ashes would make the land barren. More than that, Koreans believed that the tie between the dead and their living descendants would be cut off by this practice. Koreans believed that bones should be kept in a proper position in the grave. The elite families resisted the new system because it did not follow the requirements of geomancy and because the layout of the public cemetery would confuse the ancestor worship ceremony. There were many cases, as elderly people explain, where a dying person stated in his will that he wanted to be buried near his ancestors so that he would not be lonely in the afterworld. Compared with traditional graveyards, graves in the new cemeteries were equal in size and bore no relation to the requirements of geomancy. Through the introduction of the public cemetery system, the state trampled on the colonized people's cultural beliefs.

As well as denying space for private authority, the colonial government also suppressed the revival of private history in the name of health and development. As a counteraction, Koreans consolidated the traditional ancestor worship ritual to protect private graves as a source of memory of the past and historical consciousness.

On numerous occasions, commoners among Koreans organized a kut (shamanic ritual) to deal with unhappy spirits when they became restless and confused by the rearrangement of their houses in netherworld. Confucian scholar families, who usually rejected shamanism, reported being frequently visited in dreams by their ancestors, who complained about their uncomfortable life in the new living place. People resisted moving or removing graves because they believed that it brought the family misfortune. However, the colonial government enforced this policy, with the result that space for the living and the dead fell under colonial control.

The Colonization of Material Life

Colonial power also penetrated the realm of everyday material life. Koreans used manners, dress, and food to display their cultural superiority or to express their resistance symbolically. Dressed in a ceremonial robe (top'o) and wearing a Korean gentleman's hat (kat) or a scholar's cap (yugŏn), Confucian elites distinguished themselves from the Japanese who wore military uniforms or the Japanese haori jacket. Most Koreans did not wear the haori, deriding it as uncivilized and vulgar because it exposed the legs and breast. A Korean who wore haori was ridiculed and even despised by fellow Koreans. One day the police chief of Andong visited the primogeniture of a locally prominent lineage of the Andong Kim clan. The primogeniture was in his typical Confucian scholar's dress. The police asked the gentleman of traditional yangban status if the Koreans' hatred of wearing Japanese clothes was an expression of anti-Japanese sentiment. The Korean, with decency, asked the police how he could allow his children to be barbarous enough to destroy the thousand-year-old Korean moral system by wearing such a vulgar costume. The police chief became angry, as he felt humiliated by his colonized subject. Overwhelmed by the decency and sincerity of this statement, the police chief did not say anything and retreated.[14]

More serious confrontation between the colonial ruler and Korean society became apparent after the March First movement in 1919, when the joint forces of the military police and Japanese residents suppressed a mass demonstration for national independence through violent and fatal means.[15] After the March First movement, the new Governor-General Saitō Makoto, implemented the policy of cultural assimilation, issued special orders commanding

Koreans to speak only Japanese and strictly forbid the Korean language. At the same time, the Japanese encouraged Koreans to learn the Japanese way of life. Japanese formal education, which Koreans resisted in various ways, introduced Japanese food, dress, housing, and lifestyle. Some yangban wore Korean mourning dress and adopted the hat called p'aeraengi, which the lower classes wore. Under police interrogation, some pretended that they were in mourning while others replied that they had to wear p'aeraengi and mourning garb to mourn the death of their own country. They also said that since the whole world order had been turned upside down, they were now lower class and thus had to wear the p'aeraengi.[16]

Angry police tried to persuade the Koreans to be grateful to the emperor for their prosperity and threatened that Koreans would be treated as traitors if they continued to wear traditional mourning dress and odd hats. However, Confucian elites insisted on wearing their ritual robes for ancestral ceremonies and common people maintained their tradition of wearing Korean traditional clothing for village communal rites (tongje), as well as family rites offering the typical Korean sacrifices and making ritual addresses. The series of constant struggles between the local elite and Japanese authorities shows that ritual and ceremony became the space in which Koreans could reproduce their national identity and cultural tradition against the Japanese government policy of cultural assimilation.

To force Koreans to speak Japanese, the Government-General organized evening classes. However, Japanese officials often complained that Koreans were stupid and could not learn the Japanese language and letters.[17] When a police official or other Japanese dignitary visited the countryside, Koreans pretended not to understand, making it difficult to communicate properly. Therefore, a Korean assistant would have to be brought along as an interpreter. One day a Japanese police officer and his Korean assistant visited a peasant house in Waryong myŏn, a rural area of Andong. When they asked the Korean to prepare lunch for them, the woman gave them a bowl of boiled millet and chili pepper paste, saying that she did not have anything else to offer. The Japanese policeman was forced to eat it even though his throat was burning from the hot pepper. After that, he always carried his own lunch box. Peasants of the village still enjoy telling this story about making fun of the Japanese with coarse, hot food.[18] Thus poverty and a coarse style of life were also used intentionally by Korean peasants as vehicles of resistance.

Religious Life Space

The colonial rulers not only penetrated material life but also the spiritual sphere. Stigmatizing all Korean traditional folk religions as superstitions that produced "unhealthy" mental vices, the colonial government implemented special policies to destroy these religions in the name of science and rationality. In 1912, the government issued a special order[19] allowing the Bureau of Sanitation to investigate and purge all superstitions and "fake religions." Later, the police were given a special order to punish any antisocial religious activity at their discretion. It is significant to note that religion was defined as social pathology and came under the control of the bureaucracy and police. More significant is the fact that indigenous religions were evaluated by secular criteria for mental health, as the word "sanitation" implies, and thus were excluded from the category of "religion."

Except for the so-called world religion, the Japanese government classified all forms of native religion under the blanket term "folk belief" (*minkan shinkō*) or "folk religion" (*minzoku shūkyō*). Japanese scholars at the time invented a term, *ruiji*, literally meaning "similar but not true," as a prefix to Korean indigenous religion.

Shamans were arrested and threatened by the police to give up their practices because it was thought that they were fostering social instability and unhealthy living in the innocent populace. One day a Korean police assistant entered a place where a shamanic ritual was in process. Suddenly the spirit-possessed female shaman made a motion to chase after a devil and violently moved among the spectators to where the policeman was sitting. Terrified, he hurriedly left while the people laughed at his fear. When the police later summoned the shaman she stated that she did not even know that the man was working with the Japanese and that it was the voice of a spirit who possessed her, not her own. However, the police accused her of having ridiculed the Korean police assistant and condemning the Japanese police as evil and beat her severely.[20]

Following the advice of Japanese scholars, including Murayama Chijun (1932) the police became more concerned with shamans and kept a strict watch on their rituals.[21] The core of Korean shamanic ritual is the resurrection of a dead soul and the expression of its lamentations through the shaman's body. The spiritually possessed shaman revived all the life stories of the soul, which would be full of grievances and criticisms of contemporary life. In fact, by nodding, sighing, weeping, and dancing the spectators shared the messages the ritual generated, participated in the making of private history, and unofficially challenged official power. Making narratives of their own and giving voices to the voiceless, shamans criticized and ridiculed the official power, in ways ordinary life did not allow.[22] The colonial government believed that shamans provided negative perspectives on contemporary reality and thus deluded the world and confused the people with false beliefs (hokse mumin).

The ruthless suppression of shamans created an image of Japanese police strong enough to catch evil spirits. The shamans began to threaten the spirits by saying that the shaman would call the police to have the spirits arrested, causing spectators to burst into laughter. It became fashionable to post the words "police" or "aggressive dog" on the gate in front of one's house to expel evil spirits.[23] It took the Japanese a long time to realize that the ordinary Korean people were ridiculing the police by perceiving the police to be on equal footing with dogs.

In 1915, the government issued regulations on Confucian shrines, Buddhist temples,[24] and Christian missionary activities.[25] Through these regulations, both the corporate property and activities of religious institutions came under police examination and permission. As many Koreans had gone into exile in China to carry on the liberation movement, the colonial government was very keen on tracking down possible connections between these activists and their families and religious organizations back home. The police regularly checked not only church leaders but also relatives and lineage dignitaries of the anti-Japanese leaders in exile. The government also exercised the violence of their military authority in rather a dramatic way, in order to put all the indigenous social sectors under its control. At first, the fact that official personnel such as the police, administrative officials, and even elementary school teachers carried swords with their military uniforms shocked the Koreans. Children were terrified to see policemen with swords. Parents used to stop a child from crying by saying, "If you do not listen to me, I will call a policeman," or "If you cry too loudly, a policeman will come." These threats frightened the child into silence.[26]

While the colonizers used this symbolic gesture to prove the superiority of militarism, they also practiced the stick-and-carrot strategy toward local dignitaries and prominent lineages. Primogeniture descendants and local figures

were invited to join the advisory committee to discuss the ways mutual cooperation could be "of benefit to local people." Although the Confucian elites
and the colonialists shared antagonism toward shamanism because of their
ideas on enlightenment and modernization, they were in conflict with the
issues of national identity and cultural tradition. So some Confucians cooperated with the colonial government as long as their idea of cultural superiority
was acknowledged, while the colonial government utilized the Confucian
tradition to indoctrinate Koreans as colonized subjects.

Despite the colonial rhetoric and statistical proof of progress and development, the material conditions of life for Koreans in general worsened under
colonial rule. Especially during the 1930s when a large number of beggars and
vagabonds increased in unprecedented mass. The less fortunate poured into
cities seeking food and shelter. Some squatted or slept on the street, but most
made their shelters at the periphery of town. T'omangmin (people who live in a
shelter made of mud) became a familiar urban sight. During this period, shamanic rituals frequently revived agwi (hungry ghosts) and manse kwisin, ghosts of
those killed by police for shouting "manse!" during the March First movement.
Though the government exercised strong pressure, and the numbers fluctuated,
the number of people engaged in folk religions continued to increase.

Impoverished peasants also migrated to Manchuria during the 1930s
because the colonial government encouraged them to cultivate the vast wasteland there. Under Japanese occupation and the hardship of life in Manchuria,
shamanism began to flourish among those Korean immigrants. The following is a story of a yangban's wife who became a shaman after she migrated
to Manchuria. Mr. Kwŏn (the husband of the shaman) of Heilungjiang
Province, now Caoxianzu, recollected memories of his family history:

> At first, I did not want to leave my native place where my family had lived for
> generations. The question of who would look after the ancestors' graves in
> my absence made me feel so painful that I could not sleep. I shared with my
> wife the idea that it would be better to die of hunger in my native land than
> to fill my stomach in a foreign land. Then I saw my children who had swollen
> abdomens because of malnutrition. I asked myself—I who had failed to keep
> his fatherland—whether I was qualified even to seek a death in the stolen
> land. I deserved nothing because I could not hold onto my country while the
> monkey-like Japanese stole it from us. Though not highly educated, I was a

normal person who knew human morality and dignity, and at least I had believed that Koreans were better than those barbarous Japanese. But now I had to admit that I was nothing. I could not endure the humiliation and sense of nothingness since I was deprived of social face as well as economic means to breed even my own children. At last, I decided to escape from my hometown. For me, going to Manchuria was social suicide. I killed myself in order to give my children a chance. I fled from my ancestors since I lost face to stand before them.[27]

Kwŏn's family arrived in Heleung county in Jilin Province to settle in unoccupied land in September 1932 and found themselves in an abandoned wasteland. The cold winter had already begun in Manchuria by September. Wearing only summer clothing, they nearly froze to death. Without proper shelter, clothes, and grain, they had to earn their miserable living under Chinese landlords. Kwŏn's wife, having no proper clothing, could not expose herself during the daytime. Therefore, she went out to get water only at night. His elderly father and two of his children could not survive the hardship and died within two years. He could not bury them properly because he could not even afford coffins. Had he been in his hometown, relatives and fellow villagers would have helped the family with their needs. Chinese bandits frequently vandalized the peasants' harvest of corn and potatoes. Later, the local Chinese attacked the Koreans because they suspected the Koreans of engaging in espionage for the Japanese military forces in the region. At the same time, the Japanese Army frequently massacred Korean peasants whenever Korean guerrilla fighters took anti-Japanese military action.

Like other Korean women, Kwŏn's wife began to visit Yimgong-dang, a shrine for the spirit of General Yim Kyŏngŏp.[28] After a series of unknown illnesses, she found out, with the help of a shaman, that General Yim wanted her to be his disciple. When she became a shaman, Mr. Kwŏn, a member of the prestigious Andong Kwŏn, was embarrassed at first. In the end, he came to understand his wife and let her do her job as a shaman, though he himself continued to observe ancestor worship rites in which his wife also took part. With other Koreans, his family moved further into the northern part of Jilin Province to establish a Korean village and paddy fields. They were free to speak Korean, wear Korean garments, eat Korean food, and enjoy Korean games and festivities until the Japanese military forces relocated them.

The Japanese military police tortured Mr. Kwŏn's wife to death after she completed a serious shamanic ritual. In this ritual, a hungry ghost possessed her and described the tragic historical experiences of Koreans in the cold Manchurian wasteland by violently uttering curses on the "unidentified" evil that drove Koreans into misery. Because General Yim appeared to crush the evil in her ritual process, the military police killed Mrs. Kwŏn and destroyed the shrine dedicated to General Yim's spirit.[29]

Administrative Power over Sacred Authority

To extend colonial control down to the bottom level of the traditional authority system the colonialists felt an urgent need to reshape the structure of colonial rule. In 1920, just a year after the March First movement, the colonial government introduced a new administrative village system by incorporating traditional natural villages into larger units called ku (區). Villages had been autonomous socio-cultural communities and lineage and communal ideology were the two bases of socio-cultural life. These autonomous village units were connected to the state through the mediation of local dignitaries chosen by the villagers themselves. Local administrative officers above the village level were required to consult with these village dignitaries. Inter-village networks were the basis of society and the tie to the state. A village was a symbolic community as well as a historical one in that people lived with their ancestral spirits and shared the same historical experiences and consciousness. Through various lineage activities and communal rites (tongje), people renewed their sense of social identity and cultural tradition. When they organized the annual communal rite for the village, all the social concerns of the villagers were brought into public discussion at the village meeting, and members of the village observed religious regulations and taboos in order to perform the ritual successfully. Ritual in this context was a mechanism by which their cultural system and social structure were renewed. In other words, a communal rite provided people with a space in which the political and social autonomy of the village concerned was emphasized and regenerated by the Korean participants.

In Andong, the Government-General intentionally separated and incorporated villages that were intimately related to the traditional inter-village network system into different administrative units. In this way, the colonizers destroyed traditional autonomous units and put villages under the new colonial authority.[30] Numerous conflicts and disputes arose between newly amalgamated villages and between villages and their administrative offices. Simultaneously many villages, related through kinship and marriage networks, were separated, while yangban villages were incorporated into an administrative unit with non-yangban villages. When the colonial authorities designated an administrative unit to include small-sized yangban villages with a large, politically and socially powerful non-yangban village, the internal conflict became serious. This new administrative unit arrangement had one positive effect: it contributed to the creation of a new type of community that cut across the traditional social boundaries of class and status. However, it also introduced an agency of colonial authority into the traditional social authority system. There were cases in which men of non-yangban class became administrative heads of a rural communal society. In order to minimize any possible conflict and tension, members of prominent lineages were also appointed as village or district heads at the same time. No matter whether he was yangban or non-yangban, it was obvious that the administrative head should be under the direct administrative order system and quite often he had to compromise with the colonial authorities to handle fellow villagers' affairs and problems. Through this series of administrative intrusions in the guise of cooperative terms, colonial authorities penetrated the space of indigenous authority.

Villages that produced activists in the anti-Japanese and independence movements came under constant surveillance by the police. In addition, the Japanese police destroyed social networks across village boundaries while the administrative authorities damaged and rearranged inter-village networks and hierarchical relationships based on religious activities. The colonial administration further subdued local traditional autonomy through a series of forcefully implemented sociocultural "rural enlightenment" and "mind cultivation" campaigns.

We may note that the newly introduced administrative system eliminated the rituals of the natural village community and instead forced the people to organize communal rituals at the administratively defined village unit through permission of the local county government. As a result, traditional village rituals began to disappear. Through this series of cultural policies, the colonial government attempted not only to restructure local society but also the ritual lives of the people.

A series of police reports to the Japanese Government-General from 1919 to 1923 reveals that local authorities had great difficulty carrying out the governmental policies because of the strong resistance of the peasants. The report pointed out that shamanism lay behind the people's resistance. It did not blame Confucianism even though the resistance came from all sectors of Korean society.[31] For the colonial government, it might have been strategically and realistically more advantageous not to engage in any serious conflict with the Confucians, who held traditional, social, economic, and political power. Since shamans and their clients were mostly ordinary people lacking authority or power, it was relatively safe to crush them in a direct confrontation strategy. Because Confucians and Christians were also critical of shamanism, they supported the colonial authorities' efforts to destroy it.

Despite this suppression, the number of Koreans affiliated with folk religious sectors continuously increased. According to a statistical report, believers in "fake religion" numbered 31,071 in 1900, a figure that increased to 129,542 in 1910; to 171,101 in 1920; and notably to 511,099 in 1921 and 625,900 in 1923.[32] Twenty-three years after the turn of the century, followers of "unauthorized religion" increased nearly fivefold in Korea. After that, the number began to decrease as the ruthless counteraction of the colonial authorities tightened up.

THE MIND CULTIVATION MOVEMENT AND COLONIAL VIOLENCE

It is interesting to note, however, that after the March First movement, the colonial government took the strategy of incorporating Korean folk belief systems into the Japanese Shinto rituals. Throughout the fifteen years of critical political programs for socio-cultural transformation after 1919, the colonial authorities attempted to accomplish the restructuring of the Korean belief system as well as the sociopolitical one.

In 1933, the government launched the Rural Promotion movement (*nōson shinkō undō*) with the official goal to enlighten people's consciousness and improve the quality of life (*saengwhal kaesŏn*). First, under the heading "Down with Superstition" (*misin t'ap'a*), the government tried to quash folk belief, and shamanism was a specific target. Second, through various sanitation and orderliness educational programs the Japanese government claimed to be attempting an improvement of the living environment and an aesthetic refinement of lifestyle. Third, the program for frugal living was supposed to correct people's wasteful lifestyle. Fourth, authorities encouraged Korean women to participate in outdoor work along with men and to liberate them from the yoke of patriarchal authority.

These programs, however, were principally aimed at the destruction of the traditional folk belief system. Indigenous religious movements related to national identity and liberation ideology were denounced as fake religions that misled people through the illusions of a superstitious worldview. Shamanism became the main target because it gave people ideas about rebellion and subversion through symbolic experiences of violence against established authorities. The government emphasized the enlightenment of women because women were the main practitioners of shamanism. Local administrative governments submitted many petitions to demand intensified action by the central government to destroy the practice of shamanism among the peasants. The peasants continued to resist this series of governmental programs and folk religions remained popular.[33]

Through their sanitation and orderliness educational programs the colonial authorities encouraged people to reject the practice of traditional folk medicine and to change their everyday lifestyle into one that more closely resembled the Japanese mode. Colonizers harshly criticized the shamanic healing ritual. Where modern systems of medical care were not yet available, people had little choice but to rely upon their traditional folk medical practices. In addition, shamanic rituals provided the space for the Korean people to express their own experiences of colonialism through the use of ritual words, words that dramatized their grievances and ridiculed the Japanese authorities in the guise of religious practice. Shamanism in this context provided a space for people to construct their own moral, judicial, and historical community.

The Japanese government insisted that Koreans develop an aesthetic taste for Japanese material culture and customs. Public and official education extolled Japanese clothing, cuisine, etiquette, and protocol as replacements for the Korean counterparts. The Government-General denounced the Korean language, aesthetics, and folk customs while it promoted the Japanese lifestyle in the discourse of sanitation, science, and civilization. However, both Confucians and shamans stubbornly retained Korean traditional food and garments in their rituals believing that they were dealing with Korean spirits and ghosts. Shamans rationalized their practice of traditional customs by displaying their inability to efficiently adapt themselves to the Japanese way of life. They always proudly affirmed that they were illiterate and too stupid to master the Japanese language.

The colonial government also launched the Mind Cultivation movement (shinden kaihatsu undō) in 1936 to educate Koreans to duly appreciate colonial paternalism and to accommodate the cultural assimilation programs. The government proclaimed that the aim of mind cultivation was to give Koreans a clear idea of "nation," to promote Korean respect for the Japanese national spirit and ancestors, to cultivate Korean attitudes regarding reciprocation for indebtedness, to insist Koreans appreciate what they had been given by others, and to lead Koreans to self-reliance. The Korean people were urged to cultivate a positive view of the world in their minds and enhance their self-satisfaction, sense of responsibility, and morality as subordinate citizens of the empire (hwangguk sinmin) instead of filling their minds with the wild, unrefined thoughts full of violence, complaints, and grievances. The Japanese government proclaimed to teach the Koreans how to see the world through the prism of hope and spiritual wealth.

This program echoes the traditional Confucian teachings of self-cultivation (sugi) and the restoration of propriety through self-control (kŭkki pongnye). Many local Confucian elites were willing to cooperate with the authorities in the Mind Cultivation movement. However, disputes and debates over the movement arose among the local intellectuals and Confucian leaders. Some were critical, demanding that authorities provide a definition of proper human morality and self-cultivation. Understanding that the colonial discourse defined Koreans as uncultivated and barbarous outlaws, they said, ironically, "Let those who are well-qualified cultivate themselves. We are not intelligent enough to know how to cultivate ourselves."[34] Other leaders took the fact that the Japanese educational system trained students to be a proper examples of the emperor's children seriously, and out of their sense of cultural superiority over the Japanese urged Koreans to be honest, well-mannered, and well-behaved enough to compete with the Japanese counterparts. In this regard, it was a sense of cultural superiority that caused the Confucian elites to be cooperative or resistant to the Mind Cultivation movement.

As mentioned earlier, many prominent Confucian intellectuals sought exile in China or hid themselves in remote mountainous areas.[35] Wealthy men were robbed frequently, and this frequency in theft indicates the Korean people's impoverished economic situation. In some cases, however, thieves sent the stolen money to China for anti-Japanese activities. This was a way some of the wealthy donated money to the independence movement, since some of wealthy men were under continuous surveillance by the police. Kim Yonghwan of Andong, the primogeniture descendant of Kim Sŏngil acted like a *hallyang*, a morally fallen member of the gentry. He frequently associated with lower-class people and lost a lot of money through gambling.[36] The Japanese police regarded him as an example of a demoralized aristocrat and ignored him. Later, it was discovered that the money Kim reported to have lost at gambling was secretly sent to the Korean government in exile in China for national independence activities.[37]

People in Andong still recall that Kim Yonghwan never spoke Japanese and never wore Japanese clothes. Members of his lineage still emphasize that he always wore traditional Korean garments and ate Korean food. He never missed ancestral rituals and was very conscientious in observing all of the ritual details. From this, we understand that he deliberately disguised himself as a culturally and morally fallen man in order to resist the immoral power of the colonial government. While some Confucians accepted the Mind Cultivation campaign in hopes of keeping fellow Koreans in a state of civilization, some radical elites took part in anti-Japanese action in exile and some carried out their resistance against the colonial violence under the pretext of an uncivilized lifestyle.

Under the official discourse of agriculturalism (*nongbonjuŭi*), Koreans were taught to seek happiness through their lives as farmers. The Rural Promotion movement included a rational and scientific living campaign that meant to eliminate superstitions like shamanism and various communal rites. Here it is obvious that the colonial authorities tried to indoctrinate Koreans and confine them to the agricultural sector while leaving other fields of modern industrial and commercial capitalism in the hands of Japanese. In this way, the authorities forced the Koreans to be the main producer of grain for the industrial sector occupied by the Japanese.

However, the hidden meaning or expected result of this campaign was more significant than the simple confinement of Koreans within the agricultural sector. The authorities propagated a discourse that attributed the severe deterioration of rural economy to the supposed laziness, inactivity, backwardness, and lack of spirit of the peasants. Since rural people had been led astray by the illusion of non-agricultural work and the urban lifestyle and did not have faith in their own lives as farmers, the authorities explained, the rural economy worsened, the social order was in disarray, and all communal life was in pieces.

Through this series of campaign and educational programs that defined Korean traditional culture and replaced it with the colonial discourses of science, rationality, and civilization, assimilation to Japanese culture was enforced under the disguise of colonial nationalism. As the colonized people's resistance was stronger than had been expected, the colonial authorities issued a special order to control the folk belief system because, as we have seen, it was thought to shape the ideology of resistance through the symbolic experience of violence and subversion. The Japanese government especially criticized shamanic practice as an insanitary and unhealthy activity, one that lead people to be anti-social, idle, and dependent on a fatalistic worldview. The police and the Bureau of Sanitation were therefore given special legal power to arrest and punish anyone suspected of being a shaman or leader of an "antisocial" or "fake" religion. Shamanism was severely suppressed as a result of these colonial modernization campaigns.

The government carried out an extensive investigation of Korean customs and folk traditions,[38] and colonial scholars produced studies on premodernity and the negative nature of Korean culture, pointing out that shamanism originated in the very ancient past.[39] Based on their belief that shamanism ruled peoples' spiritual lives, scholars like Murayama Chijun and Akiba Takashi advised the colonial authorities that they must understand the political and social questions of Koreans and how these questions were expressed in shamanic ritual if the government wanted to check the possibility of antisocial movements. These scholars suggested that strategies to make Korea a healthy society could be found through an analysis of the practice of shamanism and advised the government not to forget the "importance of being serious about controlling shamanism."[40]

Teachings on frugality encouraged Koreans to be comfortable with poverty. Koreans were also encouraged to give up what they produced for the nation when the government asked them to do so. By propagandizing the desirability of sacrificing material wealth, the colonizers were able to cover their strategy of economic exploitation. Basically, the moral discourse of state capitalism distorted the quest for economic gain and manipulated Koreans into thinking they had to stick to farming and be satisfied with their lot. The government programs were intended to induce the colonized populace to acknowledge the colonial interpretation that Koreans were apathetic, idle, backward, passive, and lacking the proper vision to appreciate the Japanese socio-cultural programs for modernization and enlightenment.

The Mind Cultivation movement also demanded that the complicated traditional rituals be simplified to save time and energy for productive and rational life. Koreans performed funerals and ancestral rites through a complicated ritual process because they defined and consolidated the succession of family lines and lineages as social units. For Koreans, ritual practices were essential elements in the construction of the cultural community beyond regional boundaries and blood ties and therefore was not only a cultural but also a sociopolitical mechanism for dealing with local affairs. Participating in ancestor worship rituals, descendants also regenerated their private histories related to deceased family member. On the ancestor's death date, all the descendants within four generations gathered to observe the commemoration rite in the house of the primogeniture. Descendants also provided offerings to their ancestors on New Year's Day and the fifteenth day of the eighth month of the lunar calendar; in spring and autumn they visited the graves of their ancestors. Families of prominent Confucian scholars participated in various commemoration ceremonies held at Confucian academies where their ancestors had been enshrined. In this context, ancestor worship rituals were important cultural spaces for Koreans to revive their private histories and regenerate historical consciousness.

The Japanese, in contrast, do not have the cultural institution of worship for an individual ancestor through four generations because they do not have lineage in patrilineal succession as Koreans do. Because of this difference, the Japanese appear to be as elaborate in terms of depth in remembering the past. For Koreans, to simplify or not observe the ancestral ritual meant the elimination of history and abandonment of the mechanism of historical consciousness. The fierce resistance offered by Koreans against this colonial government campaign was quite understandable.

The colonialists also criticized communal rituals and festivals on the theory that these superstitious activities made Koreans irrationally consume energy and materials. Teachers traveled around the country to persuade peasants to stop offering sacrifices to the tree spirits and praying for good fortune in their traditional communal rites. Poor peasants were also criticized for using their grain to make cakes and wine when they frequently suffered from food shortages. The Japanese authorities pointed out that peasants were lazy and unproductive because they spent several days doing nothing but enjoying farmers' music and dancing while there were many tasks to do. It should be noted here that the Japanese *matsuri*, equivalent to the Korean *tongje* was allowed and even encouraged in Japan for promoting group solidarity and identity. At the *tongje* ritual, Koreans followed their traditional rules in terms of clothing, food, wine, language, and rituals. The Korean people observed the ritual in front of a specially designated pine tree or elm tree only, not the cherry tree. The communal ritual, therefore, was not superstitious behavior but a cultural practice in which they renewed their sense of national identity.

Shamanism was the major target of Japanese criticism because of its noise, lavish consumption, superstitious life, and its anti-social order ideas and behaviors. Again and again shamanic rituals revived hungry ghosts, entities who gave voices to the Koreans and expressed the miserable material conditions and grievances against colonial exploitation. In opposition to the official discourse that the poor living conditions were the Korean people's responsibility, shamanic ritual always disclosed that the social elements outside oneself produced the hardships of life.

Along with this, the police prohibited festivals like the stone fight (*sŏkchŏn nori*) and the chariot fight (*ch'ajŏn nori*), which the people of Andong regularly enjoyed on the fifteenth of the first month of the lunar calendar. At this time of the year, the city of Andong was traditionally divided into two teams, east and west. Each team made a huge chariot out of a pine tree trunk and rice stalks on top of which the commander took his seat and directed the motion of his team in a fierce fight. More than two hundred people took part on each team and the rest were spectators shouting in support of their team. The pine tree trunk was transported from the neighboring county of Ponghwa, and since it was regarded sacred the local magistrate of Ponghwa traditionally provided all kinds of cooperation. The chariot fight was a thousand-year-old tradition to stimulate the local people's fighting spirit and group cohesion, and Koreans believed this fight commemorated the battle of Andong where local people helped Wang Kŏn to win the decisive victory over Kyŏn Hwŏn and to establish the Koryŏ Dynasty. The colonial police prohibited the festival on the reason of the possibility of violent outbursts.

In this way, the colonizers demanded obedience and deprived the people of Andong their traditional space within which to symbolically participate in reenactments of violent confrontation and subversion. With the abolition of the festivals, the annual, traditional strengthening of interrelationships among regions that were involved in the transportation of pine trees for the *ch'ajŏn nori* deteriorated. Each region now fell under the direct administrative control of the colonial government. The Government-General thereby compartmentalized Korean regional society and the Korean people were pressured to eliminate their cultural traditions in order to be assimilated into Japanese culture.

SHINTO AND THE COLONIZATION OF CONSCIOUSNESS

It is quite interesting to note that at this time the colonialists sought to co-opt Korean shamanism into Japanese Shinto under the new cultural policy. Along with the Mind Cultivation movement, the colonialists attempted to combine Korean folk beliefs with Shinto as an effective way to control the colonized peoples' minds and achieve cultural assimilation. In July 1919, the Government-General decided to build Chōsen Jinja, a Korean Shinto shrine dedicated to worshiping Amaterasu Ōmikami (the supreme Shinto goddess) and the Meiji Emperor. The Japanese created this shrine because they regarded it necessary to rule Koreans. Korean folk religions, though denounced as superstitions, were found to have great similarities with the Japanese folk belief system. Colonial scholars like Murayama Chijun and Akiba Takashi pointed out the cultural link between Korean shamanism and Japanese Shinto and suggested the possibility of initiating cultural communication between the Japanese and Korean people through combining Shinto and shamanism.[41] Korean scholars Ch'oe Namsŏn and Yi Nŭnghwa even argued that Japanese folk religions originated from the ancient Korean folk belief systems. Ch'oe maintained that Korea and Japan, distinguished from China, consisted of one cultural unit based on shamanism and argued that Tan'gun was the supreme shaman to rule the *purham* cultural region, which he defined as the vast territory including Manchuria and the northern part of the Korean peninsula with Mt. Paektu as its central and most sacred place. The colonialists manipulated his theory to enhance their rationale for cultural assimilation.[42]

Prior to the public Shinto shrine opening on Namsan in Seoul, a group of colonial scholars suggested that the Government-General install Tan'gun together with Amaterasu Ōmikami. Their joint installment at the shrine would induce Koreans to accept the theory that the two peoples had a common origin, scholars argued. The location of the shrine had symbolic significance: while the north mountain, Pugak, was invested with the secular power of the governor-general, the south mountain, Namsan, would be invested with the sacred authority of Shinto, which symbolized the fact that all of Korea, body and soul, was invested with Japanese spirit and power.[43]

Some Koreans also believed that Tan'gun was older than the Japanese goddess and insisted that he deserved to be seated together with her. This idea provoked hot debate among Koreans. The majority opposed the idea because they believed that Tan'gun was so sacred that he should not be seated in the Japanese shrine, while other Koreans insisted that he should be treated equally with Amaterasu. In the end, the Japanese government issued an official interpretation that no other deities were allowed to challenge the supreme position of the Shinto goddess. The colonialists insisted that the Nanzan Jinja, the Namsan shrine, be the seat of the Goddess Amaterasu and the Spirit of Meiji, and compromised that Tan'gun be seated together with the spirit of Tsushima below Amaterasu and Meiji. Greatly humiliated, many Koreans opposed the installation of Tan'gun in Japanese shrines at all. The colonial government, however, forced Koreans to accept the hierarchical order of the deities and thus the superiority of Japan over Korea.

At the same time, Shinto shrines of various sizes and ranks were erected in major cities and towns, and Amaterasu was installed at the center of many of them. Many Korean traditional village shrines for communal deities were converted to Shinto shrines to accommodate Japanese deities.

In 1935, the Nanzan Jinja, the Namsan shrine, was renamed Chōsen Jingū (Chosŏn Sin'gung) and officially upgraded to a national-level temple, making it imperative for all Koreans to pay homage to the spiritual palace. At the same time, the government vigorously launched its *ichimen issha* (one district, one shrine) movement to establish one shrine in every administrative sub-county seat. As a result, even a sub-county in a remote mountain area came to have its own Shinto shrine. It was reported that most traditional communal shrines were converted to Shinto shrines, and organizations of folk religions including shamanism were nearly completely disbanded. There were 237 Shinto shrines in 1931; the number grew to 266 in 1933. In 1936, however, it increased sharply to 524, then 530 in 1939. In 1943, the number increased to 854.[44] According to a report in 1938, with Shinto and its organization at the top, all of the Korean folk religions were put into the hierarchical order under the administrative control of the colonial authority. There were two thousand three hundred Shinto shrines and the number of people paying homage to the Chosŏn Sin'gung on Mount Namsan was recorded to be 2.6 million.[45] The Government-General believed that the installation of the Shinto temple and shrines successfully implemented its goal of obliging Koreans to clarify the concept of the Japanese nation, achieving cultural and ethnic assimilation between the Japanese and Koreans and inculcating the authority of the Japanese spirit. Korean folk religion disappeared from the public scene and Koreans regularly observed rituals according to the Shinto religious calendar. Because of this, Korean religious life came under the secular power of the local colonial administration and time and space for religious life were also colonized.

In Andong, the colonial government built a Shinto shrine on Mount Yŏngnam, which was located in the east corner of the city. Traditionally Koreans erected their family shrines at the eastern or northeastern corner of their residence. The city itself had a Buddhist temple in the west and the Confucian temple in the north. A Catholic and a Protestant church were located in the western sector of the city. The Japanese, accordingly, built the Shinto shrine in the eastern sector of the city because the sun rises in the east where Japan, the land of sunrise, is located.

Teachers made students bow toward the east every morning and insisted they pray for the health of the emperor and the prosperity of Japan. For this reason, many Korean people believed that the shrine destroyed the geomantic power of sacred space for Koreans.

In Korean elementary schools, administrators built shrines at the east corner of the playground, where they required each student to bow when entering and leaving the school. Teachers watched the students bow and sometimes punished those who did not bow properly because it was a mark of disloyalty. Students were taught to cultivate themselves to be proper loyal subjects of the Japanese emperor. The principal often summoned and warned parents of "bad" students. In this way, students became reluctant to pay homage to the shrine.[46]

Mr. Kim Nosun was a young teacher at an elementary school in Andong during the period of the 1930s and early 1940s. He vividly remembered an incident that happened in his school. One morning, it was found that someone had defecated on the rear side of the shrine. As a punishment, the whole student body was ordered to sit with their legs folded on the ground until one student was found to be guilty. His father, kneeling with his son outside the principal's office, begged pardon for more than ten hours. The police brutally beat the father and ordered the son to clean toilets every day for two months. Later, a rumor began that a ghost was seen wandering late at night around the shrine. This ghost was said to have a small body with hairy arms and legs and thick eyebrows. Because he moved very swiftly, nobody could see him clearly. It was said that the ghost sometimes went to the public graveyard and sucked blood from recently buried bodies. The story was so terrifying that no one dared to approach the shrine alone even in daytime. Teachers tried in vain to find the source of the story and attempted to persuade students that it was nothing but a groundless rumor. But students refused to come near the shrine out of fear of the ghost. They even tried not to face the shrine directly because there was a rumor that anyone who made eye contact with the ghost inside the shrine would be struck by misfortune. With this in mind, students made a quick bow to the shrine at a safe distance before they hurried into the class-room. They believed if they heard someone calling, they should not look back because it might be the ghost. In this way the Shinto shrine became an object of avoidance and a subject of horror stories.

As they were being forced to bow, students depended upon other religious beliefs. It was said that the Japanese devil or ghost could not win the Korean spirit, and therefore they could expel the Japanese ghost by reciting the chants and prayers of Buddhism, Korean native folk religions, and even Christianity. So when they bowed, students silently recited these prayers of other religions with their eyes closed. "Koreans would call on Buddha, Jesus, God in Heaven, or even an ancestor in their desire to protect themselves from the Japanese ghosts."[47]

Shamanism and Resistance in Distortion

Shamanism remained the target of severe social criticism. The Christian, Confucian, and Buddhist communities reluctantly cooperated with the Japanese colonial policy on folk religion because shamanism was their common enemy. While other established religions were full of ideas of enlightenment, civiliza-tion, refinement, and modernity, religious leaders found shamanism to be filled with violence, vulgarity, excitement, fights, bribery, challenge to and ridicule of the secular authorities on the anti-structural ritual process, and so on.

Through my fieldwork in Andong, I collected many stories of the tragic deaths of shamans during this period. The police arrested and tortured shamans because they performed shamanic rituals in which many souls of the dead expressed their grievances against the colonial oppression and exploitation. In the two stories below, women recalled that the *agwi* and *manse kwisin* spirits frequently appeared in shaman's rituals.

"The Devil"

One day a Japanese official visited a rural community when he heard the sounds of a strange musical performance in the darkness of the night. As he approached the place, he found a shamanic ritual in progress. He watched the ritual out of curiosity, but he became uncomfortable when he realized that the shaman, speaking in a man's voice, mocked the Japanese emperor and colonial officials while spectators burst out laughing. He was terrified when the shaman announced that there was a devil among the spectators and pointed the sword she held as a threat to the devil directly at him. The Japanese official arrested her on the spot. He accused her of inciting people against Japan and ridiculing the sacred authority of the emperor in the guise of ritual performance. The shaman insisted that she was possessed and did not know what she was doing. She said that she could not even recognize the man as being Japanese. Nonetheless, the police sentenced her to two years in prison, and they detained the village head before releasing him at the petition of the whole village and local dignitaries.[48]

"Nephew"

A shaman performed a *kut* (shamanic ritual) for a woman's illness caused by the soul of her unmarried nephew, who Japanese military police killed while he was participating in the March First movement. The spirit of the nephew lamented his troubled life through the shaman's body and the shaman communicated with the spirit on behalf of the bereaved family.

> Shaman: Why are you so mischievous? Did I (the afflicted woman) treat you badly while you were alive? I treated you as if you were my own son, didn't I? You know how much I have missed you since you left us. You were the

hope of our whole family. You were so handsome and bright, and we all were very proud of you.

Spirit: Yes, I know you treated me well. I still remember that when we were out of grain, you gave me a bowl of barley while you did not eat. You said you had eaten and had no appetite. I know you went into the kitchen and drank a bowl of water to fill your stomach. Alas! I couldn't swallow the barley. I choked. (All the spectators burst into tears). But why didn't we have enough grain? Why did you, my beloved aunt, have to starve? We had a lot of rice paddies in front of our house [munjŏn okdap] and our field was so fertile that we had always had plenty of rice. Oh! I am scared. Look, they are coming. They are coming to eat our land and eat our houses, and now they eat our bodies. They eat everything we have. The hairy short devils (indicating the physical appearance of the Japanese) are coming. They beat me. They beat me with leather and a bull's penis. Oh! I hate the hot water with pepper flour they poured into my nostrils. (The mother and aunt burst out crying and other spectators were weeping.) Mother, I am starving, I am cold. I do not have any warm clothes. My clothes are worn out. I am lonely and restless on Mount North [pungmangsan] without a fixed address. I want to lie down beside my grandfather. Now those stranger hungry ghosts are surrounding me. Mother, I want to come home.

Shaman: My poor son, forget all that. Do not worry about the family. We have survived so many difficulties. We can survive. What else shall we be frightened of? We pray that you may go to the peaceful heaven and live comfortably with your grandfather.

Spirit: Mother, I cannot leave. How can I leave you? You reared me, you gave me rice, you gave me clothes, and you educated me. But you did not eat enough food, you did not wear any proper clothes. I had to repay your unlimited oceanic love. But I am an unfilial son. I cannot leave you. Where and how can I resolve all the grievances that fill my heart?

Shaman: Poor son, nobody's grievance can compare with mine. But I will forgive everyone. So please, you forgive everyone too. The day is coming. When the day comes, you can enjoy the fertile land and good food and good clothes. Flowers cannot last ten days, and power cannot last ten years.

Later, the police arrested and severely tortured the shaman. When they released her, she had been rendered dumb and could not move her arms and legs freely. Later, the police smashed a shrine dedicated to the spirit of Princess Noguk, the wife of King Kongmin of the Koryŏ Dynasty,[49] because the goddess was popular among shamans in the Andong area. The shaman went insane in the end. Because she shrieked and trembled so severely whenever she saw a police official, policemen themselves tried not to be seen. Children mocked her by saying the word "police" to watch her reaction.[50]

This story spread quickly throughout the country. Except for the tragic situation of the shamans, people enjoyed such tales and the phenomenon also shows us how people constructed experiences of resistance through this kind of religious conflict. Because shamans were counted as the lowest class in the traditional estate system, however, those shamans victimized by Japanese colonial cruelty were not officially recognized and thus their experiences were not documented. In this way, ordinary people were not given any place in Korean national history. Because the stories were so popular, however, they survived as unofficial history.[51]

"Manse Kwisin"

There was a kut for a soul struck by police torture after the March First movement. It was a manse kwisin (a ghost of a person killed while shouting "manse!" during the March First movement). The shaman, in the soul's mother's voice, scolded the soul for participating in the manse action and losing his life. The soul replied that there should be a master for the nation as there should be a father for a family. He was the eldest son of a poor family. When he was only nine years old, his father died leaving the son and a daughter. So, as the son, he took on the responsibility of taking care of the whole family.

The spirit, in the voice of an eighteen-year-old boy, lamented that he lost his love of life because he had lived a poor life as a fatherless son and a citizen without narannim (an honorific term for nation, state, or king). His mother again criticized him for not being responsible as the household head. She lamented that he was not filial enough to survive to help his poor mother:

Don't you know that I reared you as though I took care of gold and jade? [kŭmji ogyŏp, gold branch jade leaf] For me, a ch'ŏngsang kwabu [a young widow], you were the only hope of the family and solely for your success in the future I endured all kinds of hardships and humiliation. How many white nights did I spend with my eyes open? How many times did I dream of committing suicide? Looking at those infant children, I didn't dare kill myself. How many times did I blame my husband for having left us behind in this world of agony? Abandoned by my husband, abandoned by the *narannim*, and abandoned even by my beloved son, who else in this world is as wretched as I?

Then stories of their miserable impoverished lives were narrated as a conversation between mother and son through the shaman's mouth. Spectators were weeping when the soul described his miserable existence constantly tormented by a group of monstrous hungry ghosts. The shaman placated the hungry ghosts with rice and wine and, in the guise of General Ch'oe Yŏng,[52] and threatened them with his sword and verbal reprimands. She shouted, "You greedy little guys don't you know who I am? I am General Ch'oe. How dare you linger in front of me? Go away immediately and don't come again to torment this handsome young man." After the hungry ghosts were expelled, the mother gave her son's soul money, rice, and clothing to enjoy in the netherworld. Satisfied, the soul uttered rhythmically, through the shaman's tongue, "*Manse manse manmanse.* Long live mother, long live my family, and long live the nation. My dear brother and sister, take good care of Mother, and don't worry about me. All of you will enjoy a comfortable and wealthy life. *Manse, manse, manmanse.* Long live independence."

The police were not happy with this ritual session because it depicted the defeat of the Japanese, symbolized by the hungry ghosts and by General Ch'oe, who had defeated invading Japanese pirates during the Koryŏ Dynasty. They were also upset because the word *manse* revived memories of the March First movement. The shaman said it was good because she pacified the unsettled *manse kwisin*, but the police retaliated with physical violence in an effort to make the shaman realize the Japanese were more powerful and stronger than General Ch'oe. They released the exhausted shaman after two weeks of custody. After the incident, Koreans formed an extremely negative image of Japanese police. Several weeks later, when the Korean assistant to the Japanese police died in a car accident, people said it was General Ch'oe's punishment. Both the Japanese and the Korean police, therefore, hated, and in a sense feared, the spirit of General Ch'oe and *manse kwisin*. One evening Mr. Li, who was the Korean assistant to the Japanese police, secretly prayed to General Ch'oe to understand the agony he was undergoing and not to appear to the living.[53]

"Kongjingi"

A popular local shaman used a child spirit called a *kongjingi*, who functioned as a messenger between the shaman and the netherworld. She used to send the *kongjingi* to bring back souls. One day, at a *kut* for a sick woman, the shaman sent the *kongjingi* to the netherworld to seek the soul of the sick woman's grandmother-in-law (husband's grandmother). Unusually they waited more than an hour until the child spirit returned. When she came back, the room suddenly became chilly, and there was a whistle-like shriek, the sound of the air being torn as the child spirit flew swiftly and fiercely. When the spirit arrived, the shaman scolded it for being late, like a mother scolding her naughty child. The child spirit said that it stopped to watch a fire on the way back. It added that it could not proceed because a group of policemen were standing on the road to check people. It was afraid of police and hid itself until the police moved away. (The spirit spoke through the shaman's tongue in a child's voice). Later, people found that there had actually been a fire and police were controlling traffic in the place the child spirit mentioned.[54]

"Narannim"

The most sensitive word in these shaman performances was *nara* or *narannim*. While possessed, shamans would say, "Since *narannim* has gone somewhere unknown" or "Oh, *narannim*, please take care of us, your innocent children." Sometimes they predicted that everything would be all right once the *narannim* came back or assured people that the *narannim* accepted their agony and promised to help them. Here is a case of a shaman who was interrogated by the police, recollected by a man who was arrested as the assistant to the victimized shaman.

Policeman: What is your *narannim*?

Shaman: We are just simple *paeksŏng* [ordinary people] and *narannim* is *paeksŏng*'s *narannim*, and we are *narannim's paeksŏng*.

Policeman: You are a subject of the Great Japanese Empire, aren't you?

Shaman: I am a child of my *narannim*.

Policeman: You, wicked and foolish idiot *Chōsenjin* [Korean], don't you know that you are given special honor to be the child of Japan?

Shaman: You already said that I am *Chōsenjin*, not Japanese. My tutelary god is General Ch'oe Yŏng of the Koryŏ Dynasty. Being his spiritual daughter, I cannot change my citizenship. If I change it, General Ch'oe would kill me.

Policeman: You idiot. He [General Ch'oe] is nothing before the emperor. Forget him or bring him to become a child of the emperor, too.

Shaman: You must be careful not to be rude before General Ch'oe. I am afraid he might strike you. (At this moment, the Japanese policeman became frightened)

Policeman: How can you prove his power or efficacy?

Shaman: Well, he protects our *nara*, protects people from evil spirits. Without him, the whole nation and society would be in chaos. We owe a lot to him.

Policeman: Why don't you speak Japanese?

Shaman: I am illiterate. What I am saying in the ritual was what a spirit was saying through my tongue. You know that even souls of civilized yangban cannot speak *Waemal* [Jap language]. How can you imagine that souls of non-yangban, who were not educated, would be able to speak Japanese? *Chōsenjin* [the Koreans] can only speak *Chosŏnmal* [the Korean language] while *Waenom* [Japs] can only speak *Waemal*. Those souls I am dealing with are all Korean souls and they cannot speak Japanese. They are unhappy because their *narannim* has gone. So what should I do when they lament their losing *narannim*? If I do not resolve their grievances, then I will be killed. In order to live, I must be loyal to them and the *narannim*. Please understand me. I don't care whether this is Japan or not. I am a daughter of my *nara*. If the *nara* is pacified, everyone is happy and everything is at peace. I always pray for *kuktae minan* [that the nation be prosperous and people be safe]. Am I not a patriot? I serve the *narannim* in my own way.[55]

The policeman's assistant, who was Korean, brutally beat the shaman. He slapped her face when she said *Waenom* and *Waemal* because *wae* is a derogatory word for the word Japan, and *nom* is the derogatory word for man. It was obvious that she meant Korea by *narannim* and that there would be peace and prosperity if Koreans regained their nation.

Though the Confucians maintained a critical and scornful attitude toward shamanism in general, they recognized the shaman's bravery and lamented that some well-educated people did not feel a sense of responsibility for the nation while a socially marginalized person like the shaman resisted Japanese colonial violence. Sharing and spreading the rumors and stories about the shaman, people spread their anti-colonial ideological resistance.

Names

In 1940, Koreans were ordered to change their names in accordance with the Japanese naming system. To become the emperor's subjects, the government decreed, Koreans must change their name to the Japanese style.[56] The Korean name consists of three characters indicating clan, generation depth, and personal identity. Each character has its own meaning and by analyzing the clan name members count the relationship and social categories between them. One's name is therefore socially and spiritually important. It is registered in the clan's genealogical record book and is thus a cornerstone of social identity. Because of this cultural importance, it was a deeply disturbing experience for Koreans to change their names. For them, it amounted to selling their spirit and the entire historical succession from their founding ancestor. Actually, the name change policy's aim was the elimination of Korean national identity and the obliteration of the Korean people from the face of the earth.[57]

It is quite natural that serious conflicts arose between the colonial authorities and Koreans on this issue. Colonial authorities arrested prominent figures and even put them in prison because they refused to accept the government order. After a series of strong campaigns accompanied by torture and threats in police interrogation rooms for those who stubbornly refused to collaborate, and rewards and praise in newspapers for those who decided to change their names, the Korean people were coerced into changing their names.[58] Some Koreans changed their name using the words dog, cow, or dung, by which they ridiculed themselves and lamented that they were the same as an animal who has no sense of one's ancestors. Some people applied one of the Chinese characters from the emperor's name or challenged Japan with a name like Sŭngil, "victory over Japan"; the police authorities severely reprimanded these protestors and forced them to change their names.

There were many meetings of clans and lineages to discuss the problem. To keep their genealogical record, they needed to adopt the new clan name in the Japanese style. The government proclaimed that no one was allowed to have a public job or position without a Japanese name. Old people said that they didn't need to change their names because they were too old to have any official title or job. Young people, however, had to register their Japanese name with the authorities while they entered their names in traditional Korean style in their genealogical record book to match their ancestors. For the ritual address at the ancestral worship rites, they used their Korean names because communication between ancestors and their descendants was impossible if the descendants used a Japanese name.[59]

Shamans resisted changing their names reasoning that spirits did not need to change their names because they were not Japanese subjects. Since the spirits could not understand Japanese, it was impossible for shamans to communicate with spirits in the Japanese language. In order to cure a sickness or to solve a problem, a spirit must be identified and called back, and this was possible only by using its Korean name, they said. Interrogated by a Korean police assistant, a clever shaman explained to him that the spirit of General Ch'oe could not understand if she called him *Sai Shōgun*, as his name was pronounced in Japanese. Likewise, the name of General Yim is pronounced *Hayashi Shōgun* in Japanese, but his spirit could not respond to this Japanese name. She replied,

If a spirit cannot understand his Japanese name and thus does not make any response, I cannot liberate a soul from *han*, [the resentment in his heart]. As long as the world is full of vengeful souls, ghosts, and evils we will remain in a troubled and chaotic world. Therefore, in order to keep the country in peace and prosperity, we have to retain the spirits' original names. Though we cannot speak Japanese, we can communicate with the spirit of Emperor Meiji in the Korean pronunciation as *Myŏngch'i Ch'ŏonhwang* instead of *Meiji Tennō*. So let us keep Korean names for the sake of *kuktae minan*, the prosperity, and peace of the nation and people.[60]

The police assistant was humbled. In the end, authorities forced the shaman to change her name to the Japanese style, but she never used it.

Not all shamans resisted. Some young shamans learned Japanese and proudly displayed their Japanese language ability. They changed their names and invoked the spirit of the Japanese Emperor Meiji as their tutelary god. They even visited the Shinto shrine regularly. The Japanese police favored these shamans, but fellow shamans despised them. They tried to persuade the Korean people to enhance their health and wealth by using the power of Japanese emperor, but Korean people were reluctant to contact these shamans.

Insanity

In the early 1940s, many cases of insanity appeared among highly educated persons. Intellectuals were under continuous police surveillance because many of them harbored anti-Japanese sentiments and were active in disseminating a new political ideology among their fellow Koreans. Higher-level police, who dealt with ideology and political corrections, arrested and even tortured Korean intellectuals to death. In order to avoid police suspicion, many intellectuals pretended to be mad. Their families also attempted to protect their loved ones from the police by spreading rumors that they were insane. To prove this, families would invite a shaman to perform a healing ritual. Though rituals were not effective, people enjoyed hearing the lamentations and criticism of their life situations uttered by the shaman.

There was a man of the Andong Kim clan whose family was wealthy enough to send him to study at Waseda University in Tokyo. After several interrogations and warnings by the police about his "dangerous" thinking, he stopped studying after three years and came home under pressure from his parents to prepare for the Higher Civil Servant Examination. After a while, his behavior grew strange. People called him a genius because of his eccentricity and partly as a joke. He proved his talent by reciting the Japanese Constitution, which he had studied every day at dawn. He knew each item by heart. He wore heavy cotton clothing even on hot summer days to prove his spiritual strength and "Yamato spirit" and sometimes gave lectures on how strong the Japanese were. Sometimes he visited the Shinto shrine in Japanese clothing, too. He professed that he despised his fellow Koreans, saying, "*Chōsenjin bakayarō*," (Koreans are foolish) or "*Chōsenjin yamaga baka desu*" (Koreans are brainless). Usually Koreans became embarrassed and seriously upset when they heard this. But when they saw he was smiling, they realized that he was insane. He used to murmur, "The *Chōsenjin* are a hopeless people. You are hopeless because you are *Chōsenjin*. I am *Chōsenjin*, too. I am hopeless. Am I hopeless? I am the honorable citizen of the glorious Great Japanese Empire. I am different from you foolish *Chōsenjin*." Even though he embarrassed his family members and relatives, they enjoyed joking with him. He would play an enigmatic word game, saying,

Who are you? Since you are foolish you must be a *Chōsenjin*. Japanese are clever. I am a *Chōsenjin* so I must be foolish. If you are clever, you must be a subject of the Japanese Empire. Only subjects of the glorious Japanese Empire are clever. Koreans should be foolish. It is the order of His Royal Highness Emperor. You are subjects of the Japanese Empire. Therefore, the Japanese Empire must be a foolish empire. You are allowed to remain a *Chōsenjin* as long as you are foolish. If you prove that you are clever, then you should become the emperor's subject. But who is as clever as I in the Empire? They are foolish enough to be citizens of the Empire.[61]

He giggled and sometimes smiled when people were puzzled by his word game. One day the man took old Confucian books from his father's study and tried to burn them. Just before he set them on fire, he was stopped. He said that Confucian knowledge was useless. When his mother said that setting fires was not good, he replied, "The Japanese are very good at setting a fire since the police burnt down Hyŏptong Hakkyo. If the Japanese do it, it must be a good deed. So setting a fire is fun and good." Horrified by his speaking about a tabooed memory of the past, his mother begged the pardon of the police assistant who was once their tenant peasant. She hurriedly arranged a shamanic healing ritual in order to cure her son's sickness.[62]

It is interesting to see how this man wandered between two identities. He tried to become Japanese but realized that there was an invisible barrier to becoming genuine Japanese. He became estranged from his fellow Koreans yet was not accepted as a proper subject of the Empire. At the very moment he smiled sarcastically after denouncing his compatriots with the delirious term *Chōsenjin*, he implicitly confessed his own identity as *Chōsenjin*. He tried to differentiate himself from other Koreans, but eventually he had to admit that he was also a colonized Korean like them. At the moment his imitation of self turned out to be an illusion, he found that he had lost the cultural space for his social existence. He went mad and only in madness was he allowed to have his own voice to criticize, ridicule, and make satirical jokes about the political and social situation. Madness for him was the only space in which to attempt resistance and even subversion of the colonial reality.

It is a further irony that a person whom the colonial authorities had equipped with training in modernity and science returned to the shamanic ritual of the colonized, which was denounced as superstitious, backward, and unscientific. The man, his family, and the shaman made a space where colonial modernity and science were defined as abnormal and needing to be cured by the shamanism.

During the healing ritual, the madman grew increasingly upset. He was brought up in a Confucian elite family and was one of the most highly educated Korean intellectuals. Before they started the ritual, his mother asked for her son's understanding and cooperation in order not to ruin the hidden purpose of the ritual. She said,

> This is not only to cure your health. It is also to save our family. If you keep quiet [during the ritual process], your father will be saved, your brothers and sisters, and this poor mother will be saved. This is to save all of us, and all our families of the Kim clan. Please, please, think of our ancestors. We want to survive. You do not want our family to be dispersed in pieces by the wind [of violent punishment by the police], do you?" He agreed.

When the shaman said, "*T'aep'yŏng sŏngdae sijŏl*" (times of great peace and sagely rule), however, the man suddenly stood up to dance, saying, "If our nation is peaceful and prosperous, let's dance together. Oh, I am happy to live in this peaceful nation." As the ritual was thrown off by his unexpected rebellious act, the shaman shouted in a fearful tone of voice, "Our *narannim* went somewhere else, and the nation is like this [We lost our nation and our life is in a miserable state], our family has become like this [the family has been ruined], then you even behave in this way."

After the ritual, the police called the shaman to the station where she was interrogated and punished by the Korean police assistant, who was once the tenant of the madman's family, because she described the present living conditions of Korea as miserable and bleak.[63]

Madness

There was another case of madness. The police arrested a young man named Pak Tŏk and tortured him severely for his membership in an anti-Japanese movement circle while he was a freshman at Kyūshū Imperial University in 1940. He was released and returned home. Whenever he came across a dog, he bowed, saying, "Good morning, revered policeman," making people burst into laughter. A passing policeman slapped his cheek, but he continued to bow to dogs. Sometimes he made a speech to demonstrate his excellent Japanese in front of spectators. He would sing Japanese songs and say that he respected Japan. He also loudly insisted that the Japanese police were the most powerful and terrible police force in the world. He sometimes followed policemen, saying that he wanted to become a police officer and visited the police headquarters to apply for a job. He insisted that he was a subject of the Japanese Empire and properly qualified to become the emperor's loyal servant. He asked people to pronounce his name in the Japanese style as "Boku Doku." But often he played a game with his name, saying that "Boku" is similar to "bark" and "Doku" is pronounced similarly to that of "dog" so that his name sounded like "barking dog." In the end, however, he sighed and lamented that he had lost a strong voice to bark with. He described himself in this way: "Once a tiger, now a toothless and voiceless dog." He always bowed to dogs and policemen. When someone gave him something with a Japanese label on it, he would smell or taste it and then frown and reject it, saying that it was rotten. Japan was good, he said, but the Japanese and Japanese things were rotten and smelled bad.

Sometimes Pak threatened people, saying, "I will call the police. Don't you realize how scary the police are? You know that I have plenty of friends in the police. They all listen to my orders." People laughed at these threats. But when he saw police assistants, he would say, "There are many wild lily flowers blooming, *kaenari ka hwalch'ak p'iyŏnnae.*"[64] Because of his eccentric behavior and witty remarks, people enjoyed teasing him.[65]

Park's family invited a shaman to perform a healing ritual for him. Spectators were not satisfied when the shaman said, "In this peaceful nation, why do you ruin yourself in that way?" His mother grumbled, complaining "My son is mad and the family has become poor, but she [the shaman] describes the situation as a peaceful and prosperous state." After the ritual, the shaman said that the spirit lingering around the patient was so strong and stubborn that the family needed another ritual. However, the family complained that the ritual was not effective because the shaman did not communicate well with the spirit. The family pointed out that the spirit was a hungry ghost with a grievance against this world, but the shaman maintained that it was a prosperous and peaceful world. That was why the spirit was not happy enough to leave the patient. They quarreled with the shaman and the second ritual was not held. The family admitted that there was no possibility of healing the patient; they had held the ritual simply to resolve the psychological knot in the minds of the other family members.

Whereas the colonial police punished the shaman for Kim's ritual because she defined the world as dark and bleak, they did not intervene with the shaman for Park because she described the world as comfortable and prosperous. The actual efficacy of shamans did not concern the Korean people, rather the ritual process symbolized their own projected sense of justice, morality, and interpretation of their reality. If a shaman narrated what the people believed in their hearts, they felt liberated. But if she presented a different view of the world from theirs, they did not affirm her vision. Through the healing and ritual reconstruction of the body, the colonized Korean populace attempted a symbolic return to their own healthy and normal world.

Kwŏn Osŏl

Kwŏn Osŏl, a graduate of Waseda University in Tokyo was an active leader in organizing peasant tenure disputes against the Japanese landlords in Andong. He was one of the leading figures in the history of the early Communist movement in Korea. He was arrested as the figure to have played the leading role behind various anti-colonial activities. Finally he was tortured to death in Sŏdaemun prison in 1930. The Kwŏn clan, one of the prominent Confucian families in Andong, organized the funeral. Thousands of people paid homage to the young man despite the police's accusations that he was a Marxist traitor out to undermine the Japanese nation. The police demanded that the family observe only a three-day funeral, but the family insisted that they, as a locally distinguished Confucian elite family, had to conduct at least a nine-day funeral according to their tradition. The police had to allow them to do this in order not to affect the relationship between the government and the local dignitaries. The bereaved family treated all of the visitors to only a bowl of millet gruel instead of the traditional well-prepared food and wine. Eating the coarse millet gruel, guests conveyed the message that, Koreans lacking their own country were not deserving of good food. The mother said that though they were poor in having only millet gruel, Koreans should not forget to fight against the Japanese, who filled their stomachs with the rice that they robbed from Korean peasants.[66]

Several months later, a shamanic ritual was held in a neighboring village for a man of the Kwŏn clan who had gone insane. The shaman discovered that this man had been afflicted by the soul of Kwŏn Osŏl. After the ritual, the police interrogated the shaman because she uttered "treacherous" words in her ritual.

Instead of *Tae Ilbon Cheguk* (Great Japanese Empire), she used the name *Haedong Chosŏn'guk* (Chosŏn, East of the Sea), to indicate the patient's residence. She also said, "Since *narannim* has gone somewhere unknown, the world is dark and the innocent people are fearful and uncomfortable." Since the word *narannim* is an honorific term for the nation or the head of the nation, the police demanded the shaman to clarify what she mentioned. The police asked whether by stating this she meant Korea, the late King Kojong,[67] Japan, or the Emperor Hirohito. They also wanted to know what she meant by "gone somewhere unknown." Police also required the shaman to explain why she described the world as dark and the people as fearful and uncomfortable. At first, she answered that she could not remember what she had said because the spirit made the utterance while she was possessed.

After a series of severe torture sessions, she replied that she could not speak Japanese so that she had to use the Korean words for the man's residence. Then the authorities asked her to learn Japanese, she responded that the spirits could not understand Japanese. If she could not communicate properly with a spirit, then there would be a tragedy, she added. The police ordered her to stop her shamanic practice, but she refused, explaining that the spirit would kill her if she resisted it. At last, she bravely confessed that she meant Korea by narannim and declared that she would not stop being a shaman as long as people wanted her to soothe those many poor souls. The police beat the shaman severely and she died several months after she was released.

When she was close to death, the shaman often mentioned that Min Hwanghu (Empress Min)[68] appeared in her dreams. After her death, the shaman's relatives and friends feared the possibility of Empress Min's vengeance, so they organized a ritual to resolve her grievances. In the ritual, the vengeful spirit of Min Hwanghu appeared and a shaman described how cruel the police had been and how dreadful the torture was. Whenever the shaman vividly described the torture and terror the empress was subjected to, the spectators looked on in horror and shivered. Torture narratives allowed Korean people to experience the violence of colonial power while maintaining their own grievances against the terrifying immorality of the colonialists. Rituals such as these positioned the spectators between the realm of colonial domination and the front line. Though this ritual was performed secretly lest it be exposed to the police, the latter arrested those who participated. The participants tried to rationalize that they were contributing to the stability of the social order by appeasing the vengeful spirit of the dead shaman. They also attempted to persuade the police to accept that more cruel treatment would engender endless shamanic rituals. The police were so nervous on the issues connected with Min Hwanghu, Emperor Kojong, and Chosŏn that they prohibited shamanism.[69] They expelled some of the principal shamans and released others from Andong after two weeks in custody.

Meanwhile the family of the Kwŏn brothers was asked to organize a shamanic ritual to liberate souls of the brothers. Their mother as the primogeniture daughter-in-law of the locally prominent Confucian elite family, however, flatly rejected the suggestion on the ground that people should control their emotions with reason and that only when the Korean nation was restored, would the souls of her sons be automatically liberated from grievance and agony. Members of the lineage, as Confucian elites, were also aloof to the shaman's case, maintaining that people should manage their life issues with Confucian rationality rather than shamanic disillusionment.

Thus, the colonial government, Confucian circles, and the Christian community criticized, denounced, and ostracized shamanism. It is well known that throughout the Chosŏn Dynasty the government had formally suppressed shamanism; Christian missionaries also supported the rhetoric of colonial modernity against shamanism. At the turn of the century, under the patronage of Min Hwanghu (Empress Myŏngsŏng), the most vehement political opponent to her father-in-law, the Prince Regent (Taewŏn'gun), shamans frequented the royal palace and thus corrupted social morality and bureaucratic politics. After the Japanese killed Min Hwanghu and made their dominance over Korea visible, many politically oriented shamans turned to pro-Japanese agents. Suryŏn, a trusted shaman of Emperor Kojong, even performed a special ritual to console the soul of former Resident-General Itō Hirobumi who was shot to death by An Chunggŭn in 1909. Not only Confucian elites but also ordinary people were shocked by her act and became deeply antagonistic toward shamanism.

Despite official denouncements, however, peasants at the local level constantly practiced popular shamanism. The violent spirits these rituals revived were mostly hungry ghosts and the souls of those killed by the police. As a consequence of the constant attacks by the government, many shamans eventually disappeared, while others compromised with the colonial authorities by paying regular homage to the Shinto shrine and accepting the Japanese spirit as their tutelary god.

CONCLUSION

The completion of the process of assimilating folk religions was officially reported by 1935 and the seasonal observations of religious life in Korea were transformed in accordance with the dictates of Shinto. On the eighth day of every month, the Korean people had to pay homage to Shinto shrines. All schools, companies, and villages organized a group visit, which was followed by a communal picnic and other related activities, such as athletic meetings, essay or poetry contests, and so on. On October seventeenth of every year, the Japanese organized the largest festival at the Shinto shrines to offer the year's harvest. The emperor made a special sacrifice to Amaterasu Ōmikami, the Japanese goddess of heaven, and with this as a signal all the shrines began their rituals and festivals for the deities enshrined. Since Koreans observed the traditional Korean harvest ritual (Chusŏk) in October, Chusŏk was effectively abolished. The main object of worship at the newly implemented autumn festival was Amaterasu Ōmikami, flanked by the spirit of the Emperor Meiji, while the god of Tsushima and Tan'gun were seated below.

Through this religious arrangement the Japanese colonized indigenous customs, history, time, and space. The new religious calendar introduced a new mechanism for social memories, and "foreign" deities came to occupy indigenous sacred space. The Korean cultural system was subordinated to the Japanese one, and a hierarchical order of history was imposed. After 1936, many shamans began to frequent Shinto shrines to pay homage to Amaterasu because they were indoctrinated to believe her to be the supreme goddess of shamanism, while some shamans identified Meiji as their tutelary god.

However, Koreans strongly resisted the colonial attempt to control time and space. Apathy and inaction were deliberate forms of resistance in everyday life. People tried to maintain, invent, and reproduce a "backwardness" by which they displayed their resistance to Japanese colonial rule. Conservatism was also a part of their strategy in adapting the colonial change in the fields of politics, economics, and culture.

Needless to say, colonial policies changed over time during the thirty-six year period of Japanese rule. While colonial authorities officially denounced Korean shamanism, they also tried to incorporate shamanism with the Japanese religious system of Shinto in other ways. Shamanism at the practical level maintained a conservative stance and resisted social transformation initiated by the colonial government by generating a challenging ideology against the colonial authority. Shamanism also provided the symbolic experience of subversion to colonial reality. Not only shamans, but also the Confucians and Christians maintained a strategic stance in dealing with colonial violence, attempting to maintain their sacred authority through strategic cooperation with the colonial authority.

In other words, the Japanese colonial policy to destroy Korean culture did not succeed.⁷⁰ The Japanese achieved their goals of economic exploitation and political domination in the secular sphere but could not enjoy absolute domination in the field of culture and religion. After Korea liberation, nearly all of the Shinto shrines were either demolished in a day or two or were totally deserted.

When they realized that shamanism acted as a cultural instrument, one that dramatically reproduced the experience of resistance and imagination of subversion, Koreans came to manipulate it to revive their national identity and history. Through the ritual process, spectators participated in one way or another to criticize, challenge, and ridicule the colonial authority and narrated their grievances and grudges against the reality of colonial violence in the disguise of ritual possession. During the rituals, people witnessed the resurrection of the dead and thus the revival of the muted history of the colonized, and publicized the officially disqualified memories of the past. Through vehement accusations and violent fights against evil, as dramatized by shamans in the ritual process, spectators experienced and shared the counter-colonial rhetoric of their reality. Shinto, however, does not provide this kind of space for dramatic imagination and violent ritual processes that revive and contact souls, ghosts, and spirits. Through vivid narration and counter-discourse on reality in people's everyday language, a shamanic ritual liberates both the dead and living from their unresolved grievances and resentments, thus attempting a symbolic achievement of negation and subversion of the colonial reality.

Of course, this does not necessarily mean that all Koreans overwhelmingly supported shamanism. As we have seen, the Confucian bureaucracy imposed continuous pressure on shamanism during the Chosŏn period. However, in a special political situation like colonial rule, ordinary people deprived of power and voice came to re-evaluate shamanism as a cultural instrument for their political resistance against the secular power of colonialism.

As it has been redefined and distorted by various powers, however, it should be noted here that shamanism did not maintain its original form and nature. Colonial authorities and scholars manipulated shamanism for their cultural assimilation policy, and local Confucians and Christians formally denounced shamanism. Even the shaman community was divided into two factions, the pro-Japanese "enlightened" group and the conservative "backward" group.

Korean intellectuals also invented and redefined shamanism along their own political and ideological lines. They emphasized the ancient history of Korean shamanism in their effort to prove the superiority of Korean culture over the Japanese, or support the theory of a common cultural root between Korea and Japan. Shaman practitioners themselves, however, were not highly educated enough to theorize their practice in relation to political symbolism other than for religious purposes. Rather, nationally oriented local scholars, intellectuals, and Japanese scholars acting as colonial agents defined and shaped shamanism.

My contention in this chapter is that the Korean shamans might have not been conscious of their role as anti-colonial resistors. In fact, it is neither certain nor easily proved that shamans constructed their ritual performance and manipulated their responses to the police as an intentional reaction against or resistance to colonial power. It should be noted here that the Korean people in general were not enthusiastic about shamanism *per se*. However, they implicitly recognized the ritual and enjoyed participating in it. Through their conscious indifference to shamanism, they enjoyed seeing their own hidden agenda against the colonial authorities exposed, dramatized, and shared through the agency of shamanic rituals denounced and rejected by the colonial powers. Even Confucians and Christians actively participated in repeating and spreading the stories about shamans and their colonial encounters. They participated, in short, by non-participation. Koreans constructed a collective experience of anti-colonial resistance and produced their own social memory out of the private experience of the shamans whom they marginalized. The ambiguous attitude toward shamanism and the multifaceted and distorted stance of shamanism, therefore, should be understood in the context of conflict and compromise within a specific colonial situation.

NOTES

1. This chapter was written between the years 1998 and 2000 as a part of a project sponsored by the Korean Research Foundation.
2. See Jean Comaroff and John Comaroff, *Of Revelation and Revolution*.
3. Kwang-Ok Kim, "Cultural Community."
4. Clifford Geertz, *Interpretation of Culture*.
5. Kwang-Ok Kim, "Rituals of Resistance."
6. Nicholas B. Dirks, *Colonialism and Culture*; Nicholas Thomas, *Colonialism's Culture*.

7. Mun Okp'yo, "Ilche ŭi singminji munhwa," 3.

8. In fact, older Koreans are not willing to revive or verbalize their miserable memories of the colonial experience. They have a strong tendency to select only happy memories to relay to their children, by which they think they can maintain face before their descendants. It is not easy to encourage old people to recall their shameful experiences as well.

9. Jean Comaroff and John Comaroff, *Of Revelation and Revolution*.

10. Before he left, lineage elders tried to persuade Yi Sangyong to remain at home to fulfill the responsibilities of the primogeniture descendant. However, he flatly rejected this advice, saying that there was no reason to maintain one's lineage when one's nation was lost. It is interesting to note that members of his lineage intentionally purchased his house and fields in their effort to keep them as the lineage corporate property.

11. Kim Sŏngil (1538–93), of the Ŭisŏng Kim lineage, organized and led militia and died in the battlefield when Toyotomi Hideyoshi's Japanese Army invaded Korea in 1592. Also, one of the founding members of the school was Tongsam Kim who went into exile in Manchuria to lead the liberation movement. Thus, the village and lineage as a whole had very strong anti-Japanese and nationalistic sentiments.

12. Interview by the author with Kim Siwu, the primogenital descendant of Ŭisong Kim lineage of Andong.

13. The Government-General issued the regulations on grave sites, cremation sites, and burial and cremation. Chōsen Sōtokufu, "Sōtokufu rei dai 123 gō" [Government-General of Korea Order no. 123], June 1912.

14. This story was not a story from a specific family. Similar stories are told by members of many other lineages in Andong.

15. Kim Ŭltong, *Andogp'an tongnip undongsa*, 211–328.

16. Secret Reports on Intellectuals by the Andong Police in 1925.

17. A Short Record of the Secret Police in 1934.

18. Anonymous interviews by the author with elderly citizens in the area, 1985.

19. Chōsen Sōtokufu, "Sōtokufu rei dai 40 gō" [Government-General of Korea Order no. 40].

20. Park Eul Sun, interview with the author, 1986. In 1986, Ms. Park was eighty-five years old. She was an ex-shaman.

21. "Special regulations to watch and control the eighteen thousand shamans in Korea was implemented," *Tonga ilbo*, June 10, 1934 (reprinted).

22. Kwang-Ok Kim, "Rituals of Resistance."

23. Head police chief Imamura ridiculed Koreans saying that they were so stupid and superstitious that they posted the words "police" on their house gate in order to expel evil spirits or misfortune. See Imamura Tomo, *Chōsen fūzoku shū*.

24. Chōsen Sōtokufu, "Sōtokufu rei dai 82 gō" [Government-General of Korea Order no. 82].

25. Chōsen Sōtokufu, "Sōtokufu rei dai 83 gō" [Government-General of Korea Order no. 83].

26. The author was also brought up in such an atmosphere. Until the 1960s the image of police as horrible monsters prevailed among children of Korea. This image of police was regenerated by people who suffered from the Japanese police surveillance during the colonial period.

27. Mr. Kwŏn, interviewed by the author in 1998. At that time he was eighty-five years old and living in Heilungjiang Province, China.

28. After the Manchus invaded and devastated Korea in 1627 and 1636, General Yim plotted military retaliation, but his secret mission was discovered by the Manchu court and he was beheaded.

29. Mr. Kwŏn, interviewed by the author in 1996, Heilungjiang Province, China.

30. Kim Ikhan, "1930-nyŏndae Chosŏn ŭi chibang."

31. Shocked by the March First movement, the Government-General of Korea intensified police control over Koreans. Under the direction of Murayama Chijun, the colonial government carried out in-depth research for the project "Chosŏn sahoe sajang kosa," [Investigation of affairs in Korean society], 1919–23. And there were many secret reports made by local police stations. See Aono Masaaki, Chōsen nōson no minzoku shūkyō.

32. Murayama Chijun, Chōsen no ruiji shūgyo. See also Chōsen Sōtokufu, "Chōsen ch'ongdokbu t'ongye ny," 1923.

33. A Japanese anthropologist, Abito Itoh maintains that the Rural Promotion movement of the Japanese colonial government promoted "village autonomy, economic recovery" and aimed at encouraging "mutual friendship, diligence, education, reducing consumption, reforming corrupt customs. . . . " Abito Itoh, "Coordination and Brokerage," 158–9.

34. Anonymous interviews by the author with elderly Confucian leaders in Andong.

35. Yi Yuksa, one of Yi T'oegye's descendants and a sociologist who studied at Peking University, wrote a famous poem "Green Grapes" in which he expressed his dream of recovering the nation. Another poet Yi Sanghwa wrote "I Wonder Whether Spring Comes Even to The Robbed Land." These poets died in prison and their poems were forbidden, but students circulated them secretly. Students loved to use numbers three or sixty-four on their athletic uniforms because these numbers when pronounced are the sounds sam of Kim Tongsam and yuk-sa of Yi Yuksa, respectively. After liberation in 1945, these two poems were printed in the new high school textbook of Korean literature (국어). Almost all Koreans know these poems; they are now regarded "national" poems.

36. Kim Yonghwan seriously damaged his lineage properties and even sold a sword that was the clan's treasure given by the king. Clan dignitaries held a special meeting and bought the sword back. Once, the clan council discussed removing him from the position of primogeniture because he failed to maintain a decent lifestyle and shirked

his moral obligation to uphold the clan's reputation. His grandfather, Kim Hŭngnak, was regarded in the Confucian academic community as the greatest Confucian philosophy scholar in the school of T'oegye at the turn of the century. Therefore, his clan was distinctively proud of their clan identity. Despite warnings by the clan council, however, Kim Yonghwan continued to gamble.

37. Song Chihyang, *Andong hyangt'o chi*; "Chōsen shisei no kaizen."

38. For a detailed examination, see Park Hyŏnsu, "Illche ŭi Chosŏn chosa."

39. For a detailed analysis, see Kim Sŏngnae, "Musok chŏnt'ong ŭi tamnon."

40. Murayama Chijun, *Chōsen no ruiji shūkyō*.

41. Murayama Chijun, *Chōsen no ruiji shūkyō*; Akamatsu Chijo and Akiba Takashi, *Chōsen fuzoku no kenkyū*.

42. Yi Nŭnghwa, "Chosŏn musokko"; Ch'oe Nam-sŏn, "Salman'gyo ch'agi."

43. Namsan is important to the extent that it is mentioned in the Korean national anthem, "Evergreen pine trees on Namsan represent our Korean spirit. . . . " Traditionally Namsan was the sacred place where Korean national rituals were held.

44. Chōsen Sōtokufu statistics, 1936.

45. Chōsen Sōtokufu statistics, 1943.

46. Anonymous interviews by the author with elderly citizens of the area on their school life during the Japanese period.

47. Kim Nosun, interview by Kwang-Ok Kim, 1982. At the time of the interview Mr. Kim was seventy-five years old.

48. This story is based on my personal interview in 1990 in Andong with Pak Pansul (b.1905). He recalled an incident he witnessed while he was serving as an assistant at a police box in a suburb village of Andong in 1927.

49. King Kongmin (1351–74) tried to strengthen the independent position of Koryŏ from the rule of the Yuan even though he married the Mongol princess, Noguk Taejang Kongju. When the Red Turbans invaded Koyrŏ in 1361, the king and queen fled to Andong because it was the home of the king's most loyal supporters. Later, the queen died at a young age of natural causes and the king was poisoned to death. The people of Andong were sympathetic to the couple and shamans began to worship their spirits.

50. This is based on my personal interviews with two women in Andong in 1998. They were Kim Chŏmnye (김점례, b.1905) and Chang Ch'asun (장차순, b. 1910). Despite their old ages, these women had vivid memories and revived what had happened in late 1930s.

51. The cruel treatment of Koreans by the police produced many tragic deaths and therefore many miserable spirits and ghost stories. Many Koreans believed that shamans were needed to console these spirits and ghosts. In this way, the Japanese police unwittingly contributed to the survival of shamanism.

52. Ch'oe Yŏng, the supreme commander of the Korean Army in the late Koryŏ

Dynasty, is remembered as an exemplary pure-minded patriot in Korean history. He sent the army to attack Ming in order to retake land in Manchuria but was beheaded by the rebellious deputy commander Yi Sŏnggye in 1388.

53. This story was told by three women in Andong in 1996. They were Kwŏn Sunim (권순임, b. 1912), Yi Mallyŏ (이말녀, b. 1915), and Chongnye Im (임종례, b. 1919). Though both Ms. Kwŏn and Ms. Yi were from yangban families; they depicted the story in detail. Yim was from a non-yangban family. She heard the story from her elder brother who was once an assistant of the Japanese police.

54. Kim Punŏ (김부녀, b. 1923), a woman in Andong told me this story in 1994.

55. Pak Suri (박술이, b. 1905) was an assistant of a locally well-known shaman. During my interview with him in 1988, he still vividly recalled the terrifying experiences he and the shaman underwent when the Japanese police interrogated both of them in 1940.

56. Miyata Setsuko et. al., Sōshi kaimei.

57. Ki-baik Lee, A New History of Korea, 353.

58. Major daily newspapers like the Tonga ilbo and Chosŏn ilbo reported and praised many nationally known figures, such as Yi Kwangsu for having decided to change their names.

59. Anonymous interviews with dignitaries of local lineages in Andong. Many dignitaries told me the same stories at interviews.

60. Mr. Park Suri, interview by Kwang-Ok Kim. Mr. Park was well acquainted with the shaman.

61. Kim Hokyu, interview by Kwang-Ok Kim. Kim Hokyu was a classmate of this man in elementary school and a member of the same lineage.

62. Kim Nosun, interview by Kwang-Ok Kim, 1982.

63. Ibid.

64. In Korean, kae means dog and nari means lily flower. However, nari is also a homonym for a term of address for an official. So kaenari, literally "wild lily," is used here to imply a dog-like official.

65. Pak was from the family of a hereditary official at the local magistrate office of Andong during the Chosŏn period. When the Korean War (1950–53) broke out, his family moved somewhere and never returned, while Pak himself remained in Andong. He died in 1978. During my fieldwork I found people in Andong still enjoyed the many anecdotes about him.

66. Song Chihyang, Andong hyangt'o chi.

67. King Kojong established the Taehan Empire and became emperor in his effort to maintain Korea as an independent nation; he struggled against the Japanese imperialists until he was poisoned to death. Although his death was not clearly investigated, people regarded it as a Japanese plot.

68. In the year 1895, a group of Japanese samurai invaded the royal palace, killed Empress Min (Min Hwanghu) and burnt her body with kerosene on the spot because

she tried to block Japanese influence on Korean politics.

69. Empress Min, General Ch'oe, General Yim, Princess Noguk, and King Kongmin were the most popular tutelary gods or goddesses for shamans in the Andong region. These figures were associated with histories of foreign invasion and plunder, mostly by Japanese marauders and armies as well as Chinese armies and bandits that devastated the Korean nation. They were respected patriots who tried to preserve the Korean nation in the face of massive foreign invasions.

70. Mun Okp'yo, "Ilche ŭi singminji munhwa," 21.

9

The Korean Family in Colonial Space—Caught between Modernization and Assimilation

CLARK W. SORENSEN

After Korean liberation in 1945, two powers with different agendas immediately occupied the Korean peninsula. In the North, the Soviet Union facilitated a revolutionary transformation of Korean society designed to free
Koreans from feudal (ponggŏnjuŭijŏk) social and class relations. This
required the elimination of authoritarian family ties founded on male control of property, women, and children. Laws abolishing licensed prostitu-
tion and bride wealth payments and declaring the equality of the sexes were
quickly put into place. In the South, however, the United States military
government preserved most of the institutions and the legal system
bequeathed by the Japanese. In so doing, substantially more continuity
existed between the Southern colonial and post-colonial society than in the
North. Under these conditions, a number of conflicting tendencies appeared
in the South. On the one hand, many of the South Korean intelligentsia
wanted to transform Korea into a prosperous, modern country. With this in
mind, they introduced new discourses on sex, love, marriage, and the family designed to modernize Korean family practices and bring them up-to-
date. These modernizers felt that family law should quickly be revised to
reflect "modern" (Western) norms of martial freedom, divorce, property
ownership, and sexual equality. Other Koreans, however, felt that rebuilding
the nation and restoring Korean tradition should take precedence over the
introduction of bourgeois freedoms. Reacting to Japanese assimilation pressures, many in this camp felt the most urgent concern for the Korean family legal system was the restoration of Korean tradition. Seeing the family
as the locus classicus of ethno-national identity this group tended to look

askance at the idea that modernizing reforms harmed public morality (*p'unggi mullan*), and they worried more about the fraternization of Korean women with occupying troops and *après guerre* sexual license (*ap'ŭre*) than about the modernization of Korean family relations.[1]

Up until the democratizing reforms of the 1980s and 1990s when feminist reformers united with civil society groups to introduce epochal changes in South Korean family law, it was the ethnic restoration approach that by in large had the most influence on the legislation regarding the family. South Korean family law remained quite conservative for two generations after liberation. Japan meanwhile enacted the 1947 Constitution which abolished the traditional Japanese corporate family, the *ie*, in favor of a Western-type nuclear family system.[2] In Korea the corporate family, or *ka*, survived at least in vestigial form until 2005, when the legislature agreed to abolish the household registration system.

This ethnic restoration approach that dominated post-liberation South Korean family law seems a post-colonial reaction to colonial assimilation attempts. Yang, however, problematized the "traditionality" of the post-colonial Korean family. She criticized the equation of tradition with an essentialized Confucianism and noted the past montage "invented" as "custom" under colonialism.[3] One would agree with Yang's points here, yet Yang treats postcolonialism as a temporal category—that which follows colonialism. This treatment tends to downplay the structural features of colonialism per se—ethnic stratification, overwhelming colonial power, colonial discourses of superiority and inferiority, and the defensive, social, and intellectual positions the colonized adopted to deal with imperial power and discourse—and thus creates space for Yang to criticize post-liberation South Korean family law as insufficiently modern. Here I would treat post-coloniality as a social formation, a reaction to colonial power and discourse that continues after the colonial regime is no longer in place. Korean tradition was constructed, of course, but constructed in specifically colonial space. As Chatterjee pointed out, when the British colonial administrators assumed sovereignty in India they introduced the modern technology and institutions that facilitated their rule. They *also* introduced registration and census practices that classified the Indian people under their rule, as well as Orientalist discourses that juxtaposed Western rationality to Indian mysticism and traditionalism. Lacking the agency of citizenship, Chatterjee notes, colonial subjects create, in reaction, an "inner domain of sovereignty" based on their local language, religion, and family life that becomes the locus of native identity formation. One can see this phenomenon in Korea as well as in India. Under Japanese rule Koreans also sought an autonomous domain of sovereignty by cultivating native literature and folklore and creating new, indigenous religions such as Ch'ŏndogyo,[4] and such defensive traditionalism, in my view, crowded out space for modernity.

By Korean colonial space I refer to the totality of lifeways possible within the structural constraints of colonialism. The Japanese used their administrative power to control and classify Koreans. They thus enforced the legal distinction between ethnic Japanese residents of Korea (*naijijin*) who were treated as citizens with political rights, and Koreans (*Chōsenjin*) who were treated as imperial subjects without political rights. Ethnic stratification ensured that positions of power and authority were restricted to the Japanese. The national language became Japanese, which was used in schools and all other public contexts, while Korean was reduced to the status of a local dialect. The Japanese naturally used their power and control of the educational system and the media to disseminate discourses of Korean inferiority and inability to achieve modernity as necessity for Japanese rule.[5] These kinds of features are typical of most colonies but the colonial space in Korea was, for a number of reasons, more constrained than in many other colonies. The Japanese established the Protectorate (Chōsen tōkanfu) in 1905 with indirect rule similar to the French rule of Tongking or British rule over much of India, but they quickly moved in 1910, to direct rule with a Government-General (Chōsen Sōtokufu). Responsible only to the Japanese emperor, the governor-general ruled by decree with minimal input from native advisors. Because the Koreans were neighbors and racially and culturally similar to the Japanese, rather than an entirely alien and distant people, the Japanese imagined they could assimilate the Koreans and mobilize them for the modernization of Japan proper. As Caprio pointed out, while there was much discussion during the colonial period about the speed by which assimilation could realistically be achieved, that linguistic and cultural assimilation of Koreans was Japan's ultimate goal was rarely questioned by Japanese.[6]

While one might hypothesize that Koreans would try to preserve intact, traditional Korean families during the colonial period as an "inner domain of sovereignty," this kind of defensiveness was, in fact, difficult to achieve because ideologies of modernity imported from the West (including important Christian missionary activity) had already penetrated the Korean peninsula before colonial take-over in 1905. As early as the 1890s, the necessity of adopting at least some modern family forms for national development had already been widely accepted among the elites.[7] Modernizing reforms had, in fact, already been applied to Korean families during the Kabo Reforms of 1894.[8] This made it difficult for Koreans during the latter part of colonialism to protect a family-based "inner domain of sovereignty" through rejection of modern reforms to the traditional family system. The colonial state in Korea thus used its power of legislation by decree and its dense and effective colonial bureaucracy, to move in the direction of transforming the ethnic Korean family structure to an approximation of that of Japan.

As the Japanese were the earliest successful modernizers in East Asia it was difficult in any case for the Koreans to distinguish between innovations introduced by the Japanese from that which was modern. In Korea's colonial space, the family continued to be a locus of internal sovereignty and preserved the Korean ethnic identity within the Japanese Empire. However, Koreans were caught between the need to modernize the family for national survival and the pressure to assimilate into Japanese culture which would negate Korean ethnicity. The colonial authorities' incremental changes in Korean family law served first to transfer legal control of family matters, through a system of family records (hojŏk) to the colonial state bureaucracy first, and then to gradually transform the Korean family toward Japanese norms. While most of the obvious Japanization decrees—most notoriously the creation of Japanese house names and the introduction of Japanese-style uxorilocal marriage (iri muko, muko yōshi)—had been reversed after liberation in order to restore the ethno-national purity of the Korean family,[9] the South Korean state did not relinquish control over the family after liberation. Nor did the South Korean state relinquish the colonial project of creating standardized bourgeois family structures in which patriarchal authority could be used to maintain social order. Nevertheless, while family law seemed to "restore" the traditional Korean Confucian family after liberation, this restored family was not identical to the pre-colonial Korean family, for tradition had been redefined within colonial space, and many modern colonial innovations had become indigenized by the time of liberation.

Thus when anthropologists and sociologists began to do modern field studies of Korean social organization after 1945,[10] what these field workers found—though it seemed by and large an only slightly modified version of the traditional, Confucian, patriarchal family—was, in fact, something which had already been significantly transformed.[11] Although anthropologists and historians are now aware that the patriarchal, patrilineal family system, which has come to be considered traditional in Korea, was a result of the Confucianization of Korean society in the fifteenth and sixteenth centuries and probably became widespread throughout the middle class by the eighteenth century,[12] the possibility that the system, as handed down through the colonial period (1910–45), had already been significantly modified by the colonial experience has not been sufficiently explored. Those interested in changes in the Korean family have, in general, been content with the simple dichotomy of traditional and modern or have dealt with changes in the Korean family in terms of modernization.[13] Work by Ch'oe Chaesŏk and Ch'oe Paek, on the other hand, suggest that Korean family organization passed down through the colonial period had already been substantially modified by the Japanese.[14]

COLONIAL LEGAL PLURALISM

At the time of Japanese take over in 1905,[15] the Japanese had been active in Korea for some time, had collected a good deal of information about their new colony from government-sponsored surveys, and had made plans for the modernization and transformation of Korean society as a way of protecting Japanese trade interests and preventing control of Korea, their nearest continental neighbor, by hostile nations (especially the Russian and Qing empires). Already during the Protectorate (Chōsen Tōkanfu), the Japanese had forced reforms on the Koreans and separated the administrative and judicial functions of local government that theretofore had been combined in Chinese-style magistrates. Finding the Koreans uncooperative, the Japanese began directly taking over the courts after 1907.[16] The Japanese justified these measures by expressing the "urgent necessity of applying progressive and remedial measures in order to rescue the (Korean) people from the evil effects of centuries of misrule and to promote national improvement."[17] This also facilitated Japanese control over uncooperative political elements. From the beginning Japanese control over the legal system was seen as necessary to facilitate the promotion of reforms favorable to Japanese national interest. Thus in 1909, after they decided in principle to annex Korea outright, the Japanese began to place the Korean courts under the direct control of the Japanese.

With formal annexation in 1910, establishing a stable government and society was Japan's first priority. Plans for the transformation of Korean society and culture had to be tabled to commence the immediate task of building a colonial administration. The Emergency Declaration of August 19, 1910, established the principle that the colonial administration would regulate Korea based on Japanese law and would decide later which Japanese laws would apply to the Korean colony and which would not. However, the Korean laws in effect at the time of annexation were simply confirmed. It was not until 1912, when the Japanese promulgated the Decree on Korean Civil Affairs (Chōsen minji rei), that the introduction of the Japanese Civil Code began to affect Korea to any significant degree. The Decree on Korean Civil Affairs regulated a number of legal areas and established that legal areas not covered by decree should be treated according to the Japanese Civil Code.[18] People's legal ability, family relations, and inheritance, however, were treated according to Korean custom (J. kanshū, K. kwansŭp).[19] Hence, during the first few years of the colonial administration, laws relating to family relationships and inheritance were not modified in any deliberate way.

A modern state strives to create legal uniformity throughout its domain of sovereignty as an expression of the nation, however,[20] and modern civil administrations cannot rely on unwritten custom. In order to determine precisely what Korean custom was, the Investigation Office (Torishirabe kyoku) of the colonial government studied Korean family customs. The Government-General published the results of their investigation in 1912 under the title "Report on the Investigation of Customs" (Kanshū chōsa hōkokusho). In this report, that runs for more than 400 pages in small print, reference to various provisions in the Korean legal code such as the fifteenth-century Kyŏngguk Taejŏn and the later Soktaejŏn, supported by reference to Chinese precedents—especially the Ming Code (Da Ming Lü) which had been the ultimate backup authority during the Chosŏn Dynasty (1392–1910)—and manuals of ritual practice such as Zhu Xi's Family Ritual (Jiali) or its simplified Korean version Handbook of the Four Rituals[21] (Sarye p'yŏllam) answered questions about Korean customary practice. Importantly for the ethnologist, Japanese authorities also conducted interviews on customary practices with knowledgeable people from all areas of Korea. This work, along with the interpretations and clarifications of Korean customary practices (kwansŭp) distributed by various colonial ministries such as the Legal Office (Hōmu Kyoku), the Civil Affairs Office (Minji Kyoku), and the High Court of Korea (Chōsen Kōtō Hōin), formed the basis for family law in Korea during most of the colonial period.

Though in principle the colonial authorities wanted a European-style Civil Code system[22] for family that uniformly regulated both Japan and Korea, they in fact ended up with a pluralistic system that is common in colonial societies. A legal distinction was made between ethnic Japanese residents in Korea (naijiin) to whom the Japanese Civil Code applied in its entirety, and Koreans (Chōsenjin) for whom a combination of Korean statute, Chinese precedent, informal custom, and colonial administrative regulations prevailed in matters of family and inheritance. This reliance on custom meant that differences based on former Chosŏn-period status continued to be relevant for determining the legality of family relations. For example, the Japanese authorities noted that in most cases a marriage ceremony was necessary for a marriage to be valid, but not always. This was because upper- and middle-class marriages were always accompanied by substantial negotiation, dowry, and ceremony, while in the lower-class a girl might simply have walked to her new home with a few things after the family had negotiated a match. Lower class women might have encountered divorce simply by being "sent home" by their mothers-in-law.

THE COLONIAL STATE TAKES CONTROL

Interpretations of Korean family relations based on custom (kwansŭp), however, were soon joined by positive measures to transform the Korean family system. In 1915, the authorities created a system of family registration records (hojŏk) to be kept by mayors (puyun) and township heads (myŏngjang),[23] and in 1918 they set up a Revision Research Committee (Kaisei Chōsa Iinkai) to investigate whether customs should be changed, or if a new family system should be set up. In part, this research was motivated by considerations of modernization or "whether an aspect of these customs has become inappropriate to the contemporary social system."[24] While changes were justified in the name of modernity, however, even at this early date the colonial authorities were explicit about their ultimate goals of assimilation "in light of long-range plans to unify the Japanese and Korean legal systems."[25] As a result of these investigations, a series of decrees issued in late 1921, 1922, and 1923 made large areas of Korean family law subject to the provisions of the Japanese Civil Code and altered the basis of the Korean legal system.

The areas affected by these decrees of the early twenties included parental rights over children (ch'inkwŏn), the councils of kin (Ch'injok hoe) which represented those without legal ability (munŭngnyŏk cha), the age of legal marriage, divorce by judicial decisions, recognition of illegitimate children (inji), recognition of inheritance, and the separation of inherited estates. All of these issues became subject to the provisions of the Japanese Civil Code. In addition, the partition of younger sons from their natal household, the revival of died-out family lines, marriage, divorce by mutual consent, adoption, and dissolution of adoption by mutual consent, all of which had traditionally been accomplished without state intervention and judged by de facto criteria, now depended on registration with the proper authorities and entry into the household register (hojŏk) in order to be considered legal.

In one sense the changes introduced by these decrees were quite substantial because the legality of family relations depended on registration with state authorities, rather than on evidence from ordinary daily life. In addition, areas of family affairs that had been governed by Korean customary law were now being regulated by the Japanese Civil Code. This was quite a considerable intrusion of the colonial state into family affairs. At this time, however, there were few changes to Korean family structure per se. Areas regulated by the Japanese Civil Code were not fundamental to the Korean family system at that time. Many of the new regulations dealt with matters that only happened occasionally to families. Moreover, comparison of the traditional Korean system as described in the Report on the Investigation of Customs with the Japanese Civil Code reveals that in many cases the areas affected were not changed in substance, and when there were changes, these changes had precedents in previous Korean legal codes or could be considered modernization rather than Japanization. Perhaps this is why few Koreans raised objections at this time.

In the Japanese Civil Code, the age of permissible marriage was eighteen completed years for men and fifteen years for women. These legal ages were higher than was customary in Korea at that time. I found in my own fieldwork in western Kangwŏn Province, for example, that those villagers who had married in the 1920s had a modal age of marriage of seventeen for males and fifteen for females. A substantial number of males and females had married below these modal ages—some as young as eleven. One woman had been a child bride (min myŏnŭri) married before the age of eleven.²⁶ Although on the surface this seems a clear case of change introduced by the Japanese, in actual fact the legal age of marriage did not change from what had already been part of Korean law in 1910. Kyŏngguk Taejŏn had set the legal age of marriage at fourteen completed years for males and thirteen for females. This could be lowered to eleven for females, if one of the parents was over fifty, or an invalid. Customary practice in Korea during the early twentieth century in general seems to correspond with this code: that is, thirteen or fourteen years was usually the minimum respectable age of marriage for children, and when marriages were made at a younger age they had to be rationalized by extenuating circumstances. For commoners and the lower classes the state made no particular effort to enforce these regulations, so child marriage remained an evil custom (aksŭp) that came under increasing attack as Korea tried to modernize. During the 1894 Kabo Reforms when Korea was still independent, the age of marriage had been raised to twenty. This age was reduced to seventeen for males and fifteen for females by royal decree in 1907. The *Report on the Investigation of Customs* quotes King Sunjong's decree:

> We say: In this life a man marrying when he reaches thirty, and a woman being married off when she reaches twenty was the glorious law of the three dynasties of antiquity [Xia, Shang, Zhou], and so turning to the present, there is no cause of sickness among the people more serious than the vice of early marriage. Thus a few years ago [1894] there was a prohibition [on early marriage], but it has not yet been implemented. How could this be anything but a failure in our duties. Now that we come upon this autumn of restoration [yusin] the improvement of customs is our most urgent duty. Given that we must consult the past and consider the present, one may begin to permit marriage of males at seventeen completed years and females at fifteen completed years. Respect this without opposition.²⁷

Of course in 1907 when the legal age of marriage was lowered by law from twenty to seventeen for boys, and fifteen for girls, Korea was already a Japanese protectorate, and Japanese advisors were in control of the legal system. No changes could be made in the law without their approval, and it is not hard to imagine that a Korean minister with a Japanese advisor looking over his shoulder might well find the provisions of Japan's Civil Code a source of inspiration. The ages actually chosen, however, were in fact appropriate for Korea's aspirations to modernity.

Most of the changes in Korean family and inheritance law brought about by the decrees of the 1920s were similar to the case of the age of marriage. Although the provisions sometimes did not precisely correspond with traditional Korean practices, they could be justified in terms of administrative convenience and the requirements of modern society. They did not necessarily lead to changes in the fundamental principles of the kinship or inheritance systems, nor were they attempts at Japanization of traditional Korean practices. In spite of their ultimate goal of absorbing the Koreans, the Japanese were quite aware at this time that the changes they were making were not fundamental. Their analysis of the fundamental differences between the superficially similar Japanese house system and the Korean patrilineal stem family system was actually quite sophisticated, and they felt fundamental changes could not be introduced into the Korean family until the time was ripe. Modifications that the Japanese thought would have to wait included the system by which Korean spouses kept their birth surname at the time of marriage into a household (because this is an expression of a kinship system based on patrilineal bloodlines, rather than house lines as in Japan), and the Japanese system of adopted sons-in-law (mukoyōshi) and uxorilocal marriage (nyūfukon) by which sons-in-law could be brought in as the head of household.[28]

Administrative Rulings

More important than changes to the laws by colonial authorities and the courts during this period were the interpretations of Korean customs. Although the Japanese had organized the Committee for the Investigation of the Old Customs and System (Kukan to Seido Chōsa Iinkai) in 1921 as a way of making decisions about Korean customs, those in charge of the administration of Korea did not necessarily follow the findings of the committee. In any case, administrative decisions introduced important changes in the Korean family even before the committee had been organized. In at least three of these cases, fundamental changes in the Korean family system were introduced by way of the back door of an administrative fiat. Concubines lost their legal status as family members by being refused registration on family registration ledgers in 1915.[29] In 1917, the district legal office of Hwanghae Province issued a decision (which was subsequently confirmed in other jurisdictions) that allowed unmarried sons to partition from their natal family.[30] This was in spite of the fact that research of the "Report on Research on Korean Custom" (Kanshū chōsa hokokusho) had shown that in Korean custom this was not permissible. In a similar fashion, the High Court of Korea on March 3, 1933 declared that the inheritance of the obligation to perform ancestor worship—a religious task—was not properly a concern of the state, and with one stroke abolished the legal status of ancestor worship in the family system. This was done in spite of the fact that traditionally the inheritance of the house headship and house property had been thought to follow from the inheritance of the ancestor worship obligation, which served as the market *par excellence* for those qualified for succession.

THE MOVE TO RAPID ASSIMILATION

As we have seen, then, Korean family law through the 1920s remained relatively stable. Those changes that were introduced, for the most part, were a consequence of the Japanese desire to promote social order and establish definite administrative proceedings. This led to state intrusion into family formation and pressure toward making the system more uniform, but did not lead to assimilation. Those administrative changes that were more substantive—such as abolishing concubinage, allowing the partition of eldest sons, or abolishing ancestor worship as a concern of the state—were mostly ignored by Koreans many of whom continued organizing their families as before on a *de facto* basis.[31] The increasing militarization of the Japanese Empire after 1933, however, induced the authorities to step up integration of the various parts of the Empire and move to a policy of rapid assimilation, the so-called transformation into imperial subjects policy (kōminka). So far as family law was concerned, attention was focused on those laws having to do with patrilineal succession—inheritance of names and uxorilocal marriage— laws that had been identified in 1922 by the Civil Affairs Office as crucial structural differences between the Japanese and Korean family systems and not yet "ripe" for change. The rapid assimilation policy or the policy of "making imperial subjects" (kōminka) came to a head in 1939 with a series of Decree on Civil Affairs (Chōsen minji rei) revisions designed to transform Korean family organization into a facsimile of that of Japan.

The Japanese revised the policies to provide for the creation of Japanese-style names for Koreans. Adoption of children with different surnames was allowed, and marriage within the household was permitted so long as adopted sons-in-law could be arranged. On the surface, none of these revisions seems particularly earth shattering, though the attempt to force Japanese names on the Koreans was bitterly resented. In fact, each revision was deliberately aimed at a fundamental feature of the Korean family system which, if changed, would bring the Korean family into conformance with that of Japan.

Sŏng, Ssi, and the Name Change Controversy

Beginning in the early Chosŏn period, Koreans placed increasing ethical significance on the preservation of the patriline and its purity.[32] Preservation of the patriline is, of course, an expression of the cardinal virtue of filial piety (hyo), but it is also a symbol of universal order and the preservation of society from ungovernable chaos. The Korean surname, or sŏng, like its Chinese counterpart, came during this period to be a marker of a patrilineal bloodline. Most are monosyllabic such as Kim, Pak, Yi, Ch'oe, or Hong, but a few are bisyllabic such as Nam-gung or Sŏn-u. A child would take the surname of his or her own biological father in all circumstances in which the father was known.[33] Just as one cannot change one's own biological father, one cannot change one's surname. Those with the same surname, however, were not necessarily related. Surnames were further distinguished by pon'gwan—the place of origin of the apical ancestor of the patriline. All persons with the same surname and pon'gwan are considered patrikin descended in the male line from a common ancestor, and until 1997 were prohibited from marrying no matter how distant the relationship.[34]

The ethics of kinship and succession, thus, revolve around the preservation of knowable patrilineal bloodlines. In this system, a woman never takes her husband's name upon marriage, since her marriage does not change her bloodline. Before the twentieth century many women did not have a formal given name. She would be listed in genealogies as the daughter of her father. Informally she would be known by her social position (new bride, daughter-in-law), by teknonymy (Suni's mother), or geonymy (the girl from Pusan). Even adoptions were arranged so that the spirit of the patriline would not be violated. Only boys with the same surname and pon'gwan were eligible for adoption, for they would move into the house to take over the succession. Most ideal for adoption were patrilateral nephews—i.e. the child of a brother.

Under the Meiji Civil Code the Japanese surname or *shi* though often described by writers using a patrilineal-like idiom, was in fact a house name rather than the name of a bloodline. Because of this it was thought proper that all the members of the house have the same name. Women who married in, took the house name even though they were not of the same bloodline as the husband. Men coming into the house would also take the house name. There were a number of institutions by which men could enter a house into which they were not born. They could be adopted (*yōshi*), they could make one of two different sorts of uxorilocal marriage, or they could become an adopted son-in-law (*mukoyōshi*).

Adoption was rather straightforward: a house head without a suitable successor simply adopted a son to serve as successor. The son, by virtue of the adoption (*engumi*), became eligible for all the rights and duties of a natural son. In Japan, unlike Korea, there was no regulation about the bloodline of the son. Collateral relatives, even a younger brother, could be adopted in addition to completely unrelated individuals.

The institution of adopted sons-in-law was more complex. This could take place if a house had a suitable daughter, but no suitable son for succession. The son-in-law would be simultaneously, or almost simultaneously married to the daughter of the house head and adopted by the house head as successor. Actually, whether the two transactions—the marriage and the adoption—took place at the same time or not could be quite important. If the adoption and marriage took place simultaneously and then subsequently the house head had a natural male heir, the natural son would succeed in preference to the adopted son-in-law. However, if the adoption took place first and the marriage was subsequent to the adoption, then the adopted son-in-law would be legally considered an ordinary adoptee that could not be displaced by any subsequent natural male issue of the house head. Thus it was legally possible for an adopted son to marry his adopted sister. In fact, the prudent son-in-law would wait, if only for a couple of hours, between the filing of his adoption and that of his marriage.

Uxorilocal marriages were similar to adopted sons-in-law in that the husband entered the house of his wife and took her name, rather than vice versa. However this could be done either with the wife remaining head of household, or the husband becoming the head of household, depending upon how the marriage was registered.[35]

Uxorilocal marriage was also known in Korean custom, but the Korean forms of uxorilocal marriage did not have the property and succession implications of the Japanese forms. In Korean uxorilocal marriage, known as *teril sawi* (accompanying son-in-law), *ch'osŏhon*, or *ch'wesŏhon* the husband did indeed move into the wife's house. He never took his wife's surname, however, nor had any right to succeed to the position of the house headship of his father-in-law. Neither did his wife usually succeed to the headship in propertied families because agnates of the clan council (*chokch'inhoe*) had the right to force the adoption of a clansman for purposes of inheritance and succession. Conceptually the accompanying son-in-law was just that: a son-in-law who is head of his own household living for convenience in his father-in-law's house. When the father of the house died, the successor to the house headship could only be a male of the same surname and clan origin, and he would have to be adopted. If there was no property to motivate an adoption, the line of the father-in-law would simply die out.

The differences between the Korean and Japanese systems of naming, marriage, and succession, then lay in three points. Korean surnames (*sŏng*) referred to patrilineal bloodlines, while Japanese names referred to lines of house heads and their spouses that were not necessarily bloodlines. Succession to the house headship in Korea could go only to an eldest son or to an adoptee of the same surname and *pon'gwan*,[36] while in Japan eldest sons were favored, but a variety of persons including daughters, adopted sons, adopted sons-in-law, and uxorilocally married sons-in-law could succeed to the house headship. Finally, in Korea strict and wide-ranging rules of exogamy excluded persons of close collateral and any degree of agnatic kinship from marrying, while in Japan only the closest collateral kin were prevented from marrying, and adopted sons were allowed to marry the daughter of the household—something that would be incest twice over in the Korean system.

One final difference between Japan and Korea was never harmonized, however. Japan had a system of impartible inheritance: "Inheritance of family authority [*katoku sōzoku*] is succession of one person to the entirety of the social status and property rights as inheritor of the house headship, and no room exists for the commencement of property inheritance as a separate estate only."[37] Korea, however, had partible inheritance. The right to ancestor worship devolved solely on the eldest son in the male line, and younger sons had to travel to their oldest brother's house to participate in ancestor worship. Succession to the house headship was similar to ancestor worship, except that the temporary succession to wives or daughters was permitted. At the death of a house head, property was divided according to the wishes of the deceased house head. Generally it was considered fair that the eldest son responsible for ancestor worship should receive more than what other sons received—often twice more. Younger sons were entitled to a share, though in poor families or in cases when the father died without dividing the property, younger sons sometimes received nothing.

The devolution of the responsibility of ancestor worship on only the eldest son combined with partible inheritance favoring the eldest son in Korea fostered the creation of small-scale lineages made up of brothers and agnatic cousins who had separate households, but who shared ancestor worship. Younger sons would partition from the main household (the big house, or k'ǔn chip) and be set up with whatever property the main house could spare to form their nearby branch houses (chagǔn chip). Over time, a clan village of nested main and branch houses would form.

The 1939 revisions to the Decree on Korean Civil Affairs that mandated the creation of Japanese-style surnames and allowed the adoption of children with different names, within-household marriage, and the adoption of sons-in-law as successors to the house headship thus struck at the heart of the Korean kinship system. Japanese surnames were not simply an issue of linguistic assimilation but also a matter of structural assimilation. The 1939 decrees strictly speaking did not abolish Korean patrilineal sŏng but simply added house names (ssi) and made ssi the legally effective names for public use. The accompanying decrees about marriage and succession, however, were intended to break up the Korean lineages and turn them into ie-like corporate families without wide-ranging kinship ties. The limitation of succession to members of the same bloodline in Korea was not simply an old custom, but also a means to create and maintain lineage that linked, ranked, and organized households into large kinship groupings. The vast majority of villages in Korea were, in fact, clan villages. The successful introduction of Japanese-style names would separate these lineages into vertically integrated households with narrower kin ties, and the allowance of different-name adoption and adopted son-in-law marriages would have the same effect. This would have done nothing less than transform the Korean patrilineal stem family system into the Japanese house system with ambilateral filiation.

AFTER 1939

Although the decrees of 1939 introducing Japanese names, marriage, and succession practices into Korea would, if maintained, have completely altered the Korean family and kinship system, these policies were introduced too late to have much lasting effect. Although all Koreans were forced to take Japanese house names, inspection of the household records at my disposal from three villages in South Korea shows that those who were members of well-organized lineages all took the same Japanese surname—often constructed from the Japanese reading of some of the Chinese characters in their pon'gwan. Kims sometimes took the new Japanese name of Kaneyama from the Japanese reading of Kim (kane=money) to which they added yama to get "mountain of money." In other cases, when persons did not choose a Japanese surname, they were arbitrarily given a name—often by clerks simply adding "moto" to the Japanese reading of their Korean surname so that Pak could become Bokumoto, a name that would be instantly recognizable as Korean even in Japanese. Many of the latter people were probably illiterate and may not have even been aware of their new house names unless they had contact with official authorities (say, to register children in school).

No matter how strong their assimilationist rhetoric and activity, the colonial authorities were not prepared to abolish the legal distinction between ethnic Japanese (naijijin) who had political rights, access to the ethnic Japanese school system, and access to the best jobs in Korea, and the ethnic Koreans (Chōsenjin) who lacked political rights, access to the ethnic Japanese school system in Korea, and who were subject to discrimination. The Japanese still organized their families in Korea according to impartible inheritance, while the Koreans were still subject to customary law. The assimilation policy, as Caprio pointed out, was doomed to fail because of Japan's inability to accept even the assimilated Koreans as citizens.[38]

In any case, as we all know, Japan went to war with China in 1937, and eight years later Korea was liberated by the Allied Forces' defeat of Japan. Koreans then began the postcolonial task of restoring Korean families and cultural traditions. Most of the decrees that would have led to a radical change in the Korean kinship system were speedily repealed under the American occupation. On October 10, 1946, the American Military Government declared Japanese house names invalid.[39] In 1947, a circular put out by the Justice Department (Sabŏpbu) found adoption of persons of different surnames, or of sons-in-law to be invalid.[40] Finally, the Constitution of the Republic of Korea that was promulgated in 1948 rendered invalid colonial laws on subjects, such as family, that were dealt with directly in the Constitution.

Laws which were not dealt with in the Constitution, however, were left as they were. Thus, the great bulk of the customary laws and many of the official and judicial decisions of the colonial period were not visible and did not have the political ramifications that the change of name regulation did and remained on the books until the promulgation of the New Civil Code in 1960 (Sin minpŏp). The New Civil Code again prohibited the partition of the eldest son from the family (a regulation that stood until 1989), but even the New Civil Code is not entirely without colonial influence. The system of household registration continued. The Japanese-introduced system of uxorilocal marriage (J. nyūfukon, K. ippuhon) in which the husband enters his wife's house, the wife is house head, and the children take the name of the mother was retained, though such marriages, while common in Japan, remained quite rare in Korea.

CONCLUSION

The Korean family changed significantly during the colonial period. While the most obvious changes to the Korean family during this period were Japanese attempts to transform and assimilate the Koreans, these changes in the end seem to have failed. The Koreans found these changes shocking and infuriating. They ignored them as much as they could while these changes were part of the legal code, and they repealed them as soon as they had a chance after 1945. Investigation of family records in several villages revealed no example of Japanese-style succession practices in rural areas (though it is possible that there were urban cases). Other changes motivated by administrative convenience and modernization—especially those changes that were the result of administrative interpretation of customary practice—quickly became part of the system. These changes have been so thoroughly incorporated, in fact, that few people today are conscious of them. The net result, however, seems to have been that the membership boundaries of the corporate family have been clarified and narrowed so that fewer people can lay claim on family resources. The system by which younger brothers partitioned from the main house, a drawn out practice whose point of break was traditionally unclear,[41] was clarified with the creation of new household records for partitioned families. The use of the Japanese house head system to codify Korean customary law probably enhanced the autocratic power of the house head, as it did in Japan. The domestic groups that emerged in the twentieth century, though not Japanese-style house groups, did become corporate stem families with clear membership boundaries, property rights, and succession practices.

Perhaps the most interesting colonial influence on the family, however, may have been the post-colonial reaction to Japanese assimilation attempts: (1) the post-liberation attempts to restore Korean tradition by re-institutionalizing in the New Civil Code of 1960, i.e. the patrilineal, patriarchal stem family with prohibition of marriage for people of the same surname and pon'gwan; (2) obligatory succession to the house headship by the eldest son; (3) partitioning of younger sons; (4) transfer of daughters at marriage to their in-law's house; and (5) partible, unequal inheritance in which the eldest son—who must maintain ancestor worship—expected to receive about twice as much as other sons as had been codified in customary law (kwansŭp pŏp) during the colonial period. The fact that this traditional family organization has been almost completely swept away by a series of revisions to family and inheritance law since democratization in the 1980s suggests that the re-traditionalized family did not meet the needs or desires of large segments of urban Korean society. Would the patrilineal, corporate stem family have been revived after 1945 if the Japanese had not attempted cultural and structural assimilation? Perhaps a more culturally sensitive modernization of the family during the colonial period would have led to a more muted post-Colonial re-traditionalization.

NOTES

1. Yi Chŏnghŭi, "Haebang konggan ŭi yŏsŏngji ŭi nat'anan sŏng/sarang."

2. While legal support for the ie was abolished in 1947, ie-like thinking has been widely documented in contemporary Japan. See Jane Bachnik, "Recruitment Strategies for Household Succession" or Dorinne K. Kondo, Crafting Selves, for examples.

3. Hyunah Yang, Envisioning Feminist Jurisprudence in Korean Family Law.

4. Partha Chatterjee, The Nation and Its Fragments.

5. Stefan Tanaka, *Japan's Orient*; Peter Duus, *The Abacus and the Sword*.

6. Mark Caprio, "Koreans into Japanese," 251–52.

7. Yi T'aejin, *Kojong sidae ŭi chae chomyŏng*.

8. The family reforms introduced in 1894 included prohibiting early marriage, allowing the remarriage of widows (who up until that time had been considered concubines if they remarried), and exempting criminals' families from punishment. These may well have been suggested as part of "Particulars of an Outline Plan to Reform Domestic Administration" (Naejŏng kaehyŏk pangan kangnyŏng semok) proposed by Japanese envoy Ōtori Keisuke in July 1894 to the new Deliberative Council (Kunguk kimuch'ŏ) headed by Kim Hongjip and Yu Kiljun. Kim Tuhŏn, Chosŏn Kajok Chedo Yŏn'gu, 447. The degree of Japanese and/or of Korean inspiration for these reforms, however, is extremely difficult to tease out. In the first stage of the Kabo Reforms (July–October 1894) during which this place was presented, for example, the Deliberative Council under Kim Hongjip and Yu Kiljun was pro-(Japanese-inspired) reform but was not a rubber stamp for the Japanese. Japanese control was more oppressive after Japanese victories over China at which time Count Inoue Kaoru took over from Ōtori as Japanese pro-consul (October 1894–July 1895) and Japanese advisors were forced on all Korean ministries. The anti-Japanese Min faction returned to significant influence in July 1895, however, and when King Kojong fled to the Russian Legation in February 1896, Japanese influence ended. It is notable that the end of Japanese influence did not end the reform project, indicating the reform had some internal traction within Korea that did not depend on the Japanese.

9. Kim Tu-hŏn, *Chosŏn kajok chedo yŏn'gu*, 611–15.

10. I do not mean by this statement to slight the ethnological work done during the colonial period by Son Chin-t'ae, Murayama Chijun, Zenshō Eisuke, Akiba Takashi, and others. Their work, excellent as it is however, did not, as a rule, involve the long term participant-observation and concern for the interaction of various elements of social organization according to their context that is the hallmark of modern field studies.

11. For examples see Chungmin Choi Han, *Social Organization of Upper Han Hamlet*; Cornelius Osgood, *The Koreans and Their Culture*; Ko Ponggyŏng, Yi Hyojae, Yi Mangap, and Yi Haeyŏng, *Han'guk nongch'on kajok ŭi yŏn'gu*; Kim T'aekkyu, *Tongjok purak ŭi Saenghwal Kujo Yŏn'gu*; William Eugene Biernatzki, *Varieties of Korean Lineage Structure*; Vincent S. R. Brandt, *A Korean Village Between Farm and Sea*; Roger Janelli and Dawnhee Yim, *Ancestor Worship and Korean Society*; and Clark W. Sorensen, *Over the Mountains are Mountains*.

12. Yi Tuhyŏn et.al., *Han'guk Minsokhak Kaesŏl*; Martina Deuchler, "The Tradition: Women during the Yi Dynasty"; Martina, Deuchler, *The Confucian Transformation of Korea*; Edward W. Wagner, "Two Early Genealogies"; Mark A. Peterson, *Korean Adoption and Inheritance*, 3.

13. Kim Tu-hŏn, *Chosŏn kajok chedo yŏn'gu*; Yi Kwanggu, *Han'guk kajok ŭi sajŏk yŏn'gu*.

See Dae-hong Chang for a different point of view. Dae-hong Chang, "The Historical Development of the Korean Socio-Family System."

14. Ch'oe Chaesŏk, "Chosŏn sidae ŭi sangsokche e kwanhan yŏn'gu—punjaegi ŭi punsŏk e ŭihan chŏpkŭn"; Ch'oe Paek, "Han'guk ŭi chip—kŭ ŭi kujo punsŏk."

15. The Japanese occupied Korea militarily at the beginning of the Russo-Japanese War in 1904. After the conclusion of the Treaty of Portsmouth on September 5, 1905 in which Russia recognized Japan's paramount interest in Korea, Japan forced a protectorate treaty on Korea on November 17, 1905. Formal annexation of Korea took place on August 29, 1910.

16. Already by 1908 more than two-thirds of the judges and procurators in the Korean court system were ethnic Japanese. Edward Baker, "The Role of Legal Reforms," 21.

17. Quoted in Edward Baker, "The Role of Legal Reforms," 17.

18. By Japanese Civil Code, I mean the New Civil Code which Japan enforced from July 16, 1898. De Joseph Ernest De Becker, Elements of Japanese Law, 10.

19. Chŏng Kwanghyŏn, Han'guk kajokpŏp yŏn'gu, 22.

20. M. B. Hooker, Legal Pluralism, 1.

21. The four rituals were (1) coming of age (kwallye); (2) marriage (hollye); (3) funeral (sangnye); (4) ancestor worship (cherye).

22. The Meiji Civil Code of 1889 was based largely upon the Napoleonic Code but was never enforced. It was revised by reference to the codes of Germany, France, Belgium, Holland, Switzerland, Great Britain, and the United States. The revised New Civil Code that was implemented in 1898 is what I refer to as the Japanese Civil Code. Joseph Ernest De Becker, Elements of Japanese Law, 10.

23. Chŏng Kwanghyŏn, Han'guk kajokpŏp yŏn'gu, 129.

24. Nagumo Kōkichi, Genkō Chōsen shinzoku sōzoku hō ruishū, 6.

25. Ibid.

26. The custom of min myŏnŭri (a bride with loose hair) was found among the poorest classes because such marriages did not require an expensive wedding and relieved the girl's birth family of the necessity of feeding her. Girls were typically between six and eleven years of age. See Youngsook Kim Harvey, "Min Myŏnŭri: The Daughter-in-Law Who Comes of Age." In addition to this case in western Kangwŏn, I have also encountered cases in South Ch'ungch'ŏng where one informant explained that "she grew up in her husband's arms."

27. Chōsen Sōtokufu, Torishirabe Kyoku. Kanshū chōsa hōkokusho (1912), 302.

28. Nagumo Kōkichi, Genkō Chōsen shinzoku sōzoku hō ruishū, 14.

29. Ibid., 146. Administrative Circular No. 240 of August 1915 and Directive No. 47 of the same month regarding the implementation of the Family Registration Law (Minseki hō) prohibited adapting regulations for husbands and wives to accommodate concubines and prohibited the registration of new concubines from that time on. Concubines who

were already registered at that time, however, were allowed to remain. Prior to this time concubines (ch'ŏp) entered into a sexual relationship with their husbands by mutual consent, supposedly for purposes of providing sons to a sonless man. The children of these unions were considered nothoi, legitimate children who did not inherit the social status of their father and had attenuated inheritance rights. The concubine could be brought into the husband's house and had a right to subsistence as a family member.

30. Nagumo Kōkichi, Genkō Chōsen shinzoku sōzoku hō ruishū, 72.

31. My investigation of Family Registration Records (hojŏk) of three villages in South Ch'ungch'ŏng Province, for example, shows that for the period 1911–45 approximately 5 percent of the families showed evidence of concubinage, though after 1916 concubines were no longer registered as family members; this percentage dropped markedly after 1945.

32. Prior to the Chosŏn period the Korean family seems to have been bilateral. Yi Kwanggyu, Han'guk kajok ŭi sajŏk yŏn'gu; Martina Deuchler, "The Tradition: Women during the Yi Dynasty"; and Martina Deuchler, The Confucian Transformation of Korea.

33. An illegitimate child (sasaengja) whose father is not known will take his mother's surname, but fathers commonly recognize (inji) children born out of wedlock. These children are not considered illegitimate but rather nothous (sŏja)—children having a legally recognized mother and father but who cannot succeed to the social position of the father.

34. In 1997, the Constitutional Court ruled article 809 unconstitutional, which had prohibited people with the same surname from marrying.

35. Joseph Ernest De Becker, Elements of Japanese Law, 250.

36. Technically an unmarried daughter could succeed to the house headship if there were no sons, but she lost that headship the minute she married, and in most cases that involved significant property. Clan leaders had the ability to force the adoption of an agnate to fill this position.

37. Murayama Michio, Chōsen sōzoku seirei, 16.

38. Mark E. Caprio, "Koreans into Japanese."

39. Chŏng Kwanghyŏn, Han'guk kajok pŏp yŏn'gu, 65.

40. Ibid.

41. Ch'oe Paek, "Han'guk ŭi chip—kŭ ŭi kujo punsŏk."

Bibliography

Akamatsu, Chijō, and Takashi Akiba. *Chōsen fuzoku no kenkyū* [A study of Korean shamanism]. Tōkyō: Ōsakayagō Shoten, 1937.

An Pyŏngjik. "Han'guk kŭnhyŏndaesa yŏn'gu ŭi saeroun p'aerŏdaim: kyŏngjesa rŭl chungsim ŭro" [A new paradigm for research in modern Korean history with an emphasis on economic history]. *Ch'angjak kwa pip'yŏng* 98 (1997): 39–58.

An Pyŏngjik, and Chungch'on Chŏl [Nakamura Satoru]. *Kŭndae Chosŏn kongŏphwa ŭi yŏn'gu: 1930-45yŏn.* [A study of modern Korea's industrialization: 1930–45]. Sŏul: Iljogak, 1993.

An Soyŏng. "Haebanghu chwaik chinyŏng ŭi chŏnhyang kwa kŭ nolli" [Conversion and its logic for the leftist camp after the liberation]. *Yŏksa pip'yŏng* 24 (1994): 288–303.

Anderson, Benedict. *Imagined Communities.* London: Verso, 1983.

Aono Masaaki. *Chōsen nōson no minzoku shūkyō: shokuminchi no Tendōkyō: Kongō Daidō o chūshin ni* [The folk religion of Korean villages: Centering on Ch'ŏndogyo and Kŭmgang]. Tōkyō: Shakai Hyōronsha, 2001.

Aoyagi Namei. *Sōtoku seiji shiron* [On the history of the politics of the governor-general]. Keijō: Keisei Press, 1928.

Armstrong, David. *Political Anatomy of the Body: Medical Knowledge in Britain in the Twentieth Century.* Cambridgeshire: Cambridge University Press, 1983.

Arnold. David. *Colonizing the Body: State Medicine and Epidemic Disease in Nineteenth-Century India.* Berkeley: University of California Press, 1993.

Asada Kyoji. "Hang-Il nongmin undong ŭi ilbanjŏk chŏn'gae kwajŏng" [The general process of anti-Japanese peasant movements]. In *Hang-Il nongmin undong yŏn'gu* [Studies on anti-Japanese peasant movements]. Sŏul: Tongnyŏk, 1984.

———. "Singminji Han'guk esŏ ŭi nongmin chojik ŭi palchŏn sanghwang" [The development of peasant organizations in colonial Korea]. In *Hang-Il nongmin undong yŏn'gu* [Studies on anti-Japanese peasant movements]. Sŏul: Tongnyŏk, 1984.

Bachnik, Jane. "Recruitment Strategies for Household Succession: Rethinking Japanese Household Organization." *Man* 18 (1983): 160–82.

Baker, Edward. "The Role of Legal Reforms in the Japanese Annexation and Rule of Korea, 1905–1910." In *Studies on Korea in Transition*, edited by David R. McCann, John Middleton, and Edward Schultz, 17–42. Honolulu: Center for Korean Studies, University of Hawai'i, 1979.

Balandier, Georges. "The Colonial Situation: A Theoretical Approach." In *Social Change: The Colonial Situation*, edited by I. Wallerstein. New York: John Wiley and Sons, 1966.

———. *The Sociology of Black Africa: Social Dynamics of Central Africa*. Translated by Douglas Garman. New York: Praeger, 1970.

Baldwin, Frank P. Jr. "The March First Movement: Korean Challenge and Japanese Response." Ph.D. diss., Columbia University, 1969.

Barlow, Tani E. *Formations of Colonial Modernity in East Asia*. Durham, NC: Duke University Press, 1997.

Beasley, W. G. *The Rise of Modern Japan*. London: Weidenfeld and Nicolson, 1990.

Bechelli, L.M. "Advances in Leprosy Control in the Last 100 Years." *International Journal of Leprosy and Other Mycobacterial Diseases* 41, no. 3 (July–September 1973): 285–97.

Beillevaire, Patrick. "The Family: Instrument and Model of the Japanese Nation." In *A History of the Family*, edited by André Burguière, Christiane Klapische-Zuber, Martine Segalen, and Françoise Zonabend, translated by Sarah Hanbury Tenison. Cambridge, MA: Harvard University Press, 1996.

Bellah, Robert N. "Continuity and Change in Japanese Society." In *Stability and Social Change*, edited by Bernard Barber and Alex Inkeles. Boston, MA: Little, Brown and Company, 1971.

Benhabib, Seyla. "Models of Public Space: Hannah Arendt, the Liberal Tradition, and Jürgen Habermas." In *Habermas and the Public Sphere*, edited by C. Calhoun. Cambridge, MA: MIT Press, 1992.

Berry, Mary Elizabeth. "Public Life in Authoritarian Japan." *Daedalus* 127, no. 3 (Summer 1998): 133–65.

Biernatzki, William Eugene. "Varieties of Korean Lineage Structure." Ph.D. diss., St. Louis University, 1967.

Blumer, Herbert. *Industrialization as an Agent of Social Change: A Critical Analysis*. New York: A. de Greuter, 1990.

Bobbio, Norberto. "Gramsci and the Concept of Civil Society." In *Civil Society and the*

State, edited by John Keane. London: Verso, 1988.

Brandt, Vincent S. R. *A Korean Village between Farm and Sea*. Cambridge, MA: Harvard University Press, 1971.

Brody, Saul Nathaniel. *The Disease of the Soul: Leprosy in Medieval Literature*. Ithaca, NY: Cornell University Press, 1974.

Burger, Thomas R. *A Long and Terrible Shadow: White Values, Native Rights in the Americas, 1492–1992*. Vancouver, BC: Douglas and McIntyre, 1991.

Calhoun, Craig, ed. *Habermas and the Public Sphere*. Cambridge, MA: MIT Press, 1992.

Caprio, Mark E. "Assimilation Rejected: The *Tonga ilbo*'s Challenge to Japan's Colonial Policy in Korea." In *Imperial Japan and National Identities in Asia*, edited by Li Narangoa and Robert Cribb 119–45. New York: Routledge Curzon Press, 2003.

Caprio, Mark E. *Japanese Assimilation Policies in Colonial Korea, 1910–1945*. Seattle: University of Washington Press, 2009.

———. "Koreans into Japanese: Japan's Assimilation Policy." Ph.D. diss., University of Washington, 2001.

Cha Kibyŏk, ed. *Ilche ŭi Han'guk singmin t'ongch'i* [Japanese colonial rule in Korea]. Sŏul: Ch'ŏngunsa, 1985.

Chandra, Vipan. *Imperialism, Resistance, and Reform in Late Nineteenth-Century Korea: Enlightenment and the Independence Club*. Berkeley: Institute of East Asian Studies, University of California Press, 1988.

Chang, Dae-hong. "The Historical Development of the Korean Socio-Family System Since 1392—A Legalistic Interpretation." *University of Manila Journal of East Asiatic Studies* 11, no. 2 (September 1967): 1–124.

Chartier, Roger. *The Cultural Origins of the French Revolution*. Translated by Lydia Cochrane. Durham, NC: Duke University Press, 1991.

Chatterjee, Partha. *The Nation and Its Fragments: Colonial and Postcolonial Histories*. Princeton, NJ: Princeton University Press, 1993.

Chi Sŭngjun. "1930-yŏndae sahoejuŭi chinyŏng ŭi chŏnhyang kwa Taedong Minuhoe" [The "conversion" of the socialist camp and Taedong Minuhoe in 1930s]. M.A. thesis, Chungang Taehakkyo, 1996.

"Chian jōkyō [Security situation]." *Nitteika shakai undoshi shiryō sōsho* [Collection of materials regarding social movements under Japanese colonial rule]. Sŏul: Koryŏ Sŏrim, 1992.

Chikei kyōkai [Association of rule for criminals]. *Chikei* [Rule for criminals] 15 no. 3 (1937); 17 no. 1 (1937); 17 no. 4 (1939).

Chin Tŏkkyu. "1920-nyŏndae kungnae minjok undong e kwanhan koch'al" [A study of 1920s' domestic nationalist movements]. In *Han'guk minjokchuŭi non 1* [On Korean nationalism, vol. 1], edited by Song Kŏnho et al. Sŏul: Ch'angjak kwa Pip'yŏngsa, 1982.

Cho Sŏkkon. "Sut'allon kwa kŭndaehwaron ŭl nŏmŏsŏ" [Beyond exploitation and modernization]. Ch'angjak kwa pip'yŏng 96 (Summer 1997): 355–70.

———. "T'oji chosa saŏp kwa kŭndaejŏk chise chedo ŭi hwangnip" [The land survey and the establishment of the modern land tax system]. In Chosŏn t'oji chosa saŏp ŭi yŏn'gu [Studies in the land survey in colonial Korea], edited by Kim Hongsik, et al. Sŏul: Minŭmsa, 1997.

Cho Sŏngho. "Zōshinsho" [Statement of submission]. Sisōkeppō [Monthly report of thought] 3, no. 4 (1933): 27–30.

Cho Tonggŏl. "Han'guk kŭndae haksaeng undong chojik ŭi sŏnggyŏk pyŏnhwa" [Organizational changes in Korean student movements in modern Korea]. In Han'guk kŭndae minjok undongsa yŏn'gu [A history of modern nationalistic movement], edited by Han'guk Yŏksa Yŏn'guhoe. Sŏul: Ilchogak, 1993.

———. Ilcheha Han'guk nongmin undongsa [History of peasant movements under Japanese colonialism]. Sŏul: Han'gilsa, 1979.

Ch'oe Chaesŏk. "Chosŏn sidae ŭi sangsokche e kwanhan yŏn'gu—punjaegi ŭi punsŏk e ŭihan chŏpkŭn" [A study of the inheritance system of the Chosŏn period—An approach based on the analysis of inheritance records]. Yŏksa hakpo 53, no. 4 (1972):103–50.

Ch'oe Chinok. "1860-nyŏndae ŭi millan" [Popular uprisings in the 1860s]. In Chŏnt'ong sidae ŭi minjung undong [Popular movements in the traditional period]. Sŏul: P'ulbit, 1981.

Ch'oe Chun. Han'guk sinmunsa [History of Korean newspapers]. Revised Edition. Sŏul: Ilchogak, 1990.

Ch'oe Minji. Ilcheha minjok ŏllon saron [A study of the history of nationalist journalism in the Japanese colonial period]. Sŏul: Irwŏl Sŏgak, 1978.

Ch'oe Namsŏn. Puram munhwaron. Sŏul: Uri Yŏksa Yŏn'gu Chaedan, 2008 [original 1925].

———. "Salman'gyo ch'agi" [Selections on shamanism] Kyemong 19 (May 1927): 2–51.

Ch'oe Paek. "Han'guk ŭi chip—kŭ ŭi kujo punsŏk" [The Korean household—Its structural analysis]. Han'guk munhwa illyuhak 13 (1981): 119–36.

Ch'oe P'anok. "Hikōhō undo kara kōhō seikatsu heno sakebi" [Voice to legal life from illegal movement]. Kotōkei satsuhō 3 (1934): 22–29.

Ch'oe Sŏgyŏng. Ilcheha musongnon kwa singminji kwŏllyŏk [Theory of shamanism and colonial power under Japanese rule]. Sŏul: Sŏgyŏng Munhwasa, 1999.

———. Ilche ŭi tonghwa ideollogi ŭi ch'angch'ul [Creation of the Japanese imperialist ideology of assimilation]. Sŏul: Sŏgyŏng Munhwasa, 1997.

Ch'oe Wŏn'gyu. "Hanmal Ilche ch'ogi t'oji chosa wa t'ojibŏp yŏn'gu" [Cadastral survey and land law in the late period of the Korean Empire and the early colonial period].

Ph.D. diss., Yŏnse Taehakkyo, 1994.

Ch'oe Yongdal. "Kansōroku" [Record of impression]. Sisōihō 24 (1940): 298–310.

Chŏng Chaech'ŏl. Ilche ŭi tae-Han'guk singminji kyoyuk chŏngch'aeksa [Japan's colonial educational policies toward Korea]. Sŏul: Ilchisa, 1985.

Chŏng Chinsŏk. Han'guk ŏllon sa [The history of Korean journalism]. Sŏul: Nanam, 1990.

Chŏng Chinsŏk, ed. Ilche sidae minjokchi apsu kisa moŭm [A collection of articles confiscated from national newspapers during the Japanese colonial period]. Sŏul: LG Sangnam Ŏllon Chaedan, 1998.

Chŏng Chinsŏk, et al. Han'guk kŭndae ŏllon ŭi chae chomyŏng [Re-examining modern Korean journalism]. Sŏul: Minŭmsa, 1996.

———. "Tonga wa Chosŏn ŭi ŏllon ŭrosŏ ŭi sŏngkyŏk kwa panghyang e." Han'guk tongnip undong sa yŏn'gu 5 (1991).

Chŏng Chinsŏng. "Ilcheha Chosŏn e issŏsŏ nodongja chonjae hyŏngt'ae wa chŏimgŭmja: 1930-nyŏndae rŭl chungsim ŭro" [Situation of the laborer and low-wage earner under the Japanese Empire 1930s]. In Han'guk chabonjuŭi wa imgŭm nodong [Korean capitalism and wage labor], 13–94, edited by Pak Hyŏnjae. Sŏul: Hwada, 1984.

Chŏng Kŭnsik [Jung, Keunsik]. "'Singminjijŏk kŭndae' wa sinch'e ŭi chŏngch'i" ['Colonial modernity' and politics of the body]. Sahoe wa yŏksa 51 (June 1997): 211–65.

Chŏng Kwang-hyŏn. Han'guk kajokpŏp yŏn'gu [A study of Korean family law]. Sŏul: Sŏul Taehakkyo Ch'ulp'anbu, 1967.

Chŏng Sehyŏn. Hang-il haksaengsa [A history of anti-Japanese students]. Sŏul: Ilchisa, 1975.

Chŏng T'aehŏn. "Sut'allon ŭi songnyuhwa sok e sarajin singminji " [The colony lost in the midst of the vulgarization of exploitation]. Ch'angjak kwa pip'yŏng 97 (Fall 1997): 344–57.

Chŏng Yondŏk. "Ilcheha (1932–35) chŏnhyang kongjak e taehan okchung t'ujaeng ki" [Record of struggles in prison against conversion operation (1932–35)]. Record Group 242, Records Seized by U.S. Military Forces in Korea. Yŏksa pipyŏng 21 (1993): 371–77.

"Chōsengo to Nihongo" [Korean and Japanese]. Keijō nippō, September 1, 1910.

Chōsen Sōtokufu [Government-General of Korea]. Chōsen. Keijō: Chōsen Sōtokufu, 1920–27.

Chōsen Sōtokufu. Chōsen kokusei hōkoku [Korean census report]. Years 1926, 1930, 1935, 1944. Keijō: Chōsen Sōtokufu, (published various dates).

———. "Chōsen naini okeru sisō tenkō no jōkyō" [Trend of thought conversion in colonial Korea]. Kotōkei satsuhō [Report of the higher police] 3 (1934): 1–22.

———. Chōsen ni okeru kyoiku no gaikyo [A brief survey of education in Korea]. Keijō: Chōsen Sōtokufu, 1941.

———. *Chōsen ni okeru shuppanbutsu gaiyō* [Korean publication survey]. Keijō: Chōsen Sōtokufu, 1930.

———. *Chōsen no gunshū* [The Korean crowd]. Keijō: Chōsen Sōtokufu, 1926.

———. *Chōsen no kosaku kankō* [Tenancy customs in Korea]. 2 vols. Keijō: Chōsen Sōtokufu, 1930.

———. *Chōsen no kosaku kanshū* [Tenancy customs in Korea]. Keijō: Chōsen Sōtokufu, 1929.

———. *Chōsen no shakai jigyō* [Social work in Korea]. Keijō: Chōsen Sōtokufu, 1936.

———. *Chōsen Sōtokufu tokei nenpo* [Statistical yearbooks of the Government-General of Korea]. Keijō: Chōsen Sōtokufu, 1932–38, 1942.

———. *Chōsenjin no shisō to seikaku* [The ideological orientations and character of Korean people]. Chōsa shiryō Vol. 20, 1927.

———. *Chosŏn t'ongch'i pihwa* [The secret story of ruling Korea]. Translated by Yi Ch'ungho and Hong Kŭmja. Sŏul: Hyŏngsŏl Ch'ulp'ansa, 1993.

———. "Chosŏn ŭi ch'ian sanghwang [State of public order in Korea]." In *1930-nyŏndae minjok haebang undong* [The national liberation movement of the 1930s]. Sŏul: Kŏrŭm, 1984.

———. "Daidō minyūkai no ketsuzyō narabi sonokatsudō kaikyō" [The establishment of Taedong Minuhoe and its overall activity]. *Sisōihō* [Assorted report on thought]13 (1937): 37–86.

———. "Dokuritsu undō ni okeru minzoku undo no kōgai" (January 1927) [A summary of the people's movement from the cessation of the independence movement]. *Saitō Makoto kankei monjo* [Official papers regarding Saitō Makoto], reel 97, Japanese National Diet Library.

———. Gakumukyoku [Ministry of education]. *Chōsen shogakko ichiran* [Prospectus of schools in Korea]. Keijō: Chōsen Sōtokufu, 1921.

———. Gakumukyoku [Ministry of education]. *Chōsen shogakkō ichiran, Shōwa jūyonnen* [Prospectus of schools in Korea], Keijō: Chōsen Sōtokufu, 1939.

———. Gakumukyoku Gakumuka [Bureau of education, education branch]. *Gakuji sango shiryo* [Reference data for educational policy]. Keijō: Chōsen Sōtokufu, 1937.

———. Kanbō bunshoka. [Official documents office]. *Chōsen no kenron to sesō* [Korean journalism and the world]. Keijō: Chōsen Sōtokufu, 1927.

———. Keimukyoku [Police administration bureau]. *Chōsen chian chōgyo* [Korean security situation]. Keijō: Chōsen Sōtokufu, 1922.

———. Keimukyoku [Police administration bureau]. "Chōsen naini okeru sisō tenkō no jōkyō" [Trend of thought conversion in colonial Korea]. *Kotōkei satsuhō* [Report of the higher police] 3 (1934): 1–22.

———. Keimukyoku. *Chōsen no shuppan keisatsu gaiyō* [Korean publication police survey]. Keijō: Chōsen Sōtokufu, 1939.

———. Keimukyoku. *Saikin ni okeru Chōsen chian jōkyō* [Recent conditions of public security in Korea]. Keijō: Chōsen Sōtokufu, 1933, 1938.

———. Keimukyoku. *Chōsen ni okeru dōmei kyūkō no kōsatsu* [A survey of student strikes in Korea]. Keijō: Chōsen Sōtokufu, 1929.

———. Keimukyoku toshoka. *Onmon shimbun saatsu kisi shūroku: Chōsen nippō* [A collection of articles confiscated from vernacular newspapers: *Chosŏn ilbo*]. Keijō: Chōsen Sōtokufu, 1932.

———. Keimukyoku toshoka. *Onmon shimbun saatsu kisi shūroku: Tōa nippō* [A collection of articles confiscated from vernacular newspapers: *Tonga ilbo*]. Keijō: Chōsen Sōtokufu, 1932.

———. Keimukyoku toshoka. *Ri denka no shikyo ni saishi "shinbunshi wo tōshite mitaru" Chōsenjin no shisō keikō"* [Tendencies in Koreans' thoughts "as seen through newspapers" at the time of the death of the Yi Highness]. Keijō: Chōsen Government-General Secret Report, 1926.

———. Keishō hokudo keisatsusho. [North Kyŏngsang Province, police department]. *Kōtōkei satsu yōshi*. Keijō: Chōsen Sōtokufu, 1934.

———. Naimu Kyoku [Bureau of interior]. *Chōsen chihan jaisei yoran* [A summary of regional finance in Korea]. Keijō: Chōsen Sōtokufu, 1924–38.

———. Nōrinkyoku [Bureau of agriculture and forestry]. *Chōsen nōchi nenpō* [Annual reports on Korean agricultural lands]. Keijō: Chōsen Sōtokufu, 1940.

———. *Seikatsu jōtai chōsa go: Chōsen no juraku zenhen* [A survey of living conditions 5: Korean villages part one]. Chōsa shiryō [data series] Vol. 38, 1938.

———. *Seikatsu jōtai chōsa: Kōryō gun* [A survey of living conditions: the case of Kangnŭng-gun (county)]. Chōsa jiryō [data series] Vol. 32, 1931.

———. *Seikatsu jōtai chōsa: Suigen gun ich* [A survey of living conditions: the case of Suwŏn-gun (county) part 1]. Chōsa shiryō [data series] Vol. 28, no.1, 1929.

———. *Shisei Shanjunenshi* [The thirty-year history of government in Korea]. Keijō: Chōsen Sōtokufu, 1940.

———. *Showa go nen Chōsen koku seitsusa chensenhen dai ichi hen* [Census report of Korea in 1930, vol.1]. Keijō: Chōsen Sōtokufu, 1935.

———. *Showa jugonen Chōsen koku seitsusa ketka yoyaku* [Census summary report of Korea in 1940]. Keijō: Chōsen Sōtokufu, 1940.

———. *Shisōihō* [Assorted reports on thought] 3 (1935); 12 (1937); 15 (1938).

———. *Shisōkeppō* [Monthly reports on thought] 3 no. 9 (1933).

———. "Sōtokufu rei dai 123 gō" [Government-General of Korea Order no. 123], June 1912.

———. Torishirabe Kyoku [Research office]. *Kanshū chōsa hōkokusho*. [Report on the investigation of customs]. Keijō: Chōsen Sōtokufu, 1912.

"Chōsen shisei no kaizen" [Reforms in Korean administration]. In *Saitō Makoto monjo* [Saitō Makoto official papers]. Vol. 2. Sŏul: Koryŏ Sŏrim, 1990.

Chosŏn Ilbosa. *Chosŏn ilbo myŏng sasŏl obaeksŏn* [A selection of 500 famous editorials from the *Chosŏn ilbo*]. Sŏul: Chosŏn Ilbosa, 1972.

———. *Chosŏn ilbo 80-nyŏn sa* [The eighty-year history of the *Chosŏn ilbo*]. 2 vols. Sŏul: Chosŏn Ilbosa, 2000.

Chu Ponggyu. *Ilcheha nongŏp kyŏngjesa* [History of agricultural economics under the Japanese colonial rule]. Sŏul: Sŏul Taehakkyo Ch'ulp'anbu, 1995.

Chu Yohan. *An Tosan chŏnsŏ* [The complete works of An Tosan]. Sŏul: Pŏmyangsa, 1990.

Chung, Young-Iob. *Korea under Siege, 1876–1945*. New York: Oxford University Press, 2006.

Clark, A. *Kyohoe ŭi sahoe saŏp* [Social work of the church]. Korean Christian Books, 1932.

Colonna, Fanny. "Educating Conformity in French Colonial Algeria." In *Tension of Empire: Colonial Cultures in a Bourgeois World*, edited by Frederick Cooper and Ann Laura Stoler. Berkeley: University of California Press, 1997.

Comaroff, Jean. "The Diseased Heart of Africa: Medicine, Colonialism, and the Black Body," In *Knowledge, Power, and Practice*, edited by Shirley Lindenbaum and Margaret Lock, Berkeley: University of California Press, 1993.

Comaroff, Jean, and John L. Comaroff. *Of Revelation and Revolution* Vol.1. Chicago: University of Chicago Press, 1991.

Crone, Patricia. *Pre-Industrial Societies*. Oxford, UK: Blackwell Publishers, 1989.

Cumings, Bruce. *Korea's Place in the Sun: A Modern History*. New York: W.W. Norton and Company, 1997.

———. "The Legacy of Japanese Colonialism in Korea." In *The Japanese Colonial Empire, 1895–1945*, edited by Ramon H. Meyers and Mark R. Peattie. Princeton, NJ: Princeton University Press, 1984.

———. "The Origins and Development of the Northeast Asian Political Economy: Industrial Sectors, Product Cycles, and Political Consequences." In *The Political Economy of the New Asian Industrialization*, edited by Frederic C. Deyo. Ithaca, NY: Cornell University Press, 1987.

———. *The Origins of the Korean War*. Vol. 1. Princeton, NJ: Princeton University Press, 1981.

"Daily Life of Prince and Princess Yi." Seoul Press. December 20, 1910, 2.

De Becker, Joseph Ernest. *Elements of Japanese Law*. Washington, DC: University
Publications of America, Inc, 1979. Reprint. Originally published in Yokohama, 1916 .

de Certeau, Michel. *The Practice of Everyday Life*. Berkeley: University of California Press, 1984.

Deuchler, Martina. *The Confucian Transformation of Korea: A Study of Society and Ideology*.
Cambridge, MA: Harvard University Press, 1992.

———. "The Tradition: Women during the Yi Dynasty." In *Virtues in Conflict: Tradition
and the Korean Woman Today*, edited by Sandra Mattielli. Seoul: Royal Asiatic Society,
Korea Branch, 1977.

Devine, Richard. "Japanese Rule in Korea after the March First Uprising: General
Hasegawa's Recommendations." *Monumenta Nipponica* 52, no. 4 (Winter 1997): 523–40.

Dirks, Nicholas B., ed. *Colonialism and Culture*. Ann Arbor: University of Michigan
Press, 1992.

Dong, Wonmo. "Assimilation and Social Mobilization in Korea." In *Korea under Japanese
Colonial Rule*, 146–82, edited by Andrew Nahm. Kalamazoo: Western Michigan
University Press, 1973.

Duncan, John B. "Non-Elite Perceptions of the State in the Late Chosŏn."
(Unpublished paper).

Duus, Peter. *The Abacus and the Sword: The Japanese Penetration of Korea, 1895–1910*.
Berkeley: University of California Press, 1995.

———. "Chōsenkan no keisei—Meijiki no sihaiimēzī" [The formation of the
Chosŏn'gwan—The dominant image of the Meiji period]. In *Teikoku to iukensō:
Daitōakyōeiken no sisō to kenzitsu* [The illusion of empire: Ideology and practice in the
Greater East Asia Co-Prosperity Sphere], edited by Peter Duus and Hideo Kobayashi.
Tōkyō: Aoki-shoten, 1998.

Eckert, Carter. "Exorcizing Hegel's Ghosts: Toward a Postnationalist Historiography of
Korea." In *Colonial Modernity in Korea*, edited by Gi-Wook Shin and Michael Robinson.
Cambridge, MA: Harvard University Asia Center, 1999.

———. *Offspring of Empire: The Koch'ang Kims and the Colonial Origins
of Korean Capitalism, 1876–1945*. Seattle: University of Washington Press, 1991.

———. "Total War, Industrialization, and Social Change in Late Colonial Korea." In
The Japanese Wartime Empire, 1931–1945, edited by Peter Duus, Ramon H. Myers, and
Mark R. Peattie. Princeton, NJ: Princeton University Press, 1996.

Eckert, Carter J., and Ki-baek Yi. *Korea, Old and New: A History*. Seoul: Published for the
Korea Institute, Harvard University by Ilchokak, 1990.

Ekeh, Peter P. *Colonialism and Social Structure*. Ibadan, Nigeria: University of Ibadan, 1983.

Em, Henry. "The Nationalist Discourse in Modern Korea: *Minjok* as a Democratic

Imagery." Ph.D. diss. University of Chicago, 1995.

Enuma Jiroy. "Ilcheha Chosŏn ŭi nongŏp hyŏngmyŏng" [Agricultural revolution in colonial Korea]. In *Singminji sidae Han'guk ŭi sahoe wa chŏhang* [Resistance movements in Korean society in the colonial period]. Sŏul: Paeksan Sŏdang, 1983.

Femia, Joseph. *Gramsci's Political Thought: Hegemony, Consciousness, and the Revolutionary Process*. Oxford [Oxfordshire]: Clarendon Press, 1981.

Field, Norma. "War and Apology: Japan, Asia, the Fiftieth, and After." *Positions: East Asia Cultures Critique* 5, no. 1 (1993): 1–49.

Fisher, Galen M. "Revisiting Japan."*Amerasia* 1, no.1 (1937): 219–24.

Fletcher, A. G. "Country Clinics or Dispensaries for Treatment of Cases of Leprosy." *Leprosy Review* 3.2 (1932): 58–66.

Foster, Philip. *Education and Social Change in Ghana*. Chicago: University of Chicago Press, 1965.

Foucault, Michel. *The Archaeology of Knowledge*. Translated by A. M. Sheridan Smith. New York: Pantheon Books, 1972.

———. *The Order of Things: An Archaeology of the Human Sciences*. New York: Vintage, 1973.

Fuzino, Yutaka. *Japanese Fascism and Medical Problems*. Tokyo: Iwanami, 1993.

Frank, Arthur W. "For a Sociology of the Body: An Analytical Review." In *The Body: Social Process and Cultural Theory*, edited by Mike Featherstone, Mike Hepworth, and Bryan Turner. London: Sage, 1992.

Fujino Yutaka. *Kyōseisareta kenkō: Nihon fashizumu-ka no semei to shintai* [Forced health: Life and body under Japanese fascism]. Tōkyō: Yoshikawa Kōbunkan, 2000.

Geertz, Clifford. *Interpretation of Culture*. New York: Basic Books, 1973.

Geuss, Raymond. *The Idea of a Critical Theory: Habermas and the Frankfurt School*. Cambridge, NY: Cambridge University Press, 1981.

Giddens, Anthony. *The Consequences of Modernity*. Stanford, CA: Stanford University Press. 1990.

Gilman, Sander L. *Disease and Representation—Images of Illness from Madness to AIDS*. Ithaca, NY: Cornell University Press, 1988.

Goffman, Erving. *Asylums: Essays on the Social Situation of Mental Patients and Other Inmates*. New York: Anchor Books, 1961.

———. *Stigma: Notes on the Management of Spoiled Identity*. Englewood Cliffs, NJ: Prentice Hall, 1961.

Gondō Yorōsuke. *Yi ōkyū hishi* [Secret history of the Yi royal palace]. Keijō: Chōsen Shinbunsha, 1926.

Government-General of Korea. *See* Chōsen Sōtokufu.

Gragert, Edwin H. *Landownership under Colonial Rule: Korea's Japanese Experience, 1900–1935*. Honolulu: University of Hawai'i Press, 1994.

Grajdanzev, Andrew. *Modern Korea*. New York: John Day Co, 1944.

Gramsci, Antonio. *Selections from Political Writings 1921–1926*. Translated and edited by Quintin Hoare. New York: International Publishers, 1978.

Grob, Gerald N. *From Asylum to Community*. Princeton, NJ: Princeton University Press, 1991.

Gussow, Zachary. *Leprosy, Racism, and Public Health*. Boulder, CO: Westview Press, 1989.

Ha Sangnak. "Ilche sidae ŭi sahoe pojang" [Social security in Colonial Korea]. *Ŭiryo pohŏm* [Medical insurance] 66 (February 1984): 27–31.

Ha, Yong chool. "*An Analysis of School Registrars Preliminary Summary.*" Unpublished memorandum, 1997.

———. "Late Industrialization, the State, and Social Changes: The Emergence of Neofamilism in South Korea." *Comparative Political Studies* 40, no. 4 (April 2007): 363–82.

Habermas, Jürgen. *Between Facts and Norms: Contributions to a Discourse Theory of Law and Democracy*. Cambridge, MA: MIT Press, 1996.

———.*The Structural Transformation of the Public Sphere: An Inquiry into a Category of Bourgeois Society*. Cambridge, MA: MIT Press, 1989.

Haggard, Stephen, David Kang, and Chung-In Moon. "Japanese Colonialism and Korean Development: a Critique." *World Development* 25, no. 6 (1997): 867–81.

Hahm, Pyong-Choon. *The Korean Political Tradition and Law*. Seoul: Hollym Corporation Publishers, 1967.

Hakkyŏn Chunp'o [Tsurumi Shunsuke]. *Ilbon chegukchuŭi chŏngsinsa* [The mental history of Japanese imperialism]. Translated by Kang Chŏngjung. Sŏul: Hanbŏt, 1982.

Hallin, Daniel. "The American News Media: A Critical Theory Perspective." In *Critical Theory and Public Life*, edited by John Forester. Cambridge, MA: MIT Press, 1985.

Hamada Kenji. *Prince Itō*. Tokyo: The Sanseido Co., 1936.

Hamano Kikuo. "Han'guk ŭi nabyŏng" [Leprosy in Korea]. *Saebit* 3 no. 7 (1965).

Hamilton, A., Herbert Henry Austin, and Masatake Terauchi. *Korea: Its History, Its People, and Its Commerce*. Boston and Tokyo: J. B. Millet Co., 1910.

Han, Chungmin Choi. *Social Organization of Upper Han Hamlet in Korea*. Ph.D. diss., University of Michigan, 1949.

Han Haŭn. "Naja ŭi sahoe pokkwi esŏ ŭi silchejŏk munje" [Some problems in lepers' return to society]. *Saebit* 3 no. 6 (1965).

Han Kiŏn. "Ilche ŭi tonghwa chŏngch'aek kwa Hanminjok ŭi kyoyukchŏk chŏhang." [Japanese imperialist assimilation policy and the educational resistance of the Korean nation]. In *Ilche ŭi munhwa ch'imt'alsa* [A history of cultural plunder under Japanese imperialism]. Sŏul: Hyŏnŭmsa, 1982.

Han Paeho. "Samil undong chikhu e Chosŏn singminji chŏngch'aek" [Chosŏn colonial policy after the March First movement]. In *Ilche ŭi Han'guk singmin t'ongch'i* [Korean colonial rule under the Japanese Empire], edited by Ch'a Kibyŏk. Sŏul: Chŏngŭmsa, 1985.

Han Ugŭn. *Tonghangnan kiin e kwanhan yŏn'gu* [A study of the causes of the Tonghak Rebellion]. Sŏul: Sŏul Taehakkyo Ch'ulp'anbu, 1971.

Han Uhŭi. "Pot'ong hakkyo e taehan chŏhang kwa kyoyungnyŏl" [Resistance to and educational zeal for colonial primary schools]. *Kyoyuk iron* [Educational theory] 6 (1991): 63–77.

Han, Woo-keun. *The History of Korea*. Edited by Grafton W. Mintz and translated by Kyung-Shik Lee. Honolulu: University of Hawai'i Press, 1974.

Han'guk Kŭnhyŏndae Sahakhoe. *Han'guk tongnip undongsa kangŭi* [Lecture on the Korean independence movement]. Sŏul: Hanul Ak'ademi, 1998.

Han'kukhak Munhŏn Yon'guso. *Tonghak sasang charyo chip* [Collection of materials on Tonghak thoughts]. Sŏul: Asea Munhwasa, 1979.

Han'guk Munhak Yŏn'guhoe, ed. *1930-yŏndae munhak yŏn'gu* [A study of the literature of 1930s]. Sŏul: P'yŏngminsa, 1993.

Hanminjok tongnip undongsa [History of the independence movement of the Korean nation]. Vol. 8. Sŏul: Taehan Minjok Mun'gyobu, 1990.

Harvey, Youngsook Kim. "Min Myŏnŭri: The Daughter-in-Law Who Comes of Age in Her Mother-in-Law's Household." In *Korean Women: View from the Inner Room*, edited by Laurel Kendall and Mark Peterson, 45–61. New Haven, CT: East Rock Press, 1983.

Hashitani Hiroshi. "1930–40 nyŏndae Chosŏn sahoe ŭi t'ŭkchil e taehayŏ" [On the nature of Korean society in the 1930s and 1940s]. In *Han'guk kŭndae sahoe kyŏngjesa ŭi che munje* [Problems of modern Korean socio-economic history], edited by Yi Haeju and Ch'oe Sŏngil. Pusan: Pusan Taehakkyo Ch'ulp'anbu, 1995.

Hayashi Fusao. "Tenkō ni tsuite" [On thought conversion]. *Hayashi Fusao Tsyosakusyū* [Collected works of Hayashi] III. Tōkyō: Yokushoin, 1969.

Henderson, Gregory. *Korea: The Politics of the Vortex*. Cambridge, MA: Harvard University Press. 1968.

Hewitt, Martin. "Bio-politics and Social Policy: Foucault's Account of Welfare." In *The Body: Social Process and Cultural Theory*, edited by Mike Featherstone, Mike Hepworth, and Bryan Turner. London: Sage, 1992.

Honda Shuōko. "Tenkō bungakuron" [Theory of conversion literature]. In *Iwanami kōza bungaku* Vol. 5. Tōkyō: Iwanami Shoten, 1954.

Hong Sŏngch'an. *Han'guk kŭndae nongŏp sahoe ŭi pyŏndong kwa chijuch'ŭng: 20-segi chŏnban'gi Chŏnnam Hwasun-gun Tongbok-myŏn iltae ŭi sarye* [Changes in Korean modern rural society and landlords: The case of Tongbok-myŏn, Hwasun-gun, South Chŏlla Province in the first half of the twentieth century]. Sŏul: Chisik Sanŏpsa, 1992.

———. "Ilcheha chijuch'ŭng ŭi chonjae hyŏngt'ae" [Patterns of landlords in Korea under colonial rule]. In *Han'guk kŭnhyŏndae ŭi minjok munje wa sin'gukka kŏnsŏl* [National issues of modern Korea and new state building], edited by Han'guk Sahak Nonch'ong Kanhaeng Wiwŏnhoe [Korean history research series publication committee]. Sŏul: Chisik Sanŏpsa, 1997.

Hoare, Quintin, and G. Smith, eds. *Selections from the Prison Notebooks*. New York: International Publishers, 1971.

Hooker, M. B. *Legal Pluralism: An Introduction to Colonial and Neocolonial Laws*. Oxford: Clarendon Press, 1975.

Hori Kazuo. "Ilbon chegukchuŭi ŭi Chosŏn esŏ ŭi nongŏp chŏngch'aek: 1920-nyŏndae singminji chijuje ŭi hyŏngsŏng" [The agricultural policy of Japanese imperialism in Korea: The formation of the colonial landlord system in the 1920s]. In *Kŭndae Tongasia wa Ilbon chegukchuŭi* [Japanese imperialism in early modern East Asia], edited by Kim Yŏngho. Sŏul: Hanbat Ch'ulp'ansa, 1993.

Hoston, Germaine A. "*Ikkoku Shakai-shugi*: Sano Manabu and the Limits of Marxism as Cultural Criticism." In *Culture and Identity: Japanese Intellectuals during the Interwar Years*, edited by J. Thomas Rimer. Princeton, NJ: Princeton University Press, 1990.

———. "Tenkō: Marxism and the National Question in Prewar Japan." *Polity: The Journal of the Northeastern Political Science Association* 16 (1983): 96–118.

Hwang Hyŏn. *Tonghangnan: Tongbi kiryak ch'ogo* [The Tonghak rebellion: A draft history of the Tonghak rebellion]. Translated by Yi Minsu Sŏul: Ŭryu Munhwasa, 1985.

Hwang Minho, ed. *Ilcheha chapchi palch'we singminji sidae charyo ch'ongsŏ Vol. 15: Ŏllon* [A collection of colonial era sources: excerpts from magazines under Japanese imperialism vol. 15: Journalism]. Sŏul: Kyemyŏng Munhwasa, 1992.

Ikegami Shiro. "Doshigakukaigi ni okeru seimusōkan kunji" [Address of vice governor-general in a provincial school inspector's meeting]. In *Yukoku kunji enshutz shoran 1* [Collections of advices, admonitions, and addresses 1], edited by Chōsen Sōtokufu, branch of secretariat and records. Keijō: Chōsen Gyosei Gakki, 1941.

Im Chongguk. *Ilcheha ŭi sasang t'anap* [Repression of thought under Japanese imperialism]. Sŏul: P'yŏnghwa Ch'ulp'ansa, 1985.

Im, Henry. "Nationalist Discourse in Modern Korea: Mijok as a Democratic Imaginary." Ph.D. diss., University of Chicago, 1995.

Im Kyŏngsŏk. "1910-nyŏndae kyegŭp kusŏng kwa nodongja nongmin undong" [Class composition and the social movements of peasants and workers in the 1910s]. In *Minjok haebang undong yŏn'gu* [A study on the March first national liberation movement]. Sŏul: Ch'ŏngnyŏnsa, 1989.

Imamura Tomo. *Chōsen fūzoku shū* [A compendium of Korean customs]. Keijō: Kidōkan, 1915.

Inaba Iwakichi. "Chōsen no bunka mondai" [Cultural issues in Korea]. *Tōa Keizai Kenkyū* [East Asian economic studies] 6 (1922).

Inch'on Kinyŏmhoe. *Inch'on Kim Sŏngsu chŏn* [A biography of Inch'on Kim Sŏngsu]. Sŏul: Inch'on Kinyŏmhoe, 1976.

Ingold, M.B. "Dispensary Notes." *The Christian Observer*. March, 1902.

Itō Akira. *Tenkō to tennōsai* [The Tenkō and the tennō system]. Tōkyō: Keiso Books, 1995.

Itoh, Abito. "Coordination and Brokerage: Leadership in Community Development in Rural Korea." In *The Anthropology of Korea: East Asian Perspectives*, edited by Mutsuhiko Shima and Roger L. Janelli. Osaka: National Museum of Ethnology, 1998.

Iwashita Takeki. *Shonen no hi no haisen nikki: Chōsen hantō kara no kikan* [A diary of wartime defeat in the days of my youth: Returning from the Korean peninsula]. Tōkyō: Hōsei Daigaku Shuppankyoku, 2000.

"Japs Up to Her Old Tricks Again" (July 30, 1944). *Miguk kungmusŏng Han'guk kwan'gye munsŏ* [Papers of the United States Department of State, related to Korea]. Internal Affairs of Korea, 1940–1944. Sŏul: Wŏnju Munhwasa, 1993.

Janelli, Roger, and Dawnhee Yim. *Ancestor Worship and Korean Society*. Stanford, CA: Stanford University Press, 1982.

Jung, Keunsik. *See* Chŏng Kŭnsik.

Kaebyŏk, 1920–26.

Kamasuka Dasuku. "Genkon kyoiku no hei o joshi sono kaizenten ni ronkyosu" [Arguments on the abuse of current education and its remedy]. *Bunkyo no Chōsen* [Educational policy of Korea] 9 (1938): 7–30.

Kang Tŏksan. *Yŏ Unhyŏng hyōten 1: Chōsen san-ichi dokuritsu undō* [A critical biography of Yŏ Unhyŏng, 1: Korea's March first movement]. Tōkyō: Shinkansha, 2002.

Kang Munsu. "Senjin shisōhan tenkōsyawai kanaru hogowo kibōsuruka" [What protection the Korean thought criminal converts are wishing for]. *Shisōihō* [Assorted report of thought] 6 (1936): 100–102.

Kang Munsu. "Zōshinsho" [Statement of submission]. *Shisōkeppō* [Monthly report of thought] 4, no. 3 (1934): 40–50.

Kang Sangjung. *Orient'allijŭm ŭl nŏmŏsŏ* [Beyond orientalism]. Translated by Yi Kyŏngdŏk and Im Sŏngmo. Sŏul: Isan, 1997.

Kang Tongjin. *Ilche ŭi Han'guk ch'imnyak chŏngch'aek sa* [A history of Japanese imperialist aggression in Korea]. Sŏul: Han'gilsa, 1980.

——. "Munhwajuŭi ŭi kibon sŏnggyŏk" [The fundamental character of culturalism].
In Han'guk sahoe yŏn'gu 2 [Korean social research 2]. Sŏul: Han'gilsa, 1984.

Kashima Setsuko. "Kaisetsu: Kwangju gakusei undō" [Analysis: The Kwangju student
movement]. In Shokuminchi shita Chōsen: Kwangju gakusei undō no kenkyū [Korea under
colonial rule: Research on the Kwangju student movement], edited by Mukuge no kai.
Kobe: Mukuge no kai, 1990.

Kasuya Kenichi. "Chōsen Sōtokufu no bunka seiji." [The cultural politics of the
Government-General of Korea]. Kindai Nippon to shokuminji 2 [Modern Japan and col-
onies]. Tōkyō: Iwanami, 1992.

Kawashima Takeyoshi. Kawashima Takeyoshi chosaku shū 10: kazoku oyobi kazokuhō 1 kazoku
seido [Collection of the works of Kawashima Takeyoshi vol. 10: Family and family law
part 1 family system]. Tōkyō: Iwanami Shoten, 1986.

Keikidō Naimufu [Department of home affairs, Kyŏnggi Province]. Keikidō nōson shakai jijyō
[The state of Kyŏnggi Province's agricultural society]. Keijō: Keikidō Naimufu, 1927.

Kelly, Gail P. "Colonial Schools in Vietnam: Policy and Practice." In Education and
Colonialism, 96–121, edited by Philip G. Altbach and Gail P. Kelly. New York and
London: Longman, 1978.

Kelly, Gail P., and Philip G. Altbach. Education and Colonialism. New York and
London: Longman, 1978.

Kerr, Edith A., and George Anderson. The Australian Presbyterian Mission in Korea, 1889–
1941, Sydney: Australian Presbyterian Board of Missions, 1970.

Kim, C. I. Eugene, et al., eds. Korea's Response to Japan: The Colonial Period. Kalamazoo:
Western Michigan University, 1975.

Kim Ch'angho, and Kang Sŏkhŭi. Chōsen tsūshi [Korean history]. P'yŏngyang: 1995.

Kim, Chin'gyun, and Chŏng Kŭnsik, eds. Kŭndae chuch'e wa singminji kyuryul kwŏllyŏk
[Modern subject and colonial discipline power]. Sŏul: Munhwa Kwahaksa, 1998.

Kim, Christine. "The King is Dead: Monarchism and National Identity in Modern
Korea, 1897–1919." Ph.D. diss., Harvard University, 2004.

Kim Chunyŏp, and Kim Changsun. Han'guk kongsanjuŭi undong sa 2, 3 [A history of the
Korean communist movement]. Sŏul: Ch'unggye Yŏn'guso, 1986.

Kim, Dong-No [Kim Tongno]. "Peasants, States, and Landlords: National Crisis and
the Transformation of Agrarian Society in Pre-Colonial Korea." Ph.D. diss., University
of Chicago, 1994.

Kim Hakchun. Koha Song Chinu p'yŏngjŏn [A critical biography of Koha Song Chin'u].
Sŏul: Tonga Ilbosa, 1990.

Kim Hoil. "Ilcheha '6–10 haksaeng undong' ko" [The "6–10 student movement" under imperial Japan]. In Han'guk kŭndaesa nonch'ong [Papers of modern Korean history], edited by Yun Pyŏngsŏk. Sŏul: Han'guk Kŭndae Nonch'ong Kanhaeng Wiwŏnhoe, 1990.

Kim Ikhan. "1930-nyŏndae Ilche ŭi chibang chibae wa haengjŏng" [Japanese colonial regional rule and administration in the 1930s]. Han'guk Saron 37 (1997): 207–51.

Kim Inho. T'aep'yŏngyang chŏnjaeng sigi Chosŏn kongŏp yŏn'gu [A study of Korean industrialization during the era of the Pacific War]. Sŏul: Sŏul Taehakkyo Ch'ulpansa, 1998.

Kim, Joong-seop. "In Search of Human Rights: The Paekchong Movement in Colonial Korea." In Colonial Modernity in Korea, edited by Gi-Wook Shin and Michael Robinson. Cambridge, MA: Harvard University Asia Center, 1999.

———. The Korean Paekjŏng Under Japanese Rule. London: RoutledgeCurzon, 2003.

Kim Keongil. "Chŏnsigi Ilbon ŭi Taedonga Kongyŏnggwŏn kusang kwa ch'eje" [The wartime structure and system of the Japanese Greater East Asia Co-prosperity Sphere]. Ilbon yŏksa yŏn'gu 10 (1999): 221–46.

———. "Intellectual Context of Korean Studies: Universalism and Particularism in Colonial Korea." Review of Korean Studies 1 (1998): 53–75.

Kim Kŭnbae. Hwang Osŏk sinhwa wa Taehan Min'guk kwahak [The myth of Hwang Osŏk and Science in the Republic of Korea]. Sŏul: Yŏksa Pip'yŏngsa, 2007.

———. Ilche sigi Chosŏnin kwahak kisul illyŏk ŭi sŏngjang [The growth of Korean scientists and technicians under the Japanese colonial rule]. Ph.D. Diss. Sŏul Taehakkyo, 1996.

———. "20-segi singminji Chosŏn ŭi kwahak kwa kisul" [Science and technology of colonial Korea in the twentieth century], Yŏksa pip'yŏng [Historical criticism], No. 56 (Fall 2001), 297–313.

Kim, Kwang-Ok (Kim Kwangok). "The Confucian Construction of a Cultural Community in Contemporary South Korea." In The Anthropology of Korea: East Asian Perspectives, edited by Mutsuhiko Shima and Roger L. Janelli. Osaka: National Museum of Ethnology, 1998.

———. "Cultural Community and Local Level Politics: With Reference to Localized Elite Lineage in a Modern Situation." Korean Social Science Journal 22 (1996): 121–44.

———. "The Reproduction of Confucian Culture in Contemporary Korea: An Anthropological Study." In Confucian Traditions in East Asian Modernity, edited by Wei-ming Tu. Cambridge, MA: Harvard University Press, 1996.

———. "Rituals of Resistance: The Manipulation of Shamanism in Contemporary Korea." In Asian Visions of Authority: Religion and the Modern States of East and Southeast Asia, edited by Charles C. Keyes, Laurel Kendall, and Helen Hardacre. Honolulu: University of Hawai'i Press, 1994.

———. "Socio-Political Implications of the Resurgence of Ancestor Worship in

Contemporary Korea." In *Home Bound: Studies in East Asian Society*, edited by Chie Nakane and Chiao Chien. Tokyo: Center for East Asian Cultural Studies, 1992.

Kim Kwang-Ok (Kim Kwangok). "Ilche sigi t'och'ak chisigin ŭi minjok munwha insik ŭi t'ŭl" [Conceptual framework of national culture among native intellectuals under Japanese colonialism]. *Pigyo munwha yŏn'gu* 4 (1998): 79–120.

Kim Kŭnsu, ed. *Ilche ch'iha ŏllon ch'ulp'an ŭi silt'ae* [The reality of journalism and publication under Japanese imperial rule]. Sŏul: Yŏngsin Ak'ademi Han'guk Yŏn'guso, 1974.

Kim Kyuhwan. *Ilche ŭi tae-Han ŏllon, sŏnjŏn chŏngch'aek* [Japanese colonial policy on journalism and propaganda in Korea]. Sŏul: Iu Ch'ulp'ansa, 1978.

Kim Minch'ŏl. "Ilcheha sahoejuŭijadŭl ŭl chŏnhyang nolli" [The conversion logic of communists under Japanese imperialism]. *Yŏksa pip'yŏng* [Critical review of history] 28 (1995): 230–46.

Kim Namch'ŏn. *Maek* [Barley]. Sŏul: Sŭlgi, 1987.

Kim Pyŏngch'an, et al, eds. *Ch'in-Il munhak chakp'um sŏnjip* [Selected works of pro-Japanese literature]. Sŏul: Silch'ŏn Munhaksa, 1986.

Kim Sangman. *Tonga ilbosa* [The history of the *Tonga ilbo*] Vol. 1. Sŏul: Tonga Ilbosa, 1975.

Kim Sŏkpŏm. *Tenkō to shinnitsiha* [Conversion and the pro-Japanese]. Tōkyō: Iwanami, 1993.

Kim Sŏngnae. "Musok chŏnt'ong ŭi tamnon punsŏk" [Discourse analysis of the shamanist tradition]. *Han'guk munhwa illyuhak* [Korean cultural anthropology] 22 (1990): 211–43.

Kim Sŏngsik. *Ilcheha Han'guk haksaeng tongnip undongsa* [Korean student movements under Japanese colonial rule]. Sŏul: Chŏngŭmsa, 1974.

Kim T'aekkyu. *Tongjok purak ŭi saenghwal kujo yŏn'gu* [The cultural structure of a consanguineous village]. Taegu: Silla-Kaya Munhwa Yŏn'guwŏn, 1964.

Kim Tongmyŏng. "Chibae wa tongnip ŭi chŏpchŏm" [The point of contact between control and independence]. In *Han'guk chŏngch'i oegyosa nonch'ong* 21(1) [Collected essays on Korean political and diplomatic history]. Sŏul: Han'guk Chŏngch'i Oegyo Sa Hakhoe, 1999.

———. "1920-nyŏndae Chosŏn esŏ ŭi Ilbon chegukchuŭi ŭi chibae ch'eje ŭi tongyo" [The upheaval of the Japanese imperial system of control in 1920s' Chosŏn]. In *Ilbon yŏksa yŏn'gu* 8 [Studies on Japanese history]. (1998): 65–95.

———. "1920-nyŏndae singminji Chosŏn esŏ ŭi chŏngch'i undong yŏn'gu" [A study on 1920s political movements in colonial Korea]. *Han'guk chŏngch'i nakhoe po* [Korean political science review] 32, no. 3 (1998): 139-61.

Kim Tohyŏng. "Ilche ŭi nongŏp kisul pogŭp kwa nongmindŭl ŭi taeŭng" [The response of peasants to the diffusion of agricultural technology by Japanese imperialism]. In *Han'guk minjok undongsa yŏn'gu* [A study of the history of the Korean nationalist movement]. Sŏul: Nanam, 1997.

Kim Tongno [Kim, Dong-No]. "Singminji sidae ŭi kŭndaejŏk sut'al kwa sut'al ŭl t'onghan kŭndaehwa" [Modernization and exploitation in the colonial period of Korea]. *Ch'angjak kwa pip'yŏng* 99 (1998): 112–32.

———. "Singminji ŭi minjokchuŭi rŭl nŏmŏ kŭndae ro" [Overcoming colonial nationalism]. *Tong Asia pip'an* [East Asia critique]. April 2001.

Kim Tu-hŏn. *Chosŏn kajok chedo yŏn'gu* [A study of the Korean family system]. Sŏul: Sŏul Taehakkyo Ch'ulp'anbu, 1948.

Kim Tujŏng. *Bōkyō sensen syori no hitsuzensei* [The necessity of victory on the frontier for anti-communism]. Keijō: Zensen sisō hōkoku renmei, 1939.

Kim Ŭltong. *Andong p'an tongnip undongsa* [The History of the independence movement in Andong] Andong: Taehwa, 1985.

Kim Unt'ae. *Ilbon chegukchuŭi ŭi Han'guk t'ongch'i* [Japanese imperialist rule in Korea]. Sŏul: Pagyŏngsa, 1986.

Kim Yangsik. "Kojongjo millan yŏn'gu" [A study of popular revolts during the reign of King Kojong]. In *Han'guksa ŭi ihae: Kŭnhyŏndae p'yŏn* [Understanding Korean history: The early modern and modern periods]. Sŏul: Munhak kwa Chisŏng, 1990.

Kim Yong-dŏk. *Han'guk kajok chedosa yŏn'gu.* [A study of the hisory of Korean systems] Sŏul: Ilchogak, 1983.

Kim Yŏnggŭn. "1920-nyŏndae nodongja ŭi chonjae hyŏngt'ae e kwanhan yŏn'gu" [A study of the existence of labor in Korea during the 1920s]. In *Ilcheha Han'guk ŭi sahoe kyegŭp kwa sahoe pyŏndong* [Social class and social change in Korea under Japanese colonial rule], edited by Han'guk Sahoesa Yŏn'guhoe. Sŏul: Munhak kwa Chisŏng, 1988.

Kim Yongjik [Kim, Yong-Jick]. "Han'guk chongch'i wa kongnonsŏng: Yugyojŏk kongnon chŏngch'i wa konggong yŏngyŏk" [Korean politics and publicity: Politics of Confucianism and the public sphere]. *Kukchejŏngch'i nonch'ong* [Collected essays on international politics] 38, no. 3 (1998): 63–80.

———. "Han'guk minjokchuŭi ŭi kiwŏn: Chŏngch'i undong kwa konggong yŏngyŏk." [Origins of Korean nationalism: political movements and public spheres]. *Sahoe pip'yŏng* [Social criticism] 11 (1998): 353–83.

Kim, Yong-Jick [Kim Yongjik]. "Formation of a Modern State and National Social Movement in Modern Korea: The March First Movement in a Comparative Historical Perspective." Ph.D. diss., University of North Carolina–Chapel Hill, 1992.

———. "The Political Tradition of Kongnon Politics and the Public Sphere: Democratic Origins of Modern Korea." A paper presented at the eleventh international conference on Korean Studies. Seoul: Academy of Korean Studies, June 28, 2000.

Kim Yŏngmo. *Ilchesi taejiju ŭi sahoejŏk paegyŏng kwa idong* [Social background and change among large-scale landlords in the colonial period]. *Asia yŏn'gu* 14, no. 1 (1971): 107–25.

Kim Yunsik. "Chŏnhyangnon" [The theory of conversion]. *Han'guk kŭndae munye pip'yŏngsa yŏn'gu* [History of modern Korean literary criticism]. Sŏul: Ilchisa, 1976.

————. "Sasang chŏnhyang kwa chŏnhyang sasang" [Thought conversion and converted thought]. *Han'guk kŭndae munhak sasangsa* [History of modern Korean literary thoughts]. Sŏul: Han'gilsa, 1984.

————. *Yi Kwangsu wa kŭ ŭi sidae* [Yi Kwangsu and his era]. Sŏul: Han'gilsa, 1986.

Ko Ponggyŏng, Yi Hyojae, Yi Mangap, and Yi Haeyŏng. *Han'guk nongch'on kajok ŭi yŏn'gu* [A study of the Korean rural family]. Sŏul: Sŏul Taehakkyo Ch'ulp'anbu, 1963.

Ko Sŭngje. "Kŭnse hyangch'on chedo ŭi punggoe wa ch'ollak sahoe ŭi kujojŏk pyŏnhwa" [The decline of the village system and the structural transformation of the village society in early modern Korea]. *Haksurwŏn nonmunjip* 14 (1975): 91–119.

Kobayashi Hideo. "Tōarenmei undō" [On the Tōarenmei movement]. In *Teikoku to iukensō: Daitōakyōeiken no sisō to kenzitsu* [The illusion of empire: Ideology and practice in the Greater East Asia Co-Prosperity Sphere], edited by Peter Duus and Hideo Kobayashi. Tōkyō: Aoki-shoten, 1998.

Kokuritsu Kyoiku Kenkyujo [National research center of education]. *Nihon kindai kyoiku hyakunenji 1–kyoiku seisaku* [One hundred-year-history of modern education in Japan 1–educational policy]. Tōkyō: Bunchodo, 1974.

Kolhi, Atul. "Where Do High Growth Political Economies Come From? The Japanese Lineage of Korea's 'Developmental' State." *World Development* 22, no. 9 (1994): 1269–93.

Komagome Takeshi. *Shokuminchi teikoku Nihon no bunka togo* [Cultural integration of the Japanese colonial empire]. Tōkyō: Iwanami Shoten, 1996.

Kondo, Dorinne K. *Crafting Selves: Power, Gender, and Discourses of Identity in a Japanese Workplace*. Chicago: University of Chicago Press, 1990.

Korean Central News Agency. "June 10, 2001 edition." http://www.kcna.co/jp/item/2001/200106/news06/10.htm.

Korea Web Weekly. "Kim Il Sung Memoirs." http://www.kimsoft.com/war/r-2-1.htm.

Ku, Dae-yeol. *Korea Under Colonialism: The March First Movement and Anglo-Japanese Relations*. London: Royal Asiatic Society, 1985.

Ku Han'guk woegyo munsŏ Vol II. [Old Korea diplomatic documents, September 1889–July 1894]. Han'guk Taehakkyo, Asea Munje Yŏn'guso, 1967.

Kublin, Hyman. "The Evolution of Japanese Colonialism." *Comparative Studies in Society and History* 2, no.1 (October 1959): 67–84.

Kuksa P'yŏnch'an Wiwŏnhoe, ed. *T'onggambu munsŏ* [Residency-general papers] Vol. 9.

Kwach'ŏn: Kuksa P'yŏnch'an Wiwŏnhoe, 1999.

Kukhak Charyowŏn. *Han'guk amhŭkki sinmun sasŏl charyo ch'ongsŏ* [A collection of newspaper editorials from the dark (colonial) age of Korea]. 12 vols. [*Tonga ilbo* vols. 1–4 *Chosŏn ilbo* vols. 5–12]. Sŏul: Kukhak Charyowŏn, 1996.

Kukhoe Tosŏgwan, ed. *Tosan An Ch'angho charyojip* 2 [Source materials on An Ch'angho]. Sŏul: Kukhoe Tosŏgwan, 1998.

Kuksa P'yŏnch'an Wiwŏnhoe. *Kabo yangnyŏk.* [A short history of 1894]. Kwach'ŏn: Kuksa P'yŏnch'an Wiwŏnhoe, 1959.

Kungnip Sorokto Pyŏngwŏn. *Sorokto pyŏngwŏn 80-nyŏnsa: 1916–1996.* [Eighty-year history of Sorokto hospital]. Chollanam-do, Kohŭng-gun: Kungnip Sorokto Pyŏngwŏn, 1996.

Kwŏn Hyŏnhŭi. *Chosŏn esŏ on sajin yŏpsŏ* [Postcards from Korea]. Sŏul: Minŭmsa, 2005.

Kyŏngsang-pukto Sa P'yŏnch'an Wiwŏnhoe. *Kyŏngsang-pukto sa* [The history of North Kyŏngsang Province], 3 vols. Taegu: Kyŏngsang-pukto Sa P'yŏnch'an Wiwŏnhoe, 1983.

Laclau, Enesto, and Chantal Mouffe. *Hegemony and Socialist Strategy: Towards a Radical Democratic Politics.* London: Verso, 1985.

Law, Jane Marie ed. *Religious Reflections on the Human Body.* Bloomington: Indiana University Press, 1995.

Lee, Chong-Sik. *The Politics of Korean Nationalism.* Berkeley: University of California Press, 1963.

Lee, Ki-baik. *A New History of Korea.* Translated by Edward W. Wagner and Edward J. Shultz. Cambridge, MA: Harvard University Press, 1984.

Lee, Peter H., et.al. *Sourcebook of Korean Civilization: From Early Times to the Sixteenth Century* Vol. 1. New York: Columbia University Press, 1993.

Lee, Peter H., et al. *Sourceboook of Korean Civilization: From the Seventeenth Century to the Modern Period Vol. 2.* New York: Columbia University Press, 1996.

Lew, Joon. *A Korean Model for the Healing of Leprosy.* Seoul: Lew Institute for Biomedical Research, 1993.

Loomba, Ania. *Colonialism/Postcolonialism.* London: Routledge, 1998.

MacCarthy, D.M.P. *Colonial Bureaucracy and Creating Underdevelopment: Tanganyika, 1910–1940.* Ames: Iowa State University Press, 1982.

Mackenzie, Helen. *Mackenzie—Man of Mission.* Melbourne: Hyland House, 1995.

Maeil sinbo, 1920–30.

Mann, Michael. "The Autonomous Power of the State: Its Origins, Mechanisms and Results." In *States in History*, edited by John A. Hall. Oxford, UK: B. Blackwell, 1986.

Maruyama Masao. *Hyŏndae chŏngch'i ŭi sasang kwa haengdong* [Thought and action in modern politics]. Translated by Kim Sŏkkŭn. Sŏul: Han'gilsa, 1997.

Marx, Karl. Capital: A Critique of Political Economy Vol. I. New York: International Publishers, 1967.

Masuda Shūsaku. "Chōsen ni okeru buraku chūshin jinbutu ni tukiteno ichi kōsatu" [An observation of major village figures in Korea]. Chosen 257 (November 1936): 86–110.

McKenzie, F. A. Korea's Fight for Freedom. Seoul: Yonsei University Press, 1969.

McNamara, Dennis L. The Colonial Origin of Korean Enterprise, 1910–1945. Cambridge, MA: Cambridge University Press, 1990.

Memmi, Albert. The Colonizer and the Colonized. Boston, MA: Beacon Press, 1967.

Mercier, P. "Problems of Social Stratification in West Africa." In Social Change: The Colonial Situation, edited by I. Wallerstein. New York: John Wiley and Sons, 1966.

Meyers, Ramon H., and Mark R. Peattie. The Japanese Colonial Empire, 1985–1945. Princeton, NJ: Princeton University Press, 1984.

Mich'ell Rich'adŭ [Mitchell, Richard]. Ilche ŭi sasang t'ongje [Japanese imperialist thought control]. Translated by Kim Yunsik. Sŏul: Ilchisa, 1982.

Mignolo, Walter D. "Colonial and Postcolonial Discourse: Cultural Critique or Academic Colonialism?" Latin American Research Review 28 (Summer 1993): 120–34.

Ministry of Education. "Fundamentals of Our National Polity" [Kokutai no hongi], 1937. In Sources of Japanese Tradition II, edited by Wm. Theodore de Bary. New York: Columbia University Press, 1958.

Mitchell, Richard H. [Mich'ell Rich'adŭ]. Thought Control in Prewar Japan. Ithaca, NY: Cornell University Press, 1976.

Miyata Setsuko, Kim Youngdal, and Yang Taeho. Sōshi kaimei [Creation of clan name and change of personal name]. Tōkyō: Akashi shōten, 1992.

Mizda, Kenske. "Condolence for the Death of Chief Suho." Eisei 12, no. 8 (1942).

Mizuno Rentarō. Mizuno Rentarō kaisōroku, kankei bunsho [Memoirs and official papers of Mizuno Rentarō], edited by Nishio Rintarō. Tōkyō: Yamagawa Shuppansha, 1999.

Moore, Barrington Jr. Social Origins of Dictatorship and Democracy. Boston, MA: Beacon Press, 1966.

Morris, Ivan I. Nationalism and the Right Wing in Japan: A Study of Post-War Trends. London: Oxford University Press, 1960.

Mun Okp'yo. "Ilche ŭi singminji munhwa chŏngch'aek" [The colonial cultural policy of the Japanese colonial period]. In Ilche ŭi singmin chibae wa saenghwalsang [Japanese colonial rule and life in Korea], edited by Han'guk Chŏngsin Munhwa Yŏn'guwŏn. Sŏngnam: Han'guk Chŏngsin Munhwa Yŏn'guwŏn, 1990.

Mun Sojŏng. "Ilcheha nongch'on kajok e kwanhan yŏn'gu" [A study of rural families under colonial rule]. In Ilcheha Han'guk ŭi sahoe kyegŭp kwa sahoe pyŏndong [Social class and social

change in Korea under Japanese colonial rule], edited by Han'guk Sahoesa Yŏn'guhoe
[Korean Social History Research Association]. Sŏul: Munhak kwa Chisŏng, 1988.

Murata, Shota. " The Problem of Leprosy Relief in Korea." *Japan and Japanese* 821 (1921).

Murayama, Chijun. *Chōsen no fūgeki* [Female and male shaman of Korea]. Keijō: Chōsen
Sōtokufu, 1932.

———. *Chōsen no ruiji shūgyo* [Pseudo-religions of Korea]. Keijō: Chōsen Sōtokufu, 1935.

Murayama, Michio. *Chōsen sōzoku seirei.* [The decree on Korean inheritance tax]. Keijō:
Chōsen sōtokufu, Zaimu kyōkai, 1934.

Myers, Ramon, et al., eds. *The Japanese Colonial Empire 1895–1945.* Princeton, NJ:
Princeton University Press, 1984.

Nakamura Satoru. *See* Chungch'on Ch'ol.

Nagumo, Kōkichi. *Genkō Chōsen shinzoku sōzoku hō ruishū.* [Compendium of currently
practiced Korean kinship and inheritance law]. Osaka: Yago Shoten, 1935.

Nahm, Andrew, ed. *Korea under Japanese Colonial Rule: Studies on the Policy and Techniques of
Japanese Colonialism.* Kalamazoo: Western Michigan University, 1973.

Nairn, Tom. *The Break-up of Britain: Crisis and Neo-Nationalism.* London: New Left Books, 1981.

Navon, Liora. "Internal Exclusion of Leprosy Sufferers: Dual Ambivalence and Its
Theoretical Implications." *Qualitative Sociology* 19, no. 4 (1996): 453–69.

Nettleton, Sarah. *The Sociology of Health and Illness.* Cambridge, UK: Polity Press, 1995.

Nomura Chōtarō. "Chōsen kazoku seido no suii" [Trends in the Korean family system].
Chosen 296 (January 1940): 17–37.

O Chiyŏng. *Tonghaksa* [The history of the Tonghak]. Sŏul: Yŏngch'ang Sŏgwan, 1940.

O Ch'ŏng. "Chōsen no shinzoku kankei" [Family relations in Korea]. *Chōsen* (December
1927): 77–105.

O Chuhwan. "Ilche ŭi tae-Han ŏllon chŏngch'aek" [The Korean media policy of
Japanese imperialism]. In *Ilche ŭi munhwa ch'imt'al sa* [A history of cultural invasion by
Japanese imperialism], edited by Han Kiŏn. Sŏul: Hyŏnŭmsa, 1982.

O Sŏngch'ŏl. "1930-nyŏndae Han'guk ch'odŭng kyoyuk yŏn'gu" [A study of Korean
primary education during the 1930s]. Ph.D. diss., Sŏul Taehakkyo, 1996.

———. *Singminji ch'odŭng kyoyuk ŭi hyŏngsŏng* [The making of colonial primary education in Korea]. Sŏul: Kyoyuk Kwahaksa, 2000.

Onishi, Norimitusu. "Japanese Remarks about Taiwan Anger Beijing." *The New York
Times,* February 6, 2006.

Ono Ichiro. "Che ilch'a taejŏn hu ŭi singmin chŏngch'aek non: Chosŏn munje rŭl tullŏ
ssago" [On the colonial policy after World War I: The Korean problem]. In *Kŭndae Tong
Asia wa Ilbon kwa chegukchuŭi* [Modern East Asia and Japanese imperialism], edited by

Kim Yŏngho. Sŏul: Hanbat, 1983.

Osgood, Cornelius. *The Koreans and Their Culture*. New York: The Ronald Press, 1951.

Ōtani Fuzio. *History of Abolition of Leprosy Protection Act in Japan*. Tokyo: Keiso Press, 1996.

Ōwa Kazuaki. "1920-nendai zenhanki no Chōsen nōmin undō: Zennan Junsen-gun no jirei o Chōshin ni" [Korean peasant movements in the early 1920s: A case in Sunch'ŏn County, South Chŏlla Province]. *Rekishiteki kenkyū* 502 (1982): 18–33.

Pae Yŏngsun. "Hanmal Ilche ch'ogi ŭi t'oji chosa wa chise kaejŏng e kwanhan yŏn'gu" [A study of the cadastral survey and the change of land tax in the late Chosŏn Dynasty and early colonial period]. Ph.D. diss., Sŏul Taehakkyo, 1988.

Pak Ch'ansŭng. *Han'guk kŭndae chŏngch'i sasangsa yŏn'gu* [A study of the history of modern Korean political thought]. Sŏul: Yŏksa Pip'yŏngsa, 1992.

Pak Chihyang. *Chegukchuŭi:sinhwa wa hyŏnsil* [Imperialism: Myth and reality]. Sŏul: Sŏul Taehakkyo Ch'ulp'ansa, 2000.

Pak Hyŏnsu. *Ilbon chegukchuŭi ŭi Chosŏn chibae* [The domination of Japanese imperialism in Korea]. Sŏul: Ch'ŏnga, 1986.

———."Ilche ŭi Chosŏn chosa e kwanhan yŏn'gu" [A study of the investigation of Chosŏn by the Japanese Government-General]. Ph.D. diss., Sŏul Taehakkyo, 1993.

Pak Kyŏngsik. *Ilbon chegukjuŭi ŭi Han'guk chibae* [Japanese imperial rule of Korea]. Sŏul: Ch'ŏnga Ch'ulp'ansa, 1986.

Pak Kyŏngsik, ed. *Chōsen mondai shiryō sōsho* [Collection of colonial document series] vol. 8. Tōkyō: Asia Mondai Kenkyŭsho, 1983.

Palais, James B. *Confucian Statecraft and Korean Institutions: Yu Hyŏngwŏn and the Late Chosŏn Dynasty*. Seattle: University of Washington Press, 1996.

———."Nationalism: Good or Bad?" In *Nationalism and the Construction of Korean Identity*, edited by Hyung Il Pai and Timothy R. Tangherlini. Berkeley: Institute of East Asian Studies, University of California, 1998.

Peattie Mark R., and Ramon H. Myers, eds. *The Japanese Colonial Empire, 1895–1945*. Princeton, NJ: Princeton University Press, 1984.

Peterson, Mark A. *Korean Adoption and Inheritance: Case Studies of a Classic Confucian Society*. Ithaca, NY: Cornell University Press, 1996.

Poggi, Gianfranco. *The State: Its Nature, Development, and Prospects*. Stanford, CA: Stanford University Press, 1990.

Positions: East Asia Cultures Critique 1, no. 1 (Spring 1993).

Pye, Lucian, ed. *Communication and Political Development*. Princeton, NJ: Princeton University Press, 1963.

Rankin, Mary B. "The Origins of a Chinese Public Sphere: Local Elites and Community

Affairs in the Late Imperial Period." *Études Chinoises* 9, no. 2 (1990): 13–60.

Robinson, Michael E. [Robinsŭn, M]. "Colonial Publication Policy and the Korean Nationalist Movement." In *The Japanese Colonial Empire 1895–1945*, edited by Ramon Myers, et al. Princeton, NJ: Princeton University Press, 1984.

———. "Forced Assimilation, Mobilization, and War." In *Korea Old and New: A History*, edited by Carter J. Eckert, et al. Cambridge, MA: Harvard University Press, 1990.

———. "Ideological Schism in the Korean Nationalist Movement, 1920–1930: Cultural Nationalism and the Radical Critique." *The Journal of Korean Studies* 4, no. 1 (1982): 241–68.

Robinsŭn, M [Robinson, Michael E.]. *Ilcheha munhwajŏk minjokchuŭi* [Cultural nationalism in colonial Korea]. Translated by Kim Minhwan. Sŏul: Nanam, 1990.

Rothman, David J. *The Discovery of the Asylum*. Boston, MA: Little and Brown Co., 1971.

Ryan, Michael, and Avery Gordon. *Body Politics*. Boulder, CO: Westview Press, 1994.

Said, Edward. *Culture and Imperialism*. New York: Alfred A. Knopf, 1993.

———. *Orientalism*. New York: Random House, 1978.

Saitō Makoto. *Saitō Makoto bunsho* [The collected documents of Saitō Makoto]. Sŏul T'ŭkpyŏlsi: Koryŏ Sŏrim, 1990.

Saitō Shishaku Kinenkai. *Shishaku Saitō Makoto den* [Biography of Baron Saitō Makoto]. Tōkyō: Saitō Shishaku Kinenkai, 1942.

Sakai, Naoki. "Modernity and Its Critique: The Problem of Universalism and Particularism." In *Postmodernism and Japan*, edited by Masao Miyoshi and H. D. Harootunian. Durham, NC: Duke University Press, 1989.

Schmid, Andre. "Japanese Propaganda in the United States from 1905." Paper presented at the International Impact of Colonial Korea Conference, University of Washington–Seattle, November 19, 2010.

———. *Korea Between Empires, 1895–1919*. Irvington, NY: Columbia University Press, 2002.

Scott, David. "Colonialism: Anthropological Approaches to Colonialism." *International Social Science Journal* 49 (December 1997): 453–562.

Scott, James C. *Domination and the Arts of Resistance: Hidden Transcripts*. New Haven, CT: Yale University Press, 1990.

———. *Seeing Like the State*. New Haven, CT: Yale University Press, 1998.

———. *Weapons of the Weak: Everyday Forms of Peasant Resistance*. New Haven, CT: Yale University Press, 1985.

Seoul Press. *Administrative Reforms in Korea*, Seoul: Seoul Press, 1919.

Shiga, Kiyoshi. "Studies on the History of Leprosy." *Chōsen Shakai Jigyō* 9, no. 3 (1931).

Shilling, Chris. *The Body and Social Theory*. London: Sage, 1993.

Shin, Gi-Wook. *Peasant Protest and Social Change in Colonial Korea*. Seattle and London: University of Washington Press, 1996.

Shin, Gi-Wook, and Michael Robinson, eds. *Colonial Modernity in Korea*. Cambridge, MA: Harvard University Press, 1999.

Shin, Jiwon. "Recasting Colonial Space: Nationalist Vision and Modern Fiction in 1920s Korea." *Journal of International and Area Studies* 11, no. 3 (2004): 51–74.

Sim Chŏnhwang. *A, 70 nyŏn— challanhan sŭlp'ŭm ŭi Sorokto* [Ah, seventy years—Sorokto of brilliant sorrow]. Sŏul: Tongbang Ch'ulp'ansa, 1993.

Sin Yongha. *Chosŏn t'ojichosa saŏp yŏn'gu* [A study of the land cadastral survey in the colonial period]. Sŏul: Chisik Sanŏpsa, 1982.

————. *Han'guk hyŏndae sahoesa yŏn'gu* [A study of modern Korean social history]. Sŏul: Ilchisa, 1987.

————. *Ilche singminji kŭndaehwaron pip'an* [A critique of colonial modernization theory]. Sŏul: Munhwa kwa Chisŏngsa, 1998.

————. " 'Singminji kŭndaehwaron' chaejŏngnip sido e taehan pip'an" [A critique of the reformulation of colonial modernization theory]. *Ch'angjak kwa pip'yŏng* 98 (Winter 1997): 8–38.

Sisō no Kagaku Kenkyūkai, ed. [Association for the scientific study of thought]. *Kyōdō kenkyū-Tenkō* 1 [Collective studies on conversion]. Tōkyō: Heibonsha, 1959.

Skocpol, Theda. *States and Social Revolutions: A Comparative Analysis of France, Russia, and China*. Cambridge, NY: Cambridge University Press, 1979.

Smethurst, Richard J. "The Military Reserve Association and the Minobe Crisis of 1935." In *Crisis Politics in Prewar Japan: Institutional and Ideological Problems of the 1930's*, edited by George M. Wilson. Tokyo: Sophia University Press, 1970.

Smith, Anthony. *Segye sinmun ŭi yŏksa* [The newspaper: An international history]. Translated by Ch'oe Chŏngho and Kong Yongbae. Sŏul: Nanam, 1990.

Sŏ Chungsŏk. *Han'guk hyŏndae minjok undong yŏn'gu* [A study of modern Korean nationalist movements]. Sŏul: Yŏksa Pip'yŏngsa, 1991.

————. "Ilche sidae sahoejuŭijadŭl ŭi minjokkwan kwa kyegŭpkwan" [The socialists' perspectives on nation and class in the Japanese colonial era]. In *Han'guk minjokchuŭi ron 3* [On Korean nationalism, vol. 3]. Sŏul: Ch'angjak kwa Pip'yŏngsa, 1985.

Song Chihyang. *Andong hyangt'o chi* [Andong gazette]. Sŏul: Taesŏng Munhwasa, 1983.

Sonntag, Susan. *Illness as Metaphor*. New York: Vintage, 1979.

Sorensen, Clark W. *Over the Mountains are Mountains: Korean Peasant Households and Their Adaptations to Rapid Industrialization*. Seattle: University of Washington Press, 1988.

Steinhoff, Patricia Golden. "Tenkō: Ideology and Societal Integration in Prewar Japan."

Ph.D. diss., Harvard University, 1969.

Suzuki Keifu. *See* Yŏngmok Kyŏngbu.

Taehan Na Hyŏphoe. "Han'guk nabyŏngsa" [Korean history of leprosy]. *Pokchi*, 1988.

T'akchibu [Ministry of Finance]. *Toji chosa ch'amgosŏ* [Reference book for the land survey]. Sŏul: T'akchibu, 1909.

Takeda, Shoji. *Segregation as Disease*. Tokyo: Gotosi, 1997.

Tama Zenshōen Kanja Jichikai. *Kue issho: Kanja ga tsuzuru Zenshōen no shichijūnen* [Gathered together in one place: Seventeen years of Zenshōen compiled by the patients]. Tōkyō: Ikkōsha 1979.

Tanaka, Stefan. *Japan's Orient: Rendering Pasts into History*. Berkeley: University of California Press, 1993.

Taussig, Michael. *Shamanism, Colonialism, and the Wild Men*. Chicago: University of Chicago Press, 1987.

Tehranian, Majid. "Communication and Development." In *Communication Theory Today*, edited by David Crowley, et al. London: Polity Press, 1994.

Thomas, A. F. "Japan's National Education." *Transactions and Proceedings of Japan Society London* 36 (1938–39): 29–52.

Thomas, H. L. "A Study of Leprosy Control—R.M. Wilson Colony." *American Mission to Lepers*, 1947.

Thomas, Nicholas. *Colonialism's Culture*. Cambridge, UK: Polity Press, 1994.

Tilly, Charles. *Coercion, Capital, and Europe States AD 990–1990*. Oxford and Cambridge: Basil Blackwell Publishers, 1991.

Tonga ilbo. 1921–28.

Tonga Ilbosa. *Tonga ilbosa sa* [A history of the Tonga Ilbo Company]. Vol 1. (1920–45). Sŏul: Tonga Ilbosa, 1975.

———. *Tonga ilbo sasŏl sŏnjip vol 1* [An anthology of *Tonga ilbo* editorials]. Sŏul: Tonga Ilbosa, 1977.

Tongnip Undongsa P'yŏnch'an Wiwŏnhoe. *Tongnip undongsa 9: Haksaeng tongnip undongsa* [History of the independence movement vol. 9: History of the student independence movement]. Sŏul: Koryŏ Tosŏ, 1980.

———. "Tongnip undongsa charyojip vol 12" [Collected sources on the history of cultural struggle Vol 12]. In *Tongnip undongsa charyojip*. [Collected sources on the history of independence movement]. Sŏul: Tongnip Undongsa P'yŏnch'an Wiwŏnhoe, 1977.

Tsurumi, E. Patricia. "Colonial education in Korea and Taiwan." In the *Japanese Colonial Empire, 1895–1945*, edited by Ramon H. Myers and Mark R. Peattie, 275–311. Princeton, NJ: Princeton University Press, 1984.

———. *Japanese Colonial Education in Taiwan, 1895–1945*. Cambridge, MA: Harvard University Press, 1977.

Tsurumi Shunsuke [Hakkyŏn Chunp'o]. *Senjiki Nihon no seishinshi, 1931–1945 nen*. [A history of Japanese psychology in wartime, 1931–1945].Tōkyō: Iwanami Shoten, 1983.

Turner, Brian S. *Regulating Bodies: Essays in Medical Sociology*. London: Routledge, 1992.

Ueda Tatsuō. *Chōsen no mondai to sono kaiketsu* [The Korean question and its solutions]. Keijō: Shogaku kenkyūjo, 1942.

Ugaki Kazushige. "Dotsishikaigi ni okeru sōtoku kunji" [Address of Government-General in a provincial governor's meeting]. In *Yukoku kunji enshutz shoran* 1 [Collections of advice, admonitions, and addresses 1], edited by Chōsen Sōtokufu, Branch of secretariat and records. Keijō: Chōsen Gyosei Gakki, 1941.

Unschuld, Paul. "Traditional Chinese Medical Theory and Real Nosological Units: The case of Hansen's Disease." *Medical Anthropology Quarterly* 17, no. 1 (1985): 5–8.

Valencia, L. B. "Social Science Research on the Social Dimension of Leprosy." *International Journal of Leprosy and Other Mycobacterial Diseases* 57, no. 4 (December 1989): 847–63.

Vaughan, Megan. *Curing Their Ills: Colonial Power and African Illness*. Stanford, CA: Stanford University Press, 1991.

Wada Ichiro. *Chōsen tochi chizei seido chōsa hōkokusho* [A study of land tax in Korea]. Keijō: Chōsen Sōtokufu, 1920.

Wagner, Edward W. "Two Early Genealogies and Women's Status in Early Yi Dynasty Korea." In *Korean Women: View From the Inner Room*, edited by Laurel Kendall and Mark Peterson, 23–32. New Haven, CT: East Rock Press, 1983.

Wang Sunbong. "Senjinsisō han tenkō shawa ikanaru hogowo kibōsuruka" [What protection the Korean thought criminal converts are wishing for]. *Shisōihō* 6 (1936): 98–100.

Watts, Sheldon. *Epidemics and History: Disease, Power, and Imperialism*. New Haven, CT: Yale University Press, 1997.

Weber, Max. *The Protestant Ethic and the Spirit of Capitalism*. New York: Charles Scribner's Sons, 1930.

Wells, Kenneth. *New God, New Nation: Protestants and Self-Reconstruction Nationalism in Korea 1896–1937*. Honolulu: University of Hawai'i, 1990.

Wilson, R.M., and Unger, J. Kelly. *Leper Work in Korea at Biederwolf Home*. Sunchon, s.n, 1928.

Wilson, R.M. "In Heroic Mould." *Korean Mission Field* 10 (1930).

———. "Industrial Work in a Leper Home." *Without the Camp* 102 (1922).

———. "Leprosy in Korea." *The Journal of the American Medical Association* 87, no. 15 (1926): 1211–12.

———. *Korean Mission Field* (1929).

————. "Occupational Therapy in Leprosy." *The China Medical Journal* 46 (1932).

————. *Without the Camp* 67 (1913); 70 (1914); 97 (1921); 109 (1924); 118 (1926); 124 (1927); 126 (1928); 128 (1928); 140 (1931); 150 (1934); 159, (1936).

Wolf, Eric. *Peasant Wars of the Twentieth Century*. New York: Harper and Row, 1969.

Wunsch, Richard. *Fremde Heimat Korea—Ein deutscher Arzt erlebt die letzen Tage des alten Korea (1901–1905)*. [Foreign home Korea—a German doctor experiences the last days of old Korea]. Munich: Simon and Magiera, 1983.

Yamamoto, Junichi. *Hansenbyo Nihon no rekishi* [History of leprosy in Japan]. Tokyo: Tokyo University Press, 1993.

Yang, Hyunah. *Envisioning Feminist Jurisprudence in Korean Family Law at the Crossroads of Tradition/Modernity*. Ph.D. diss., New School of Social Research, 1998.

Yasuda Mikita. "Chōsen ni okeru kazoku seido no hensen" [The development of the family system in Korea]. *Chōsen* 296 (January 1940): 7–16.

Yi Chongbŏm. "19-segimal 20-segich'o hyangch'on sahoe kujo wa chose chedo ŭi kaep'yŏn: Kurye-gun T'oji-myŏn Omi-dong: 'Yu ssi ka munsŏ' punsŏk" [A study of the social structure of local provinces and the reform of tax systems in the late nineteenth to the early twentieth century: An analysis of the Yu family papers of Kurye County, T'oji Township, Omi village]. Ph.D. diss., Yŏnse Taehakkyo, 1994.

Yi Chŏnghŭi. "Haebang konggan ŭi yŏsŏngji ŭi nat'anan sŏng/sarang (romaensŭ) kyŏrhon ŭi tamnon" [Discourses on sex, love (romance), and marriage appearing in female periodicals in liberation space]. *Yŏksa minsokhak* 21 (2005): 141–70.

Yi Hongnak. "Singminji ŭi sahoe kujo" [Social structure of colonial Korea]. In *Han'guksa 14: singminji ŭi sahoe kyŏngje (2)* [History of Korea 14: Society and economy of colonial Korea (2)], 139–99, edited by Kang Man'gil. Sŏul: Han'gilsa, 1994.

Yi Kwanggu. *Han'guk kajok ŭi sajŏk yŏn'gu* [An historical study of the Korean family]. Sŏul: Ilchisa, 1977.

Yi Kwangsu. "Sinteki sintaisei to Chōsen bunka no sinrō" [Spiritual new system and the leading way of Korean culture]. *Mainichi sinpō*, September 5–12, 1940. In *Ch'in-Il munhak chakp'um sŏnjip* [Selected works of pro-Japanese literature], edited by Kim Pyŏnggŏl et al. Sŏul: Silch'ŏn Munhaksa, 1986.

————. "Na ŭi kobaek" [My confession]. *Han'guk hyŏndae munhak chŏnjip 2* [Contemporary Korean literary works] 2. Sŏul: Samsŏng, 1978.

Yi Kyŏnghyŏng. "Osun ŭi pinnanŭn ch'ottae" [A shining candle of five decades]. *Saebit* 10, no. 9, 10 (1972).

Yi Nŭnghwa. "Chosŏn musok ko" [A study of Korean shamanism]. *Kyemong* 19 (May 1927): 1–85.

Yi T'aejin. *Kojong sidae ŭi chae chomyŏng* [A re-illumination of Kojong's era]. Sŏul: T'aehaksa, 2000.

Yi Tuhyŏn, Chang Sugŭn, and Yi Kwanggyu. *Han'guk minsokhak kaesŏl* [An outline of Korean folklore]. Sŏul: Minjung Sŏgwan, 1974.

Yi Yŏn. *Ilcheha ŭi Chosŏn chungang chŏngbo wiwŏnhoe ŭi yŏkhal* [The role of the Chosŏn central information committee during Japanese imperial rule]. Sŏul: Nanam, 1993.

Yi Yŏnghun. "T'oji chosa saŏp ŭi sut'alsŏng kŏmt'o" [An investigation of exploitation in the land survey]. In *Chosŏn t'oji chosa saŏp ŭi yŏn'gu* [Studies of the land survey in colonial Korea], edited by Kim Hongsik et al. Sŏul: Minŭmsa, 1997.

Yŏngmok Kyŏngbu [Suzuki Keifu]. *Pŏb ŭl t'onghan Chosŏn singminji chibae e kwanhan yŏn'gu* [A study on legal aspects of colonial rule in Korea]. Sŏul: Koryŏ Taehakkyo, 1989.

Young, Crawford. *The African Colonial State in Comparative Perspective.* New Haven, CT: Yale University Press, 1994.

Young, Louise. *Japan's Total Empire: Manchuria and the Culture of Wartime Imperialism.* Berkeley: University of California Press, 1998.

Yu Sŏkch'un. "Singmin chibae ŭi tayangsŏng kwa t'alsingmin chibae ŭi chŏn'gae" [The variations in colonial rule and the development of post-colonial rule]. *Chŏnt'ong kwa hyŏndae* (Fall 1999): 44–45.

Yun Chŏngmo. *Kŭrigo hamsŏng i ttullryŏtta* [And then a shout was raised]. Sŏul: Songhyŏn Ch'ulp'ansa, 1990.

Yun Imsul. *Han'guk simmun sasŏl sŏnjip* vols. 3, 4 [Selected editorials Korean newspapers]. Sŏul: Pang Iryŏng Munhwa Chaedan, 1995.

Zenshō Eisuke. "Chōsen ni okeru dōzoku buraku no kōzō (1)–(3)" [Structure of clan villages in Korea (1)–(3)]. *Chōsa geppō* [Research monthly]. (October–December, 1940).

Zheng, Bijian. " 'Peaceful Rising' to Great-Power Status." Foreign Affairs (September–October 2005): 18–24.

Contributors

HONG YUNG LEE is currently professor of Political Science at the University of California–Berkeley. His research areas of interest include the domestic politics of China and Korea and political economy and international relations in East Asia. He authored *Politics of Chinese Cultural Revolution* (1978) and *From Revolutionary Cadres Party Technocrats in Socialist China* (1991) and edited *Korean Options in a Changing International Order* (1993); *Political Authority and Economic Exchange in Korea* (1993), and *Prospects for Change in North Korea* (1994).

YONG CHOOL HA is the Korea Foundation Professor of Korean Social Science at the University of Washington. His interests in Korean studies include bureaucracy, democratization, civil society, and political economy. Dr. Ha has long been working on expanding Korean cases into comparative perspectives with a focus on the emergence of socially meaningful units under state-led industrialization cases, such as Japan, Prussia, and the Soviet Union. Also he has been teaching and writing on international politics of late industrialization. His articles, monographs, and books have been published in Korean, English, Japanese, and Russian languages. The most recent one is "Late Industrialization, the State and Social Change: The Emergence of Neofamilism in South Korea" (*Comparative Politics*, April, 2007). He is currently finishing a book on late industrialization and social consequences and preparing one on clashes of institutions. Since he led a trans-Siberian railroad research trip for the first time in the year 2000, Prof. Ha has been engaged in the future of the Northeast Asia regional order in terms of community building.

CLARK W. SORENSEN is the director of the Center for Korea Studies at the University of Washington and co-editor of *Reassessing the Park Chung Hee Era: Development, Political Thought, Democracy, and Cultural Influence* (2011). He is editor-in-chief of *The Journal of Korean Studies*.

MARK E. CAPRIO is professor in the College of Intercultural Communications at Rikkyo University, Tokyo, Japan. His research interests include Japan-Korean relations over the twentieth century, particularly the period of Japanese colonial occupation and the present North Korean nuclear issue. He has published a monograph titled *Japanese Assimilation Policies in Colonial Korea, 1910–1945* (2009) and an edited volume titled *Democracy in Occupied Japan: The U.S. Occupation and Japanese Politics and Society* (2007). He has also written on post-liberation Korean repatriation from Japan and on contemporary North Korea-United States-Japan relations.

KEUNSIK JUNG is a professor in the Department of Sociology at Seoul National University. He was chair of both the Korean Critical Sociology Association and the Korean Social History Association. He has edited several books including: *T'allaengjŏng kwa Han'guk minjujuŭi* (The Post-Cold War and Korean democracy, 2010); and *Singmin kwŏllyŏk kwa kŭndae chisik: Kyŏngsŏng Cheguk Taehak yŏn'gu* (Colonial authority and modern knowledge: A Study of Keijō Imperial University, 2011).

DONG-NO KIM is a professor of sociology at Yonsei University. He has written many articles and books on modern Korean history including: *Kŭndae wa singmin ŭi sŏgok* (Prelude to modernity and colonialism, 2009); and "The Transformation of Familism in Modern Korean Society," *International Sociology* 5 no.4 (1990).

KEONGIL KIM is a professor of sociology at the Graduate School of Korean Studies, Academy of Korean Studies. He is concerned with issues on historical sociology, labor history, feminist history, Korean modernity, and East Asian solidarity. He is the author of several books including: *Kundae ui gajok, kundae ui yosong* (Modern family, modern women), Sŏul: Pureun-yeoksa, 2012; *Yŏsŏng ŭi kŭndae, kŭndae ŭi yŏsŏng* (Women's modernity, modern women, 2004); *Han'guk kŭndae nodongsa wa nodong undong* (Modern Korean labor history and the labor movement, 2004); *Pioneers of Korean Studies* (2004); *Yi Chae-yu, na ŭi sidae na ŭi hyŏngmyŏng* (Yi Chae-yu, my era my revolution, 2007); and *Cheguk ŭi sidae wa tong Asia yŏndae* (The Age of Empire and East Asia Era, 2011).

KI-SEOK KIM is a professor at Seoul National University. Dr. Kim serves as the chief executive for Educators without Borders and is the author of *Kyokyuk yŏksa sahoehak* (Historical Sociology of Education, 1999).

KWANG-OK KIM is a professor of anthropology at Seoul National University. He is the author of *Issues of Development in the Yellow Sea Region* (1997); and "Rice Cuisine and Cultural Practice in Contemporary Korean Dietary Life," *Korea Journal* 50 no. 1 (2010). He works on the anthropology of China, as well as Korea.

YONG-JICK KIM is a professor of political science at Sungshin University.

SEONG-CHEOL OH is a professor for the Department of Primary Education at Seoul National University. He is the author of *Kyoyuk kwahaksa: Singminji ch'odŭng kyoyuk ŭi hyŏngsŏng* (History of the science of education: The formation of primary education, 2000).

Index

Duncan, John B., 7
Duus, Peter, 203n51

East Asian League, 220
Eckert, Carter, 22–23, 25–28
economic system category, modern
    nation-states, 144, 169n6
economics issues, as methodological
    problems, 10–12, 14–15, 21–25, 27.
    See also agricultural policies; labor/
    employment; poverty conditions;
    tenant disputes, peasant movements
education policies, leprosy asylums,
    250–53
education systems: overview, 33; in colo-
    nial space model, 51, 52–57, 68–69;
    in cultural rule reforms, 194; curricu-
    lum characteristics, 73n27, 131–34,
    210, 272, 288–89; enrollment pat-
    terns, 8–10, 54–56, 73n30, 119–25,
    130; expansion process, 125–31; goal
    conflicts, 8–9, 114, 131, 134–37; insti-
    tutions for, 57, 111n37, n39, 115–19,
    267–69; and yangban changes, 65–66
Ekeh, Peter P., 48–49, 72n16
elementary education. See education sys-
    tems
entrance examination, primary schools,
    124, 126
Evergreen Association, 61
extrapolation tendencies, as method-
    ological problem, 25–28

False conversion tactics, as policy resis-
    tance, 225–27
family organization, Japanese role: over-
    view, 35, 315–18, 330–31, 332n8; with
    administrative fiat, 323–24, 333n29;
    in colonial space model, 49, 52–53,
    64–70; concubine status, 323–24,
    333n29, n31; inheritance system, 321,

324, 327–28; with legal system
    changes, 318–20; marriage customs,
    67, 320, 321–23, 325–29; name
    change controversy, 296–98, 324–30;
    post-colonial changes, 314–15, 329–
    30; registration system, 320–21;
    research reports, 319–21
Federation of Workers and Peasants in
    Korea, 97
Federation of Youth in Korea, 97
festival restrictions, 284–85
Field, Norma, 229n7
Fletcher, A. G., 237, 256
folk religion label, 265. See also indig-
    enous religion, as contested culture
food, as cultural resistance, 272, 282
Forsythe, W. H., 237
Foster, Phillip, 136
fragmented vs. totality perspectives, as
    methodological problem, 21–23,
    42–45, 70–71
French model, colonial rule, 25, 93–94
frugality teachings, in Rural Promotion
    program, 279–80, 283–85
funding, education system expansion,
    128–30
Fuzino Yutaka, 263n62

Gender patterns, education system, 115,
    123
geomancy, 270, 288
Goffman, Erving, 52, 73n19
Grajdanzev, Andrew, 69
Gramsci, Antonio, 89
graveyards, 270–71, 309n13
Greater East Asia Co-Prosperity Sphere,
    47, 213, 221, 223–25, 232n64
Greater Korean Independence Party, 190
"Green Grapes" (Yi Yuksa), 310n35
Gussow, Zachary, 238, 260n10, 261n17

www.ingramcontent.com/pod-product-compliance
Lightning Source LLC
Chambersburg PA
CBHW022259280326
41932CB00010B/912